Reflective Teaching for Student Empowerment

Elementary Curriculum and Methods

Dorene Doerre Ross
University of Florida

Elizabeth Bondy
University of Florida

Diane Wells Kyle
University of Louisville

Macmillan Publishing Company
New York

Maxwell Macmillan Canada
Toronto

Maxwell Macmillan International
New York   Oxford   Singapore   Sydney

This book is dedicated with love to
   Jack, Kate, and Sarah
   Bill, Charlie, Sam, and Molly
   Grace, Jack, Joanne, and Kathy
Our students who challenge us to continue to grow and develop
as reflective teachers

Cover photo: Reginald Wickham
Editor: Robert B. Miller
Production Editor: Sharon Rudd
Art Coordinator: Peter A. Robison
Cover Designer: Robert Vega
Production Buyer: Pamela D. Bennett
Electronic Text Management: Ben Ko, Marilyn Wilson Phelps
Artist: Jane Lopez

This book was set in New Baskerville and Swiss by Macmillan Publishing Company and was printed and bound by R. R. Donnelly & Sons Company. The cover was printed by New England Book Components.

Macmillan Publishing Company
866 Third Avenue
New York, New York 10022

Macmillan Publishing Company is part of the
Maxwell Communication Group of Companies.

Maxwell Macmillan Canada, Inc.
1200 Eglinton Avenue East, Suite 200
Don Mills, Ontario M3C 3N1

Library of Congress Cataloging-in-Publication Data
Ross, Dorene Doerre.
   Reflective teaching for student empowerment : elementary
curriculum and methods / Dorene D. Ross, Elizabeth Bondy, Diane W.
Kyle.
      p.   cm.
   Includes bibliographical references and index.
   ISBN 0-02-403960-8
   1. Elementary school teaching—United States.   2. Education,
Elementary—United States—Curricula.   I. Bondy, Elizabeth.
II. Kyle, Diane W.   III. Title.
LB1555.R67   1993
372.11'02—dc20   92–19800
                                                                 CIP

Printing: 1 2 3 4 5 6 7 8 9   Year: 3 4 5 6 7

Photo credits: National Education Association, Joe DiDio

Preface

We have taught elementary curriculum courses for 8 to 14 years. During that time, we have expressed concern about the nature and quality of texts available to both undergraduate and masters-level students. At one extreme, we found highly theoretical texts that explored abstract issues irrelevant to the needs of practicing teachers. These texts preserved the complexity and richness of teaching, but required much supplementation and adaptation to make them relevant to the needs of teachers. At the other extreme, we found simplistic "cookbooks" that presented assorted sets of guidelines drawn from a variety of theoretical perspectives. These books provided no consistent theoretical or research-based framework for interpreting the guidelines presented and thus implicitly suggested that good teaching means following a set of rules laid out in a text.

Reflective Teaching for Student Empowerment is a synthesis of the best in both kinds of elementary curriculum texts. It is intended for courses commonly titled Elementary Curriculum, General Methods in Elementary Education, or Principles and Practices of Elementary Education. It also could be used in a seminar accompanying a practicum in elementary education. The text is designed for instructors who believe teaching involves the coordination of a complex array of knowledge (e.g., knowledge of children, learning theory, available research, educational aims, the particular teaching context, available resources, background knowledge and experiences of the children, collected evidence about student learning) in order to make and continually revise decisions. We intend for the text to be used as a tool to assist in the professional empowerment of teachers.

Content and Organization

The book uses the concept of reflective teaching to present a theoretically coherent approach that provides a unique combination of practical and conceptual issues. It is grounded in a constructivist view of learning, a view of the teacher as a reflective decision maker, and in a commitment to student empowerment as an essential aim of elementary education. In Part 1, we define reflective teaching and curriculum. We also help students see the variety of perspectives about curriculum that exist within the field. We guide students to see the central importance of determining their educational aims as a first step in becoming empowered as reflective teachers.

In Part 2, we synthesize research to develop instructional guidelines on topics considered most important by today's elementary teachers: development of literacy, development of problem-solving abilities, use of teacher effects research, use of cooperative learning, development of social skills, development of thinking skills, working with students at risk for academic failure, and helping students become self-disciplined (classroom management). These topics also are consistent with recommendations from various national reports recommending reform within elementary education. We help the reader to see how these topics are applicable across the various subject areas of the elementary curriculum. We discuss practical and theoretical issues throughout the text.

In Part 3, we present a practical approach to teacher empowerment, a feature that distinguishes our text from other available curriculum texts. We help students identify the key features of empowering school contexts, help them learn micropolitical strategies necessary for the collaborative empowerment of teachers, and help them learn strategies and skills necessary for reflective self-evaluation.

Reflective Teaching as a Central Focus

Reflective teaching is a common term in teacher education; however, the term is used in many—and often conflicting—ways because many authors fail to define it. Our definition of reflective teaching is grounded in 15 years of study and research with preservice and in-service teachers committed to the development of reflective teaching. Within this text, we define reflective teaching as making rational and ethical choices about what and how to teach and assuming responsibility for those choices. We introduce students to a cycle describing the reflective process, sets of attitudes and abilities that influence the quality of teacher reflection, and a set of criteria that reflective teachers use to evaluate their decisions.

After developing this definition, reflective teaching for the purpose of student empowerment becomes the organizing focus for the text. Part 2 provides teachers with the information about schools, classrooms, children, and teaching that is necessary for them to engage in reflective decision making. Part 3 focuses on the teacher empowerment that is necessary to make reflective practice a reality. Throughout the book we help readers develop ideas about what needs to be done in today's schools, and we provide them with images of teachers who are doing it. However, developing ideas is insufficient unless readers also learn strategies for gaining and maintaining the autonomy to implement their ideas within today's schools. Thus, we considered it essential to devote Part 3 to helping readers acquire knowledge designed to help them become instructional leaders within schools. This approach is highly compatible with current efforts in school restructuring.

Strong Research Base

Since the 1960s, the knowledge base for teaching has expanded greatly, yet few comprehensive syntheses of research important for elementary teachers exist. Grounding the development of instructional guidelines in available research and integrating research across chapters helps students and instructors draw on this rich source of information to guide teacher thinking and teacher action. The syntheses of research provided in this text also are grounded in a constructivist view of learning. Thus, the text specifically directs student attention to conflicts in various research findings and uses the constructivist perspective to help students develop a framework for making decisions when confronted with conflicting research findings. For example, in Chapter 5 we describe instructional implications from teacher effects research, then we present critiques of this research based upon a constructivist view of learning. We then help readers see how the research can be modified to help resolve the problems presented in the critique.

Linking Theory to Practice

It is our view that research informs practice *and* that practice informs research. As a result we have tried, throughout the book, to stress the connections between theory, research, and practice. Syntheses of research, no matter how thorough, are of little use to teachers who either find them too boring to read or too loosely connected to the daily practice of teaching. We have tried to help our readers "see" the connections between theory and practice by providing vignettes of teaching practice, particularly in Part 2. These vignettes clarify and exemplify discussion of common problems in elementary teaching. The vignettes also present alternative instructional guidelines and the nature of students' responses to instruction. For example, in Chapter 8, we help readers develop an understanding of the role of culture in the ways that at-risk students respond to schooling by describing the schooling experiences of some children typically perceived as at risk for academic failure. Most vignettes are drawn from actual classroom practice.

Activities That Invite Student Interaction and Participation

While it is valuable for teachers to read about teaching, reading is not enough. We incorporate features within this text to invite student interaction with the ideas presented and with one another. This interaction is considered to be a key component of the development of reflection. Within each chapter readers will find focus boxes. These focus boxes include (1) activities that facilitate the assessment of entering beliefs, (2) activities that encourage assessment of comprehension, and (3) practical application activities. The activities within the focus boxes stimulate student thought and interaction and make the book highly readable for students and easy for instructors to use.

Activities that facilitate the assessment of entering beliefs are found in most chapters in Part 2. These activities provide a vehicle for students to examine their entering beliefs related to the content presented and to reanalyze those beliefs after reading the content. Current research on teacher learning suggests that entering beliefs can be powerful constraints to change for teachers. Exercises that help readers reveal their entering ideas enable them and their instructors to confront these ideas and challenge them as necessary. These activities also enable readers to connect more personally to the content of the text.

Comprehension activities provide questions and/or situations that encourage readers to respond to the content presented within each chapter. We encourage readers to respond individually. In many activities, readers also are given guide questions for group discussion in which they compare and contrast answers and discuss the significance of any differences they discover. These exercises encourage readers to confront and discuss possible contextual constraints to the implementation of strategies presented in this book.

Practical application activities provide students with suggestions for the application of ideas and strategies presented in the text. Practical application activities include ideas for role play, for hypothetical lesson development and/or revision, and for use of strategies within classroom settings.

Acknowledgements

It is exciting—and a relief—to conclude a project that has consumed our lives and the lives of those close to us for over 4 years. Many people have supported us technically, conceptually, and emotionally through this process. We all wish to thank Robert Miller for his patience throughout this project, and Debbie Payne, whose careful work in copyediting this manuscript has been invaluable and Sharon Rudd, Robert Vega, and Pam Bennett of Macmillan's production department for helping us turn the manuscript into a book. We also are indebted to the reviewers who thoughtfully critiqued our work and provided encouragement and many suggestions that have improved the book. Reviewers for this project included Renee M. Casbergue, Tulane University; Renee T. Clift, University of Illinois at Urbana–Champaign; Paul F. Cook, Brigham Young University; Leah Engelhardt, Purdue University–Calumet; Nathalie J. Gehrke, University of Washington; John M. Kean, University of Wisconsin–Madison; J. Gary Knowles, University of Michigan; John E. Merryman, Indiana University of Pennsylvania; Alan R. Tom, University of Arizona; and Richard Uhleman, Edinboro University of Pennsylvania.

Our other acknowledgments are presented in two parts. While this has been a collaborative process in every way, we are housed in two distinct locations and have distinct sources of support.

From Diane: I would like to thank my colleagues in the Department of Early and Middle Childhood Education at the University of Louisville for their interest and encouragement and for the champagne toast I'm sure they must be planning when the book is published. Colleagues Ric Hovda, Mark Condon, Marjorie Kaiser, and Chuck Thompson (University of Louisville) and Amos Hatch (University of Tennessee) deserve special thanks for taking the time to read early drafts and provide very helpful suggestions for improvement. As always, I am grateful to my parents and sisters who have always let me know that they believe I can accomplish what I try. I also want to acknowledge my wonderful friends who have provided needed support throughout all phases and the highs and lows of this project. I especially want to thank Maureen Awbrey for that support and also for reading many drafts, for long talks about the ideas, and for her marvelous perspective that comes from over 20 years of teaching young children.

From Dorene and Buffy: We are particularly indebted to Rodman Webb (University of Florida) and Jesse Goodman (Indiana University) who have influenced our thinking and helped us over many rough spots in the preparation of this book. We want to thank them for their depth of knowledge and their willingness to share it. We also thank Rod for all the technical tips along the way and Jesse for taking time to read and critique early drafts of many chapters. We wish to thank Joe Vaughan (U.S. Department of Education), Renee Clift (University of Illinois), Sharon Feiman Nemser (Michigan State University), Ken Zeichner (University of Wisconsin-Madison) and Dan Liston (University of Colorado) for dialogue and feedback that has helped shape our orientation to and definition of reflection. Others who have contributed to the development of our ideas or critiqued early drafts include Deborah Ball (Michigan State University), Dwight Rogers (University of North Carolina-Chapel Hill), and Steven Ball (King's College London).

As we developed drafts of chapters, we used them in our classes. We owe tremendous gratitude to colleagues who have taught with us, critiqued the chapters, and helped us see what readers did and did not understand. Many thanks to Sam Andrews, Bob Blume, Mary Brownell, Paula DeHart, Cynthia Griffin, Lynda Hayes, Sharen Halsall, Karen Kilgore, Peggy Johnson, and Bill Smith. We also wish to thank the countless PROTEACH (University of Florida) students who have asked questions that challenged us to clarify our ideas and improve our writing. Of course, we could not have completed this project without the emotional support provided by our families. We thank our parents, our parents-in-law, and our siblings and their families who have shown great interest in this project and unfailing confidence that we would complete it. We thank our husbands for technical and conceptual support, for Friday night pizza, beach weekends, the Park Plaza Hotel, and other forms of emotional support. And we thank our children for hugs, playground outings, picnics, and continual reminders about the wonder and excitement of learning.

Dorene Doerre Ross
Elizabeth (Buffy) Bondy
Diane Wells Kyle

Contents

Chapter 5

Promoting Literacy: Implications of Teacher Effects Research   105

Chapter 6

Chapter 7

Chapter 8

Chapter 9

PART 3

Maximizing Professional Autonomy   287

Chapter 10

Selecting a Professional Environment   290

Chapter 11

Working Within the Social System of the School   302

Teaching Methods and Key Topics Locater Guide

An Introduction to Reflective Teaching

This book uses the concept of reflective teaching to provide a novel approach to elementary curriculum. Many teachers view curriculum as a highly theoretical, and thus impractical, field or as a set of prepackaged information to be delivered to students. This book presents a unique combination of practical and conceptual issues. It is grounded in a view of the teacher as a reflective decision-maker and in a commitment to student empowerment as an essential aim of elementary education. Within this framework, the book synthesizes research to develop instructional guidelines on topics considered most important by today's elementary teachers. A brief overview of the focus of each section of the book will be useful.

Part 1 of the book introduces you to the concept of reflective teaching. Reflective teaching has become a common term in teacher education; however, the term is used in many and often conflicting ways because many teacher educators fail to define it. We provide a comprehensive definition of and rationale for reflective teaching and multiple examples of the practice of reflective teaching to help you to develop reflective capacity and to develop and use criteria for evaluating your effectiveness as teachers. In addition, we provide an analysis of the practicality of reflective teaching by exploring whether reflective teaching is possible or merely an idealized but impractical view of teaching. A major conclusion from this exploration is that one of the most significant influences on teachers' abilities to teach reflectively is their educational aims for students because these aims provide the starting point for making decisions about teaching. Consequently, Chapter 3 is designed to help you clarify your aims for elementary education.

In Part 2, we share research and theory about teaching strategies that you might use to implement aims that have consistently been of highest priority to teachers with whom we have worked. Reflection about the relative importance of various aims is of limited value unless you also have knowledge about strategies useful in achieving those aims. Over a period of 12 years we have asked graduate and undergraduate students of elementary education to identify their priority aims for education. They have consistently identified basic skills, the development of social skills, the development of creative and critical thinking abilities, the development of a desire to learn, and the development of self-motivation or self-discipline as their top priorities. As our students have written about their aims and the reasons for their importance, we have noted that their aims reflect a commitment to the development of **student empowerment**. By this we mean that elementary educators are striving to empower students to be eager and successful learners, to determine their own futures and participate productively in society, and to play an active role in making society a better place for all. Part 2 focuses on strategies that might be used across all curriculum areas in meeting these aims. That is, these chapters provide information about strategies that help children develop the **tools of empowerment**: literacy, social skills, good thinking abilities, capacity to engage meaningfully in the school curriculum, and capacity for socially responsive self-discipline. Running through the chapters of Part 2, you will find a focus on strategies for empowering students who are typically at risk for school failure.

In Part 3, we present strategies you can use to help you gain and maintain the autonomy to implement your professional ideas. In the first Parts 1 and 2, you will have learned a reflective approach to teaching and a variety of teaching strategies that can be used to support the aim of student empowerment. However, you also will have learned that many typical school practices contradict the aim of student empowerment. This is true because the culture of teaching influences the choices that teachers make about educational aims and strategies. It is not enough to develop ideas about what needs to be done. Consequently, Part 3 is designed to help you learn strategies for gaining and maintaining the autonomy to implement your ideas within today's schools.

CHAPTER 1

On Becoming a Reflective Teacher

This book is based on the assumption that the primary goal of elementary education in a democracy is to **empower** students to become active and productive participants within the community. This means teachers should help students become eager and successful learners, determine their own futures, participate productively in society, and play an active role in making society a better place for all. The purpose of this book is to help you become a more reflective teacher so that you will be able to empower your students. In this chapter, you will learn what it means to be a reflective teacher, why we believe teachers must be reflective, and what you must learn in order to teach reflectively. We will also explain why student empowerment is a critical goal for elementary educators.

What Is a Reflective Teacher?

Many educators agree that teachers need to be more reflective, but they differ in their definitions of the words *reflective teaching*. Grimmett, MacKinnon, Erickson, and Riecken (1990) describe three distinct definitions of **reflective teaching**: (1) a technique for analyzing one's teaching skills (Cruickshank, 1985), (2) a selection of the best among competing definitions of good teaching, or (3) drawing on Schon's (1983) definition, a process of problem setting, framing, and exploration within context. The third definition stresses the importance of a moral and ethical framework for reflective decision making and teacher empowerment (Zeichner & Liston, 1987). Our definition is a combination of the second and third definitions presented.

A **reflective teacher** makes rational and ethical choices about what and how to teach and assumes responsibility for those choices (Goodman, 1984; Ross, 1987; Zeichner & Liston, 1987). In doing this, the teacher must continually answer important questions, such as, What do children within a democratic society need to know and be able to do? Which teaching strategies are most likely to result in this learning? Are my teaching practices based on ethical commitments to children such as caring and/or **equity** (i.e., fairness or justice)? What evidence do I have that I am accomplishing my goals? Put simply, teachers must be thoughtful and responsible. Unfortunately, accomplishing this aim is not simple. Many forces discourage teachers from being reflective. Consider the comment of one kindergarten teacher who was asked why she drew most of her lessons from the textbook despite her professed belief that such instruction was not the best instructional approach for young children:

> I've found that with each year of teaching kindergarten it's becoming more structured, more like first grade which doesn't please me personally. . . . I'm more for the theory of let's wait until first grade. Why push them? . . . [I use the text materials because] somebody has told me, this is what you use and teach. . . . It comes not just from people in my school but from the central office. (Ross, 1978, pp. 73, 86, 87)

Because of perceived pressure, this teacher has abdicated responsibility for her instructional decisions. The attitude of this teacher is not unusual. It is difficult for today's teachers to be reflective, yet it is possible. Reflective teaching is important to those who believe teaching requires thought, rational decision making, and responsible action.

Reflective teaching requires the development of a complex array of abilities, attitudes, and knowledge. This book is designed to help you acquire them. However, you cannot learn to be reflective by reading a book. Throughout this book we will provide questions and issues to think about, classroom episodes to analyze, self-assessment tools to promote self-awareness, and suggestions of activities to try in classrooms. Although you may be tempted to skip over those sections, we urge you to try these activities and to talk about them with your peers. Dialogue is an important part of becoming a reflective teacher.

The best way to gain knowledge about reflective teachers is to observe and talk to them about their teaching; however, reflection is not easy to observe, because reflection is an internal process. Even highly reflective teachers may not be able to articulate their thought processes adequately. Although some teaching decisions are made after careful deliberation either prior to or following instruction, many others seem to be made spontaneously during instruction. Yet, spontaneous decisions also may be the result of careful reflection, because many classroom situations repeat themselves. Having confronted a dilemma on a previous occasion, teachers develop a way to respond and evaluate their decisions based on the consequences of their actions. Once the dilemma is resolved, teachers may not even remember it was ever problematic and thus may not be able to share the reasoning used to develop a solution. As we describe the reflective process and the attitudes and abilities needed for reflection, we will share the thinking of several teachers to help you understand the concept of reflection. Additionally, this chapter should help you identify reflective teachers you already know. We encourage you to seek them out and talk to them as a way to learn about reflective teaching. Before we discuss the components of reflection, we will consider why it is important.

Why Is Reflection Essential in Teaching?

Several assumptions about teaching and the role of teachers in classrooms lead to the conclusion that reflection is an essential part of teaching. Our rationale for the importance of reflection emerges from these assumptions. Throughout this book, we will ask you to complete activities that will help you examine your emerging perspectives about good teaching. The assumptions that we list are especially important, because they reveal our perspectives about good teaching. However, these assumptions are not unique to this text. Although we may have organized them somewhat differently, you probably will find these assumptions in your social and psychological foundations of education coursework.

Assumption 1: Teaching Requires an Ethical Commitment to Student Empowerment

Teaching is not and cannot be value free. The importance of an educated citizenry dedicated to democratic values is a cornerstone of American education. Teachers have a responsibility to help children grow up to be empowered citizens who are able and willing to participate fully and intelligently in a democracy (Liston & Zeichner, 1987; Moore, Mintz, & Bierman, 1987; Tom, 1984; Webb & Sherman, 1989). For example, in addition to learning basic information about our government, we expect our children to develop **democratic values**. That is, we expect them to grow up dedicated to the worth and dignity of each individual, to recognize the need to balance the rights of individuals against the rights of the rest of society, and to value and work toward the democratic ideal of **equity** (e.g., assuring that each person has equal access to knowledge, equal opportunity to speak and be heard, equal opportunity to lead a self-determined life). Goodman (1992) stresses that Americans tend to define democracy in terms of political structures and rights (e.g., voting, due process, freedom of speech) rather than in terms of individual and collective responsibility for creating a good and just society. This focus enables us to sustain the myth of *equal opportunity* and ignore the impact of factors such as race, social class, gender, and handicap on one's ability to succeed within our society. Goodman states that education for critical democracy requires that teachers actively confront issues of empowerment and equity. He believes students must:

> learn to use minds critically in order to recognize those powers that inhibit and those that work towards the creation of a more compassionate, caring and socially just world, as well as the moral courage to participate with those in the latter group. (1992, p. 159)

Even when students develop these capacities and commitments, it is difficult for them to resolve issues of equity. The rights of diverse individuals and groups vary, and there are no fixed answers. In fact, Moore et al. (1987) characterize the democratic process as the "creative resolution of conflict" and believe education in a democracy must prepare students to be inquirers ready to participate in this resolution of conflict.

Similarly Webb and Sherman (1989) state democratic societies must help children learn to value *openness* and *reason* and to engage in *conflict* and *compromise* with *civility*. Webb and Sherman (1989, pp. 69–89) argue that schools in a democratic society must empower children by helping them learn:

- openness to new ideas and an ability to listen to the ideas of others, even ideas they may not like
- the ability use reason and draw upon evidence
- the ability to accept conflict
- the ability to compromise so that the diverse needs of the population can be met
- the ability to treat others with dignity and respect

Reflective teachers are individuals who value ideas, who use reason and compromise to resolve conflict, and who treat one another with respect and dignity.

In a democratic society, reflective teachers must use **ethical criteria** to select and evaluate the content to be taught and the teaching methods used. In addition to evaluating their achievement of short-term goals, teachers must evaluate their actions in terms of the kind of people the members of a democratic society want their children to become.

The reflective process does not dictate the decisions teachers will make but rather ensures that the decisions will be constantly reevaluated in terms of their actual impact. Consider, for example, the case of a teacher who recently has begun to question the use of ability groups, a practice she and her colleagues have unquestioningly accepted in the past.

Mary and her two colleagues have always divided the children within their classes into ability groups for reading. Based on some readings in a graduate class, Mary now questions this practice. Most of the available research on ability grouping suggests that this practice has a negative impact on the achievement and self-esteem of students placed in average and low groups. Some scholars argue that ability grouping tends to disempower poor and minority students by perpetuating a cycle of failure. These scholars conclude that ability grouping should not be used (Oakes, 1985). Others conclude that ability grouping, if used properly, does not necessarily have negative effects on children in low and average groups (Hallinan, 1984; Nozick, 1974; Slavin, 1987).

Based on this evidence, Mary might decide to abandon ability groups or she might continue them. Slavin's (1987) work indicates that the negative impact of groups can be mitigated if teachers make sure the plan reduces the heterogeneity of children only within particular skills to be taught, the plan allows children to be moved from group to group as necessary, teachers vary their instruction based on the learning needs of the children, and children do not spend the majority of their instructional time in ability groups. Thus, reflection might not lead to a change in Mary's behavior, but it does ensure constant reevaluation of her practice in light of new evidence and in light of her ethical commitments to student empowerment.

Assumption 2: Teaching Requires Understanding the Student's Point of View, Because Knowledge Is Constructed Rather Than Transmitted

What students think influences what they learn and how they act. This assumption and Assumption 3 (which is the teacher parallel of this assumption) are rooted in a view that knowledge is constructed, a view of learning based in the work of cognitive psychologists. Advocates of a **constructivist view of learning** argue that learners do not simply absorb information transmitted by teachers; instead, learners construct knowledge within their minds (Glasersfeld, 1987; Piaget, 1972). Learners constantly interpret new information, trying to understand how new knowledge is related to what they already know. Previous knowledge, developed over time and in many contexts inside and outside of school, may be accurate or inaccurate and will influence how the child interprets new information. Constructivist cognitive psychologists explain that learning occurs through a process of analyzing available data in order to detect patterns; form and test hypotheses; and reinforce, refine, or revise previously existing concepts and understandings. If teachers wish to promote the development of their students' concepts and understanding, they must determine how students understand what occurs in the school. Weinstein (1983) summarizes literature on students' perceptions of teachers and schooling by saying:

> Children are active interpreters of classroom reality and they draw inferences about the causes and effects of behavior. . . . Such inferences are not always rational, and . . . children's and adults' views of classroom reality may not necessarily be synonymous. Such disparity in views may actually hinder communication. (p. 288)

Teachers must be able to understand the students' perspectives if they are to know what learning is occurring. At the simplest level, the teacher must understand the student's point of view in order to understand how each student makes sense of instruction and to design educational experiences that will help the student construct revised (and more accurate) understandings. For example, a preschool teacher doing a unit on "Where Things Come From" taught the children that fish, crabs, shells, and shrimp come from the sea; milk comes from a cow; cheese comes from milk; peanut butter comes from peanuts; and bacon comes from a pig. Toward the end of the unit, each child drew a picture and told where that animal or thing "came from." Raphi drew a picture of a shrimp and told the teacher that it "came from a pig." At first glance, Raphi's answer seems odd. How could he possibly have developed such a misunderstanding? Has he been able to understand the major concept that many common things "come from" other things, or is he simply making a random statement? Raphi's answer becomes more comprehensible when we know that he comes from a kosher

Jewish home, where many of the forbidden foods "come from pigs." Now we can understand why he might think that shrimp, a forbidden food, comes from a pig. We can see that he understands the concept and that his answer makes sense within his framework for comprehension. This example also helps reemphasize the point that teaching involves more than telling. Raphi had been told that shrimp come from the sea, but he *constructed* a different understanding. Even when students are able to "give back" a correct answer, they frequently have constructed an entirely different understanding. Determining what students are learning, then, requires that teachers ask questions that probe students' thinking.

Students' thinking influences more than their understanding of academic content. As students observe and interact with teachers and peers, they construct beliefs about things such as the nature of the classroom environment, their own ability, their ability to exert personal control over learning, the ability of their peers, and teachers' perceptions about themselves and their peers (Weinstein, 1983). For example, studies indicate that students perceive differences in how teachers interact with students of varying ability in classrooms. Weinstein (1983, p. 293) reports that students perceive differences in how teachers call on students based on ability. Teachers "call on the smart kids for the right answer. . . . They expect you to know more and won't tell answers." Teachers call on low achievers "sometimes to give them a chance" or "because they goof off."

If teachers are to understand their impact on students, they must develop the ability to see themselves, the classroom, and the instruction provided through the eyes of the students. Reflection requires viewing any situation from multiple perspectives, including the student perspective. Throughout this book, we will share research about students' understanding of content and perceptions of various aspects of instruction and classrooms. This knowledge suggests evidence you will want to collect as you assess your behavior as a teacher and the impact you have.

Assumption 3: What Happens in Teachers' Classrooms Is Influenced by What They Think

Teachers will do things differently because of differences in their beliefs about such things as the following (Clark & Yinger, 1977; Sykes, 1986; Zeichner & Liston, 1987):

- the nature of the teaching/learning process
- the characteristics of children
- the nature of motivation
- the definition of reading (math, science, art, etc.)
- the purpose of discipline
- the goals of schooling
- the potential impact of a teacher on students
- the role that school authorities should play in making instructional decisions

These differences will be apparent in classroom organization and in responses to incidents and individuals within the class. For example, a teacher who thinks of teaching as "presenting information to children" will teach differently than a teacher who thinks of teaching as "communicating with children about information." Presentation is unidirectional. The teacher lectures or demonstrates, and the students listen and observe. Communication implies much more than the skillful presentation of information. To communicate, you must do more than send a message; the message also must be received. And the meaning of the message must be negotiated so the teacher and students construct a common understanding. Thus, although both teachers may spend a great deal of time planning ways to present information to students, the second teacher will also spend time listening to students and planning activities that will make it possible to determine what students understand and how they are making sense of each lesson.

Consider another example. Mr. Waters believes that he plays a major role in influencing what children learn in his classroom. Mr. Lang believes that factors he cannot control (e.g., children's home life, their IQs, or their interest in the subject matter) have the strongest influence on what children learn in his classroom. How do you think these teachers might differ in their response to a student who failed a test?

Mr. Waters and Mr. Lang differ in their sense of **efficacy** (i.e., their power to produce an effect). This difference has been shown to influence a teacher's ability to help children achieve (Ashton & Webb, 1986). If teachers believe that factors they cannot control are the major influence on student learning, then they are unlikely to alter their instruction if students are not mastering the content. They assume that they are teaching well. The students are simply not learning well. On the other hand, teachers who believe they are a major influence on student learning are much more likely to alter instructional strategies or materials in order to improve student learning. Many teachers have a low sense of efficacy and do not believe they can influence what students learn. Why would this be? The answer to this question reveals another reason why reflection is an important part of teaching.

Assumption 4: Tacit, but Invalid, Beliefs Can Hamper Teachers' Effectiveness in the Classroom

Many beliefs teachers hold about teaching and learning are **tacit** and intuitive; that is, unexamined (Sykes, 1986; Schon, 1983). Teachers act on these beliefs, yet may not be consciously aware of them. Some of these beliefs are valid; others are not. Even excellent teachers have some unexamined beliefs that may hamper their efforts to help children learn. Beliefs about teaching, learning, and children are built through experience over a lifetime, and no teachers can possibly be aware of all of their tacit beliefs. Reflection helps to reveal tacit understandings and enables teachers to examine their thinking. By collecting evidence related to various beliefs, teachers can test the validity of each one and change invalid beliefs or alter behaviors that are inconsistent with their beliefs.

FOCUS BOX 1–1

Teachers' Sense of Efficacy: What Is It?

Teachers have a variety of beliefs that influence their teaching decisions and practices. One very important belief is a teacher's belief in teaching efficacy. Beliefs about efficacy are beliefs about one's potential influence on student learning (Ashton & Webb, 1986). Self-efficacy theory (Bandura, 1982) suggests that teachers who believe they can help students learn are more motivated to engage in activities that enhance learning. This makes sense. High-efficacy teachers believe they will be successful. Therefore, when confronted with a difficult task, they consciously search for strategies that will lead to success. For example, these teachers are likely to set goals for themselves and students, identify strategies to achieve them, assess whether they are achieved, and examine and revise their own performance when students are not successful (Ashton, 1984). That is, teachers who have high efficacy believe they *can* influence student learning and make and evaluate decisions in ways that help them achieve these goals. As a result, we find that teachers with high efficacy are likely to be judged effective by criteria such as student achievement test scores (Ashton & Webb, 1986).

In contrast, teachers with low efficacy are not convinced that they can influence student learning. They have come to believe that "some students cannot or will not learn in school and that there is nothing any teacher can do to alter this unhappy reality" (Ashton & Webb, 1986, p. 4). Therefore, when confronted with the difficult task of teaching low achieving children, low-efficacy teachers are likely to give up. Ashton and Webb (1986) have found that low-efficacy teachers give up on students readily, tend not to spend extra time or energy developing instructional strategies to reach "hard-to-teach" children, and experience little or no professional guilt as a result of their actions. Again, this makes sense. Because these teachers feel helpless, there is no motivation to spend time and energy teaching children who (in their view) simply cannot learn.

Assumption 5: There Are No Fixed Answers to the Problems of Teaching and Learning

Teaching is a highly complex and ambiguous activity, a difficult balancing act that constantly requires teacher judgment (Sykes, 1986; Zeichner & Liston, 1987). An example will illustrate what we mean. At a very general level, we may agree about educational goals. Through an historical review of goals for schooling and a study of current state documents, Goodlad (1984, pp. 50–56) derived a list of goals for schooling:

- mastery of basic skills and processes
- intellectual development (e.g., the ability to think rationally and to create, use, evaluate, and value knowledge)
- career education
- development of interpersonal skills and understandings

- development of skills, knowledge, and attitudes necessary for participation in a democratic society
- development of knowledge about our cultural heritage and its impact on society's values and traditions
- development of moral and ethical character
- development of emotional and physical well-being
- development of creativity and aesthetic expression
- self-realization (e.g., development of self-confidence, decision-making ability, awareness of one's strengths and limitations, ability to accept responsibility)

This list suggests consensus about our task, but this consensus is an illusion. No school, no teacher can achieve all of these goals. In fact, implementation of some of these goals requires that teachers attempt to achieve conflicting subgoals. For example, helping to prepare children to participate in our democratic, industrialized society requires that we help children develop independence and competitiveness. Yet, a democratic society also requires individuals who are cooperative and value collective effort. Teachers must teach children to be competitive and cooperative, yet neither goal can be overemphasized. How much time should a teacher devote to each goal? The answer to this question, like the answer to most questions in teaching, is "It depends." In a classroom of highly competitive children, a teacher might decide to devote proportionately more time to cooperative activity than in a classroom where the children are highly cooperative. Some children within the classroom may require more instruction than their peers to learn to work cooperatively with others. The balancing act is complicated further by the fact that many aspects of our educational system, such as grading, grouping by ability, and athletics, tend to stress competition, making it difficult to achieve cooperative goals rather than competitive ones. Finally, as Assumptions 1 and 2 imply, the teacher's personal beliefs will play a role. A teacher who values competition is less likely to stress cooperation in the classroom than a teacher who believes that cooperation is a very important school goal.

Many times, during your teacher education program and throughout your professional life, you will wish someone would tell you what to do and how to do it. We wish that we had the answers, but we don't. No one does, and teachers should be very wary of those who claim that they do, because such people lack an understanding of the basic nature of teaching. Making judgments about which goals to emphasize, about the appropriate balance among conflicting goals, or about the best approach to take with a class or an individual child is the most exciting and challenging part of teaching. It is also difficult and frustrating because the decisions teachers must make are not *once-and-for-always* decisions. Teachers must constantly reevaluate their judgments, because teaching is a dynamic process. Problems in education have no fixed answers. In fact, we often lack agreement about the nature of the problems. Because of this, teachers must make **pedagogical** judgments (judgments about appropriate goals, about balance among competing goals, and about appropriate teaching methods).

Assumption 6: Research Does Not Have All the Answers

We have made tremendous strides in educational research about teaching practice since the 1970s (Borko & Shavelson, 1983; Griffin, 1984; McCaleb, 1979; Sykes, 1986). Teachers today have access to a wide variety of research studies that can help increase their knowledge about such things as:

- the ways teachers communicate their expectations
- the teaching behaviors most likely to lead to higher achievement scores in basic skill areas
- the teaching behaviors related to the development of high cognitive level thinking skills
- the effectiveness of cooperative learning strategies
- the skills involved in social competence
- the stages of beginning reading and writing

However, no matter how much information is generated by researchers, we will not be able to provide teachers with a set of skills or behaviors that will assure their effectiveness with children because individual teachers must determine

Research will never have all the answers about teaching because teaching involves complex interactions among people.

whether the recommendations of individual researchers are applicable to their goals, the particular school and classroom context, and the characteristics of students in the classroom.

Research provides information, not answers. In order to make good judgments about appropriate use of research findings, teachers must become knowledgeable readers of research. Clearly, it is important to examine the quality of the research report, paying particular attention to the nature of the **sample population** (i.e., the characteristics of the subjects of the study) and to the research questions asked. For example, a study done in rural Alaska may be a very reputable study, yet may provide little information relevant to an elementary teacher in Harlem. Teachers also must remember that researchers, too, are guided by their values and goal commitments. These values guide the selection of research questions and the interpretation of results. In determining the appropriate application of research findings, teachers must examine the value commitments of

FOCUS BOX 1–2

Researchers Speak Out on the Role of Research in Teaching Practice

Directions: Read the view of each of the following researchers. Do you see any common ideas? Do you perceive any differences? Look especially at the comments made by Gage. How is his view different from the views expressed by the other researchers?

Eisner

What I do not believe holds promise in education is a prescriptive view of science. I do not believe that with greater specificity or by reducing the whole to its most essential parts we can produce the kind of prescriptions that have made the space shuttle, radar, or laser beam possible. The aspiration to create a prescriptive science of educational practice is, I believe, hopeless.

What I think scientific inquiry *can* [sic] provide in education are rules of thumb, not rules. Rules of thumb are schematics that make interpretation and judgment more accurate. Scientific inquiry can provide frames of reference that can sophisticate our perceptions, not mechanisms that will control the behavior of students, teachers, or administrators. (Eisner, 1983, p. 9)

Feiman

Those who would share research findings with teachers in the hopes of improving their practice should be explicit about the educational values which shape their work. In this way, teachers can examine recommended practices in relation to their own values and purposes. It would also encourage teachers to view research findings not as prescriptions to be followed in a routine way but rather as hypotheses to be tested and evaluated in their own situations. (Feiman, 1979, p. 78)

Gage

Both preservice and inservice teachers should be given the full story: how the research-based practices were identified, why they seem reasonable, how they work, and what questions might be raised about their scientific and moral bases. Each teacher should be asked to confront the moral issue of whether these practices can justifiably be rejected on the basis of the teacher's own experience, intuitions, hunches, or predilections. If teachers can justify a rejection of these findings on good, intellectual and moral grounds, they should do so. But if they cannot, then they should face the kinds of moral forces that led them to become teachers in the first place—forces that led them to seek to help others achieve personal goals and social values. (Gage, 1985, p. 101)

FOCUS BOX 1–3

Take a Moment to Reflect

The following paper shares the emergent beliefs of one preservice teacher about how research should be used by teachers. Consider the following questions as you read the paper:

- What are the most important points that he makes?
- With which points do you agree? Disagree? Why?

"Research Says. . . ."

By David Hoffman, Preservice Teacher, University of Florida

I'm always surprised to find "in-service" teachers so little influenced by current educational research. A field advisor [practicum supervisor] noted that most teachers respond to the statement, "research says . . .," with the question, "What research?" The question is not a search for knowledge, but an excuse for ignoring the research (at least in many cases). At first this struck me as a very poor attitude; however, there is a deep wisdom in that question if we ask it sincerely.

The truth is, we should all be sincerely asking, "What research?" each time we are presented with new findings. How can we adopt research findings to use, if we don't know the conditions under which to apply them? Does a farmer indiscriminately spray pesticide on his crops without knowing the conditions where he can expect it to work? Let's hope not—it would not only be wasteful, but dangerous. And so it is with teaching as well. . . .

I'm constantly hearing, and even saying, "Research says. . . ." Now I recoil at such an unsupported statement of "fact." I want to know who did the research and under what conditions and limitations. I want to be more circumspect in adopting research findings. I want to read the "fine print" that is often ignored. As professionals, and if we want to be considered professionals, we must apply our "remedies" as carefully as a physician prescribes his medicines. As an educator, my future practices will be much different [than what I am seeing now].

Now that you've read David's ideas, what are your own? What is the role of research in your view? Many argue that preservice teachers are overly idealistic. Do you think David is too idealistic? Why? How is your view of the role of research different than his and why?

researchers and compare them to their own. For example, research about the characteristics of effective **teacher-centered lessons** (i.e., instruction characterized by teacher lecture, large-group format, recitation, and discussion) provides us with much insight about how to design and sequence lessons. However, the research will not be useful to a teacher who wants to know the characteristics of good **guided-discovery lessons** (i.e., lessons in which the teacher plans activities or experiences designed to guide children to discover important learnings) because the goals of these research studies do not match the goals of the teacher.

In addition to assessing whether the findings of any research study are appropriate to their goals, their instructional context, and their student population, teachers must themselves become inquirers in order to make intelligent use of research. In implementing the findings of research, teachers must experiment with recommended teaching strategies and assess their effectiveness.

Assumption 7: Teaching Requires a Commitment to Professional Development and Growth

The preceding assumptions make the point that teachers are constantly encountering novel situations. No teacher education program, no matter how thorough, can prepare teachers for all the situations they will encounter. Additionally, new knowledge important for teachers is generated each year. This means that teachers must be committed to continual professional growth if they are to provide the best instruction for their students (Bagenstos, 1975; Copeland, 1986; Korthagen, 1985; Zeichner & Liston, 1987). Reflection is a process that enables teachers to direct their learning throughout their professional lives.

Perhaps even more importantly, teachers are models for their students. If teachers expect their students to be committed to learning, they themselves must be committed to learning. The students must see that their teachers are excited by inquiry and the opportunity to learn new things. Excitement and boredom are contagious. Teachers who are bored with their classrooms, who believe they have *mastered* teaching and have settled comfortably into a predictable routine, will bore their students. Teachers who reflect about their experiences have a strong impetus for growth and change that will be reflected in their classrooms. Change can help focus children's attention on new activities or revitalize their interest in learning skills that have become too routine. Change can also provide a solution to an educational problem, such as a decline in student motivation. Change keeps a teacher from stagnating. However, not all change is for the better, so efforts at change must include reflection about the impact of such changes. In this way the cycle of action-observation-reflection-revised action provides a means of both professional growth and improved practice.

Summary

Why is reflection essential in teaching? We discussed seven assumptions about teaching and the role of teachers in classrooms to support the importance of reflection. Teaching is complex. Neither research and theory, nor practical experience can provide the answers to instructional problems. Because of this fact, judgment is, in our view, the most fundamental ability a teacher must have. Yet, teachers' judgments can be good or poor, founded or unfounded. Reflection improves a teacher's ability to make founded judgments. Through reflection, a teacher is able to make tacit beliefs explicit and thus available for examination and revision if necessary. Through reflection, a teacher is able to make and assess decisions about the application of theory and research within specific practical settings. Most importantly, reflection enables teachers to assess their ongoing efforts to empower children to become full participants within a democratic society. That is, through reflection teachers can examine the students' perspectives and assess the impact of decisions on the learning and behavior of students. And through reflection, teachers can constantly reevaluate their ability to fulfill their ethical commitments to children and society.

FOCUS BOX 1–4

Take a Moment to Reflect

In this chapter, we have presented several controversial ideas. What are *your* reactions to these ideas? How do they compare to those of your peers? How do these ideas fit with your entering ideas about teaching? Whether you accept or reject these ideas, you must evaluate the evidence you use in making a judgment. What do you think of the following ideas?

- All teachers, even excellent ones, hold tacit beliefs which may hamper their efforts to help children learn.
- The problems of teaching and learning have no fixed answers. (Is teaching highly complex and ambiguous, or are we making something that is essentially simple seem too complicated? How is knowledge about teaching similar to or different from other kinds of knowledge? Do historical, scientific, or mathematical problems have fixed answers? What are the educational implications of your answer?)
- Knowledge is constructed rather than transmitted; therefore, teaching requires much more than telling. (If teaching isn't telling, what is it? What is involved in teaching? Try to give a concrete example of teaching that is not telling. Is there a role for telling? If so, what is that role?)
- Teachers in a democratic society have an obligation to help children grow up dedicated to the worth and dignity of each individual, to recognize the need to balance the rights of individuals against the rights of the rest of society, and to value and work toward the democratic ideal of equity. Do you believe this is the foremost goal for American elementary teachers? Why or why not?

Share your views with your colleagues. As you discuss your conclusions focus on the following:

1. What evidence can you provide that your conclusions are valid? (*Note:* Evidence can come from this chapter, related readings, classroom experiences, or life experiences; however, it is important that you be explicit about the source and quality of your evidence.)
2. What additional evidence might you want to collect?

What Must One Learn in Order to Teach Reflectively?

Before describing the components of reflective teaching, think about the meaning of the word *reflect*. Consider the meaning of the word in the following sentences:

1. During the frenzy of the teaching day, it is often hard to find a moment to *reflect*.
2. This paper *reflects* Alan's best writing.

In the first sentence, *reflect* means to think or to think back. In the second, *reflect* means to demonstrate or present an example. In common usage, we use one or the other meaning. In describing the elements of the reflective process, however, we must draw on both meanings simultaneously. The reflective process involves thinking but moves beyond thinking to the collection and presentation of evidence to support the conclusions of one's thinking. Thinking does not necessarily require making a decision or collecting evidence about the quality of that decision. The reflective process does. The discussion of the components of the reflective process demonstrates the importance of both definitions of the word.

The Role of Dilemmas in Reflective Teaching

According to Dewey (1933), who could be called the father of reflection, the reflective process *begins with an experienced dilemma*. A **dilemma** is a problem or problematic situation to which there is no readily identifiable correct answer. A critical ability in the development of reflective judgment is the ability to identify dilemmas. In fact, the characteristic that differentiates highly reflective teachers from their colleagues may well be the ability to see dilemmas where others do not. Learning to recognize dilemmas in the classroom where you are teaching (or student teaching) is the first ability you must develop. How can you learn to recognize dilemmas?

We previously stated that the reflective process involves both thinking and the collection of evidence. Recognition of dilemmas requires that teachers spend time thinking (reflecting) about classroom interactions. While they are teaching, teachers are unlikely to have much time to mull over each lesson and their interactions with children and other adults in the school. However, when the school day is over, reflective teachers frequently ponder the events of the day. What happened today? How did the lesson on gravity go? Did the children really understand that demonstration? Was it my imagination or did the girls seem totally uninvolved in our discussion during social studies today? What did the principal think about the fight at the water fountain today? Why did Kevin and Toby get so upset about who went first?

As a result of thinking about what occurred each day, reflective teachers identify unresolved problems or situations that they would like to improve. Perhaps the reason some teachers are able to see dilemmas where others do not is simply that they spend more time thinking and asking themselves questions about what happens in their classrooms. However, it is important to stress that thoughtful reexamination of the daily events of teaching, while important, is a limited concept of reflection. Reflection requires more than thinking back over the school day, because any teacher working in isolation is likely to have difficulty identifying dilemmas, no matter how thoughtfully practice is approached. Interaction with other teachers, with printed materials, or within staff development activities or college courses provides an important impetus for reflection. Interaction brings teachers into contact with new ideas and with alternative perspectives about practice that will enable them to perceive problems that they would like to improve.

As you begin thinking about your classroom interactions, you may have difficulty recognizing dilemmas. A key point to remember is that the dilemmas *are* present; you just have to learn to recognize them. If you have difficulty identifying dilemmas, Berlak and Berlak (1981) identify sixteen dilemmas that confront teachers. The dilemmas represent contradictions within our society that influence teachers as they engage in the work of educating children. The work of Berlak and Berlak may help you recognize dilemmas you hold tacitly. As you read this book and talk about the ideas with your peers, you probably will begin to identify dilemmas in your teaching. Reading examples of dilemmas experienced by other teachers may also stimulate your ideas. The dilemmas in Focus Box 1–5 have been

FOCUS BOX 1–5

Sample Dilemmas

When I first started teaching, I did not know how I wanted to control the behavior of my children. Because most of the teachers in my school were using a reward system for classroom management, I used this practice, too, and I have found it effective at controlling disruptive behavior. In my teacher education program we just read that extrinsic motivation can decrease the internal motivation of children. Would another method of discipline work as well? Will it be too confusing for the children if I use a method of discipline that differs from the one used by most of the other teachers in the school? Could I actually pull it off? Can I manage a classroom without the use of extrinsic rewards? Do I want to?

I've been really concerned about the low-achieving children in my classroom. I felt they were being slighted and I wanted to compensate. Boy, have I ever compensated. Today one of the brightest children in the class asked me why I didn't like him. He said I never call on him in class or pick him to do things. Now I fear that I have not been treating the children more fairly. I may have started favoring a different set of children. How can I work out an appropriate balance in the classroom? Is it inevitable that someone gets shortchanged?

There was a fight on the playground today. I stopped the children by yelling at them and by taking away the rest of their play time. The fighting was stopped but I felt badly for the rest of the day. I yelled and I punished. That's not the way I envisioned my interactions with children. What could I do next time that would be effective at stopping the fight but that would make me feel better about myself?

I have just completed a reading course at the university. The course stressed that children need to spend time reading and writing for meaning if they are to become literate. This makes a lot of sense to me, and I would like to change what I am doing in my classroom. However, my school system has a long list of skills that the children must master in second grade. The reading series has lots of drills on those skills. I know the children are bored by the drills and that they are developing negative attitudes about reading, but I'm worried they might fail the skill tests if I change my approach. I just don't know what to do.

experienced by teachers or student teachers with whom we have worked. They may help you recognize dilemmas in your classroom.

The dilemmas presented in Focus Box 1–5 sound well reasoned and thoughtful, because we required students to write their dilemmas. In reality, a dilemma often begins with a sense of disquiet—a feeling that something is wrong or could be better. A dilemma need not be a problem. It frequently is, but reflection also may begin with a vague sense that a situation could be improved. Once a dilemma has been sensed, the reflective process begins.

Thus far, our discussion reveals that reflection begins with and is grounded in the thinking of the teacher, and involves making decisions and evaluating the quality of those decisions. In the sections that follow, we will describe the fundamental structure of the reflective process and the knowledge base essential to reflection. Then we will discuss the abilities and attitudes that must be developed to support the reflective process. The basic structure of reflection in action is a synthesis of Schon's (1983) work on reflective practice and Kemmis and McTaggart's (1982) work on action research. If you are interested in a more thorough discussion of the components of reflection, read the research by Schon (1983) or Ross (1987). In our discussion of the structure of reflection, it sounds as if the teacher follows a series of steps; however, in reality the *steps* are less distinct than suggested. Many of the components are mental processes that may occur simultaneously or may occur in a different order. Reflection involves all of these components, but there is no fixed order in actual practice.

The Cycle of Reflective Teaching

In presenting a model for the cycle of reflective teaching, we have adapted a cycle Kemmis and McTaggart (1982) suggest as appropriate **action research** (i.e., research done by teachers to answer questions important to the practice of teaching) (see Figure 1–1).

Figure 1–1

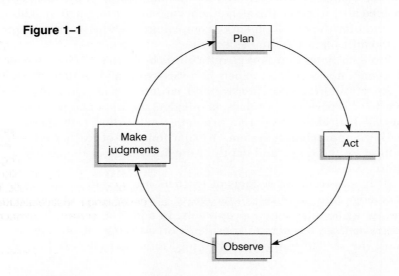

Although action research, which will be described in more detail in Chapter 12, is more systematic than day-to-day reflective teaching, the basic processes are the same.

PLAN.   Each component of the reflective process is important; however, planning sets the stage for the rest of the cycle. **Planning** involves consideration of two important issues: (1) definition of the problem, and (2) an active search for a desirable solution.

Problem definition is critical, because some definitions will narrow the range of alternatives considered and tried, therefore precluding successful resolution of dilemmas. Consider, for example, a teacher who observes a student, Jayne, dawdling over reading assignments and repeatedly failing to complete them. The teacher may ask, "How can I improve Jayne's ability to complete assigned tasks?" This definition of the problem may lead the teacher to develop management systems that will encourage Jayne to complete her work. The teacher might give Jayne tokens for each assignment completed and allow her to exchange tokens for special privileges. The teacher might schedule a parent conference to ask Jayne's parents to encourage her to complete her work. The teacher might establish a classroom routine in which Jayne loses free time unless all work is completed. However, the current definition of the problem precludes the consideration of other possible solutions.

Observation of the same behavior could be interpreted in other ways. For example, another teacher might ask, "How can I encourage Jayne to practice skills and concepts necessary for the development of competence in reading?" Notice that this definition of the problem is broader than the previous one and is grounded in the teacher's ethical commitment to provide all children with access to knowledge. In addition, the teacher does not assume that the problem is rooted in Jayne's lack of ability to stay on task, leaving open the possibility of exploring alternative reasons for the problem. Asking this question might lead the teacher to analyze whether the motivational quality of the assignments might be problematic, whether the assignments are in fact targeted at skills and concepts essential for the development of competence, or whether the assignments might be too difficult or too simple.

Problem definition is very difficult. Schon (1983) notes that one difference between a novice and an expert in a variety of fields is that the expert is able to develop a more comprehensive and more relevant definition of the problem. Teachers' repertoires of values, knowledge, theories, and practices are major factors in their ability to define problems well. Schon calls these repertoires the teachers' **appreciation system**. A major function of teacher education should be to increase the range and depth of the knowledge in the appreciation system of future teachers.

If the appreciation systems of teachers are composed of extensive and valid knowledge, they are likely to recognize a broader array of educational dilemmas and to define dilemmas appropriately. In addition, comprehensive appreciation systems enable teachers to consider a broad range of possible alternative solutions, the second important planning issue. Actively searching for a desirable

FOCUS BOX 1–6

The Nature and Role of Professional Knowledge

Teachers, like all professionals, have specialized knowledge that enables them to make professional decisions. This specialized knowledge, or **appreciation system,** includes the teacher's:

- beliefs about teaching, learning, children, the subject matter to be taught, and the purposes of elementary schools within a democratic society
- knowledge of relevant theory and research (e.g, from fields such as education, sociology, psychology)
- experiences with children both within and outside the classroom setting
- knowledge of the subject matter to be taught
- knowledge of alternative teaching strategies
- knowledge of the purpose and consequences of various teaching strategies
- knowledge of the student's point of view

Teachers acquire some of this knowledge through reading and careful study of relevant literature; they acquire some of it through experience with children in classrooms and through interaction with knowledgeable colleagues. Teachers develop most of this knowledge through an interaction between research and practical experience. Theory and research inform practice; practice informs theory and research. You will note, however, that theory and research play an important role.

There is an oft-told tale in teacher education of an experienced teacher who tells the novice teacher, "Forget everything you learned up at the university. This is the real world and all that theory is useless. Here you learn what works." Undoubtedly, there are teachers who believe this. However, the number of teachers attending graduate school, subscribing to professional journals, and attending professional conferences suggests that there are many teachers who recognize that there is much to learn from theory. An appreciation system based predominantly in practical experience is incomplete and may include many unexamined beliefs that can undermine a teacher's effectiveness. The same is true, however, of an appreciation system based solely on theory. Both sources of knowledge are critical for teachers. A teacher's appreciation system is dynamic. As teachers acquire new information and experiences, the appreciation system changes.

solution to a dilemma is a mental process in which teachers consider a variety of alternative solutions and examine the potential consequences of each. Notice that we said "*a* desirable solution to a dilemma," not the best solution. While a *right* or *best* solution will be apparent at times, this will not always be the case. For example, Lampert (1985) describes an instructional dilemma in which the academic and motivational needs of the boys in a classroom conflicted with those of the girls. A solution that met the needs of one group was not useful for the other group. Using a process she calls **"dilemma management,"** Lampert opted for the least undesirable solution and continued to monitor the effect of her instructional decision on the students and to search for a more desirable resolution. You may find yourself managing, rather than resolving, dilemmas more often than you wish.

The mental process of exploring alternatives is usually not open to public examination. However, when teachers keep journals, the thinking involved in this part of the process is often revealed. Let's examine a hypothetical journal entry written by Ms. Green as she tackles the second definition of the problem posed by the student Jayne, discussed previously. Notice that as Ms. Green explores alternatives, she also continues to work on problem definition, because these two issues are integrally related. Notice how she uses evidence and professional knowledge to define the problem and consider alternatives. As teachers gain more experience, they become capable of collecting and using evidence to define dilemmas and develop alternatives.

> Well, the problem could be that Jayne lacks the self-discipline necessary to complete her work, but she has no problem completing her math work. Maybe she's just not interested in reading. Maybe she works better in the afternoon than in the morning—no that doesn't seem likely. Maybe the work is too hard, but she seems to do ok when we do similar work in the reading group. Maybe she's bored.
>
> Now that I think about it, in my reading course last semester we looked at assignments like these and decided they don't focus on skills and concepts essential for learning to read and aren't very interesting. Jayne is the only one not doing them, but I wonder how the other children feel about them. Are they learning enough from them to justify the amount of class time we spend on them? But do I feel qualified to change the entire reading program? Would the kids miss out on some essential skills if I skipped some of these assignments? What would the other third grade teachers think? I bet the principal would be on my case, too. She keeps stressing that it's important for the kids to do well on skill tests. Still, the current focus of the reading program doesn't match what I think the children should be doing. I think perhaps the low-achieving kids like Jayne are suffering more than the others. If I don't help Jayne learn to love reading, who will? What will her future be like if she is turned off by schoolwork? Then again, changing the reading program would involve an awful lot of work and I might upset the principal, parents, and other teachers. I wonder if it's worth all the trouble, but what am I going to do about Jayne! Maybe I could revise some of the assignments but keep others. Maybe I could figure out a way to make the current assignments more interesting. Maybe if Jayne worked with a friend, she would complete her work.

Essentially at this stage the teacher plays with possible ideas, considering a variety of goals and the implications of potential actions. Possible consequences for children, parents, administrators, fellow teachers, and the teacher are considered.

ACT, OBSERVE, AND MAKE JUDGMENTS.   Although these are three distinct processes, in practice they most often occur simultaneously. During the planning process the teacher makes a decision about a problem solution strategy. Obviously, the next step is to implement the plan (**act**), observe what happens (**observe**), and make a judgment about the relative success or failure of the plan in terms of one's goals and ethical commitments (**make judgments**). Teachers begin making assessments from the moment implementation begins. As they interact with students, they observe to assess student reactions (e.g., What do students say and do? What kinds of products do they produce? What are students' current understandings of these concepts and skills?). In some cases, these observations will be very informal; in others, the teacher will systematically collect information from students using such methods as questionnaires, interviews, and samples of students' work. Obviously, the more systematic the observation methods, the more valuable the information is in helping teachers make judgments. It is important to note that even when observations are informal, the reflective process is based in the collection of evidence about the impact of teaching decisions. We are not simply talking about an intuitive sense that a strategy did or did not work. We are talking about the collection of evidence that is used to draw conclusions about student learning and development. Here again, the breadth and depth of the teacher's appreciation system is critical. Teachers with comprehensive appreciation systems have greater knowledge about the range and variety of evidence they might collect and have a coherent set of values to use in making judgments about the impact of their actions.

To make judgments the teacher examines intended and **unintended or implicit consequences** of an implemented solution and evaluates whether the consequences are desirable or undesirable. Children are always learning. They just may not be learning what we intend for them to learn. At times the teacher may achieve the intended result, but due to the unintended consequences, the teacher decides to redefine the problem and begin again. Again, the range and depth of a teacher's appreciation system will be a factor in that teacher's ability to make judgments about the impact of practice. To illustrate, let's continue following Ms. Green as she attempts to improve Jayne's efforts at work completion.

Suppose Ms. Green begins by trying a token economy system for motivation. She gives Jayne tokens for completing her work and allows her to spend the tokens to purchase free time. After implementing the plan, Ms. Green observes that Jayne is completing her reading assignments, so the intended result has been achieved. However, she also observes that Jayne, who used to read trade books frequently at free time, has stopped selecting this activity. The unintended consequence of the experiment was undermining Ms. Green's broader goal—to help children develop a long-term interest in reading. Additionally, the use of a token system might lead Jayne to become dependent on Ms. Green to determine whether she is using her time productively. If Ms. Green believes that she has an ethical responsibility to help Jayne become self-sufficient and therefore able to make independent decisions about how to use time wisely, she would perceive the token system as having a negative consequence. Because neither of these consequences would be desirable, Ms. Green's reflection would probably lead her to consider additional strategies for resolving this instructional dilemma, beginning the reflective teaching cycle anew. (For more information about the evaluation of unintended consequences, see the section on implicit curriculum in Chapter 3.)

Our attempt to explain the components of the reflective process makes it appear that the reflective teacher engages in a structured form of decision making that is highly disciplined and very time consuming. At times this may be true. As we have noted, some teachers undertake action research projects, in which they systematically develop and evaluate strategies designed to resolve a problem of teaching practice. Such projects are probably the clearest example of reflective practice in action (see Chapter 12). At other times, however, the moment of reflection is quite brief; decisions seem to be made instantaneously, and the structure of the reflective process is not apparent.

In learning any complex skill, practice is, at first, cumbersome and tedious. This will undoubtedly be true as you attempt to practice reflective teaching. However, it is important to walk through each part of the reflective process in your early attempts. As you become more experienced, you will find that reflection will become a habit and that you are no longer aware of the component parts. Becoming a reflective teacher requires more than the ability to follow the parts of the cycle. That is, reflective teachers must do more than go through the motions; they must do them well. How do we recognize a good reflective teacher? Let's look at the attitudes and abilities that are required for competent reflection.

Attitudes Required for Competent Reflection

Reflective teachers spend a great deal of time thinking about classroom interactions and the intended and unintended consequences of their actions. One teacher told us that good teachers just "worry a lot" about what children say and think, how others perceive them, and whether they have done or said the right thing. In other words, good teachers are **introspective**. They engage in the thoughtful reconsideration of all that happens in a classroom with an eye toward improvement. Teachers who are not introspective are less likely to recognize dilemmas, have little impetus for change or improvement, and are unlikely to achieve their professional potential.

Another attitude that we have already discussed is a willingness to take **responsibility** for one's decisions and actions. Recall the teacher at the beginning of this chapter who taught inconsistently with her beliefs about how children learn because she had been told to do so. No teachers can achieve consistence between his/her beliefs and practice all of the time. Human behavior is simply not consistent. Additionally, the beliefs of teachers will, at times, conflict with those of parents, administrators, curriculum specialists, or other teachers; and compromises will have to be made. However, each teacher must accept the responsibility for assuring that important beliefs are not abandoned. It is one thing to compromise; it is another to allow others to make your professional decisions.

A final attitude that is critical is **open-mindedness,** a willingness to consider new evidence as it occurs and to admit the possibility of error. In one example cited previously, Ms. Green noticed that Jayne's selections during free activity time changed when she implemented a token system to reinforce work completion. She demonstrated open-mindedness by observing this change in Jayne's behavior, recognizing it as evidence related to her new instructional practice, and admitting that the token system may have been ill conceived. In the journal entry, the teacher demonstrated open-mindedness by using information gained in a university course to evaluate her current instructional practice.

Being open-minded requires one to criticize oneself. Self-criticism is hard. All of us like to be right; we like to do things well; we do not like to be reminded of our fallibility. However, teachers who are unable to acknowledge their errors tend to blame children for any problems that may arise during the teaching/learning process. If 90 percent of the class fails a test, such teachers accuse the students of not studying, not considering the possibility that the material or the approach was inappropriate. Certainly, both good and poor teachers make mistakes; however, what differentiates them is that good teachers recognize, learn from, and correct their mistakes. Additionally, open-minded teachers continually seek new information that might challenge their taken-for-granted assumptions about teaching, thus broadening their appreciation systems. Sources of new information include university courses, interactions with colleagues, journal articles, books, and staff development activities.

Abilities Required for Competent Reflection

Let's look back at Ms. Green's journal entry to identify some of the abilities of the reflective teacher. As Ms. Green considers what to do, she asks a number of questions that demonstrate her ability to *view situations from multiple perspectives*. She wonders how all the children in the class feel about the assignments from the basal. She considers what other teachers, parents, and the principal would think if she stopped using the assignments. She wonders about the impact of boring or inappropriate reading assignments on the reading motivation of low achievers. She is even quite honest about the reasons for her personal reservations about changing the curriculum—it would involve an "awful lot of work." Viewing situations from multiple perspectives is critical to a teacher's effectiveness in the classroom and in the school. Seeing things from the student perspective helps teachers understand how children interpret lessons and classroom events, making it more likely that they can present lessons in ways that children will understand. As important as this is, teachers also must be able to see things from the perspective of society and of other adults in the school setting. No matter how good teachers are, they are unlikely to teach for long if they alienate administrators, fellow teachers, and parents. Beyond survival, the ability to see things from other perspectives enables a teacher to envision a broad range of potential solutions and makes it more likely that instructional dilemmas will be resolved.

Ms. Green also *searches for alternative explanations of classroom events*. Perhaps Jayne lacks sufficient self-discipline or is not interested in reading. Perhaps the work is too hard or too boring. Settling too quickly on one explanation of behavior is the primary reason teachers define problems too narrowly, and thus limit the number of potential solutions. Viewing things from multiple perspectives helps a teacher find alternative explanations. For example, part of what the teacher needs to do in many situations is to try to "get into the child's head" to see how the child interprets the event. As the teacher tries to understand the child's perspective, many alternative explanations might be explored, as was the case with Ms. Green.

Consider a teacher who has been told by the principal that a learning center approach "just doesn't fit into this school." One explanation for this edict is that the principal does not like centers. Another is that the principal likes children to be seated and apparently working whenever an adult enters the room. Another is that the principal is concerned that this teacher is not experienced enough to run a good center-based program. An adequate search for alternative explanations makes it more likely that a teacher will discover the appropriate one, define the problem correctly, and find a solution.

Perhaps the most difficult task teachers face is to attempt to search for alternative explanations for their own behavior, yet this too is critical in a reflective approach. Consider this example drawn from the experiences of a first-year teacher:

> Mr. Weston is teaching a language arts lesson to his fourth graders. As he begins, Gregory stands and says loudly, "Tom Jones, please come to the office! Tom Jones, please come to the office." The entire class begins laughing. Mr. Weston, outraged that Gregory would interrupt in this way (not the first time he has "pulled such tricks"), is angry at him and at the class for laughing. He immediately sends Greg to the office, lectures the class about being serious about learning, and tries to continue. But the mood in the classroom is tense, and the lesson does not go well.
>
> Later that day, Mr. Weston reflects on the experience. He decides he was so angry because Gregory was disruptive, interfering with the lesson and the learning of all the other children. He begins to think of ways to control Gregory better and plans to schedule a parent conference to get parent help in stopping Gregory's outrageous behavior.
>
> Later that week, something said in a university course makes Mr. Weston rethink the reasons for his anger. Maybe Gregory's behavior was less significant than the feelings of insecurity his behavior provoked. True, Gregory was disruptive, but what made Mr. Weston so angry was the fear of being out of control, of losing the respect of the class. He begins to realize that it was his anger, not Gregory's behavior, that communicated to the class that he had lost control. A better response to Greg might have been to parlay back, "He doesn't seem to be here." The class might have laughed again, and all could have returned to the lesson. This insight helps Mr. Weston begin to relax with the class and marks the beginning of a new relationship with Gregory.

The ability to search for alternative explanations of your own behavior obviously is related to developing the attitudes mentioned previously. You must be introspective, open-minded, and willing to accept responsibility for your behavior if you are to deduce the motivations behind your behavior. This ability is of critical importance. Teaching involves the interaction between teacher and student. The teacher influences the students; the students influence the teacher. Any problem occurring in the classroom, therefore, is an interaction problem. When you hear yourself say, "I don't know what is wrong with this class today. The kids are driving me crazy. They are off the wall!" (and you inevitably will), stop and think. The problem is not "the kids"; the problem is one of interaction, and both teacher and students are involved. Remember, teaching is a difficult balancing act. One of the most difficult aspects of this involves the resolution of teacher/student interaction problems (others might call this discipline). The teacher must constantly ask the questions, "What am I doing that is contributing to this? How much of this is my problem? How much is the student's problem? How much responsibility should I accept here?" Discipline problems (interaction problems) are a major reason for teacher failure in the early years of teaching. Consequently, developing the ability to search for alternative explanations is important for both survival and effectiveness.

The last ability the reflective teacher must develop is the ability to *use adequate evidence in supporting or evaluating a decision or position*. Notice this statement has two parts. First, the teacher must be able to identify and collect adequate evidence. Then the teacher must be able to use that evidence to support or evaluate a decision, practice, or position.

By evidence we mean more than developing a feeling that children liked the lesson and are mastering the concepts taught. We are not suggesting teachers must use test scores as evidence to support their instructional decisions. Remember reflective teaching is grounded in an assumption that the teacher must understand the child's perspective because knowledge is constructed. If one accepts this assumption, one of the most important roles of the teacher is to assess the understandings constructed by students as a result of one's teaching practices. Some of these understandings will be academic (e.g., facts, concepts, generalizations). Others will involve development of perceptions of self and others, as well as the development of attitudes and values. Teachers must evaluate all of these student learnings in terms of their long-term goals and their ethical commitments to help students develop the knowledge, skills, and abilities necessary to participate fully and intelligently in a democracy. Earlier we suggested that you might collect information using strategies such as observation, interviews, questionnaires, and collection of samples of student work. As you read other chapters in this book, you will learn more about the kinds of information you might collect and ways to collect that information relative to various educational aims.

In addition to collecting evidence, teachers must apply criteria to evaluate the quality of their decisions. A great deal of evidence suggests that many teachers evaluate lessons by determining whether they *work*. This means that the lessons keep children on task and quiet. This criterion is important, but not sufficient. A teacher might require that students color all of the pictures in a primary language arts workbook. Consequently, students would spend a significant portion of their language arts period coloring pictures. Although the children would be quiet and on task, no language arts learning would occur. In fact, aside from the possibility of practicing fine motor skills, no learning would occur at all. Additionally, students might learn implicitly that they must engage in tasks simply because the teacher assigns them. This kind of passive acceptance is inconsistent with a commitment to continuous inquiry required in a democratic society.

In evaluating their decisions teachers must simultaneously use three different types of criteria (Van Manen, 1977). As you read these criteria, remember that many teachers tend to focus only on the first criterion—Does it work? Undoubtedly, this is because it is a significant challenge to keep a classroom of 30 or so youngsters well-disciplined and on task. However, it is important to remember that this criterion is not sufficient. The second and third criteria are the ones that make teaching a profession, as opposed to a technical skill.

1. Does it work? Is it possible to implement a particular strategy or approach?

2. Is the approach educationally sound? Are the children learning appropriate skills, concepts, attitudes, and values using methods consistent with good pedagogy? Is time being used productively and responsibly? Are children constructing new understandings (not parroting memorized phrases or skills)?

3. Is the approach ethically defensible? Are the children learning in ways that will enable them to grow up to be responsible citizens who can participate fully and intelligently in a democratic society? Is each child treated with dignity and respect? Are the needs of each individual child balanced equitably with the needs of the other children within the class? Are the children developing the capacity to care and be concerned about one another and their world?

In addition to using these three criteria to evaluate their own professional decisions, teachers must evaluate the evidence of others who suggest that they should change their teaching practices. Some suggestions may be inappropriate given the teacher's goals or the characteristics of the students in the class. Professional teachers must be given the autonomy to determine when and whether suggestions about teaching practice are appropriate. If teachers are granted this professional autonomy, they must be able to use adequate evidence to support a position. Parents and administrators are far more likely to accept alternative instructional practices from teachers who can marshall strong theoretical and practical evidence to support their practices than they are from teachers who simply say they "prefer to teach this way."

Summary

We have presented reflective teaching as a cycle that begins with a dilemma. During this cycle, the recognition of dilemmas, the development of plans, the collection of evidence and one's judgments about the impact of one's actions will be informed by one's appreciation system. Putting the whole cycle together

FOCUS BOX 1–7

Take a Moment to Reflect

Directions: Record your answers to the following questions to assess your understanding of the key ideas that we presented in the second half of this chapter.

1. Clarify *your* definition of and commitment to reflective teaching by answering the following questions.

   a. Explain your view of the most important elements of reflective teaching. Why is each important? Compare your ideas with those of your peers.

   b. Why do some teachers innovate and question their teaching practices when others seem to feel comfortable with very traditional practices? What could you do to maintain a questioning attitude?

2. Mr. Slater has decided to change his approach to science teaching. Instead of having children read science concepts in the text, observe his demonstration of experiments, and record their observations, he will have the children make predictions, conduct experiments, and record and explain results in terms of their predictions and further reading. He reports that the change has been "really positive because the kids really love science now, especially the science experiments."

   a. Has Mr. Slater's change been a positive one? How do you know?

   b. Is there anything else you might want to know before you draw a conclusion?

   c. From your answer to this question, can you develop any general criteria for assessing the quality of your teaching decisions?

Share your answers with your colleagues. As you discuss your conclusions focus on the following:

1. What evidence can you provide that your answer is valid? *(Note:* Evidence can come from this chapter, from related readings, from classroom experiences, or from life experiences; however, it is important that you be explicit about the source and quality of evidence.)

2. What additional evidence should you collect?

---

involves altering our original diagram to make it more complete (see Figure 1–2).

Planning involves the ability to define the problem or dilemma and to search actively for a desirable solution, using practical, educational, and ethical criteria. Once a teacher defines the problem and selects and develops an action plan, the next step is to implement the plan (act), observe what happens (observe), and make a judgment about the consequences of implementation of the plan (make judgments). Throughout the process, the teacher's appreciation system will affect the nature and quality of decisions. Additionally, teachers need to develop several attitudes and abilities to demonstrate competent reflection. As you experiment with the reflective teaching cycle, use the following questions to assess your devel-

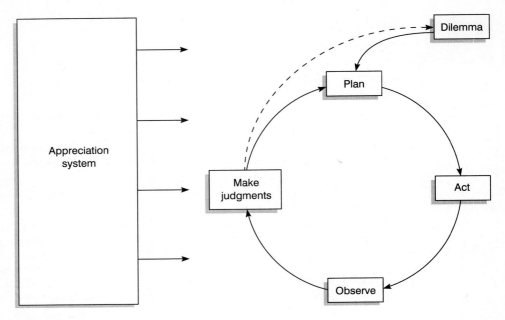

Figure 1–2

oping capacity to demonstrate the attitudes and abilities that represent competent reflection:

- Do I reconsider all that happens in my classroom with an eye toward improvement? Am I introspective?
- Do I accept responsibility for my decisions, or do I shift responsibility (or blame) to others when the decision contradicts my beliefs about good education?
- Am I willing to consider new evidence as it occurs and admit the possibility of error? Do I seek new information that might challenge my taken-for-granted assumptions about my teaching? Am I open-minded?
- Do I try to see things from multiple perspectives (e.g., those of the child, parents, administrators, society)?
- Do I search for alternative explanations of classroom events, especially for my own behavior?
- Do I use adequate evidence to support or evaluate my decisions and beliefs? Do I use educational and ethical criteria as well as practical criteria?

In conclusion, we feel it is important to emphasize the importance of the three criteria listed on page 28 that can be used to evaluate decisions. A teacher's reflective capacity depends on the ability to use all three criteria. Using the model and all the rest of the attitudes and abilities required of reflective teachers is insufficient unless the teacher evaluates practice in terms of educational, ethical, and practical criteria.

Further Readings

Eisner, E. (1983). The art and craft of teaching. *Educational Leadership, 40*. 4–18.

Goodman, J. (1984). Reflection and teacher education: A case study and theoretical analysis. *Interchange, 15* (3), 9–26.

Goodman, J. (1992). *Elementary schooling for critical democracy*. Albany, NY: SUNY Press.

Griffin, G. (1984). Why use research in preservice teacher education: A proposal. *Journal of Teacher Education, 35* (4), 36–40.

Lampert, M. (1985). How do teachers manage to teach? Perspectives on problems in practice. *Harvard Educational Review, 55* (2), 178–194.

Liston, D. P., & Zeichner, K. M. (1987). Reflective teacher education and moral deliberation. *Journal of Teacher Education, 38* (6), 2–9.

Schon, D. A. (1983). *The reflective practitioner*. New York: Basic Books.

Zeichner, K. M., & Liston, D. P. (1987). Teaching student teachers to reflect. *Harvard Educational Review, 57*, 23–48.

CHAPTER 2

Reflection and the Real World

You have learned what reflective teaching is and why it is important. You may now wonder whether such teaching is widely practiced, and if not, why not.

Is Reflection Possible?

The literature includes several examples of individual reflective teachers (e.g., Butt & Raymond, 1989; Kilgore, Ross, & Zbikowski, 1990; Ross, 1978) and of schools where reflective practice is the norm (Goodman, 1988; Goodman, 1992). However, a much larger number of studies suggests that reflective teaching is not the norm. Instead, many teacher education graduates develop a **utilitarian approach** rather than a reflective approach, focusing on practices that keep students quiet and on task with little consideration of broader educational objectives or ethical concerns (Goodman, 1986; Zeichner, 1980). Many teacher education graduates become "passive technicians who merely learn to execute pre-packaged instructional programs" (Goodman, 1986, p. 112). Wildman and Niles (1987) found that reflection is equally difficult for experienced teachers.

Research suggests that reflection is difficult, but it is not impossible; and there are indications that support for reflective practice is increasing. Major reform reports of the 1980s sent a strong message that school systems should provide teachers with increased autonomy and responsibility (Cornbleth, 1989). These recommendations recognize the importance of teaching as a profession and, if implemented, will make it more likely that schools will provide a context supportive of reflective practice.

While reflection is both important and possible, many factors can limit teachers' opportunities to be reflective. In this chapter, we will describe some of these influences. Understanding these influences will help you join the group of teachers who are able to teach reflectively, but understanding is just a first step. Throughout the book, we will suggest ways that you can empower yourself to become a reflective teacher. Before you read the rest of this chapter, complete the self-assessment in Focus Box 2–1 to determine your entering views about factors that may influence your professional development.

FOCUS BOX 2–1

Factors That Influence a Teacher's Ability to Teach Reflectively: A Self-Assessment

Directions: This activity is designed to help you think about a variety of factors that may influence your professional growth and development. Think for a minute about the teacher you want to become (i.e., your view of the ideal teacher). Then rank each of the following items from 1 to 4 to indicate your level of concern about the impact of each factor on your ability to become the teacher you want to be.

1 — Is *not* important
2 — Is slightly important
3 — Is of moderate importance
4 — Is *very* important

		1	2	3	4
1.	Decline or increase in student enrollment	1	2	3	4
2.	Changing characteristics and experiences of students	1	2	3	4
3.	Censorship of educational materials	1	2	3	4
4.	The current emphasis on accountability and testing	1	2	3	4
5.	Teacher licensure policies	1	2	3	4
6.	Legislative mandates about curriculum	1	2	3	4
7.	State adoption of textbooks	1	2	3	4
8.	The style and philosophy of my principal	1	2	3	4
9.	The nature of my professional interactions with teacher colleagues	1	2	3	4
10.	The philosophy and teaching style of my colleagues	1	2	3	4
11.	School organization and resources	1	2	3	4
12.	Mandates of school-level policies (e.g., format for planning)	1	2	3	4

Using the self-assessment: As you read the rest of the chapter, consider whether each factor now seems more or less important than when you completed the self-assessment. Compare your revised views with those of your classmates. Why are there differences? What is the significance of these differences?

Reflection and the Culture of Teaching

The culture of teaching, which influences teachers' perceptions of their role and the actions they take or do not take, can either limit or enhance a teacher's ability to be reflective. What does this mean? Before we examine the culture of teaching, let's consider what we mean by *culture*.

Culture involves the beliefs, knowledge, and behaviors shared by a particular group of people. When we think of culture, we frequently think of past civilizations, foreign countries, characteristic foods, religions, artwork, forms of government, and language. Thinking about our own culture is difficult, because we are so immersed in it that we do not usually see its distinctive characteristics. Yet, we think and act as we do because of the cultures in which we live. Note that we said *cultures* because multiple cultures exist within any society. Let's consider an example.

If you were (or are) in a sorority or fraternity during your undergraduate years in school, you most likely experienced college within a particular set of norms that influenced your behavior. Many of your friends were in sororities or fraternities. You had a number of special songs and symbols and you participated in rituals, such as pledging. Certain **norms** (informal rules) governed some and perhaps many of your social interactions. For example, you may have dressed in a particular way or dated particular people. You may have had rules about where and when you could eat, which meetings you could or could not miss. Because you belonged to the culture of sororities and fraternities, you experienced college in a particular way. However, this experience is only one component of college culture; others might stem from your major course of study, whether your parents lived nearby, whether you participated in student government, or whether you entered the school as a freshman. Because each person's college culture is a composite of multiple subcultures, describing *the* college culture is impossible. Yet it is possible to describe patterns and common threads.

This example illustrates how the subcultures in which you live influence your beliefs and your behaviors. The culture of teaching similarly is composed of many factors that exist to varying degrees and create an environment that tends to support or constrain reflective teaching. We will discuss three major categories of factors that contribute to the culture of teaching—(1) social forces, (2) state and school district policies, and (3) school-level influences.

Social Forces

Forces from the larger society can have a tremendous influence on what happens inside the schools and individual classrooms. These forces do not remain stable; they change constantly—sometimes quickly.

CHANGES IN SCHOOL POPULATION.   Two changes in school population have had and will continue to have a major impact on the culture of teaching. The first concerns changes in the number of elementary-age children. According to the U.S. Bureau of the Census (1989), the population of elementary-age children (ages 5–13) declined between 1970 and 1985, when the decline seemed to "bottom out." Many school districts with a decline in enrollment consequently faced a decline in funding.

The effects of the declining enrollments included fewer materials and activities, the omission of *frills* from the curriculum (e.g., music or art instruction in elementary school), and the transfer of teachers from school to school. Such situations can constrain teachers' reflection and decision making, as they focus their attention on the immediate problem of coping. Consider the teacher who has 15 years of experience as an elementary art teacher. Because she has seniority she can keep her job, but a decline in enrollment and funding could mean that she must transfer to a self-contained elementary classroom. In all likelihood, survival will become her main goal as she struggles to prepare herself to teach a variety of subject areas in which she has had minimal preparation and perhaps little interest.

However, data from the U.S. Bureau of the Census (1989) indicate an increase in the number of children in the elementary age group since 1985. The Bureau predicts:

> The elementary-school-age population (5 to 13 years) would be about 3 million larger in 1995 than it was in 1987 (30.8 million). . . . It is then projected to decline by 2 million between 1995 and 2005, but to remain larger than it was in 1987 until after 2030. (U.S. Bureau of the Census, 1989, pp. 6–7)

Just as a decrease in student population can constrain teacher reflection, so too can a rapid increase. Faced with too many children, school districts and teachers have to make decisions about finding enough space and materials. Adding portable units on school grounds is not uncommon. A large number of teachers and students may need to share instructional materials. Unless additional resource teachers are available, time allotments for physical education, music, art, and other special areas may be shortened in order to allow some time for everyone. In a *bursting-at-the-seams* atmosphere, teachers find little time for reflection about their decisions.

A second demographic change is even more significant. The characteristics and experiences of the students attending schools are changing, because the minority student population is increasing. Clearly, not all minority students are low achieving students. However, a great proportion of minority children are **at**

Changing demographics of the student population put more students at risk for dropping out before graduation.

risk for educational failure. From 1979 to 1980, the proportion of minority enrollment in schools rose from 21 percent to 27 percent of the total school population (Levin, 1986) due to a high minority birth rate and to immigration. Minority enrollment is increasing throughout the nation, but the data about minority enrollment in major cities (Levin, 1986) suggest the significance of these demographic changes: Miami, 71 percent; Philadelphia, 73 percent; New York, 74 percent; Los Angeles, 78 percent; Baltimore, 80 percent; Chicago, 84 percent; and Detroit, 89 percent.

Clearly, teachers must work with an increasingly diverse student population; however, research indicates that teachers enter teaching with conservative orientations, expect to teach in or near the communities where they lived as children, and expect the children they teach to be people like themselves (Paine, 1988). Consequently, many teachers will be unprepared to deal with the diversity they encounter. Although initially idealistic about their ability to make a difference with *all* children, teachers often find teaching a diverse student population extremely difficult and not at all what they expected. Again, confronted with difficult circumstances, many teachers focus on survival. As we noted in Chapter 1, experiencing failure is difficult, especially in one's early years of teaching. When a teacher is not able to reach children, self-preservation may mean that the teacher blames the children by saying, "I *am* a good teacher. Many of the children are learning. *Those* children are not learning because they come from poor environments. If they were ready to learn, I could teach them." This attitude (or low sense of efficacy) prohibits a teacher from searching for alternatives and limits the ability to be reflective. (See Chapter 1 for more discussion on efficacy.)

PUBLIC OPINION AND THE AGE OF ACCOUNTABILITY.   Public opinion has always influenced teachers. At one time, school boards issued "Rules for Teachers" which prohibited them from getting married or being out at night (except to go to church). We can be glad for social progress, but teachers still face public scrutiny, and this knowledge can affect decision making. Consider the issue of censorship and recent controversies over the use of particular books. In the last decade, textbook challenges have increased in school systems around the country, and several have become well-publicized legal battles. How might this issue limit teachers' reflection?

First, censorship might limit the range of materials teachers may select as they plan curriculum. A school system might determine that certain materials are too controversial, or a group of parents might challenge their appropriateness for elementary-age children. Second, textbook publishers, well aware of controversial topics, may omit certain topics from their publications. Therefore, teachers may find that these textbooks omit content they believe is important to teach. If they have little opportunity to supplement the text, the constraints on their decision making increase. In addition, the fear that challenges *might* occur can cause teachers to alter their selections of materials and classroom activities.

A second, and perhaps more powerful, example of the importance of public opinion is the public's demand that teachers be held **accountable** (i.e., able to account for student learning and behavior). In the 1980s accountability became a

FOCUS BOX 2–2

Take a Moment to Reflect

Is censorship a problem? Do parents have the right to ask that certain topics be omitted from the elementary curriculum? If they do, which parents decide? Should we omit anything that any parent finds objectionable? How do we make these decisions? These are not easy questions to answer. For example, which of the following materials (if any) do you think should be banned from the elementary school? Why? Do this activity individually, and then consult with a group of peers.

- A basal in which women are depicted as professionals with a variety of careers
- A basal in which women are depicted only as mothers, teachers, and nurses
- A basal in which alternative family structures are presented
- A basal in which only traditional family structure is presented
- A science text that presents evolution and creationism as equally viable, alternative explanations of the beginning of life
- A science text that presents evolution but omits creationism
- A health text with a comprehensive discussion of AIDS (Acquired Immunodeficiency Syndrome)
- Tom Sawyer
- Judy Blume's books
- Little Black Sambo

Although you may agree with others in your group, there are people within this country who would ban each of these books from our schools. What problems and questions does this raise for you as a teacher? What impact do you think this has on teaching practice?

rallying cry for critics of education who looked at declining test scores, incidence of school vandalism, and an array of problems among the nation's youth as evidence that schools have lost their sense of purpose. These critics argued for a "return to the basics" and for measures by which schools and teachers could be made accountable for student achievement. While teachers and schools clearly should be accountable for student learning, the public press for accountability has meant that testing is stressed as an objective assessment of the success or failure of each school.

The teachers with whom we have worked describe testing and accountability for material covered on the tests as two of the most powerful influences on what they teach. Comments such as the following are common:

> Each week the principal reminds us of what we should teach, if the kids are going to be ready for the test. We've changed the order of some of our units in math, because the test has some things on it we usually don't get to until later.

As a result of testing and the need for accountability, teachers decide what to emphasize, how to sequence topics, and what to omit. These decisions might be in conflict with what the teacher believes would be more beneficial or interesting. For example, a teacher might think that the students would understand better the westward expansion of the United States if they could participate in a simulation of a wagon train trip across the country. However, knowing that the activity would take several weeks to complete, the teacher might reject the idea, deciding instead to use the textbook and have the children write reports. In that way, the teacher could cover the social studies content and provide practice on punctuation and other writing skills that will be tested.

We are not arguing against teacher accountability or testing. However, teachers faced with the accountability issues often choose to adhere closely to school-selected textbooks and to the content covered on achievement tests, even when they believe that alternatives might provide better instruction. In this atmosphere, their inclination to be reflective lessens.

State and School District Policies

States and school districts frequently respond to social forces by passing legislation and establishing policies. These can shape teachers' perceptions of what is expected of them and can affect the degree to which teachers have control over instructional decisions. Consider some examples of such policies and how they might influence teachers.

TEACHER LICENSURE POLICIES.   All states have policies and regulations concerning how teachers become licensed to teach. For example, in Florida teachers must pass a pencil-and-paper test assessing content area and pedagogical knowledge. Teachers also must demonstrate satisfactory teaching performance on an observation instrument based upon teacher effects research (see Chapter 5 for information about this research). While the behaviors assessed are clearly a part of an effective teacher's repertoire, the exclusive focus on the findings from teacher effects research as the basis for evaluation may communicate to teachers that one teaching strategy (e.g., teacher-centered direct instruction) is more effective than

FOCUS BOX 2–3

Take a Moment to Reflect

We have described two major social forces—censorship and teacher accountability—and how they can affect teachers' opportunities to be reflective and to make decisions. What other social forces do you see as important and influential? We mentioned that social forces are dynamic. New ones can emerge quickly. For instance, when the Soviet Union launched Sputnik, the resulting influence on math and science instruction in this country was swift and powerful. Can you identify any social forces that have emerged very recently that might now or in the near future have an impact on teachers?

all others. In fact, several teachers have reported to us that their principals insist that they use the teaching strategies assessed on the observation instrument, even though they believe the approach is not suited to all of their instructional goals. Licensure policies do not inevitably limit teachers' instructional autonomy; however, statewide sanction of a set of instructional strategies is a powerful force that should not be underestimated.

CURRICULAR POLICIES.   State legislatures and/or boards of education frequently mandate certain areas of curriculum that must be taught in the public schools. For example, elementary schools might be required to include units on crime awareness, drug prevention, and sex education. State boards of education may regulate how many minutes should be allocated to each subject during a school week. While such policies and mandates may have sound reasons, they do limit the instructional autonomy of teachers who must, in some instances, document how many minutes they spend on each subject area.

Other curricular policies that can affect teachers' reflective decision making concern adopted textbooks and supplementary materials. Many school districts designate one or perhaps two textbooks as appropriate for each subject area, limiting teacher decision making about their most fundamental instructional decisions—what and how to teach. Research has consistently shown that the use of textbooks accounts for between 70 and 90 percent of classroom instruction (Farr & Tulley, 1985; Muther, 1985). Textbooks determine what content students should learn and shape how students should think about issues. For instance, the way a social studies text describes industrial growth can subtly communicate a pro-management or pro-labor point of view.

In addition to determining content and emphasis, textbooks can also influence teachers' instructional strategies. Many provide very specific directions that the teacher is expected to follow. This can be a problem for teachers who feel bound to the textbook but realize that their students need a different approach. Teachers may not consider alternatives seriously because they believe (1) they must use the text, (2) students may miss some important skills or concepts if teachers deviate from the text, (3) teachers lack sufficient time to develop alternatives, or (4) alternative materials are not available.

School-Level Influences

School-level influences, because they occur daily, have the strongest impact on teachers' professional lives. Because these influences vary widely from school to school, two teachers working within the same school district and operating under the same state and school district policies, may report very different levels of professional autonomy. A number of factors account for the differences in school climate.

ADMINISTRATOR STYLE AND EDUCATIONAL PHILOSOPHY.   How a principal defines leadership and good teaching practice will be a major determinant of the context of each elementary school. Effective principals provide a school climate that supports the professional growth of their teachers and thus enables them to be reflective (Brandt, 1987; Hall, 1987; Leithwood & Montgomery, 1982; Mortimore & Sammons, 1987; Wildman & Niles, 1987). Ross (1987) indicates that the most effective principals have several common characteristics. **Effective principals**:

- have clear long-range goals that stress the emotional and cognitive growth of children
- support the professional growth of teachers
- encourage teachers to develop collaborative relationships with their colleagues
- provide teachers with instructional autonomy by encouraging them to participate in making decisions
- have high expectations of themselves, teachers, and students
- monitor school performance
- provide teachers with systematic feedback
- work collaboratively with staff members to initiate and sustain school improvement efforts

Teachers who teach in schools led by effective principals have the support they need to function as autonomous professionals who are able to explore alternative solutions to instructional dilemmas.

In situations where the administrator controls decision making, holds different beliefs than those of the teachers about how instruction should occur, and makes decisions in terms of immediate concerns rather than long-range goals, teachers will feel constrained. Consider the administrative style and beliefs about appropriate instruction embedded in the following policy established by an assistant principal, "It is the feeling of the administration that materials in the textbooks are adequate and must be completed before other materials are to be introduced in the curriculum" (Kyle, 1980, p. 81). We believe such extreme cases are rare. However, the principal is a major determinant of a school climate which either supports or constrains reflection. Other factors are influential as well.

COLLEGIAL INTERACTIONS.   Aside from your interactions with children, your most direct and frequent interactions will be with your fellow teachers, and the nature of these interactions will be an important influence on you as a teacher. In schools which foster professional development, teachers spend time planning together, talking about teaching, observing and critiquing each other, and providing technical and emotional support for one another (Ross, 1987). While this type of interaction occurs in some schools, teachers commonly work in relative isolation (Feiman-Nemser, 1986). Research about the professional environment in schools indicates that teachers' interactions with their peers seldom focus on professional concerns. Teachers get support from one another, socialize with one another, and even share some instructional resources, but they tend to avoid discussing professional issues. If you listen to groups of teachers, you are likely to hear the following kinds of comments:

- "My kids are off the wall today! What about yours?"

- "I need a ditto to reinforce addition with re-grouping."
- "Kevin's mother is coming in today. It's taken me 3 weeks to schedule a conference. I hope she shows up!"
- "Did you see the ball game yesterday? It was exciting right till the last touchdown."

However, you are less likely to hear teachers explore alternative ideas about how to present content, share information from professional journals or conferences, or critique instructional strategies suggested in a text.

Feiman-Nemser (1986) summarizes the collegial environment of many schools by saying "teachers have peers but no colleagues." In such an environment, teachers are hesitant to offer help to one another, although they are often willing to help when assistance is requested. In some situations teachers must even be cautious about requesting assistance, as this can be interpreted as an admission of incompetence. For example, when one of our graduates requested help on some minor instructional problems, others became concerned about her competence as a teacher. She was observed frequently and carefully monitored. She began her second semester at this school by reporting that "neat things were happening in her classroom." She asked for no help and displayed confidence and enthusiasm whenever anyone asked how things were going. Although she had not resolved the problems in her classroom, her peers and principal believed that her teaching had improved immensely. In fact, they told her she had shown more improvement than any beginning teacher in the building. An environment in which teachers cannot ask for help with instructional dilemmas does not support risk taking by teachers. Such an environment limits teachers' abilities to explore instructional alternatives and thus their ability to reflect.

The philosophy and teaching style of your colleagues is an additional component of the school culture. What if you, as a new teacher in a school, believe your children would learn best in cooperative learning teams, but all other teachers at your grade level believe strongly in the whole-group instruction they've always used? How you respond to such a situation will depend on many factors: How committed are you to the approach? How knowledgeable are you about how to implement such an approach? How much support will you receive from the administration? How will the other teachers react to your plans? How willing are you to be perceived as "different"? This is not an uncommon dilemma faced by teachers, especially first-year teachers or those new to a school. But all teachers can find that the preferences of their colleagues shape their decisions.

The positive side to the issue of collegial influence is that once teachers have established credibility in a school, they can play a role in altering the culture of the school through collegial interactions. For example, Ross (1978) describes a teacher, Mary, who was able to encourage more professional interactions among the faculty on her teaching team by initiating such interactions. She brought in articles for others to read, initiated discussions of alternative instructional strategies, and asked fellow teachers to observe and critique her teaching. This created the impetus for other teachers to engage in similar behaviors and thus changed the professional climate of the team. One of the members of her teaching team said about Mary:

> I don't stop and think and evaluate myself enough. Mary helps me do that . . . .
> Mary brings in more things for us to do than I do. She's thinking about every
> child in here, and now I do that too. (Ross, 1978, p. 141)

Importantly, Mary was not a first-year teacher at the time of the study. Before she took action to support and encourage professional interactions among her peers, she established herself as a competent professional within the school.

SCHOOL ORGANIZATION AND RESOURCES.   A school's organization has a direct bearing on the teachers' decision making. For instance, Mary taught in an open-space school where three kindergarten teachers shared space and children. They planned together and observed each other teaching. Mary felt that this organization helped her become a more reflective teacher.

> I can't imagine not teaming and having others to interact with—to share ideas,
> materials, thoughts. (Ross, 1978, p. 142)

Mary believed all the teachers in her team gained a better understanding of children and teaching by talking about children and their needs and by sharing successful or unsuccessful lessons. In this way, each teacher drew on the knowledge, teaching skills, and ideas of three teachers rather than one. The teachers were able to clarify individual perceptions, check conclusions, explore alternatives, and receive reinforcement. They gained new insights and increased their range of alternatives.

Moreover, team teaching gives teachers the opportunity to observe other teachers and increase their knowledge about the intended and unintended consequences of teaching practices. Mary discussed this factor:

> You learn things you'd like to do or not like to do. Sometimes you see somebody
> doing something you know you do and you see it in a different light. (Ross, 1978,
> pp. 143–144)

Thus, organizing teachers into teaching teams can promote reflection by stimulating self-analysis on the part of teachers about their teaching practices, their goals, and the connections between their goals and their practices. In team-teaching situations, teachers may reflect about the connections between their goals and their practices.

However, team organization does not have a positive influence on teaching in all cases. In an open-space school, teachers must coordinate their plans, keeping in mind noise levels of activities, travel in and out of the area, and use of shared space and materials. Coordinating the schedules of several teachers can be time consuming and can limit the flexibility possible in the curriculum. Activities cannot be cut short or extended at will, and more time is spent in transition than might be spent in a self-contained classroom. Team teaching can aggravate problems if teachers differ in their philosophical orientations. For example, one of our graduates felt her autonomy was limited during her first year of teaching, because she moved into an established team with a specified, common curriculum that conflicted with her own views. Such problems may be of less concern to teachers in self-contained classrooms; however, these teachers still must consider how to schedule children's time for going to the library, gym, and music or art rooms, and the standard practices of other teachers will still be influential. For many teachers working in a departmentally or team-organized school, decisions about groupings and scheduling become primary; therefore, reflection is less likely.

The resources available in a school can either increase or decrease the probability that a teacher will be reflective within the school. As mentioned previously, administrators can place limits on the resources available and allowed for use in the classrooms, and funding can constrain the possibility of having current and sufficient resources. As a result, teachers may decide that they simply cannot implement certain classroom activities. Furthermore, the resources that are provided convey a powerful message to teachers about what type of instruction is expected. For instance, receiving science textbooks but no lab materials communicates a lack of support for experiments and inquiry in science instruction. Teachers receiving such messages might be inclined to comply, in spite of their inclination to teach in a different way.

SCHOOL-LEVEL POLICIES.   The policies set within a school will be determined by the administrator, perhaps with the advice of a small group of influential teachers. Such policies can provide teachers with a great deal of autonomy, or they may mandate that teachers follow a common discipline plan, use a common planning method, or use particular instructional strategies. If school-level policies conflict with a teacher's beliefs about appropriate educational practice, enforcement of these policies can impede the teacher's efforts at reflection. For example, let's consider the issue of planning.

Availability of instructional resources influences the learning opportunities for students.

Teachers can find a great deal of advice about how to plan. Much of this advice suggests that teachers should use a model that involves stating **objectives** (i.e., specific statements of intended student learning and criteria for evaluation), planning activities, implementing activities, and evaluating to see if the objectives have been reached (Popham & Baker, 1970; Posner & Rudnitsky, 1982). The simplicity and rationality of the model have appeal, and many school systems and school-level administrators mandate that teachers' planning should reflect such an approach. In some instances, even the planbooks provided to teachers reflect the model and indicate where to record the information.

Research on how teachers plan, however, suggests that the model has limitations when it is applied in the classroom (McCutcheon, 1980; Zahorik, 1975). Planning is not linear and simple; it is dynamic and complex. It requires a great deal of mental work by teachers, who should consider factors such as characteristics of individuals and groups of children, previous types of activities that have or have not worked, available materials and other resources, and time. At times, teachers begin by thinking about their objectives for learning. At other times, they begin by thinking about a *neat activity* and then brainstorming all the potential learning opportunities. They think about possibilities, selecting ones that seem best and feasible.

If the conception of planning used in a school reflects the first view, teachers' reflection about dilemmas and possible solutions is likely to be constrained. This is especially true if teachers are required to submit their plans to an administrator for review. Not only is their attention focused on fitting their decisions to the model, but the requirement to submit their plans for review suggests to many teachers that their professional judgment is suspect.

FOCUS BOX 2–4

Take a Moment to Reflect

In this chapter, we have discussed several factors that work together to create the culture of an individual school. Many other factors could be discussed. How, for example, might each of the following factors influence a teacher's ability to be reflective?

- the characteristics of a school's student population
- the location of a school (rural, suburban, urban)
- the level of parental support, concerns, and involvement
- the proximity of the school to a university or college
- the average length of tenure of members of the school's faculty
- the average length of tenure of the school's principals.

Can you think of any additional factors that might influence the culture of a school? Think about some schools you have attended in the past or schools in which you taught. What factors influenced the practices of teachers within those schools?

FOCUS BOX 2–5

Practical Application Activity

Directions: We have noted that school cultures vary and that school-level factors influence teachers' perceptions about their capacity to make decisions about teaching practice. The differences among schools will be more apparent if you investigate school culture on your own. First, investigate the culture at the individual school which you know best. To do this, answer the following questions based upon your knowledge of the school where you teach or where you are student teaching. If you are student teaching, you will probably want to interview your cooperating teacher in order to answer the questions.

1. Who determines the curriculum materials used in your classroom? Provide some specific examples.
2. Who determines the instructional methods used in your classroom? Provide some specific examples.
3. Has there been a time when you (or your cooperating teacher) wanted to make a change in the curriculum or operating procedures of the classroom but were unable to do so? What factors constrained your decisions and actions?
4. What evidence is there that teachers work collaboratively to solve instructional problems in this school?
5. How is your school organized (team teaching, departmentalized, open space, individual classrooms, etc.)? How does this organization affect what you do or do not do in your classroom?
6. Does the principal affect teaching practice in this school? Explain.
7. Are there school-level policies (e.g., school-wide discipline plan or policies about use of materials) that influence your teaching practice? Explain

After you have answered these questions, compare your answers with those of a group of three to five peers. Use the following questions to guide your discussion:

- What differences do you notice in school cultures?
- How do these differences seem to influence differences in teaching practices?
- Are there other school-level factors (besides the ones assessed in this activity) that you believe have an impact on teaching practice in the schools represented in your group?
- What conclusions can you draw from this activity?

Teachers can experience similar problems and frustrations with other types of school-level policies. Frymier (1987) noted that motivated people have an internal locus of control (i.e., a belief that their actions determine resultant events) and that centralized decision making that imposes highly specific demands on teachers in terms of required curriculum and policies, such as how one should plan, undermines this internal locus of control. Having the power to make decisions related to one's work increases teachers' sense of ownership and commitment to the decisions they make. Therefore opportunities for reflection, professional effectiveness, and professional growth are increased (Borko, 1986; Frymier, 1987).

Most schools will include a mix of supportive and constraining characteristics. The nature of the mix determines the overall culture of the school and has an important impact on the professional development and reflective practice of teachers within that school. In Chapter 10, you will find more information about this and some guidelines for selecting a school environment that is likely to support your professional development.

Reflection Is Possible

Now that you have read about the influences that can constrain or support reflective teaching, you might wonder how likely it is that you will have the opportunity to be reflective within a typical elementary school. We believe it is possible to be reflective. However, reflective teaching will depend on the multiple factors that create the culture of teaching for each teacher. We believe there are several reasons to be optimistic about your ability to be reflective.

First, the power individual teachers have over curriculum decisions varies across states, districts, and schools. There are many possible combinations of the influences we have discussed. Also, the strongest influences upon teachers' power over their professional life are school-based influences. In some settings, the professional autonomy of teachers is limited. In others, their autonomy is respected, and they have a great deal of influence over the instructional practices in their classrooms. The latter situation might be increasing, as more attention is given to educational reform. In more and more places, educators are paying attention to the need to create schools that acknowledge and nurture teachers as professionals (Lieberman, 1988a; Maeroff, 1988; Smith, 1987; Whitford, Schlechty, & Shelor, 1987). In these schools, teachers have the opportunity and the responsibility to be reflective, to make individual instructional choices, and to share in collegial, schoolwide decision making. Added impetus for local innovation and risk taking comes from America 2000, President George Bush's strategic plan for improving education in this country. America 2000 calls for the creation of new American schools where educational innovation will be encouraged to foster excellence in education. Such schools would seem to support the development of reflection in teachers.

Second, we know that individual teachers differ in their personalities, inclination toward self-analysis, pedagogical knowledge and experience, subject matter knowledge and experience, self-confidence, personal interests and commitments, and educational philosophies. Each difference can account for variations in how an individual teacher responds. That is, given the same environment, some teachers will exercise considerable professional autonomy and use reflection as a means to improve their instruction on a continuing basis, while other teachers will feel constrained.

Reflective teaching is possible, then, and is shaped by many factors. Although a restrictive environment can limit reflection, many teachers have some control

FOCUS BOX 2–6

Take a Moment to Reflect

Directions: Now that you have completed this chapter, answer the following questions as a way to assess your understanding of the key ideas presented in the chapter:

1. What is the difference between a *utilitarian* approach to teaching and a *reflective* approach to teaching?

2. What is *culture*? What is meant by the *cultures* of teaching? *Note:* We are asking you about the *cultures* of teaching, not the *culture* of teaching. Why is that difference important?

3. The self-assessment in Focus Box 2–1 presents a list of 12 potential factors that influence a teacher's ability to teach reflectively. Look carefully at each factor and make sure you understand how and why it influences teachers. In your view, which three factors would be most important in limiting or facilitating teachers in their efforts to teach reflectively? Why? Which three seem the least important and why?

4. Why do some teachers innovate and continually question their teaching practices when others seem to rely on and feel comfortable with a set of standard and very traditional practices? What could you do to make certain you will maintain a questioning attitude? (*Note:* We asked this same question at the end of Chapter 1. If you answered it then, note how you would change or elaborate your answer.)

5. What questions would you ask during a job interview to determine whether you would like to teach within a particular school? Why are these questions important? (*Note:* We examine this issue in Chapter 10. When you complete this activity, you might want to turn to Chapter 10 and read the questions we have suggested teachers might ask during job interviews.)

Share your views with your colleagues. As you discuss your conclusions, focus on the following:

1. What evidence can you provide that your conclusion is valid? (*Note:* Evidence can come from this chapter, related readings, classroom experiences, or life experiences. It is important that you be explicit about the source and quality of your evidence.)

2. What additional evidence might you want to collect?

---

over the context in which they will teach.[1] Even in restrictive environments, teachers can develop skills that will help them preserve their professional autonomy (see Chapter 11 for information on working within the social system of the school). Consequently, in our view, the most significant influences on a teacher's ability to teach reflectively are the personal aims of the teacher, because they provide the starting point for making decisions about teaching. These aims also affect how individual teachers react to the many influences confronting them. That is, a particular environment may limit reflection, but lack of clarity about one's aims for education prohibits it.

[1]   We recognize that beginning teachers often must take whatever job is offered. However, in time, many teachers can request transfers or choose to teach in a different community.

Further Readings

Feiman-Nemser, S. (1986). The cultures of teaching. In M. Wittrock (Ed.), *Third handbook of research on teaching* (pp. 505–526). New York: Macmillan.

Frymier, J. (1987). Bureaucracy and the neutering of teachers. *Phi Delta Kappan, 69* (1), 9–14.

Goodman, J. (1988). Democratic empowerment and elementary curriculum: A case study. Paper presented at the annual meeting of the American Educational Research Association, New Orleans.

Kilgore, K., Ross, D. D., & Zbikowski, J. (1990). Understanding the teaching perspectives of first year teachers. *Journal of Teacher Education, 41* (1), 28–38.

Kyle, D. W. (1980). Curriculum decisions: Who decides what? *Elementary School Journal, 81* (2), 77–85.

Maeroff, G. (1988). A blueprint for empowering teachers. *Phi Delta Kappan, 69* (7), 472–477.

McCutcheon, G. (1980). How do elementary school teachers plan? The nature of planning and influences on it. *Elementary School Journal, 81* (1), 4–23.

Mortimore, P., & Sammons, P. (1987). New evidence on effective elementary schools. *Educational Leadership, 45* (1), 4–8.

Wildman, T. M., & Niles, J. A. (1987). Reflective teachers: Tensions between abstractions and realities. *Journal of Teacher Education, 38* (1), 25–31.

CHAPTER 3

Deciding Your Curriculum Aims for Elementary Education

We have discussed the importance of reflective teaching and its components. We also have suggested that developing clarity about your aims is a critical element in becoming a reflective teacher. In this chapter we present information and activities that will help you to make decisions about the importance of various aims and to consider how those aims influence classroom practice.

You probably already have a general sense of your aims. Many teachers state aims such as wanting children to acquire the skills necessary to make it in the world, to learn how to work well with others, and to feel good about themselves. Although it is a good starting point, deciding your aims requires more than making a general *wish list*. Teachers must have a clear sense of what aims are possible. They must understand the potential results of selecting some aims instead of others, and must be able to see the connections between their aims and the day-to-day decisions made in the classroom. Teachers must come to terms with their aims, because those aims become part of the criteria used to make reflective judgments.

As we noted previously, reflective teachers recognize their ethical commitment to each child and to society. This commitment requires careful consideration of aims, because all **pedagogical** choices (i.e., choices of teaching methods appropriate for selected aims) reflect underlying assumptions about what and whom we value, about social issues, and about the basic purpose of schooling. For instance, suppose a teacher chooses to group students by achievement level. That choice, and the resulting modification of the curriculum, suggests that children's educational experiences should differ. What does that choice say about a commitment to educational equity? What are the potential long-term consequences for society of shaping the curriculum according to the previous achievement of the students? Such questions illustrate the moral dilemmas teachers face in selecting aims.

Furthermore, teachers must recognize that all aims are not of equal worth. For instance, solving many of the problems facing the world today will call for people skilled in cooperative decision making and consensus building. Recognizing this, a teacher could argue that aims that include cooperative learning have greater worth than those that focus solely on competition.

We will discuss the elementary school curriculum in order to help you assess your aims. One way of beginning is to answer this question, What is most important for children to learn in school within a democratic society? You could respond in several different ways, each of which has been suggested and argued for by noted experts. As discussed in Chapter 1, teachers and experts may differ in their appreciation systems. And, those differences influence their ideas about the nature of the elementary curriculum and their decisions about what takes place in the classroom. (Remember the teacher who viewed teaching as "presenting information" versus the teacher who viewed teaching as "communicating with children.") We will discuss curriculum with the intention of helping you expand your appreciation system and see its connection to decisions you make as a teacher. In this chapter you will find a discussion of what curriculum is, an explanation of theoretical models of curriculum, and an exploration of sources of aims for schooling.

What Is Curriculum?

If we asked for information about a school's curriculum, in all likelihood we would receive information about scheduling and a listing of the subjects offered. You could view this as the school's menu (i.e., the academic fare that makes up the day).

This prevalent view of curriculum is defined by many as the **explicit curriculum.** You can find summaries of the explicit curriculum in scope and sequence charts, school handbooks, curriculum guides, and teachers' planbooks. You can hear conversations about the explicit curriculum as teachers talk about what they need to cover before the test or which science experiment they will try.

However, intended goals may not be taught. For instance, a school might list "self-directed learners" as a goal, but provide few, if any, opportunities for students to make choices. Teachers may select an instructional activity for any number of reasons—habit, convenience, time of year—without being able to articulate how they plan to connect it with any intended purpose. The existence of such conflicts leads to another way of thinking about curriculum.

In any classroom, the children are always learning; they just may not be learning what the teacher intends to teach. We can broaden our definition of *curriculum* to include intended and unintended learnings. The **implicit curriculum** includes the curriculum experienced by children, the learnings they develop as part of the process of being educated. Consider, for example, two teachers intending to establish classroom rules. What else might the children learn?

Teacher 1   "OK, class. Listen up now. One of the things I want us to make sure we understand today is our classroom rules. I've put a chart of the rules up here so everyone can see it, and you won't be able to say 'I forgot.' There

	aren't many rules, but they're important. To help you learn them, I want you to write them in the front of your notebooks. First, let's read them out loud, then you can write them."
Teacher 2	"Boys and girls. Today is an important day. It's our first day together and we need to spend some time getting to know one another. One thing we need to talk about is how we can make our classroom a good place for all of us. Maybe in your family you have a few really important rules. Well, we need a few important rules, too. Let's list some rules that you think are most important. Then we'll talk about them and see which ones we agree are the best rules for our classroom this year."

In each instance, the children might learn classroom rules. But the children in Teacher 1's classroom might also learn that the teacher decides the rules and the children follow them. They might learn that their own views are not important or that their responsibility is to meet others' expectations. They might acquire some initial insights about the power of those in authority, which might later be applied in their workplaces.

The children in Teacher 2's classroom might learn that they have the right to participate in making decisions that affect them, and that power can be shared. These learnings, too, might have a long-term effect on their perceptions as adults, and their expectations that they might participate fully in making decisions that affect their lives.

Keep in mind that the implicit curriculum refers to more than a single lesson. It is conveyed by the **pervasive patterns** existing in a classroom or school; that is, by the cumulative experience of being a learner in a school.

We use the term *implicit curriculum* to discuss those learnings resulting from the cumulative experience of being a learner; however, many call this the **hidden curriculum** (Dreeben, 1968; Jackson, 1968; Martin, 1976; Sarason, 1971; Vallance, 1973/74). In our view, the word *hidden* implies that this curriculum is unknowable and, therefore, cannot become a part of what teachers consider in making instructional decisions. Instead, we suggest that teachers become aware of what can be taught implicitly and use that knowledge to make informed choices.

Some general points about the implicit curriculum should be kept in mind. First, we all have learned from the implicit curriculum. You might share with your peers an example from your own experience. As we wrote this section, we reminisced about our schooling. One of the authors of this text, Dorene Ross, recalled her sixth-grade teacher's decision to allow the advanced group to proceed independently and at a rapid pace. Because Dorene was part of the advanced group, she learned to see herself as capable and self-directed; but she now wonders what others in the class might have learned about themselves and about the children in the advanced group.

This example illustrates a second point. Individual children will interpret the implicit curriculum differently due to differences in their backgrounds, experiences, and personalities. An artist's child, for instance, probably will develop positive attitudes about the value of art, regardless of whether the school communicates a similar message.

Third, you probably noticed that in our examples we noted what children *might* learn implicitly. It is difficult to say with certainty what the implicit curriculum teaches, because the effects are subtle, cumulative, and long-term. Years later we might be able to determine that an attitude we hold has evolved as a result of what we experienced in school. And, it is important to note that attitude might be either positive or negative.

What, then, might children learn through the implicit curriculum? Although we can only suggest some possibilities, the ones we discuss can be powerful and should be considered as you think about your aims and ways of achieving those aims. The implicit curriculum teaches *what's important to learn.* For example, the implicit curriculum may tell students to concentrate on reading and math, but not to worry about art. What instructional patterns might teach this? One is the class schedule. The amount of time devoted to a subject and its placement in the schedule can announce its priority. What is taught in the morning when the children are alert? What gets relegated to Friday afternoons? If the schedule is interrupted for some reason, what is likely to be omitted? The answers to these questions communicate the relative importance of each subject. When the same types of decisions are made year after year, the pattern teaches students the school's value structure.

The testing program also suggests what's important to learn. What gets tested? Are some types of activities never evaluated? What does the report card communicate? Of course, teachers also communicate their values. Consider the teacher who "comes alive" during science but sighs when it is time for social studies. Or, think about the teacher who never misses an opportunity to quote an appropriate line of poetry. These teachers subtly convey attitudes to children.

Curriculum materials also communicate priorities to children. For instance, if children experience a pattern in textbooks that emphasizes finding one right answer, they might learn to value answers rather than questions, ideas, issues, and controversy. Furthermore, textbooks and other materials include selected information; other information is omitted. Considering the pervasive use of textbooks, it is easy to see how they become powerful influences in shaping children's views of what they should know and value and how they should learn.

The implicit curriculum also teaches *attitudes about the sources of knowledge.* Look around your classroom. What materials do you see other than textbooks? Just as children may assume that textbooks contain what's important to know, they may also assume that textbooks and teachers are the only sources of knowledge. The use of a variety of resources, on the other hand, may communicate that there are many views about an idea, and that students must actively pursue knowledge. Furthermore, students may learn about people as a source of knowledge. Depending on the types of learning opportunities provided, students may learn that the teacher alone has knowledge, or that their peers also have knowledge to share.

The implicit curriculum teaches about *the role of the teacher and that of the students in the teaching/learning process.* Our examples of how teachers introduce rules to students help to illustrate this. A hint of the teacher's view of roles exists in the arrangement of the physical environment. The placement of desks and chairs

The amount of time devoted to subjects, like music, communicates implicit messages about their educational importance.

might say, "The teacher talks, and the students listen. The teacher is at the head of the class."

Jackson (1968) notes that one of the major lessons children learn in school has to do with their roles. He identifies **three "facts of life"** in elementary classrooms—(1) children must learn to live as part of a group, (2) classrooms are evaluative settings, and (3) power is distributed unequally. What might each *fact* teach children? As a member of a group, children learn who they are and how they are perceived by others, what behaviors elicit approval from the group, and how to relate to a very significant group member, the teacher. Of course, children will differ in terms of the messages they perceive from the group and in the ways they respond. Remember, the implicit curriculum will not be the same for everyone. In any case, group living influences children's attitudes about their peers, strategies for getting attention, and ability to work in spite of distractions.

The evaluative nature of classrooms also communicates an implicit message about roles. Evaluation tells the students whom the teachers value, accept, and respect. Through this fact of classroom life, children might learn how to "read" teachers in order to please them. Or, a student could learn that he/she is a failure and cannot live up to the teachers' expectations. Teachers have the role of an authority who will make judgments, and the student has the role of worker who will be judged. The long-term influence of this experience can shape students' later attitudes about the larger world of occupations. Dreeben (1968), for instance, discusses how schooling influences a student's work ethic and attitudes about power and authority.

The issue of power is the third fact of life that Jackson identifies. Children learn that some people have more power than others. Those who possess power may be teachers. In some cases children who get good grades or live in a certain part of town have more power than others in the classroom. The fact that power is not shared equally teaches children. Some may accept the status quo and fit in to the power structure; others may challenge and question and figure out how to acquire power (though not necessarily in ways that please the teacher).

The implicit curriculum teaches *a view of society*. Many researchers have investigated the implicit curriculum of texts, raising concerns about racist and sexist stereotypes and about the portrayal of the elderly, the handicapped, and the culturally different (Baxter, 1974; Kyle, 1978; Women on Words and Images, 1974; Zwack, 1973). Of concern is whether children might develop biases about any particular group of people or assumptions about their own potential place in

FOCUS BOX 3–1

Take a Moment to Reflect

Observe a classroom. This could be your own or one you visit. What is the explicit curriculum? Where do you find it recorded? Are all facets of the explicit curriculum taught?

See if you can find some evidence to suggest what the implicit curriculum in this room might be. Where should you look? You have several choices:

- You could examine some of the curriculum materials.

- You could take a visual tour of the classroom, noting what is on the walls, what materials appear to be used, how the furniture is arranged.

- You could focus on the teacher, recording any patterns of talk or interactions with students.

- You could examine the weekly schedule and the teacher's planbook.

These are only suggestions. You can probably think of other ways of getting some insights about the implicit curriculum.

Once you have some information, discuss your findings and conclusions with your peers. As you talk about what the children might be learning implicitly, think about how this relates to the explicit curriculum. If there is a conflict between what the teacher intends to teach and what the children might be learning implicitly, what could the teacher do differently?

society. Other researchers have studied teachers' interactions with high- and low-achieving children, noting differences that might affect what children learn about themselves and others (Eder, 1983; Grant & Rothenberg, 1986; Hiebert, 1983). Still other researchers have examined free and inexpensive curriculum materials and documented how use of these materials can teach children to value certain products and to hold particular views about economics, labor, management, and various social issues (Harty, 1979).

We hope you are convinced of the importance of the implicit curriculum. As you consider your aims and how to accomplish them, pay attention to the possible implicit curriculum so that you can make better instructional decisions. Of course, your beliefs will influence your perceptions of the implicit curriculum and whether you see it as positive or negative. This is why it is so important to clarify your aims. One way of doing that is to look at how others have discussed aims. We provide several examples in this chapter. Also, Focus Box 3–1 presents an activity to help you think more about explicit and implicit curriculum.

What Should Be the Aims of Education?

In his book *Cultural Literacy: What Every American Needs to Know*, Hirsch (1987) argues that traditional subjects should form the core curriculum, and that schools must assure that all children have access to the information necessary for participating meaningfully in our culture. To help educators revise the curriculum, Hirsch provides a much-discussed list of content that schools should teach.

Hirsch's book, although current and controversial, takes its place among a collection of writings about what the curriculum should emphasize. We could even argue that the establishment of schools with the "Old Deluder Satan Act" started the debate. Our ancestors wanted schools to teach children how to read. And what did they want children to read? The Bible, of course, so they wouldn't be "deluded" by Satan. At first, then, the purpose for schools was clearly defined and caused little argument.

In the ensuing years, though, we have expanded our notion of why schools exist, resulting in a diversity of opinions about the focus of the curriculum. To help us make sense of these diverse viewpoints, researchers have categorized them in several ways (Eisner, 1985; Eisner & Vallance, 1974; Miller, 1983, Taba, 1962; Tanner & Tanner, 1980).

Although any framework could be used, we have decided to use the category system developed by Eisner and Vallance (1974) and elaborated upon by Eisner (1985) to discuss the aims of education. These authors identified five orientations to curriculum, each characterized by assumptions about what is most important to teach, how learning occurs, the roles of teachers and students, and what classrooms ought to be like. The five orientations to curriculum are as follows: (1) academic rationalism, (2) personal relevance, (3) social responsiveness, (4) cognitive processes, and (5) curriculum as technology. We will explain each orientation. Following the explanation of each orientation is a portrayal of instruction in the classroom of a teacher advocating that orientation. Reading these orientations can be a useful way of making sense of your own beliefs. Keep in mind, though, that each portrayal is presented in its pure form—but no such thing would exist in practice. Instead, we would see a tendency toward a particular orientation, with aspects of others apparent as well. Before reading about the orientations, complete the self-assessment in Focus Box 3–2 to determine your view of important aims.

Academic Rationalism

Hirsch is an academic rationalist. Advocates of this orientation argue for a **liberal education** (i.e., an education focused on conveying the best of Western cultural heritage to children). The content of the curriculum includes the academic disciplines as well as the arts and physical education. (This orientation is reminiscent of the ancient Greek commitment to "a healthy mind and a healthy body.")

FOCUS BOX 3–2

Self-Assessment of Aims

Directions: Read each statement and decide whether you agree (A) or disagree (D) with the statement based upon your beliefs. There may be some statements with which you both agree and disagree, but we want you to make a choice. Select *agree* if you agree more than you disagree with a statement. Select *disagree* if you disagree more than you agree with a statement After you finish this self-assessment, read about each orientation. The self-assessment will be used again at the end of this chapter.

____ 1. Children's interests should be of primary concern when organizing the curriculum.

____ 2. The curriculum should focus on social issues more than personal or academic ones.

____ 3. The curriculum should convey the best of our cultural heritage to the next generation.

____ 4. Children's self-actualization should be the key aim of the curriculum.

____ 5. The processes of learning are more important than the content.

____ 6. The curriculum should help children learn how to adapt to society.

____ 7. Children learn best when the curriculum includes clear aims, focused instruction, and monitored practice.

____ 8. The curriculum should help children acquire learning processes that can be applied to new situations.

____ 9. Ideas that have "stood the test of time" should form the core of the curriculum.

____ 10. The curriculum should mainly reflect research on teaching aimed at increasing children's achievement of basic skills.

Educators with this view criticize decisions about adding topics which take time away from the essentials to the curriculum. For instance, they would find fault with mandates requiring that schools provide instruction about consumer education, drug education, and any number of other topics.

It is important to note, however, that academic rationalists do not argue for a *back-to-the-basics* approach. For academic rationalists, curricular content is clearly defined; it's the "best of the best" and what has "stood the test of time." The role of teachers is critical, for it is through their expertise that the content is conveyed in such a way that students can analyze the significant ideas and events that have shaped our culture. Academic rationalists believe that it is important for all children to have access to this information. As Adler (1982) explains it, all children should get cream. (Instead, in our current system, he believes the gifted get the cream, and the low achievers get skim milk.) According to this view, a democratic society has an obligation to assure that all its members have equal access to knowledge. If we differentiate the curriculum, we assure that some students will not have the information necessary for participation in a democratic society. The ultimate result is a stratification of society.

What kind of classroom might an academic rationalist create? As we enter this classroom, we might notice things that suggest focus and purpose. For instance, some desks may be arranged into a horseshoe shape for lectures and large-group discussions, while others form clusters for ease in preparing projects. The bulletin boards, attractively arranged, display high-quality prints of famous artworks. Textbooks and reference materials such as the Great Books Series and encyclopedias sit within easy reach to assist the children as they complete reading assignments and prepare for presentations, debates, and reports.

A sense of purpose pervades the classroom. The teacher might lecture, facilitate discussions, direct group assignments, or coach children as they develop insights about important ideas and events. A visitor would be impressed by this teacher's skill in engaging the children in a dialogue about the topic at hand, always probing for underlying meanings and greater clarity and insight.

What are the concerns of critics of the academic rationalists? They wonder if, through the implicit curriculum, children might learn that school is not meaningful. Although it is possible to draw parallels between historical events and current issues, critics suggest that this is not often done; as a result, children might find little meaning in schoolwork. And, in the view of many educators, meaning is a necessary prerequisite to learning, a point basic to the next orientation.

Personal Relevance

According to proponents of this orientation, the curriculum should take into account the interests, individuality, and personal feelings of the children. Rather than viewing curriculum content as significant according to some external standard, these advocates argue for greater flexibility in deciding what to teach because they believe that significant learning *requires* personal involvement by children. Because building on students' interests is critical, the curriculum could never be completely decided before the teacher and students get to know one another. Teachers with this viewpoint want to take advantage of "teachable moments" and feel it is important to incorporate students' concerns and experiences into the curriculum, even if discussing them takes time away from academics.

Such terms as *humanistic education, personalized instruction, invitational education*, and *affective education* capture the focus of this orientation. Attention to feelings, personal meaning, and self-actualization provides a basis for curriculum decision making. Teachers place as much importance on affective concerns as on cognitive, because they believe that learning which ignores affective issues is empty. That is, these teachers believe that meaningful learning requires teachers to link the curriculum to the personal interests and needs of students. In the book *Summerhill*, Neil (1960) describes a pure application of this orientation. For example, Neil notes that some of the students at Summerhill do not learn to read until adolescence because prior to that time, they have no interest in reading. For our example, we are describing a more moderate application of this orientation.

As we enter the classroom, we might assume at first that it is disorganized—desks form clusters around the room; children move at will to get materials and work with others; the teacher circulates and only occasionally brings the entire group together; and divisions between subject areas seem blurred. Yet, after a while, we begin to realize the organizational skill needed to sustain this kind of program and the energy needed to interact knowledgeably with children about their work.

This teacher must have a wealth of information and resources at hand in order to direct children as they pursue topics of interest. This teacher must be quite perceptive, and able to motivate, challenge, and sustain a child's involvement; to stimulate a child's quest for new knowledge; and to create an appropriate balance between individual and group endeavors. This teacher must be flexible, able to deal with ambiguities and diversity. During our visit to this classroom, we might see children meeting with the teacher to plan their agendas for the day or week; working alone or in groups; checking their own work or that of a classmate; and using systems to manage time, materials, and trips in and out of the room. Although we may not easily understand the routines, the children seem to internalize them and to follow them easily.

Critics of this orientation express concern that the children might learn implicitly that they can reject learning if they are not interested in it. Certainly, the teacher would attempt to stimulate interest in new topics, but what if a child still balks? Also, critics wonder if children might learn to be so focused on their own needs and interests that they become insensitive to the needs and interests of others.

These first two orientations to curriculum, then, use either the content or the child to organize the curriculum. Another orientation begins with society as its center. Eisner (1985) uses the terms *social adaptation/social reconstruction* to describe this orientation. However, basic differences in assumptions characterize these two views, so we have chosen to label this orientation *social responsiveness*.

Social Responsiveness

Advocates of this orientation see schools as social institutions, charged with the responsibility of enabling children to take their place as knowledgeable and contributing members of the society. To accomplish this task, schools must organize the curriculum in such a way that children can understand and experience life in a democracy. In school, children should read about current and historical issues and problems of society; discuss and critique the ideas that give structure to the political, economic, and social institutions; and experience activities that communicate insights about individual and collective responsibilities in society.

Those who advocate this orientation hold different views about the basic purpose of such an approach. On the one hand are those who begin by accepting the institutions of our society as they presently exist. In other words, they believe in our present economic and political systems, although they might recognize that serious problems need attention. Schools, in their view, should help students understand the merit of these systems and learn how to function within and contribute meaningfully to society as it currently exists. In all likelihood, they would support such programs as citizenship education, economic education, student elections and student councils, and school newspapers.

On the other hand are those who begin as social critics. They suggest that basic economic and political changes must occur if we are to solve society's problems. Schools must enable students to understand, critique, debate, and challenge so that they might see the necessity of change in the social order.

Proponents of the first view far outnumber those of the second, and we find many more examples of activities designed to help students adapt to society rather than to restructure it. However, an increasing number of educators, ourselves included, argue that students need to develop the critical intelligence necessary to address the problems confronting our world. As you read this book, you will find many places where we urge teachers to help students become committed to making the world a better place. However, you will also see elements of other orientations. Let's consider now what kind of classroom a teacher of the social responsiveness orientation might create.

As we enter the room, we might notice a list of collaboratively developed classroom rules and a management system which designates students for various classroom chores. As the day begins, the teacher and students negotiate the time necessary for completing various assignments. Once this is decided, the students begin to work. Throughout the day, they engage in group tasks, simulations, and class projects, learning how to make decisions and reach consensus. They also complete individual assignments and confer with the teacher about their progress. The teacher functions as a facilitator, encouraging the children to assume responsibility, yet communicating that the teacher has the ultimate authority to make decisions.

Critics of this orientation express concern about the possibility of indoctrination. Students might learn to accept only one (e.g., radical) view about social change, or they might learn to accept the status quo unquestioningly and not look for underlying causes of society's problems.

In the next orientation, the focus is not on subject matter, the child, or society. Instead, the processes of learning organize the curriculum.

Cognitive Processes

Advocates of this orientation believe that *what* we need to know changes too rapidly for us to learn it all. Instead, we need to know *how* to acquire information. If children acquire the necessary cognitive processes, they can transfer those processes to new situations and apply them as needed.

Inquiry or discovery approaches in science and social studies illustrate this orientation. In these approaches, the students engage in problem solving by posing questions and exploring possible solutions, using content as it is needed, rather than beginning with prescribed content to be covered. In such a classroom, we would see students engaged in many projects and group activities. Many resources would be available for student use, and the teacher would be a facilitator, helping the students pose questions and discover understandings. Many solutions might be found, and students would discuss which one or ones might be best. We might also see a **guided discovery lesson** in which the teacher models how to question and hypothesize. Then students might move to individual projects in order to practice inquiry skills.

The topic of teaching cognitive skills has received much attention in the past few years, and the suggestions are varied. (This will be discussed in Chapter 7.) For example, Costa (1985) provides descriptions of over 30 approaches designed to teach such skills. Some recommend connecting these skills with regular curriculum content, while others argue for teaching the skills directly. Situations such as these reinforce our point that teachers must understand what aims they are trying to accomplish, so that they can select knowledgeably when faced with alternative suggestions.

Critics find fault with the open-ended nature of this curriculum and the possible omission of content that they consider essential. They also question whether we can assume that students will be able to transfer and apply learning processes from one situation to another.

The last orientation to curriculum focuses on making learning as efficient, accountable, and unambiguous as possible. Eisner and Vallance (1974) label this *curriculum as technology*.

Curriculum as Technology

Although it might be assumed that this orientation refers only to computer usage, more is meant by the term *technology*. It refers to the technology of teaching, specifically to the application of research on teaching. Because so much has been written on this topic, and because this orientation is so pervasive in schools, we discuss this approach extensively in Chapter 5, including examples to illustrate it in practice. We provide a brief description here.

The purpose of this orientation is to structure what is taught and how it is presented so that students' achievement is likely. Proponents do not talk about the content of instruction; they talk about efficient organization of instruction to assure student mastery of content. However, as practiced, the content taught tends to be the content that is tested. This method of instruction generally involves clear definition of the skills necessary for mastery of content, breaking skills into their component parts, designing an appropriate instructional sequence using small easy steps, and assessing student learning. In this way, instruction becomes predictable, efficient, and unambiguous.

In this classroom, we would see the teacher in charge, directing the lesson and pacing the activities. The teacher would explain to students the purpose of the lesson, present the skills in small steps, check to make sure students have mastered the skills, give them immediate feedback about their responses, and monitor them as they complete independent assignments. We would see whole-group instruction and a classroom described as purposeful and task oriented. Expectations would be clear, and little time would be wasted.

Critics wonder if students might learn implicitly to depend too much on the evaluation of the teacher and not learn to monitor their own success. They argue that such an approach might not be appropriate for teaching higher-order skills and all content areas, so these might be omitted from the curriculum or given less emphasis. The arts would be a good example, but so would creative writing, critical analysis of literature, or hands-on activities in science and social studies. Critics also argue that advocates ignore important questions about the content of the curriculum. These critics argue that content is not specified and that decisions about what content to teach are as important, if not more important, than decisions about how to teach.

FOCUS BOX 3–3

Comprehension Check

Directions: To assess your comprehension of the five orientations to curriculum, complete the following chart:

Orientation	Aims	Rationale	Teaching/Learning Process	Sample Classroom Practice
_____	___	_____	_____	_____
_____	___	_____	_____	_____
_____	___	_____	_____	_____
_____	___	_____	_____	_____
_____	___	_____	_____	_____

Usefulness of the Orientations

The five orientations to curriculum that we have discussed show how others have clarified their aims and can help you to clarify yours. Remember that no one (except a theorist) is a purist; you probably agreed with the ideas of more than one orientation and maybe all of the orientations. Although in theory we might suggest that a school should accomplish the aims specified in all of the orientations, in reality time is limited, and decisions must be made about what to do. Those decisions will reflect the teacher's aims.

The orientations provide one framework for clarifying our vision of the child we're trying to develop, our beliefs about aims, and our sense of what classrooms should be like. At times we become so involved in the day-to-day events of teaching that we lose sight of how our decisions fit into a larger context of purposes. The orientations help us think about what strategies might or might not be consistent with our overall beliefs and aims, and they help us remember the available options.

Also, the orientations can help us understand the underlying reasons for conflicts that might arise. For instance, a disagreement with another teacher might be less about the issue at hand than about differences of viewpoint about the

FOCUS BOX 3–4

Take a Moment to Reflect

Self-assessment reconsidered: Return now to the self-assessment you completed about your aims (see Focus Box 3–1, p. 54). Would you change any of your initial responses? Why or why not? You might want to discuss the self-assessment with your peers before continuing to read about aims.

Remnants from classrooms: Look over the following list of remnants of the curriculum orientations that exist in classrooms. For each, decide which curriculum orientation it might represent and why. Discuss your conclusions with your peers.

1. a collection of children's folk and fairy tales
2. boxes of mastery test dittos
3. student projects labeled "Solving the School's Litter Problem"
4. a teacher's guide for problem-solving activities
5. a display of children's favorite stuffed animals brought from home
6. a list of nominees for student council offices
7. children's books on a wide range of topics, including divorce, adoption, and death and dying
8. plants growing in paper cups as each child's science experiment
9. portraits of famous composers of classical music
10. Science Research Associates (SRA) kits (a sequenced set of independent reading activities designed to develop reading comprehension)

Whatever the curriculum model, the heart of teaching is touching the minds and spirits of young people.

intent of the curriculum. If teachers can articulate these differences, they might resolve conflicts more easily.

Also, the orientations provide a basis for analyzing curriculum materials. Many teachers feel less than well-prepared to evaluate or select textbooks; they do not know what to look for. The orientations can enable a teacher to question what assumptions are made about the content most important for children to learn, the role of the teacher and that of the student, how children learn, and what classrooms should be like and how instruction should take place.

Making Decisions About Aims

Embedded within the orientations are a number of aims for education, such as personal growth, transmission of the cultural heritage, adaptation to society, acquisition of learning processes, and development of basic skills. Although these may be important to know about, teachers often get their information about aims

FOCUS BOX 3–5

Take a Moment to Reflect

The following list of possible aims is provided as a starting point for this activity:

- interpersonal growth
- self-esteem
- crime awareness
- cooperation
- thinking skills
- visual and auditory literacy
- dressing
- motor development and physical fitness
- feeding
- empathy
- basic skills and processes
- peer relationships
- ability to use senses
- practical life skills
- positive attitudes toward school and learning
- positive attitudes toward self and others
- cognitive development

from sources other than theorists. For example, state and school district boards of education usually issue documents which spell out their aims. You and your peers might collect a sample of these lists and discuss them.

In his book, *A Place Called School,* Goodlad (1984) examined such materials from all 50 states and concluded that they lacked precision and clarity and failed to communicate which aims are essential and which are secondary. To help develop a common sense of direction, Goodlad proposed a list of aims for consideration (1984, pp. 51–56). His aims consist of the following types:

- academic (mastery of basic skills and processes and intellectual development)
- vocational (career education)
- social, civic, and cultural (interpersonal understandings, citizenship participation, enculturation, moral and ethical character)
- personal (emotional and physical well-being, creativity and aesthetic expression, self-realization).

He provides a rationale and several subgoals for each aim.

- developmental progress
- affective development
- responsibility
- communication
- drug awareness
- independence
- sex education
- aesthetic development
- home repair and maintenance
- child care
- positive self-control
- lifelong learners
- decision-making ability

Discuss the list of aims with your peers. What would you add to or delete from the list? Why?

After you have a comprehensive list of potential aims, reorganize your list to develop clusters of the aims—smaller ones grouped under larger ones. Select three broad aims that are most important to you for educating children within a democratic society. Define the components of each and be prepared to provide a rationale for why you consider these three aims to be your most important aims for teaching.

At the beginning of this chapter, we said that our purpose was to help you clarify *your* aims. One way of doing that is to find out how others have described their aims, and you have now read several different points of view. Focus Box 3–5 presents an activity designed to draw on the readings and your own thinking as you determine your personal aims for teaching.

Further Readings

Dreeben, R. (1968). *On what is learned in school.* Reading, MA: Addison-Wesley.

Eisner, E. W. (1985). *The educational imagination.* New York: Macmillan.

Eisner, E. W., & Vallance, E. (Eds.). (1974). *Conflicting conceptions of curriculum.* Berkeley, CA: McCutchan Publishing Co.

Goodlad, J. (1984). *A place called school: Prospects for the future.* New York: McGraw-Hill.

Jackson, P. W. (1968). *Life in classrooms.* New York: Holt, Rinehart, and Winston.

PART 2

Teaching Strategies for Student Empowerment

Many texts on elementary curriculum include chapters on each area of the curriculum. Rather than focusing on subject areas, we focus on teaching strategies that are necessary in all curricular areas. National assessments of student learning in all areas point to problems in critical and creative thinking abilities and in children's ability to use information they have learned in schools. For example, the National Assessment of Educational Progress indicates that only 7 percent of 17 year olds can use detailed scientific knowledge to draw conclusions and make inferences; only 5 percent are able to make interpretations based on historical facts and ideas; and only 5 percent can synthesize information well enough to understand specialized reading materials (Applebee, Langer, & Mullis, 1989; Hammack, Hartoonian, Howe, Jenkins, Levstik, McDonald, Mullis, & Owen, 1990; Langer, Applebee, Mullis, & Foertsch, 1990).

Reasons for these problems are many. For example, the increasing diversity of the student population means that many teachers find it difficult to reach significant portions of the school population. In addition, the fact that many students are having difficulty in school means that teachers must spend proportionately more time managing and controlling student behavior. This, in turn, decreases available instructional time. Many argue that these problems are created, at least in part, by the school curriculum. For example, Goodlad (1984) notes that across all areas of the curriculum, elementary teaching is characterized by:

- teacher lectures which stress factual responses by students
- large amounts of individual written work by students
- a passive rather than active student role
- little opportunity for students to become excited about or engaged with knowledge and to use their full intellectual capacities

- repetitive attention to basic skills and facts
- dominant (and almost exclusive) use of textbooks and workbooks as instructional resources (pp. 226–244)

Goodlad concludes that the educational agenda for the future is to find ways to:

> involve students in a variety of ways of thinking, to introduce students to concepts and not just facts, to provide situations that provoke and evoke curiosity, to develop in students concern for one's own performance in work and the satisfaction of meeting one's own standards, to cultivate appreciation of others through cooperative endeavors, and to be concerned about the traits of mind and character fostered in schools. (1984, p. 244)

It is true that teachers need to develop specialized knowledge in different curricular areas (e.g., art, social studies, science), and we are not arguing against this fact. However, we have proposed that the dominant aim of elementary education is **student empowerment**. We defined this as empowering students to be eager and successful learners, to determine their own futures and participate productively in society, and to play an active role in making society a better place for all. Accomplishing this requires that teachers of all subjects help children (1) develop literacy skills, (2) develop social skills, (3) become good thinkers, (4) become meaningfully engaged with the school curriculum, and (5) develop the capacity for socially responsive self-discipline. In Part 2, we suggest strategies for the development of each of these areas. Whenever possible, we have provided examples from several curricular areas so that you can see how they apply across the elementary curriculum.

As you read and think about the ideas in Part 2, keep in mind two of the assumptions discussed in Chapter 1. First, there are no fixed answers to the problems in teaching and learning. Second, research does not now, and never will, have the answers to **pedagogical problems** (i.e., problems concerning appropriate teaching methods for selected aims). Learning about the strategies that we will describe is important. We will provide you with suggestions about the use of strategies that will *help* you make decisions about when and how to use them. However, *you* are ultimately responsible for making the decisions. We will draw on the research and talk about the *appropriate* use of strategies. We want to be clear that we are not telling you when you should or should not use certain strategies. Research and theory do not tell you what to do; they help to increase your knowledge about what you might do and what the possible effects of your actions will be. Remember that individual teachers must determine the nature and relative importance of each of their educational aims. They also must determine whether the recommendations of various researchers are applicable to their goals, the particular school and classroom, and the characteristics of students in the classroom. At the end of each chapter, we will ask you to apply some of the strategies and to analyze their effectiveness. The analyses done by you and your classmates will broaden your understanding of the strategies presented in the chapter and their potential use in the classroom. As we have said before, reading is not enough. You must act, observe, reflect, and plan again.

One final comment about the translation of research and theory into practice. We are presenting research related to the component aims of the broader aim of student empowerment. We are focusing on these aims because we have found them to be of highest priority to hundreds of teachers with whom we have worked. However, there are other aims, as discussed in Chapter 2. You will acquire information about many of these aims in other coursework during your teacher education program. This knowledge also must become part of your appreciation system. Additionally, the multiple aims of education are not discrete entities. Researchers focus intensively on one aspect of a classroom so that they can develop comprehensive knowledge about that aspect. However, teachers cannot teach literacy at 9:00 A.M., social skills at 10:00 A.M., and thinking processes at 2:00 P.M. Although we discuss each of these aims in a different chapter, in actual practice teachers must teach toward all of these aims simultaneously. The recommendations of research directed toward the accomplishment of one aim often conflict with recommendations directed toward the accomplishment of another. Putting everything all together is complex and often confusing.

We will provide examples of how some teachers have used the research presented. However, their ideas and practices will not be appropriate in all situations. Even within your own classroom, decisions and strategies that are appropriate at one point in time may not be appropriate at another time. These are some of the dilemmas of teaching. There are no right answers. Although at times you will feel overwhelmed with what you need to know and the importance of the decisions you must make as a teacher, remember, this is why you cannot be replaced by a computer!

CHAPTER 4

Promoting Literacy: Implications of Reading, Writing, and Mathematics Research

In Chapter 3 we encouraged you to consider your aims for the education of elementary school students. We stated that there is no one correct set of aims and that each aim represents certain values and expectations. Which aims you decide to pursue is very important, because in pursuing them, you teach students about what is important. We assume that student empowerment is the teacher's central aim. While this broad aim provides a sense of direction, more specific aims related to empowerment are needed if the teacher is to shape a focused instructional program. One of these aims is the development of literacy. In this chapter we define literacy; describe common problems in reading, writing, and mathematics instruction; and offer guidelines for developing literacy.

What Is Literacy?

You might have been surprised to see mathematics included in a sentence about literacy. Indeed, many people think literacy is synonymous with reading and writing. The media flood us with reports of high numbers of illiterate adults in our country, and celebrities urge us to fight illiteracy by volunteering to help someone learn to read. **Functional literacy** typically refers to the possession of basic skills that enable a person to cope with the day-to-day demands of life in our society. Indeed, many people view literacy as "the sum of a set of precisely specifiable subskills" (de Castell, Luke, & MacLennan, 1986, p. 5). When terms such as *computer literacy, consumer literacy,* and *cultural literacy* are used, they, too, often refer to the mastery of specific skills, procedures, and information which enable a person to "operate effectively within existing social and economic systems" (de Castell et al., 1986, p. 11).

We agree with a number of other writers (e.g., de Castell et al., 1986; Freire & Macedo, 1987; Lankshear & Lawler, 1987; Walsh, 1991) that these definitions of literacy are too narrow. We define **literacy** as the knowledgeable use of systems of communicating. This definition includes mathematics, as the number system is a communication system with which meaning can be constructed and conveyed. While our definition does not preclude learning skills, it has a very different orientation than the definition commonly used. For instance, *knowledgeable use* implies that literacy entails "the capacity to think, reason, and judge" (de Castell et al., 1986, p. 11). Literate people do not passively receive information; instead, they have the tools which enable them to question, to wonder, to evaluate. Ultimately, literate people are able to transform the conditions of their lives and the lives of others. Notice how this definition of literacy fits with the definition of empowerment we presented in the introduction to Part 2. If teachers hope to promote student empowerment, they must be committed to developing literacy.

Goals of Literacy Instruction

Although we have defined literacy, we have yet to clarify goals for instruction. It is one thing to say, "I'm going to develop literacy in my classroom." It is another to specify the focus of this instruction. While numerous texts describe the separate focus and content of reading, writing, and mathematics instruction, we intend to describe common goals of these three dimensions of literacy. These **common goals** include the development of critical understanding, problem-solving skills, enjoyment and appreciation, and strategic application of specific skills.

Development of Critical Understanding

This is a central goal of literacy instruction to which all other goals are related. This goal means that in order for people to use systems of communication knowledgeably, they must be driven by efforts to understand and make sense of the literacy event at hand. That is, whether the task is related to reading, writing, or mathematics, the focus is the thoughtful consideration of the meaning of the task. Although the mastery of certain specific skills, such as multiplication facts or sound-symbol relationships, is necessary, this is not an appropriate end goal for literacy instruction. The appropriate end goal is for students to be able to use specific skills to understand, examine, and consider the literacy task.

Use mathematics as an example. Schoenfeld explained that "the important thing in mathematics is . . . seeing what makes things tick and how they fit together. Doing mathematics is putting together the connections, making sense of the structure" (1991, p. 328). Schoenfeld notes that when one understands how things fit together, learning mathematics requires very little memorization. Developing a deep level of understanding enables one to remember **algorithms** (rules and procedures) because they fit logically into a systematic framework. Additionally, understanding enables one to reconstruct any algorithm that is forgotten. In addition to understanding how to solve mathematics problems, this goal includes the idea of critically assessing one's understanding. By **critical**

understanding, we mean judging one's understanding by relating it to prior knowledge. Ongoing evaluation is an essential part of being a capable reader, writer, and mathematician.

Is this goal currently being met? Considerable evidence indicates that it is not. For example, research in mathematics indicates that many children lack depth of understanding about the mathematical principles that govern algorithms. The National Assessment of Educational Progress (NAEP), which evaluates student achievement at the fourth-, eighth-, and eleventh-grade levels, indicates that students of all ages perform less well on problems requiring computational estimation than they do on similar computation problems (Carpenter, Matthews, Lindquist, & Silver, 1984). That is, students are better able to compute a problem such as 18×22 than to judge the reasonableness of the answer obtained. The ability to estimate is dependent on an understanding of numbers, the relationships among numbers, and of mathematics algorithms.

Similarly, in writing, students use skills associated with the **mechanics of writing** (e.g., punctuation, capitalization) but lack understanding about how to write to accomplish a purpose. The NAEP assessed the ability of fourth, eighth, and eleventh graders to produce informative, persuasive, and imaginative writing. Sadly, it was found that students were lacking in these areas, suggesting that students spend too little time experimenting with the writing process to develop a sophisticated understanding of how to accomplish writing tasks. Langer notes:

> Results [from the NAEP, 1985] . . . suggest that schools are successful in teaching what they have set out to teach. Whether by accident or design, school curricula and the tests that go with them have rewarded relatively simple performance, and have undervalued the attainment of . . . big ideas and deeper understandings. . . . Student performance such as reported by NAEP is no surprise, since these are the ways of thinking that are highlighted in the curriculum, supported by the instructional materials, and reinforced by the tests we use and the grades we give. (1989, p. 2)

Development of Problem-Solving Skills

Although it is most obvious in mathematics, all literacy tasks involve a problem to be solved. Think of the writer who is trying to persuade readers to vote for a particular candidate. The writer faces a problem—how to use words to accomplish a purpose. What words should be used? What kind of organizational framework will be most effective? There is no clear solution to the writer's problem. In fact, few literacy problems can be solved with simple, one-step solutions. Instead, students must be taught to analyze the problem, plan a logical approach to solving the problem, and monitor the reasonableness of their efforts. In the case of the writer who is trying to persuade readers to vote for a candidate, analyzing the problem could include consideration of audience for the piece and the length of the piece. Planning a solution hinges on the careful consideration of the problem. Although there is no one correct way to plan, the writer could begin by listing key ideas and phrases, writing a rough draft at the computer, talking through plans with a friend, or even tape recording ideas. Once a general plan has taken shape, the writer begins to draft the manuscript. During the drafting process, the writer monitors the work, asking questions such as, "Does this make sense? How will my audience react to this word? Is this a persuasive argument?" The writer continues to work with the piece until satisfied with the solution to the problem.

Now think of the reader who encounters the piece about the political candidate. The reader must solve a problem: "What is the best way to read this text to meet my purposes?" Again, there is no clear solution. The reader must consider elements of the problem, such as the reason for reading and ways to approach the text to meet this purpose. If the reader is preparing for a debate to support this candidate, it will be necessary to approach the text in a particular way. If the reader is skimming the newspaper on the way out the front door in the morning, it is likely that the text will be approached differently.

Writing researchers have found that students fail to approach writing tasks from a problem-solving orientation. To determine how well students are learning the skills necessary for managing the writing process, the NAEP included items that focused on students' problem-solving strategies (Applebee, Langer, & Mullis, 1986). The researchers found that although students reported using a number of problem-solving strategies, they in fact used very few. For instance, in planning what to write, students reported using specific, as opposed to general, strategies. While 81 to 85 percent of the students reported thinking before writing (a fairly general strategy), only 44 to 63 percent looked up facts or considered how to write for different audiences (a narrower focus). And, when given the opportunity to write planning notes as part of the assessment activity (a much more specific strategy), only 8 percent of the fourth graders and 19 to 20 percent of the eleventh graders did so.

Development of Enjoyment and Appreciation

Developing literacy skills serves little purpose if students are not interested in using their skills. In other words, the *will* to engage in literacy tasks is as important as the *skill* to engage in those tasks (Winograd & Greenlee, 1986). In fact, evidence from the NAEP suggests that, by the eleventh grade, students with positive attitudes about writing tend to be better writers (Applebee et al., 1986). This goal focuses teachers' attention on helping students to like reading, writing, and mathematics. It suggests that teachers should help students to see literacy tasks as interesting, challenging, and rewarding.

Research has revealed that most children do not seem to develop an attitude that writing is personally rewarding. Although 57 percent of fourth graders in the NAEP study reported that they liked to write, only 41 percent of eighth graders and 39 percent of the eleventh graders agreed. Consider their responses to some of the other items. To the statement, "I am a good writer," 58 percent of the fourth graders, 42 percent of the eighth graders, and 41 percent of the eleventh graders agreed. To the statement, "I write on my own outside of school," 48 percent of the fourth graders, 35 percent of the eighth graders, and 29 percent of the eleventh graders agreed.

Children must develop the will to engage in literacy tasks.

Think of your experiences learning to read, write, and do mathematics. Were your teachers successful in helping you to enjoy literacy? Many of our students have said no, particularly in the area of mathematics. What was it about your literacy instruction that resulted in your lack of enjoyment?

Development of Strategic Application of Specific Skills

The word *skill* has been used several times in our discussion of literacy instruction. A **skill** is a learned procedure that a person applies automatically as the result of repeated drill (Routman, 1988). Although literate individuals must be able to perform certain procedures, the procedures must be performed strategically. **Strategic application** is thoughtful and intentional. Literate individuals make judgments about what to do, when, why, and how, in order to solve the problem at hand. They select and orchestrate a variety of skills appropriate for the demands of the task.

There are many literacy skills to be learned, yet it often happens that students master skills but are not good readers, writers, or mathematicians. For instance, the NAEP has shown that by age 13, over 90 percent of students have mastered the basic facts in addition, subtraction, multiplication, and division (Carpenter et al., 1984). However, the level of mastery of more complex concepts is much lower. This means that when it comes to solving problems, students are severely limited. They are not able to make good decisions about what procedures to use at which times. Similarly, in writing, Applebee et al. concluded that "American students can write at a minimal level, but cannot express themselves well enough to ensure that their writing will accomplish the intended purpose" (1986, p. 9). You may have observed young readers who are able to say the words on a page (they have mastered decoding skills), but who are unable to interpret or evaluate the content of what they have read. In other words, these students can apply a number of skills, but fail to apply them strategically to solve the literacy problem at hand. Knowing how to do a skill is not enough; students must be able to determine when and why to use it to accomplish their purposes. Clearly, this goal is related to the importance of developing in-depth understanding and a problem-solving orientation.

The goals of literacy instruction are interrelated. Helping students to focus on the meaning of the task and to think critically about the task is central to the development of literate citizens. It is evident that these essential goals are not being met. Consequently, it is not surprising that research on literacy instruction in elementary classrooms has revealed little attention to these goals. Now we will look at common problems in literacy instruction.

Problems in Literacy Instruction

Studies of literacy instruction have revealed two significant problems: (1) too little instruction occurs, and (2) the instruction that is provided is of poor quality.

Too Little Instruction

Various studies by reading researchers have illustrated the point that too little instruction occurs. In a study of 15 first-, third-, and fifth-grade teachers, Durkin (1984) found that little or no time was devoted to teaching new vocabulary, to helping students access and develop relevant background information, or to considering prereading questions to establish a purpose for reading. The *only* instruction observed addressed **phonics skills** (i.e., the relationship between letters and sounds). Another strong pattern was the emphasis on written assignments. This is not surprising, as other researchers have noted that students spend as much as 70 percent of their reading period engaged in written work, typically filling out workbook and worksheet pages (Fisher, Berliner, Filby, Marliave, Cohen, Dishaw, & Moore, 1978). In other words, students spend considerably more time on written assignments than in reading instruction.

A similar picture emerges in math studies. Good and Grouws (1987) found that the development of math concepts involves only 14 percent of the instructional time. Typically, teachers spend a very brief period introducing concepts and then assign practice activities. The critics of math instruction are not suggesting that students do not need practice; however, practice should follow a significant period of instruction.

Poor Quality Instruction

There are several related problems with the quality of literacy instruction. These include fragmentation, decontextualization, overemphasis on accuracy, and limited student involvement.

FRAGMENTATION.   Fragmented instruction focuses on the pieces of reading, writing, or math rather than on the whole, meaningful process. By "pieces" we mean the specific skills associated with each dimension of literacy (e.g., grammar and punctuation skills in writing). In a review of eight language arts textbook series, Graves (1977) concluded that activities focusing on grammar and punctuation accounted for 52 to 93 percent of writing instruction; only 3 to 29 percent of the activities asked the children to compose (i.e., write original text). Bridge and Hiebert (1985), wanting to know if textbooks had improved, analyzed four series. Their findings echoed those of Graves' earlier study:

> Texts still stress the mechanics of grammar, punctuation, and spelling in word- or sentence-level tasks. (Bridge & Hiebert, 1985, p. 169)

In reading and math the picture is the same. Teachers tend to focus on to-be-tested skills rather than on integrated, problem-solving processes. The fragmented approach fails to promote the **strategic application** of skills (i.e., learning how, when, and why to apply skills). To learn to apply skills strategically requires that students "spend more time reading legitimate materials for legitimate purposes and less time practicing discrete skills in isolation" (Winograd & Greenlee, 1986, p. 18).

DECONTEXTUALIZATION.   This problem is related to fragmentation. When teachers emphasize specific skills in isolation from the process of reading, writing, or math, they decontextualize instruction. This means that skillwork is not grounded in real literacy tasks; it is without context. For example, if a teacher has students complete a grammar exercise in which they are to circle sentence subjects and underline predicates, but fails to help students see how such an activity is related to their own writing, the teacher has failed to contextualize the work. This is a common occurrence in reading instruction, when students complete workbook pages on skills such as finding the main idea of the paragraph. When students are not helped to see the role of such skills in real reading, they are unlikely to recognize much purpose to the assignment. Also, one wonders how likely students are to transfer these decontextualized skills to real reading tasks.

We can think about the problem of decontextualized instruction in another way. When students are given decontextualized skillwork, they are not likely to feel personally involved in the activity. Workbooks and practice sheets do not engage students in personally meaningful experiences. These exercises are not connected to students' prior knowledge or to their experiences outside of the classroom. Decontextualized instruction, then, is cut off from what matters to students. It is removed from the context of real literacy tasks, and it is removed from the context of students' lives.

OVEREMPHASIS ON ACCURACY.   In all areas of literacy instruction, there is the tendency to emphasize accuracy over depth of understanding. Writing instruction emphasizes neat handwriting, correct spelling, and complete sentences. In reading, fluent oral reading is valued. In math, correct computations are valued. The problem with overemphasizing accuracy is apparent in math research. When teachers stress memorizing procedures to get right answers, children have difficulty understanding concepts and solving problems that are different from those used in class (Vobejda, 1987). Students come to believe that learning math means acquiring information developed by others by memorizing rules and finding right answers (Romberg & Carpenter, 1986). Schoenfeld (1991) has said that schooling leads to a suspension of sense making by students. In other words, students come to believe that math just does not always make sense. Both Schoenfeld (1991) and Hiebert (1984) note that children enter school with an analytical approach to problem solving. After a few years of schooling, they shift to a mechanical and meaningless approach to mathematics (Hiebert, 1984). One sixth grader's explanation of how to solve problems exemplifies this approach:

> You look at all the numbers in the problem. Then you go to the next to the last period and read on from there. That tells you what to do. (Lester & Garofalo, 1982, p. 10)

In short, an overemphasis on accuracy diverts students' attention from the thoughtful consideration of literacy tasks as they focus on the form rather than the sense of their response.

LIMITED STUDENT INVOLVEMENT.   Carpenter, Corbitt, Kepner, Lindquist, and Reys (1981) noted that students report spending their math period listening to and watching the teacher and completing pencil-and-paper tasks. The students seldom used manipulative materials or did exploratory activities. Similarly, Davis (1983) reported that most mathematics instruction neglects student experimentation and invention, fails to teach concepts and principles, and instead focuses on highly verbal presentation of facts and procedures. Bridge and Hiebert (1985), in their research on writing instruction, found that students in six elementary classrooms spent most of the writing period copying others' speech and texts from workbooks, textbooks, and the chalkboard. First graders filled in blanks on workbook pages; third graders copied sentences in order to correct capitalization and punctuation errors; and fifth graders copied words in order to correct spelling

FOCUS BOX 4–1

Researchers Speak Out: Problems in Literacy Instruction

Directions: Read the statements of reading, writing, and mathematics researchers about problems in literacy instruction. Synthesize a list of the problems they describe. Then go over the discussion questions with a group of your peers.

Researchers' Statements

Schoenfeld

Teachers give you rules for solving problems, which you memorize and use. Those rules don't have to make sense, and they may not, but if you do what you're told, you'll get the right answer and then everybody will be happy. The result in the short term is that some students manage to solve word problems that they might not otherwise be able to solve. The result in the long term is that students come to understand that school mathematics is arbitrary, that the situations described in so-called real problems aren't real at all, and that you don't have to understand them to solve them. (1991, p. 323)

Good and Grouws

Teachers and textbooks view mathematics as characterized by certainty. Both teachers and text-books see their function as helping students to do problems quickly and accurately. (1987, p. 780)

Calkins

If students are going to become deeply invested in their writing, and if they are going to draft and revise, sharing their texts with each other as they write, they need the luxury of time. If they are going to have the chance to do their best, and then to make their best better, they need long blocks of time. Sustained effort and craftsmanship are essential in writing well, yet they run contrary to the modern American way. We live in a one-draft-only society, a land of instant diets, frozen waffles, and throw-away razors. . . . Like our society, our schools have adopted a one-draft-only mentality. Their motto seems to be "get it done" and "move along." (1986, p. 23)

Hillocks

We know that the teaching of traditional grammar has virtually no impact on the quality of writing and cannot be expected to have. (1986, p. 90)

---

errors. As in mathematics instruction, these writing students minimally were involved in the literacy process. They did not imagine, create, and manipulate their own texts. When student involvement in the learning process is limited, there is concern about the students' depth of understanding and the attitudes they are developing toward literacy.

Mentioning, a concept coined by Durkin (1978–79), is useful in describing the nature of literacy instruction. Durkin found that teachers often provided very little instruction at all. Rather than explicitly explaining skills and concepts, teachers "mention" the new material, give and check assignments, and interrogate students on the content they have read. This "mentioning" kind of teaching is unlikely to promote the goals of literacy we have discussed; teachers tell students just enough about a skill to enable them to do an assignment.

What is good literacy instruction? You will explore each dimension of literacy in depth in your education methods classes. Although we cannot provide a thor-

Taylor
> The methods of instruction that are now dominant dictate that, when a young child comes to school, "learning" to read is presented as an orderly, linear, hierarchical sequence of tasks. How a child measures up to this "theory of instruction" becomes the benchmark of his or her early reading development. When an individual child's learning does not fit the instructional training program, "problems" are diagnosed and "remediated," using more intensive doses of linearly sequenced decoding skills. Children are labeled and pigeonholed, and their own learning is denied. (1989, p. 186)

Position statement, Commission on Reading, NCTE
> So much time is typically taken up by "instructional" activities (including activities with workbooks and skill sheets) that only a very slight amount of time is spent in actual reading—despite the overwhelming evidence that extensive reading and writing are crucial to the development of literacy. (1988)

Discussion Questions

1. Do the researchers' descriptions of teaching practice match the experiences you had when you were in school? Explain the similarities and the differences.

2. Do the researchers' descriptions of teaching practice match what you do in your classroom when you teach literacy (or what you have seen other teachers doing)? Explain the similarities and the differences.

3. Do you think these researchers are overly critical of elementary teachers? If so, what are some other explanations for the problems in literacy achievement?

4. If you do not think these researchers are overly critical of elementary teachers, why do you think some teachers have difficulty teaching literacy?

ough discussion of reading, writing, and mathematics instruction, we have synthesized instructional guidelines that can help teachers promote literacy among elementary school students.

Guidelines for Developing Literacy

In this chapter, you will not find everything you need to know about teaching reading, writing, and mathematics. Instead, you will find several general guidelines to use as you plan and implement literacy instruction. These guidelines are not meant to be followed in sequence. Rather, they form a foundation that supports the specific materials and activities of any literacy lesson. These guidelines range from very formal to very informal.

Develop an Understanding of Literacy Processes

Your success in accomplishing the goals of literacy instruction rests on your understanding of the processes you seek to develop. You cannot expect to rely on basals and other technology because these programs typically are not designed to promote the goals we have described. Durkin's (1981) analysis of five basal reading programs revealed that while the teacher's manuals stressed the subskills of reading, they offered practice exercises on these subskills rather than suggestions for explicit instruction. In addition, the manuals rarely clarified the connection between subskills and the whole process of reading. As a result, explained Durkin, "All these activities become ends in themselves. . . . The children receiving the instruction never do see the relationship between what is done with reading in school and what they should do when they read on their own" (1981, p. 542).

Current mathematics textbooks place more emphasis on drill than on understanding and do not place sufficient emphasis on underlying concepts (Lindquist, 1984) or on developing knowledge of the relationships among numbers (Reys, 1984). Although this emphasis is changing, the problem is still pervasive. The emphasis of texts on procedural knowledge and drill means that the teacher's level of expertise in mathematics is a critical factor in the quality of instruction. Unfortunately, many teachers lack a comprehensive understanding of the nature of mathematics. Consequently, improving math instruction requires more than learning some new teaching strategies. It requires teachers to think differently about math, and to increase their understanding of math concepts and principles.

The situation is similar for writing instruction. In a survey conducted by Bridge and Hiebert (1985), 233 first-, third-, and fifth-grade teachers rated their preparation for teaching writing. On a scale of 0 (poor) to 3 (excellent), the teachers rated their undergraduate preparation with an average of 1 and their graduate preparation with an average of .8. Furthermore, many teachers do not perceive themselves as effective writers and do not choose writing as a personally rewarding activity. Given these circumstances, it is not surprising to find poor quality writing instruction in elementary classrooms. If teachers are to make intelligent decisions about literacy instruction, they must understand how these processes of reading, writing, and mathematics work.

READING.   Before you read our description of the reading process, clarify your beliefs about reading by completing the self-assessment on reading instruction that is found in Focus box 4–2. As we discussed in Chapter 1, it is important to recognize your beliefs because they influence what you see as important and how you interpret information presented to you.

Good reading is a dynamic process of selecting and adjusting the most appropriate skills for a given set of variables. To what variables do good readers respond? These variables include the readers' purpose(s), their level of interest in the material, familiarity with the topic, and knowledge of words and concepts in the text. These variables determine the manner in which students will read a par-

FOCUS BOX 4–2

Self-Assessment on Reading Instruction

Directions: Read each statement and decide whether you agree (A) or disagree (D) based on your current knowledge and beliefs about reading. There may be some statements with which you both agree and disagree, but we want you to make a choice. Select *agree* if you agree more than you disagree with a statement. Select *disagree* if you disagree more than you agree with a statement.

_____ 1. In order to learn how to read, children must first know the sounds of the letters.

_____ 2. Children figure out letter sounds after they have spent a lot of time being read to and memorizing/reading texts.

_____ 3. Good readers rarely misread a word.

_____ 4. Teachers should read to beginning readers instead of requiring beginning readers to read to them.

_____ 5. The best way to teach children to read is to be sure they master the necessary subskills.

_____ 6. Good readers read for meaning more than for accuracy.

_____ 7. Good readers adjust their reading behaviors to fit with the purpose for reading a particular text.

_____ 8. When children can figure out what the words say, they are well on their way to becoming good readers.

_____ 9. Reading can best be defined as the application of a set of rules for decoding print.

_____ 10. Good readers make a lot of decisions while in the process of reading.

_____ 11. Beginning readers require concentrated decoding instruction, while better readers require more instruction in comprehension.

_____ 12. Workbooks are useful because they provide instruction on essential reading skills.

_____ 13 Although it is sometimes boring, learning to read requires repetitive drill so that decoding skills can be applied automatically.

_____ 14. It is a waste of valuable time to let "nonreaders" engage in independent reading (i.e., sustained silent reading).

_____ 15. Reading ability can be improved by developing a child's ability to speak, listen, and write.

ticular text. Poor readers are less likely to adjust their reading in response to these variables.

In what ways do readers adjust their approach to text? This is where the strategic application of skills referred to earlier is important. Good readers actively process print by selecting and orchestrating a variety of skills appropriate for the demands of the text at hand. For instance, they predict meaning of text before reading, recognize and use relevant background knowledge to interpret text, create mental images, monitor understanding, and attempt to correct themselves when they realize they have not understood. This active, intentional approach to reading has been called **strategic reading**. Strategic reading entails making judgments about what to do in order to process and comprehend text. Look back at your reading self-assessment. If you agreed with items 2, 4, 6, 7, 10, and 15 on the self-assessment, you appear to agree with the definition of reading we have presented.

WRITING.   Before you read about the writing process, clarify your beliefs about writing by completing the self-assessment on writing instruction found in Focus Box 4–3.

Good writing is also a dynamic process. Good writers adjust their approach to the writing task according to their purpose and their audience. If you take a minute to think of the many times you have used writing over the past week, you will see that you have written for a variety of purposes. Think further, and you will see that you managed tasks differently according to your purpose.

FOCUS BOX 4–3

Self-Assessment on Writing Instruction

Directions: Read each statement and decide whether you agree (A) or disagree (D) with the statement based upon your current knowledge and beliefs about writing. There may be some statements with which you both agree and disagree, but we want you to make a choice. Select *agree* if you agree more than you disagree with a statement. Select *disagree* if you disagree more than you agree with a statement.

_____ 1. Children learn best how to write by trying to make their writing look like good models of writing.

_____ 2. We should let young children spell in any way that makes sense to them.

_____ 3. Students who drill and practice grammar and punctuation skills will be better writers.

_____ 4. Young children's scribbles can be understood as writing.

_____ 5. We should consistently correct children's spelling errors, so they can learn to spell well.

_____ 6. Children should be able to finish a written piece with one draft and a final copy.

_____ 7. Writing instruction becomes much more important after second grade when children have had a chance to develop the basic spelling and grammar skills.

_____ 8. Children need to learn to get their ideas written down first and to worry about grammar and punctuation later.

_____ 9. Writing instruction needs to focus more on the processes than the product.

_____ 10. If children learn how to write to the teacher, they will be able to transfer that ability and be able to write for any audience.

Good writers know how to keep the purpose and audience in mind as they compose. They know how to analyze and assemble information; they know how to organize ideas in order to convince others; and they know how to express thoughts and feelings in imaginative and creative ways. To accomplish these things, good writers depend on many strategies. For instance, they may make additions and deletions, rearrange the order of ideas, ask others to critique their works, throw their first drafts away and start over, and check their spelling and punctuation for accuracy. Strategies like these fit into several **stages of the writing process**. These stages include prewriting or rehearsal, drafting, sharing, revising, editing, and publishing. Within each of these stages, writers use varied techniques to help them accomplish the task.

According to Flower and Hayes (1981), the process of writing is recursive; that is, a writer moves back and forth among the stages. Planning may lead to writing, but writing may suggest the need for more planning. Similarly, revision may point out a need for further writing or even more planning. Now check your writing self-assessment. If you agreed with items 2, 4, 8, and 9, you appear to agree with the definition of writing presented here.

MATHEMATICS.   Before you read about the process of mathematics, complete the self-assessment on mathematics instruction that is found in Focus Box 4–4.

Most people view mathematics as getting correct answers (Good & Grouws, 1987) or as "a specific collection of explicit algorithms" (Davis, 1983, p. 101). Yet mathematicians define mathematics as an open-ended process that involves finding ways to approach and solve problems (Davis, 1983; Good & Grouws, 1987). Mathematics involves the coordination of a variety of complex problem-solving techniques such as the following:

- recognizing and defining mathematics problems and terms
- analyzing problems to recognize patterns of similarity to and difference from other problems
- creating mental representations
- searching one's memory for appropriate algorithms
- constructing or revising algorithms
- using algorithms flexibly and appropriately
- setting appropriate goals and subgoals (i.e., deciding what should be done first, second, third)
- making hypotheses
- making discoveries
- developing arguments and proofs and debating their validity

Math is not the pursuit of predetermined right answers. Rather, it is a dynamic process that requires high-level reasoning skills and, most importantly, a strong propensity to analyze and understand (Schoenfeld, 1991). Refer to the math self-assessment you took earlier. If you agreed with items 3, 4, 6, 7, 9, 11, and 14, you appear to agree with this definition of mathematics.

FOCUS BOX 4–4

Self-Assessment on Mathematics Instruction

Directions: Read each statement and decide whether you agree (A) or disagree (D) with the statement based upon your current knowledge and beliefs about mathematics. There may be some statements with which you both agree and disagree, but we want you to make a choice. Select *agree* if you agree more than you disagree with a statement. Select *disagree* if you disagree more than you agree with a statement.

_____ 1. One of the most important skills in learning mathematics is the ability to memorize algorithms (i.e., rules and procedures).

_____ 2. Essentially, problem solving in mathematics involves selecting the appropriate procedure and doing the computation correctly.

_____ 3. In mathematics there is very little need for students to memorize if they learn to construct relationships among numbers.

_____ 4. Individual students have different but equally appropriate ways of solving mathematics problems.

_____ 5. Mathematics can best be defined as a collection of explicit rules and procedures for manipulating numbers.

_____ 6. The ability to set goals and subgoals is important in mathematics.

_____ 7. The least important skill in learning mathematics is the ability to memorize algorithms.

_____ 8. Mathematics primarily involves learning numbers and operations on numbers.

_____ 9. Mathematics can best be defined as an open-ended collection of techniques (i.e, individuals are free to invent new techniques).

_____ 10. In mathematics it is important to follow the correct procedures, step by step.

_____ 11. Mathematics provides students an opportunity to use their creativity and reasoning.

_____ 12. Although it is sometimes boring, mathematics learning requires a great deal of repetitive drill so that facts and procedures become habit.

_____ 13. Mathematics primarily requires convergent thinking (i.e. thinking that leads to the one right answer).

_____ 14. Solving mathematical problems frequently involves the construction or revision of mathematical rules and procedures.

_____ 15. If a group of children cannot understand the reasons behind a math procedure, it is best to teach them a memory device that will enable them to do the correct calculations. Understanding can come later.

Although the processes of reading, writing, and mathematics are distinct, they have much in common. All are dynamic processes directed by the individual. All require the student to coordinate many specific skills and techniques. All revolve around the construction of meaning and understanding. Teachers who understand these processes are equipped to understand their students' misunderstandings, to plan lessons appropriate for their students' current needs, and to facilitate students' growth as literate individuals. The guidelines that we will discuss next direct-ly address what the classroom teacher should do to promote literacy instruction.

Determine What Students Already Understand

Literacy researchers have emphasized the importance of providing instruction that matches learners' current understanding. Y. Goodman (1978) has promoted the concept of the teacher as "kid watcher," who studies children's behavior for clues to their understanding and then provides instructional experiences that meet students where they are, cognitively speaking. Similarly, Harste, Woodward, and Burke (1984) have described students as "curriculum informists." That is, through close observations of students, teachers can become informed about what to do next; the students inform the curriculum.

The concepts of the teacher as a kid watcher and students as curriculum informists have powerful implications. If teachers accept these concepts, they accept the responsibility to direct curriculum and instruction in their classrooms. Although teacher's guides and lists of objectives provide teachers with some direction, they should not determine what is taught to whom and when. These decisions should be based on students' current levels of understanding. Let's see how a teacher might do this.

Lampert (1986) described a series of mathematics lessons she taught to 28 het-erogeneously grouped fourth graders. She began by trying to determine what students already knew about multiplication by observing the students, analyzing their errors, and drawing on research studies of children's errors (e.g., Brown & Van Lehn, 1980; Brown & Burton, 1978). The children's mistakes suggested to her that they did not understand the relationship of composition, decomposi-tion, or place value in solving multiplication problems. Based on the following typical errors of children, Lampert explained their current understanding. See if you can determine the system each child used to compute the problems. (See Focus Box 4–5 for an explanation of how the children solved the problems.)

Child A	Child B	Child C	Child D
86	86	86	86
$\times\ 3$	$\times\ 3$	$\times\ 3$	$\times 3$
2438	278	2418	222

Lampert explained:

> In each of these cases, the child knew that $3 \times 6 = 18$, that $3 \times 8 = 24$, and that these two multiplications needed to be done to find the answer. These are not errors of fact. . . . They are errors that seem to indicate that the students reached an impasse in their knowledge of what to do when they got to the carrying part of the procedure and they invented a way to cope with it. . . . [The errors] are not "misconceptions" about place value; rather, they suggest that place value is simply not a relevant consideration to these children in the process of doing computation. There is no attempt to apply any other knowledge about multipli-cation besides the procedural. (1986, p. 314)

An Explanation of How Children Solved the Problems

You may have easily figured out how the children solved the problem, 86 × 3. Or you may find that one or two stumped you. The following explanations will help you understand the reasoning used by each child. We have recorded the "thinking" that might have guided the children as they solved the problem.

Child A: (Note the child worked the problem from right to left, beginning with the one's column)

$$
\begin{array}{r}
86 \\
\times\,3 \\
\hline
38
\end{array}
$$
3×6 is 18.
Write down the 8.
Now bring down the 3.

$$
\begin{array}{r}
86 \\
\times\,3 \\
\hline
2438
\end{array}
$$
Now 3×8 is 24.
Write down 24.
The answer is 2438.

Child B: (Note the child worked the problem from right to left, beginning with the one's column)

$$
\begin{array}{r}
86 \\
\times\,3 \\
\hline
8
\end{array}
$$
3×6 is 18.
Write down the 8.

$$
\begin{array}{r}
86 \\
\times\,3 \\
\hline
278
\end{array}
$$
3×8 is 24. Add the 3.
Write down 27.
The answer is 278.

Child C: (Note the child worked the problem from right to left, beginning with the one's column)

$$
\begin{array}{r}
86 \\
\times\,3 \\
\hline
18
\end{array}
$$
3×6 is 18.
Write down 18.

$$
\begin{array}{r}
86 \\
\times\,3 \\
\hline
2418
\end{array}
$$
3×8 is 24.
Write down 24.
The answer is 2418.

Child D: (Note that the child worked the problem from left to right, beginning with the ten's column.)

$$
\begin{array}{r}
4 \\
86 \\
\times\,3 \\
\hline
2
\end{array}
$$
3×8 is 24.
Write down the 2. Carry the 4.

$$
\begin{array}{r}
86 \\
\times\,3 \\
\hline
222
\end{array}
$$
3×6 is 18. Add the 4.
Write down 22.
The answer is 222.

Based upon her assessment of their errors, Lampert concluded that the students had stopped trying to make sense of math and were trying (unsuccessfully) to apply memorized procedures. To stress the meaning of concepts, she recognized that her instruction needed to begin with problems in which the students would be able to do meaningful calculation with numbers. Consequently, she began with identification of the value of coins and with single-digit multiplication activities that the children could understand.

Assessment of student understanding should be done prior to and during instruction. The teacher must continually assess student thinking to determine what sense they are making of instruction. For example, when Lampert found that her students were surprised that alternative groupings of the same number result in the same answer (e.g., $86 \times 3 = (80 + 6) \times 3 = (40 + 3 + 40 + 3) \times 3$), she decided she must do a variety of problems stressing multiple ways to group within multiplication problems.

Ground Instruction in the Real World

Students come to school with knowledge about literacy. Before they have had any formal instruction, they have had multiple experiences with print and numbers. Some children enter school believing that they can read and write, only to find that by school standards they are not readers or writers. This happens because teachers fail to use what students know to shape formal literacy instruction. Instead, teachers let publishers tell them what, when, and how to teach. If you think this guideline is related to the previous one, you are correct. Because students come to school with literacy knowledge, teachers should ground literacy instruction in the real world of students. By providing students with meaningful, contextualized literacy tasks, teachers encourage students to use the knowledge they have constructed over time to manage the task and to solve new literacy problems.

The whole-language movement speaks to the principle of grounding instruction in the real world. K. S. Goodman (1989) identified "a positive view of human learners" as one of the key characteristics of whole language. Teachers who view learners as capable and knowledgeable respect learners' knowledge and use that knowledge to help learners develop their literacy. In the classroom, this means that teachers engage students in real-life talking, listening, reading, and writing activities. In real life, language is used for a purpose. Therefore, in this context of meaningful language use, children work out their understandings of how language functions and what words mean.

In one second-grade classroom, students decided to write to one of their favorite authors, Roald Dahl. The teacher used students' interest to create various language experiences. The teacher divided the class into groups, and each group came up with ideas about what they wanted to say to Mr. Dahl and in what form. Each group assembled their lists of ideas. The whole class reconvened to discuss the ideas and make a plan. Once the class had agreed that they wanted to write a book to let Mr. Dahl know how they felt about his books, there were additional tasks to be accomplished. The general plan for the book had to be developed. Groups of students became responsible for the various aspects of book pro-

Grounding instruction in the real world of students helps increase literacy learning.

duction. During this four-week project, students were immersed in talking, listening, reading, and writing, as they worked to complete literacy tasks that were personally meaningful and important. Along the way, they used a number of specific skills identified in the second-grade language arts text and the basal reader, but they used them in the context of real language activities. The teacher taught a number of mini-lessons on skills such as writing complete sentences and using quotation marks. Students saw the relevance of these lessons because they were grounded in meaningful language tasks.

By grounding instruction in the real world, teachers help students use what they know to make sense of what is new. Also, when students see purpose and relevance in schoolwork, they become more engaged with their schoolwork.

Focus on the Strategic Application of Skills

As we stated earlier, knowing how to do skills does not guarantee thoughtful, reasoned literacy. Students can know how to perform a particular skill, such as identifying details that support a main idea, but fail to use that skill to write a descriptive paragraph. This is why the strategic use of skills is so important. Knowing how to perform the skill is necessary, but knowing why, when, and where to use the skill are also essential to literacy.

Helping students become strategic in their approach to literacy tasks means helping them develop awareness and control of their cognitive activity. This cognitive control is known as **metacognition**. (We shall discuss metacognition in depth in Chapter 7.) According to Garner (1987), metacognition refers to knowledge of the factors that affect the way a learning activity should be conducted as well as control of these factors. Three kinds of factors that are important in reading are (1) knowledge of oneself as a reader, (2) the demands of particular reading tasks, and (3) the strategies one can use to manage reading tasks successfully. These same factors are important in writing and mathematics. How can teachers help students to develop this kind of knowledge and control? Let's look at an example from a reading lesson.

The central focus of much recent research on reading instruction is on the teacher's explanations to students of the cognitive activities engaged in by good readers. At the other end of the instructional spectrum from *mentioning*, the kind of explanation referred to here is detailed, precise, and explicit. Notice how Mrs. Gregory helps her first graders focus on the cognitive and metacognitive processes used by good readers:

Mrs. Gregory:	The story we're going to read today is called "Mr. Fig" (Early, Cooper, & Santeusanio, 1979). When I read that title, some thoughts come to my mind. I'm thinking about the story we read yesterday.
Nadia:	Mr. Fig was in that story.
Melissa:	It was his house, really.
Mrs. Gregory:	I'm picturing that house in my mind.
Josh:	It was really small, in the grass.
Mrs. Gregory:	Hmm. It was a tiny house in the grass. I wonder what that tells us about Mr. Fig.
Melissa:	He's not a real person because he's tiny.
Josh:	Yeah, I think he's a magic person because he was flying with animals on the book cover.
Mrs. Gregory:	Oh, yes, good thinking. So we did have more information about Mr. Fig, didn't we?
Nadia:	Yeah, and the book's called *Magic Afternoon*, so he could really be magic.
Mrs. Gregory:	Good for you. You children are really pulling together a lot of information here. Let's see. We know Mr. Fig lives in a tiny house in the grass and that he can't be a real person. We said he could be magic because there's a picture of him flying with some animals, and the name of the book is *Magic Afternoon*. So, we already know a lot about Mr. Fig. I think this story will probably tell us even more about him.
Dwayne:	Yeah, it might tell us if he's really magic.
Mrs. Gregory:	That sounds like a reasonable prediction. Do you think we're ready to read this story?

Students: Yes!

Mrs. Gregory: We've done a lot of important thinking even before we started to read! All
                  that good thinking will help us understand the story. Let's read the first
                  page silently and then we'll talk about it.

This excerpt from a first-grade reading lesson may sound more like casual conversation than a formal lesson. However, if you attend closely, you will see that while the tone may be casual, the teacher is pursuing a definite agenda. Notice how she draws the students' attention to their own knowledge and thinking. She uses the words *thoughts*, *thinking*, and *mind*. She engages the students in extensive discussion of relevant background knowledge before they begin to read. And, she points out that this kind of "prereading" thinking is very helpful (e.g., "All that good thinking will help us understand the story about Mr. Fig"). With this comment we can see that Mrs. Gregory is teaching her students more than how to assemble relevant background knowledge before reading; she is teaching them *why* it is important to use this skill. This is what is meant by the strategic application of skills. Even first graders can be helped to gain control over reading skills. The teacher must help them to see why the skills are important and when they should be used.

Notice how Mrs. Gregory models her own thinking for students. The practice of sharing one's thinking processes with others, or **think alouds**, has received attention in all areas of literacy instruction in recent years. When teachers use think alouds, they focus students' attention on the thinking and reasoning that underlie skilled performance. This is an essential aspect of developing strategic literacy. By stressing the processes by which tasks are accomplished, teachers help students develop depth of understanding.

Imagine additional practices a math teacher might use to help students focus on reasoning. Lampert (1986) uses practices like praising students for their attempts as well as for correct solutions, requiring them to develop alternative solutions to problems, and requiring them to explain the reasoning behind the answer. Kantowski (1981) notes that teachers who wish to foster students' ability to reason must evaluate more than correct answers because the criteria used in evaluation communicate to students what is valued by the teacher. If teachers judge the mathematical competence of their students by assessing their ability to obtain correct answers, students will inevitably view mathematics as a set of procedures for obtaining answers.

Use Supportive Dialogue to Help Children Construct Understanding

In this guideline we elaborate on teaching methods that are appropriate for helping students acquire complex cognitive tasks such as reading, writing, and mathematics. **Cognitive apprenticeship**, a "learning-through-guided-experience" model based on traditional apprenticeship, is one example of a set of strategies useful in providing supportive dialogue. In this model an expert models task performance, coaches the novice, and gradually withdraws assistance as the novice becomes more adept at the task (Collins, Brown, & Newman, 1989). This kind of teaching is not something that is done by the expert to the novice; rather, the two work together to move the novice toward expert performance. The teacher, then, is a collaborator who participates with students as they begin to internalize the various strategies involved in accomplishing literacy tasks.

Supportive dialogue between teacher and students is an integral part of the apprenticeship model. As teacher and students work together to solve a literacy task (e.g., reading a passage, writing a letter, solving a math problem), the teacher provides just as much support as the students need to accomplish the task. The teacher acts like a coach, who closely observes the learners and provides help and feedback when needed.

Collins, Brown, and Newman (1989) have described **six component methods of cognitive apprenticeship**. You will notice that they are integrated rather than distinct. We discuss them separately to help you see the components of instruction that fosters depth of understanding. However, in the context of real teaching, the components are neither distinct nor sequential.

MODELING.   The student observes the teacher in order to build a mental model of the task, so the teacher models by demonstrating the cognitive dimensions of the task. For instance, Mrs. Gregory models how she makes predictions:

> It helps us understand what we read if we think about what might happen next. To make good predictions we have to think about what's happening in the story and then wonder what the author might tell us next. Then as we read, we can see whether we were on the right track. So far we've found out about Mr. Fig, who's a little, magical creature with a big hat. I think the author will probably tell us more about Mr. Fig.

COACHING AND SCAFFOLDING.   Because scaffolding is a critical component of coaching, we discuss these two methods together. Based on observation of student performance, the teacher **coaches** by offering suggestions, providing support (scaffolding), providing feedback, and designing new tasks in order to move the student closer to expert performance. **Scaffolding** is the way that the teacher provides support, such as physical help or hints, so that students can successfully complete tasks. That is, the students and teacher work together to accomplish a complex task. The teacher does the parts of the task that are too advanced for the students. An important part of scaffolding is that the teacher removes these supports as soon as students are capable of completing the task without them. Mrs. Gregory provides us with an example of coaching and scaffolding:

Mrs. Gregory:	Mark, can you make up a good question about the page we just read?
Mark:	Okay, um—Mr. Fig did what—um—Did he do what kind of—No, that's not right.
Mrs. Gregory:	What do you want to ask about, Mark?
Mark:	The magic.
Mrs. Gregory:	Can you start the question with the words, "What kind?"
Mark:	Uh, what kind did he, did Mr. Fig—

Mrs. Gregory: How about saying, "What kind of—"

Mark: What kind of magic did he, did Mr. Fig, do?

Mrs. Gregory: I think you've got it!

Notice how Mrs. Gregory helped Mark formulate his question. First she asked him what he wanted to focus on, so that the question would be his rather than hers. Then she offered him the first two words of the question. When these supports did not lead to success, she added a third word. With that help, Mark was able to formulate an appropriate question.

ARTICULATION.   Explaining how you accomplished a task is known as articulation. When students are asked to articulate cognitive strategies, they gain greater awareness of and control over those strategies. Mrs. Gregory asked Mark to articulate his understanding of the process of summarizing:

Mark: A good summary for this page would be "Mr. Fig does happy magic in the afternoon."

Mrs. Gregory: And how did you figure out such a good summary, Mark?

Mark: Well, the important ideas are Mr. Fig and the magic in the afternoon. So, I just put them together in a sentence.

REFLECTION.   You have already read an entire chapter about reflection and what it means to be a reflective teacher. The meaning of the word *reflection* here is somewhat different. When students compare their efforts at carrying out a cognitive task to that of an expert, they are engaging in reflection. Reflection helps students develop precise understandings of cognitive tasks. They are able to see clearly what features are necessary for skilled performance. Here's how Mrs. Gregory built reflection into her reading lesson:

Mrs. Gregory: Now, everybody think about how you'd summarize the page. (*Long pause*) I think I would summarize the page by saying that on a sunny afternoon, Mr. Fig sat in a little chair wearing his big, magic hat. Was your summary like mine?

Josh: Sort of, except I was thinking that Mr. Fig and the house and the chair were all little.

Mrs. Gregory: In a summary, would we need to say that each of those was little?

Melissa: No, because it's supposed to be short.

Mrs. Gregory: What do we know about making summaries?

Melissa: You just say the important ideas.

Mrs. Gregory: Is it important that things are little?

Josh: Yeah, because Mr. Fig is so little.

Mrs. Gregory: Okay, so how could we do that without using too many words in the summary?

Mrs. Gregory asks the students to compare their summaries with hers. She encourages them to think deeply about how to summarize. You may have noticed that she also acts as a coach in this excerpt, by observing Josh's comment about his summary and tailoring her feedback to address his particular difficulty.

EXPLORATION.   Exploration occurs when the teacher removes all supports and has students perform cognitive tasks on their own. During exploration, students practice and refine strategies that they jointly had developed with the teacher. Exploration moves students toward independent use of strategies and transfer of strategies to novel situations. Mrs. Gregory provided the occasion for exploration at the end of the lesson:

Mrs. Gregory: The last thing we're going to do today is read the song I've written on the chart paper and make up summaries for it. We'll also talk about how you handled any tricky parts you came across. I'll read it to you first.

To help you understand this guideline about using supportive dialogue, we have focused on one reading lesson. Our purpose was to avoid confusing you with examples drawn from all three dimensions of literacy. By restricting our example to one reading lesson, we do not mean to imply that student-teacher collaboration and the methods of cognitive apprenticeship apply only to reading instruction. This approach to teaching and learning is equally applicable to mathematics and writing instruction. For example, Lampert (1986) has demonstrated this approach to teaching math. In the area of writing, Langer and Applebee (1987) use the term *instructional scaffolding* as an image of the kind of structure teachers need to create in helping students gain control of the processes of prewriting or rehearsal, drafting, revising, and editing. We include an example of a writing lesson to illustrate the use of this guideline in writing instruction:

> For her fourth graders, Anita [the teacher] set up a revision and editing lesson when she realized that some of their stories were drawing out narratives by using *and then* too often. She overloaded her own composition with these connectives, wrote it on a huge sheet of lined paper, displayed it on an easel before the group, and announced, "You know how I feel about my stories. I think they're terrific. Here's a true story about my dog Barney, who's a little bit of a coward." She read:
>
> **Barney's Walk on the Beach**
> One day I took my dog Barney for a walk on the beach. We went down the cliff stairs and then headed west. Then Barney saw something way up ahead and started to run toward it. Then he stopped. Then he started walking slowly and cautiously. Then he began to sniff so then I began to follow him. . . . Then I saw it too. Something was moving at the water's edge. Then Barney started barking and barking. Then I began to laugh. The moving object at the water's edge was a feather!
>
> "Do you think that's a perfect story?"
>
> Students respond by asking about Barney and telling of their visits to the beach.
>
> "What could I do to make it better?"
>
> Cindy suggests, "You say *Barney* too many times. You could put in *he* or *my dog* or something like that."

"Oh, that's so. Are there any other words that are repeated a lot?"

Students count up the number of times *Barney* is used and also discover eight occurrences of *then*.

"Is that a lot?"

"Yes!" several chorus.

"What should we do about that?"

Eric says, "Change it!"

Rich adds, "Cross some out!"

Anita smiles and reaches for a black felt-tip marker. As they together start to cross out some *thens*, Kevin remarks, "You always wreck your stories." (Carter, 1983, pp. 42–43. By permission of University of Chicago Press.)

We can see that Anita built her lesson on something the students already understood and knew—that a written piece sounds better and is clearer if a word is not repeated unnecessarily. Children's already-acquired language sense can provide such support as they make judgments in writing.

The students used the support, the scaffold, to help them learn strategies they could apply in other situations as they attempted to solve problems in their own writing. For instance, Anita demonstrated how she asked the students questions about her writing. The students witnessed and begin to understand the concept of "wrecking" your writing until you get it to be its very best. By learning what kinds of questions to ask and what it means to revise and edit, these students may be more likely to apply such strategies to their own compositions. As Langer and Applebee explain, "The student learns to do new language tasks by being led through them in the context of a supportive dialogue" (1987, p. 143). This means shifting away from teaching skills and procedures in isolation and toward teaching processes that reflect the natural stages of writing.

Create a Classroom Environment That Values Literacy

As stated earlier, knowing how to perform literacy tasks does not ensure that students will enjoy and value these processes. If teachers hope to develop students' *will* to be literate, they must attend to the nature and tone of classroom literacy events and lessons. A number of the guidelines we have discussed can contribute to students' positive attitudes toward literacy.

One of the points we have made is that teachers must respect what students already know and build instruction on that knowledge. In other words, we must shape the curriculum to meet the students where they are, rather than expect the students to catch up with the curriculum. Therefore, students are likely to feel capable and intelligent. A second point, grounding instruction in the real world, is also likely to contribute to positive attitudes toward literacy. When students find instruction to be relevant and purposeful, they are apt to enjoy it and become more deeply engaged in it than they would in activities for which they see little purpose. Third, when learning becomes a collaborative effort between the teacher and the students, students actively pursue understanding in a sup-

Providing projects like writing a class newspaper communicates that literacy is valued.

portive context. Teachers help the students to be successful at and to engage thoughtfully in literacy tasks.

There are additional things that teachers can do to create an environment in which literacy is valued. For example, teachers can talk about literacy in positive ways and help students see how central it is to our very existence. In and out of school, people engage in literacy events countless times during the day. Because literacy is a natural part of social life, people often take it for granted. By talking about literacy events, teachers can help students become more aware of their existence and importance. Also, teachers can support students' efforts, even rudimentary ones, at literacy. This means, for example, allowing time for children to scribble and talk about what those marks say. It means valuing children's spelling (i.e., **invented or developmental spelling**), instead of focusing on "correct" or "grown-up" spelling. Teachers can balance formal literacy lessons with informal literacy experiences. Students need formal lessons to help them understand and use particular literacy strategies; however, students also need to engage in informal literacy experiences where they can experiment with, practice, and construct literacy skills. This can be as simple as giving students 15 minutes to share new library books with classmates. More focused activities, such as working with a small group to invent a useful machine, give students the chance to use literacy skills in a natural context.

A Summary of Instructional Guidelines

We have described a set of instructional guidelines that are appropriate for the development of literacy. The guidelines are equally applicable to instruction in reading, writing, and mathematics because the three processes share important dimensions. As we discussed earlier, the goals of reading, writing, and mathematics instruction are similar. We suggested that teachers follow these instructional guidelines:

1. Develop an understanding of the processes of reading, writing, and mathematics.
2. Determine what students already understand, by acting as "kid watchers" and by viewing students as curriculum informists. Linked to gaining insight into the students' understanding is planning lessons that build on this understanding.
3. Ground instruction in the real world so that students see its purpose and relevance. Also, instruction that is connected to students' lives helps them make use of their background knowledge to tackle new tasks.
4. Focus on the strategic application of skills so that students learn to approach tasks thoughtfully. Help students learn why, when, and where to use their skills.
5. Help children construct understanding of strategies through supportive dialogue. The teacher works with students to build skill in and an understanding of literacy processes.
6. Create a classroom environment in which literacy is valued in order to promote enjoyment and appreciation of reading, writing, and mathematics.

We think of this kind of instruction as **collaborative instruction**. That is, teachers and students work together to develop understanding. While teachers are responsible for directing the action, they take their cues from the students so that teaching and learning are interactive processes. This is quite different from the traditional transmission model of teaching and learning, in which teachers are viewed as delivering knowledge to learners. In a transmission approach,

FOCUS BOX 4–6

Practical Application Activity

Activity 1:   Select a lesson from any elementary mathematics, language arts, or reading teacher's manual. Use the instructional guidelines presented in this chapter to adapt the lesson so that it can be taught using collaborative instruction. Ask one or more peers to critique your plan and make suggestions for improvement.

Activity 2:   Choose a particular educational objective in the area of reading, writing, or mathematics instruction. (Teacher's manuals always list objectives.) Using the guidelines from this chapter, develop a lesson to help students construct the understanding(s) necessary to meet this objective.

Activity 3:   Use audio- or videotape to record yourself as you teach a literacy lesson using the instructional guidelines presented in this chapter. Analyze the recording for evidence of the different guidelines. You might do this with a peer. Then the two of you could suggest improvements to one another.

teachers are tellers and students are listeners and absorbers. In the collaborative model, learning is an active, social process in which children construct under-standings as they interact with others to complete meaningful tasks (Vygotsky, 1978). Collaborative instruction recognizes the social basis of conceptual growth and the supportive role of the "expert" in helping the "novice" to learn.

Although there is no one right way to conduct collaborative instruction, it should reflect the general guidelines we have presented. Specific instructional models have been developed based on the collaborative orientation. **Reciprocal teaching**, for example, is a technique developed for reading instruction (Palincsar & Brown, 1984). We saw bits of a reciprocal teaching lesson in the excerpts about Mrs. Gregory and her students. The purpose of reciprocal teaching is to help students become strategic readers. Original reciprocal teaching lessons were designed to focus on self-questioning, summarizing, clarifying con-fusing parts of text, and predicting, as these strategies promote comprehension. The basic procedures are as follows:

1. Teacher and students silently read a passage of text.

2. Teacher and students take turns leading the discussion of the passages. Initially, the teacher models, but students gradually take over responsibility.

3. The individual acting as teacher does the following in relation to the pas-sage: asks a potential test question; summarizes the content; clarifies any dif-ficult parts; and predicts future content.

4. As the acting teacher performs these tasks, other group members make com-ments and ask questions. The group tries to maintain a natural dialogue.

5. When the students acting as teachers have difficulty performing the tasks, the teacher provides one or more kinds of assistance:

    a. *prompts*— "Can you start the question with the words, *What kind?*"

    b. *instruction*—"To make good predictions we really have to think about what's happening in the story and then wonder what the author might tell us next."

    c. *activity modification*— "If you're having a hard time summarizing, why not try to predict what you think we'll find out about next?"

    d. *models*—"A question I might have asked is. . . ."

6. The teacher reminds students that they can use these activities when they read independently to help them understand better.

7. The teacher encourages students to compare their performance of cognitive tasks to the expert model and to articulate the processes used.

8. The students apply cognitive tasks in new contexts.

    In the reciprocal teaching model, we see evidence of the six methods of cognitive apprenticeship: modeling, coaching, scaffolding, articulation, reflection, and exploration (Collins, et al., 1989). Together these methods enable students to acquire cognitive and metacognitive skills, refine and gain control of problem solving strategies, and develop independence in carrying out processes and defining problems. The model is collaborative in that it is based on ongoing interaction between teacher and students. Students participate in the literacy task and receive the support they need from the teacher to be successful.

    Reciprocal teaching is an example of a formal application of collaborative instruction but the model need not be this formal. The guidelines can come into play as a teacher interacts with a single student over a composition or with a group trying to figure out the dimensions of the classroom. Collaborative instruction gives teachers a way to think about their interactions with students.

    Although we believe the collaborative orientation provides a productive framework for literacy instruction, we recognize that it presents some challenges to teachers. In the final section of this chapter we turn to the questions this approach to instruction raises for teachers.

Meeting the Challenges of Collaborative Instruction

How Do I Shift Away From a Transmission Model of Teaching?

Collaborative instruction embodies principles that run counter to traditional teaching models. Many teachers are guided by what Barnes (1976) called a "transmission" model of teaching. In this model of teaching, "the role of the teacher is to be the purveyor and evaluator of ideas, and the role of the student is to be the recipient of them" (Langer, 1984, p. 113). Collaborative instruction calls for a change in student and teacher roles.

    What should teachers do? First, teachers must monitor their talking. Collaborative instruction requires that teachers learn when to be quiet. Running a tape recorder during a lesson can give teachers a clear sense of who talks and when. Too much teacher talk can turn the lesson into a one-way street. A second

FOCUS BOX 4–7

Comprehension Check

Directions: Check your comprehension of the major ideas presented in this chapter by answering the following questions:

- What are appropriate goals for literacy instruction?
- What does a competent reader, writer, and mathematician need to know and be able to do?
- Are children currently learning to be good readers, writers, and mathematicians? Do the data reported in this chapter confirm or contradict your observations of children in classrooms?
- What problems exist in current literacy instruction?
- Which of the strategies presented in this chapter stand out to you as especially important? Evaluate this list of strategies using your list of goals for literacy instruction. Doing this can help you identify goals for literacy that you might be likely to underemphasize.

When you finish, compare your responses with those of your peers. Pay attention to similarities and differences in your answers. Did some of you omit things that others considered important? What might this tell you about your understanding of literacy instruction?

suggestion is to avoid trying to make overnight transformations. It would be wiser for teachers to gradually integrate the collaborative instructional model into their instructional repertoire. Careful self-assessment will help teachers come to grips with the features of collaborative instruction and improve their ability to teach in this manner. A third suggestion is that teachers consider their goals for literacy instruction. We have argued in this chapter that instructional goals include developing depth of understanding, problem-solving skills, the ability to use specific skills strategically, and an enjoyment and appreciation of literacy. Collaborative instruction can address all of these goals as well as many others (e.g., to develop positive attitudes toward school, teachers, and learning; to develop and demonstrate respect for self and others).

How Do I Know How Much and What Kind of Scaffolding to Use?

The idea is to give students only as much support as they need to accomplish the task. In order to do this, the teacher must continually assess the student's level of competence and determine how much and what kind of assistance is necessary. The unpredictability of this feature of the model may pose problems for teachers (Pearson & Dole, 1987).

What should teachers do? The key is for the teacher to tune in to students' behavior. The teacher should observe students. What do they understand? Insight into students' thinking enables teachers to provide productive assistance.

Sometimes other students understand a peer's difficulties better than the teacher does. Teachers should be sensitive to this possibility and encourage students' comments, questions, feedback, and suggestions.

How Do I Model Mental Activity?

The oral reporting of your mental activity may not come easily. In addition to the difficulty of this task, some teachers may be embarrassed to model thought processes (Pearson & Dole, 1987). It may feel strange to present your thinking patterns to students, especially if you have never done it before.

What should teachers do? Developing the ability to model requires that teachers tune in to their own mental activity. Teachers can start to pay attention to what they are thinking as they, for instance, pick up a piece of reading material, begin to read, misread a word, and stop reading. After identifying what they do and think, teachers can try to report those activities in a step-by-step, clear manner.

How Do I Deal With the Expectations of Others?

School personnel and parents have assumptions about good teaching and appropriate classroom activity. Teachers who want to experiment with instructional alternatives face a challenge when others in the school community expect that instruction will proceed in a particular way.

What should teachers do? Essential to securing the support of colleagues, parents, and supervisors is the teacher's sound understanding of collaborative instruction and the rationale behind it. Teachers will have more credibility when they can explain their plans intelligently. Low-key, reasoned explanations, coupled with assurances that you are not abandoning all traditional practices and materials, are likely to win people's confidence. It can be especially helpful to involve colleagues in your exploration of collaborative instruction and other new practices. Small groups of teachers working together can promote professional growth, build confidence, and improve teaching practice. (The micropolitical strategies described in Chapter 11 may help you as you work to deal with the expectations of others.)

How Do I Combine This Approach With Basal Materials?

Basals are based on the notion that reading, writing, and mathematics consist of sequential hierarchies of subskills that should be taught through teacher-directed lessons. On the other hand, collaborative instruction is based on the idea that reading, writing, and mathematics are holistic processes that can best be learned through the social interaction of experts and novices.

What should teachers do? The key to success is to rethink the skills identified in the basal in terms of strategies (Duffy & Roehler, 1987). This means that the focus must shift from mechanics ("This is the word *magic*") to metacognition ("How can we figure out what this word is in the story?"). In mathematics, instead of saying, "When you see the words *all together* in a word problem, you know you have to add" (a mechanical orientation), you might say, "Let's see if we can draw a picture of this problem to figure out what to do" (metacognitive orientation). Skills identified in the basal can still be addressed but with an aim toward helping students understand when, why, and how they are useful in the real world. For instance, when the teacher's manual lists "finding details" as a comprehension skill, working on summarizing with students provides the opportunity to talk about story details and their value. Rather than dealing with details in workbook pages unrelated to real reading, the teacher would help students see the role of details within the context of the story. Students can even be taught to use phonics skills strategically. They must learn how, when, and why to apply their knowledge of phonics to unfamiliar text.

What Kinds of Independent Assignments Are Compatible?

Teachers who use this model will want to think about appropriate practice activities for students. Traditional workbook and worksheet exercises do not provide appropriate independent practice.

What should teachers do? Students should be given opportunities to practice independently the strategic approach to literacy. This means that some seatwork time should be devoted to whole reading, writing, and mathematics tasks, as opposed to practicing pieces of those tasks. For example, students could alternate reading paragraphs with a partner, providing a summary of each paragraph. The pairs could report back to the reading group concerning problems, progress, and questions. Predicting could be exercised by having students choose any five stories in the basal and predict the content of those stories using all available cues except the story text. The teacher could ask the students to make a list of all cues they used for each story. Assignments such as these stress the reader's role as active participants. Similarly in math, students could solve a small number of problems with a partner. Rather than merely recording answers, the teacher could tell partners to come up with several alternative solution strategies. They could be responsible for explaining the reasoning behind each alternative.

Is there any role for workbook pages? Teachers must remember the emphasis of collaborative instruction on the social development of strategies within the context of literacy tasks. The problem with most workbook pages is that they have little to do with real literacy and focus on the mechanics of performing subskills. Still, there may be reasons for having students do workbook pages. Teachers who want students to become familiar with the style of future tests may want to assign an occasional workbook page. Similarly, students' ability to complete a workbook page correctly may indicate that they have mastered the mechanics (though not necessarily the metacognitive aspects) of a skill. Teachers might consider the following guidelines when assigning workbook pages:

1. Assign only those pages addressing skills that are directly related to real literacy tasks.

2. Clarify the purpose of doing a given page. Make sure that the skill is related to reading, writing, or mathematics.

3. Omit pages covering already mastered skills.

4. Occasionally have students complete a page with a partner and report back to the group any differences of opinion and how they were resolved.

5. Redesign workbook pages to serve your purposes—you don't have to use them exactly as they appear!

6. Never make workbook pages the only assignment—real reading, writing, and mathematics should always be part of students' independent work.

FOCUS BOX 4–8

Yes, These Look Like Good Ideas, but . . .

Whenever teachers encounter new ideas, they have to try to fit them within their current understandings about children, their knowledge of and beliefs about appropriate instructional strategies, their current knowledge base, and their specific teaching context. Because of this you probably found yourself raising questions about the feasibility of the alternative practices we suggested in this chapter. We suspect at times you found yourself thinking, "Yes, these look like good ideas, but. . . ?" Work with a small group of peers to raise and try to answer your questions about the strategies associated with collaborative instruction. The following questions may help to guide your thinking:

- What is your overall reaction to the collaborative instructional approach presented in this chapter? Does it look like something you might like to try? Why or why not?

- As you think about trying to implement this approach, what concerns do you have?

- If you were to implement this approach, what skills, abilities and/or knowledge would you need to develop? How would you go about doing this?

- What contextual barriers do you see that might make implementation of this approach difficult? How could you work around these contextual barriers? (Note: By **contextual barriers**, we mean circumstances specific to your teaching situation. For example, you may teach or student teach in a school where teachers are required to "cover" every unit in the mathematics text or where students are tested on specific mathematical facts and procedures. You may teach in a team-teaching situation where teachers are expected to cover the same content within the same time frame.)

- What are the implicit curriculum implications of this model? How do they fit with the aims you have identified as important for elementary education?

It is important to raise these kinds of questions and to explore the answers with your peers. Failure to confront these questions probably means you will not make any significant changes in your literacy instruction.

Summary

In this chapter, we defined literacy as the ability to use communication systems knowledgeably. In the elementary school, developing students' intelligent use of reading, writing, and mathematics is one of the teacher's priorities. We introduced you to the broad area of literacy instruction by focusing on the commonalities in these three processes: common goals, common problems of literacy instruction, and guidelines for developing literacy. Remember that this chapter is not meant to replace your language arts, reading, and mathematics methods texts! It would be impossible to tell you everything you need to know about these areas in a single chapter. Instead, we wanted to introduce you to a coherent way of thinking about literacy instruction and encourage you to read widely in these areas.

Further Readings

Calkins, L. M. (1986). *The art of teaching writing*. Portsmouth, NH: Heinemann.

Carter, J. (1983). Characteristics of successful writing instruction: A preliminary report. *The Elementary School Journal*, *84* (1), 40–44.

Collins, A., Brown, J. S., & Newman, S. W. (1989). Cognitive apprenticeship: Teaching the craft of reading, writing and mathematics. In L. B. Resnick (Ed.), *Knowing, learning and instruction: Essays in honor of Robert Glaser* (pp. 453–494). Hillsdale, NJ: Erlbaum.

de Castell, S., Luke, A., & MacLennan, D. (1986). On defining literacy. In de Castell, S., Luke, A., & Egan, K. (Eds.), *Literacy, society, and schooling* (pp. 3–14). New York: Cambridge University Press.

Duffy, G. G., & Roehler, L. R. (1987). Teaching reading skills as strategies. *The Reading Teacher*, *40*, 414–418.

Durkin, D. D. (1984). Is there a match between what elementary teachers do and what basal reader manuals recommend? *The Reading Teacher*, *37*, 734–744.

Goodman, K. S. (1989). Whole–language research: Foundations and development. *The Elementary School Journal*, *90* (2), 207–221.

Goodman, Y. (1978). Kid watching: An alternative to testing. *The National Elementary Principal*, *57*, 41–45.

Hiebert, J. (1984). Children's mathematics learning: The struggle to link form and understanding. *The Elementary School Journal*, *84* (5), 497–513.

Lampert, M. (1986). Knowing, doing, and teaching multiplication. *Cognition and Instruction*, *3* (4), 305–342.

Langer, J. A. (1984). Literacy instruction in American schools: Problems and perspectives. *American Journal of Education*, *93* (1), 107–131.

Palincsar, A. S., & Brown, A. L. (1984). Reciprocal teaching of comprehension–fostering and comprehension–monitoring activities. *Cognition and Instruction*, *1*, 117–175.

Pearson, P. D., & Dole, J. A. (1987). Explicit comprehension instruction: A review of research and a new conceptualization of instruction. *The Elementary School Journal, 88,* 151–165.

Romberg, T. A., & Carpenter, T. P. (1986). Research on teaching and learning mathematics: Two disciplines of scientific inquiry. In M. Wittrock (Ed.), *Third handbook of research on teaching* (pp. 850–873). New York: Macmillan.

Routman, R. (1988). *Transitions.* Portsmouth, NH: Heinemann.

Schoenfeld, A.H. (1991). On mathematics as sense–making: An informal attack on the unfortunate divorce of formal and informal mathematics. In J. F. Voss, D. N. Perkins, & J. W. Segal (Eds.), *Informal Reasoning and Education* (pp. 311–343). Hillsdale, NJ: Lawrence Erlbaum Associates.

CHAPTER 5

Promoting Literacy: Implications of Teacher Effects Research

In Chapter 4, we defined literacy, described common problems in literacy instruction, and offered guidelines for promoting literacy in elementary students. The goals and strategies we suggested were grounded in a definition of *literacy* as the mastery and knowledgeable use of systems for communicating. However, we also noted that some educators draw upon different assumptions about the definition of literacy and about how teachers develop and measure mastery. For example, some researchers define literacy as the ability to score well on standardized tests of achievement that measure the subskills of reading, mathematics, and writing. The research that these researchers have produced has been powerful and influential in the field of education. This body of literature is frequently called *teacher effectiveness* research. It has been used to develop a six-step model of "effective" instruction that is widely taught and used to assess the competence of many teachers, especially beginning teachers. We are discussing this model in a chapter on the development of literacy because most of the research on the model comes from reading or mathematics research. However, note that the model has been suggested as appropriate for instruction in all subject areas so its potential impact upon students is great.

Because of the pervasiveness of this six-step model, we believe it is important for you to understand and use it. However, as you read about the teacher effects model, you may notice that it is not completely consistent with the guidelines for literacy instruction that were discussed in Chapter 4. That is, the six-step model is based upon the assumption that learning is transmitted to students rather than that it is collaboratively constructed by teachers and students. Therefore, within this chapter we also present a critique of the model and share guidelines that will enable you to modify the model so that you can use it to collaboratively construct knowledge with students.

Teacher Effects Research

The **teacher effects research** identified and validated instructional strategies to improve achievement as measured by standardized tests in reading and mathematics. In much of the literature, this research is called "teacher effectiveness research." Following the logic of Brophy and Good (1986), we use the term *teacher effects research* because we believe it more accurately represents this body of literature. Brophy and Good state:

> It is a misnomer to refer to it as "teacher effectiveness" research, because this equates effectiveness with success in producing achievement gain. What constitutes "teacher effectiveness" is a matter of definition, and most definitions include success in socializing students and promoting their affective and personal development in addition to success in fostering their mastery of formal curricula. (1986, p. 328)

Gage (1985) and Cuban (1986) have noted the predominance and persistence of **teacher-centered instructional practices**: "lecturing, large-group instruction, reliance on a textbook and chalkboard, seatwork assignments, recitation, discussion and the use of teacher-made quizzes and tests" (Cuban, 1986, p. 8). Despite repeated efforts of educators, the majority of teachers seem to prefer teacher-centered instruction. Teacher effects research reveals teacher behaviors that define *good* teacher-centered instruction (i.e., active teaching or the six step model mentioned previously). Because teacher-centered instruction is pervasive, it makes sense that researchers have investigated the strategies that will maximize its effectiveness. Note, however, that teacher effects research does not state that other teaching styles are ineffective. Brophy and Good (1986) stress that the researchers studied existing practice and found that active teaching was not the common mode of instruction. If more teachers used active teaching, the characteristics that differentiate more effective and less effective teachers might be more subtle. In other words, the differences might be more related to the **qualitative aspects of instruction** (i.e., things we cannot count and measure) than to the **quantitative aspects of instruction** (i.e., things we can count and measure).

Teacher effects research has centered on finding management and instructional strategies that will help increase students' scores on standardized reading and mathematics achievement tests. Good (1979) noted three major conclusions from the research. First, teachers do make a difference. How teachers organize their classrooms, what they do and say have potential significance in terms of student achievement. Second, the classroom environment is very important. Teachers who provide an organized, task-oriented, yet emotionally warm environment, promote higher achievement among their students. And third, effective elementary teachers use a specific pattern for instruction in reading and mathematics. Although the more commonly used term for this pattern is **direct instruction**, Good and Grouws (1979) use the synonym, *active teaching*, a term we prefer because of its emphasis on the *active* role of the teacher.

Research about creating an appropriate classroom environment will be presented in Chapters 6 (social skills), 8 (student engagement) and 9 (self-discipline). Here we

FOCUS BOX 5–1

What Is Good Teaching? A Self-Assessment

You have spent a considerable amount of time as students in classrooms, developing conclusions about the nature of good teaching. You also have had experience teaching or student teaching in elementary classrooms. In this activity, we want you to focus on only your experiences as a student because what we do as teachers in classrooms may not always be consistent with what we think we should do. Thinking about your experiences as a student can be a useful way to uncover some implicit assumptions you may hold about good teaching, assumptions which may or may not be reflected in your teaching practices.

Directions for individual activity: Think about one of the best teachers you have ever had. List this teacher's teaching behaviors. Be careful to list specific instructional behaviors, not general characteristics. For example, a good teacher may be described as enthusiastic, but that is a general characteristic. Instead, you might note that the teacher demonstrated love and excitement about the subject matter by using varied instructional techniques such as dressing as historical characters and by telling interesting stories about famous people. If you cannot think of a specific behavior, list the general characteristic. List as many behaviors as you can.

Directions for group activity: Work with a group of your peers. Help each other turn general characteristics into specific behaviors by asking questions like, How do you know? Can you think of an example? How was this teacher different from other teachers? After you are confident each person's list is as specific as possible, compare your lists by answering the following questions:

- Do you seem to have a common definition of good teaching?
- Are there some behaviors that all good teachers seem to use? Are there others that are used by some teachers and not others?
- Is there any pattern to the similarities and differences that you noted?

Save your individual and group responses. We will return to these after you complete the sections describing active teaching.

---

will focus on research describing the elements of active teaching. The implications of this literature are strongest in the areas of reading and mathematics for primary grade levels but have been supported to some extent across subjects and grade levels. Let's look first at your entering assumptions about the nature of good teaching. Complete the self-assessment in Focus Box 5–1 before reading any further.

What Is Active Teaching?

Low-achieving students and children from low socioeconomic status (SES) homes typically do not score well on achievement tests. To help low achievers score higher than expected scores on these tests, researchers recommend that teachers use direct instruction or active teaching. Note the language here: The specified goal is higher than *expected* scores because these students typically do not score well. The result of teachers' efforts may not be high scores in an absolute sense; they simply help students make more rapid progress than they might otherwise have made on standardized achievement tests.

Note well: Keep the purpose of this research in mind as you read about active teaching. **Active teaching** increases the amount of time students engage in and experience success on tasks related to the skills tested on achievement tests (i.e., **engaged time**). If researchers had set out to determine the strategies that would be most effective in reaching other educational goals (e.g., higher-level thinking, creative thinking, mathematical problem solving, scientific processes and attitudes), their findings might have been very different.

According to Rosenshine, "The major components [of active teaching] include teaching in small steps with student practice after each step, guiding students during initial practice, and providing all students with a high level of successful practice" (1986, p. 2). Before we examine the steps of active teaching, let's consider the focus and pace of instruction that provide an important framework for the active teaching sequence.

Focus and Pace of Instruction

Teachers who are effective in helping children improve their achievement test scores have a clear focus on academic goals and provide extensive coverage of content in basic skills areas. Classroom teachers determine, to a large extent, what will be taught and how much time will be devoted to various subjects and skills. Differences among teachers in content coverage and in the time allocated to content in basic skill areas contribute to differences in children's achievement. Consider differences found by researchers in the Beginning Teacher Evaluation Study:

> While observing fifth grade teachers, it was noticed that one teacher could find only 68 minutes a day for instruction in reading and language arts, while another teacher was able to find 137 minutes a day. . . . In mathematics the same variability was shown. One second grade teacher allocated 16 minutes a day to instruction in mathematics, another teacher constrained by the same length of the school day somehow found 51 minutes a day. (Berliner, 1984, p. 54)

Obviously, children learn mathematics and reading content and skills when they spend more time practicing in these areas. Teachers who maintain an academic focus help children score higher scores on achievement tests. Other aspects of active teaching indicate how effective teachers maintain a strong academic focus.

As we have just noted, students only have the opportunity to learn the content presented by the teacher. The teacher who presents information at a faster pace covers more content. The more content the teacher covers, the more the students will learn—unless, of course, the teacher moves too rapidly and the students are unable to master the content. The pace of instruction in different achievement groups seems particularly important. Shavelson (1983) reported that high-ability

FOCUS BOX 5–2

Take a Moment to Reflect

The differences in the amount of time devoted to basic skill subjects are interesting. You probably have noticed such differences in teachers you observed or among teachers with whom you teach. Similar differences exist in how teachers use time allotted to a single subject area. For example, given the same amount of time in a standard school day, some teachers devote substantially more time to comprehension activities than do other teachers. Berliner (1984) reports that one fifth-grade teacher spent 5,646 minutes on reading comprehension and another spent only 917 during half of the school year. What do you think might account for the differences observed among the teachers in the content covered and level of focus on academic concepts and skills? What attitudes and beliefs do you have that might influence the amount of time you spend on various subjects? As you try to answer this question consider the following:

- Would you rather read a book or watch television? Why?
- Which of these courses would you prefer to take—"Advanced Mathematics" or "English Literature Classics"? Why?
- Would you rather teach a unit on "Our Families" or one on "Hurricanes"? Why?
- Would you rather teach one large-group lesson or several small-group lessons (which requires planning instructional activities for the remainder of the class while you work with each small group)? Why?
- Is it easier to teach from a textbook or to plan your lessons independently? Which way of planning do you prefer? Why?

Discuss the answers to these questions with your peers, focusing especially on the reasons for your preferences. What does this tell you about choices you might make as a teacher?

groups were paced up to 15 times faster than low-ability groups, suggesting that low achievers have less opportunity to learn than high achievers and that choice of pace influences student achievement.

A Definition of Active Teaching

It is logical that children will learn more when interacting with an adult than when working independently. Effective teachers assume a dominant role in the classroom and actively teach and supervise the instructional activities of children. Active teaching (Good & Grouws, 1979), or explicit teaching (Rosenshine, 1987), is a multiple-step process involving many related teaching behaviors. Most often, active teaching will be done using a large-group instructional format because this increases the amount of time each individual child spends actively attending to the teacher. However, small-group instruction is recommended for children in early grades, especially during reading instruction.

Teachers' Use of Classroom Time

Are teachers who devote more time to reading and math instruction making good use of classroom time? While it may seem self-evident that devoting more time to reading and mathematics is an educational good, we feel the most appropriate answer here is, "It depends." It depends on what a teacher does with the extra time. Berliner's (1984) research pointed out that one teacher was able to devote 137 minutes per day to reading while a colleague devoted only 68 minutes. If teachers lose 69 minutes of instructional time due to inefficient organization of time, materials, and pupils, these data clearly suggest a problem that must be confronted (and research suggests this happens in far too many classrooms). However, if teachers use these 69 minutes to provide daily instruction in the arts, an area frequently underemphasized in elementary classrooms, they may be making a wise instructional decision. In fact, there is some evidence that increasing attention to the arts increases rather than decreases literacy achievement, even if less instructional time is devoted to reading instruction (Simandl, 1979; Williams, 1980). Remember, the teacher effects research tells us that, in general, children in classes where more instructional time is devoted to academic skills and content score better on achievement tests. This finding is probably true because a significant amount of instructional time is wasted in many classrooms. However, this finding does not mean that it is always better to increase the amount of time devoted to basic skill instruction. Whether this is a wise decision depends on an assessment of how available classroom time is used.

By following the **steps in active teaching**, teachers (1) *help students see a purpose for each lesson* by reviewing and establishing the connection to previous and future learning; (2) *actively present skills and concepts in small easy steps*, using careful organization, a structure that calls attention to important points and frequent review of important points; (3) *check student understanding* and assure student engagement through appropriate use of questions and group practice exercises; (4) *provide regular and immediate feedback* about the accuracy of student responses; (5) *monitor independent practice* by circulating as students work to assess lesson difficulty and to ensure students have a high success rate; and (6) *review important learnings* periodically. Notice that we have stated that the teacher must provide *active*, teacher-centered instruction. We stress this because teacher-centered instruction is not necessarily active. In fact, much of the teacher-centered activity in elementary classrooms does not really qualify as instruction. Consider the following example.

Ms. Gunther: Okay, class, today we are going to learn about nouns and verbs. Who knows what a noun is? Gary?

Gary: It's like a person.

Ms. Gunther: Yes, that's right. Are there any other kinds of nouns? [Silence from the class.] Well, remember you've learned that a noun names a person, place, or thing, right? Okay. Now who knows what a verb is? [Three children raise their hands.] Tonya?

Tonya: It, well, um, a verb tells about doing something like running or cooking.

Ms. Gunther: Right. Now today we are doing a paper on nouns and verbs. Kevin, please pass out the papers. Now look at the first sentence: "Jennifer ran to the store." Who can tell me the noun in the sentence? Michael?

Michael: Jennifer.

Ms. Gunther: Right. Now what you do is draw a circle around the noun, so you would draw a circle around "Jennifer." Does anyone else see a noun in the sentence? [Silence] Look in the sentence and see if you see a person, place, or thing. [Silence] Think, people. Look at the end of the sentence. Stephanie?

Stephanie: Store?

Ms. Gunther: Yes, of course. So you draw a circle around "store," too. Remember to look at the beginning and the end of the sentence when you are looking for nouns. Okay, now who knows the verb? [Six hands are raised.] Stephanie?

Stephanie: Ran?

Ms. Gunther: Right, ran—so you would draw a line under the word "ran." Notice that the verb follows the first noun in the sentence. Now what you do is draw a circle around all the nouns and draw a line under all the verbs for all the sentences on this page. Any questions? Okay, get started. [As the children begin working, Ms. Gunther calls one reading group to come and work with her.]

In the preceding example, it looks like the teacher is presenting information to the students and providing practice with a worksheet. However, in truth, this teacher is not actively teaching. She presents the children with just enough information to complete a worksheet (a practice called **mentioning behavior** that we discussed in Chapter 4 (Durkin, 1978–79), but she does not teach the concepts using presentation or demonstration. The teacher does not assess student understanding before assigning independent work. In fact, the teacher has *no* concrete indication that students have mastered the skills involved. Few students raise their hands. At one point, the teacher has to prod and give clues to encourage a response. During the whole lesson, there are only five responses from students, and two of those are from one student. The students' successful completion of a worksheet might provide evidence of their understanding. However, in this case, it seems possible that the students could complete the work without understanding the concepts. Recall that the teacher tells students to look at the beginning and end of the sentences to find the nouns. The teacher also tells the students that the verb follows the first noun. That is, the teacher directly teaches the students a **response pattern** that the students can use to find the nouns and verb. Using this strategy to complete the sheet does not mean that students can recognize nouns and verbs. Finally, the teacher does not circulate as students begin working, so she is unable to identify misunderstandings or to give feedback to those having difficulty.

Clarifying the Steps in Active Teaching

Now that we have discussed the differences between teacher-centered instruction and *active* teacher-centered instruction, let's look specifically at active teaching. Researchers have summarized the teacher effects research into a series of six steps that teachers can follow. The following synthesis is based upon work by Brophy and Good (1986); Murphy, Weil, and McGreal (1987); Rosenshine (1987); and Webb, Ashton, and Andrews (1983).

STEP 1: HELP STUDENTS SEE THE PURPOSE OF THE LESSON.   In this step the teacher establishes a framework for student understanding by relating the current lesson to previous learning. Researchers recommend the following strategies to help students understand why the skills and concepts to be presented are important and how they relate to previous and future learning:

- Review and check previous work.
- State the purpose and/or objectives of the lesson.
- Help students recall related knowledge or experiences.
- Help students recognize relation of lesson to future learning and goals.

Although this step is of vital importance, teachers all too often skip it. For example, Durkin (1981) has noted that teachers seldom connect reading skill lessons to one another or to "real" reading. Similarly, researchers have found that many children do not understand the purpose behind independent practice exercises. Over the past several years, we have encouraged teachers to ask children why they believed they had to do particular assignments. The teachers report that most children respond, "Because it is our work," or "So I can go outside." When children do not understand the reasons behind assignments, the result is that they spend many hours practicing skills that have no meaning to them and "master" skills which they cannot apply.

STEP 2: ACTIVELY PRESENT SKILLS AND CONCEPTS IN SMALL EASY STEPS.   The teacher must structure (organize) information so that students can learn it with a minimum of confusion. The teacher's goal is to present the information through lecture and demonstration using strategies which facilitate the students' memory and help them relate pieces of information to each other and to some integrated whole. The following strategies provide a means for structuring information.

- Begin instruction with overviews and advance organizers. An **overview** presents a preview of the big picture. For example, look at the section in this chapter entitled "A Definition of Active Teaching." Here we provide a concise summary of the elements of active teaching, highlighting the important points. **Advance organizers** indicate how the lecture will be organized (i.e., what will come first, second, third), and foreshadow the important points to come. For example, during our discussion of active teaching, we explained that we would discuss general characteristics that support active teaching and then describe the steps involved in active teaching.

- Provide an outline, when appropriate. An outline, providing a summary of the total picture and highlighting important points, is another way to overview information and provide advance organizers.

- Call attention to important points and transitions by reviewing periodically and reminding students what the next step will be. For example, in a lecture, we might say, "We have just learned that teachers should begin instruction by helping students see the purpose of the lesson using strategies such as reviewing previous learning and connecting current learning to past learning. Now we will describe how a teacher should structure lectures and presentations."

- Make important points clear by providing many vivid examples and by using models that show how the parts are connected and sequenced. For example, in this chapter, we clarified the difference between teacher-centered instruction and active teaching by describing a scene from a classroom and then analyzing it in terms of the characteristics of active teaching.

- Alter the pace of instruction based on the content of the lesson and the students being taught. Difficult content must be structured into smaller steps and presented at a slower pace than easy content. Whatever the content, high achievers can handle a faster instructional pace than low achievers.

- Repeat important points often and review them at the end of the lecture or demonstration.

Notice that each of these strategies helps students identify and remember important information. In addition to using these strategies, the teacher should present lessons using an interesting, enthusiastic style. The purpose of active teaching is to increase the amount of time students spend *attending to* instruction (engaged time). Bored students do not pay attention. Teacher enthusiasm is contagious and very important. One of the authors of this book, Dorene Ross, still remembers reading Strunk and White's (1959) *Elements of Style* with interest because her English teacher introduced it with such flair and excitement. Rereading it years later, Dorene marvelled at the skill of that teacher who could spark interest in the book. (It deals, after all, with grammar!) While it is not always possible to make boring material seem interesting, it is inevitable that a boring presentation will stifle even the most diligent student. It is difficult, but remember, even when you are tired or depressed, you must be on as a teacher.

STEP 3: CHECK STUDENT UNDERSTANDING.   Practice problems and/or questions are necessary to encourage student participation and to check student understanding. It is important to note that this is not independent "seatwork," but a group task. Teachers might assign one or two practice problems that each student must complete so they can assess student comprehension. When the class discusses the practice problems, the teachers should try to maximize the participation of students and check the understanding of low achievers. More commonly, teachers would lead a question/answer session in order to check student understanding. (This process is called **guided practice**.)

Teacher enthusiasm stimulates student interest and on-task behavior.

When they answer teachers' questions, the students have an opportunity to demonstrate skill and concept attainment, summarize what they have learned, provide examples, and apply skills and concepts to new situations. Brophy and Good (1986) provide an excellent review of the research on questioning strategies. The following points are important. Many of them also are applicable during class discussion of practice problems.

- When teaching skills and simple concepts, teachers should ask many **low-level cognitive questions** (i.e., those that focus on recall and comprehension). Questions should have a single, correct response, and most (80 percent) should be answered correctly by students.

- When teaching complex concepts, teachers should ask **high-level cognitive questions** (i.e., those that focus on application, evaluation, or synthesis). These questions will have no single correct answer, and the number of correct responses may be low. Note that even lessons that stress complex concepts will include more low- than high-level cognitive questions. (i.e., only 25 percent of the questions will be high-level cognitive questions).

- Teachers should state questions clearly and ask only one question at a time. Less effective teachers tend to string a series of questions together before calling on a student to respond. Because the initial question is not well phrased, the teacher finds it necessary to rephrase it several times before a student can answer. A teacher should not need to restate a question in order for students to respond. The appropriate pattern is "question-response, question-response."

- Teachers should ask the question, wait 3 seconds, and then select a respondent (Rowe, 1974a; 1974b). Less effective teachers tend to allow very little **wait time** (i.e., the time between asking a question and selecting a student respondent). Although 3 seconds may not seem like a long time, it can seem very long in a quiet classroom. If teachers force themselves to wait, they will find that more students are ready to respond. A brief *wait time* limits the opportunity for low achievers to participate and thus limits their achievement. Rowe (1974a) also suggests waiting 3 seconds *after* a student responds to improve interaction among students.

- Teachers should make sure each student has the opportunity to participate, especially in small groups and in early grades. Less effective teachers tend not to call on low achievers. One reason for this may be that teachers do not wish to embarrass these students; however, limiting student opportunity to respond limits achievement. In most situations, teachers need to develop a system to limit students' calling out answers so that eager students do not limit the involvement of others. However, in classes where students are hesitant to respond (which may be the case if the majority of students are low achievers), the teacher may need to allow calling out answers to stimulate student response. When it is impossible to call on every student, teachers should try to call on students representing various achievement levels. Over time the teacher should use a system to assure that all students have equal opportunity to participate.

Appropriate use of practice problems and questions enables a teacher to assess student learning, reteach if necessary, and decide when students are ready for independent practice. In addition the recitation period provides practice for students, and helps to focus their attention on critical features of the material (Gall, 1984). The next step tells us how teachers should respond to student responses.

STEP 4: PROVIDE REGULAR AND IMMEDIATE FEEDBACK.   **Feedback** from teachers (i.e., teacher response to student responses) helps students to know whether they are understanding new skills and concepts. Before the teacher can give feedback, however, the student must respond to the teachers' questions. Many students have learned that teachers will "move on to someone else" if they just sit quietly and say nothing. For these students, it is easier to say nothing than to risk failure by responding, a phenomenon called **learned helplessness**. Teachers do not help students by "moving on." You may feel it is cruel to put a student "on the spot," but it is more cruel to allow a child to progress through school without learning important skills and concepts. Teachers can encourage a response by increasing the amount of wait time and by requiring a response, even if the response is, "I don't know."

What Is "Learned Helplessness?"

Perhaps you have heard the saying, "It is better to keep your mouth closed and have people think you a fool, than to open your mouth and remove all doubt." This is the essence of **learned helplessness**. Covington (1984) notes that humans have a strong need to succeed and to be perceived as successful. Therefore, children and adults try to avoid situations in which others will perceive them as lacking in ability (and worth). However, some children experience failure from their first days of school. This is particularly true for impoverished children. Based upon a history of repeated school failure, these children approach new tasks believing they will fail. Because they expect to fail, they are unlikely to exert much effort. However, not trying is also a protective action. Covington (1984) notes that if children don't try, the reason for the ultimate failure is not certain. Perhaps they failed because they didn't try. Thus, not trying can protect the self-esteem of children, enabling them and others to believe they could have succeeded if only they had tried.

These children are described as having an **external locus of control**. That is, they believe that their success is determined by luck or difficulty of a task, factors which they cannot control. In contrast, students with an **internal locus of control** believe that effort and ability are the major determinants of their success (Hunter & Barker, 1987). When students believe that their behavior has no impact on their success or failure, their performance in school steadily declines even when they are presented with tasks they could master (Hoy, 1986; Hunter & Barker, 1987). Teachers who fail to break this cycle, fail these children. Webb and Sherman explain,

> As poor youngsters come to view themselves as helpless in academic settings, as they begin to see achievement to be a result of luck rather than of ability and effort, they are made unknowing conspirators in their own bondage. Insofar as schooling increases the disadvantages faced by impoverished children, it fails in its task to equalize opportunity. (1989, p. 483)

It is the responsibility of teachers to help children break out of the cycle of learned helplessness. A number of strategies can prove helpful. In this chapter, we make suggestions for encouraging students' responses and for responding to their responses. In Chapters 7, 8, and 9, you will find additional strategies designed to help students develop and accept responsibility for their own learning. To counter learned helplessness, Covington also recommends the use of cooperative learning activities (see Chapter 6) and a focus on "learning to learn" rather than on the accumulation of facts (see Chapters 7 and 8).

When many students give incorrect responses, reteaching is necessary. Webb et al. (1983) recommend using different examples when reteaching. Explaining the skills in a new way may help students master them. After reteaching, the teacher should begin asking questions again to assess student understanding.

Teacher effects research provides guidelines for responding to students. In responding, teachers should communicate to the students that they expect them to try hard and that they are accountable for the quality of their work (Hunter &

Barker, 1987; Webb et al., 1983). Brophy and Good (1986) provide an excellent summary of the important guidelines about feedback.

- Affirm correct responses; however, praise is generally not necessary. If the teacher does praise a student, the praise should be specific, focused on the content of the answer, and contingent upon the quality of the response. Praise is most appropriate for low achieving, dependent, and/or anxious students. Generally, the teacher will make an overt statement indicating that a response is correct. However, during fast paced drill, the teacher may simply ask another question if the students understand that no response means the answer was correct. For more information about the appropriate use of praise, see Focus Box 5–5.

FOCUS BOX 5–5

To Praise or Not to Praise?

At one time, teachers were advised to praise their students frequently. In fact, people believed "the more praise, the better." However, studies of the effects of praise suggest that this was not good advice. There clearly are times when praise is important, but there are other times when praise can have negative effects on children. Consideration of *how* to praise is as important as consideration of when to praise. The following recommendations will be useful as you make decisions about when and how to praise.

When to Praise

There are two situations in which teachers might want to avoid or limit their use of praise because of potentially negative effects upon children. First, avoid praising children for participating in tasks which are intrinsically motivating. Researchers have found that children who are rewarded for participating in tasks which initially were attractive, subsequently have less interest in those tasks (Deci, 1971, 1972; Morgan, 1984). That is, praise can decrease intrinsic motivation. Second, limit your use of praise if your goal is the development of social autonomy in children. Rowe (1974b) found that children in classrooms where teachers used relatively little praise demonstrated higher levels of task persistence, self-confidence and social problem-solving ability than did students in classrooms where teachers used praise frequently. Brophy (1981a) emphasizes both these points:

> [Praise] is a type of extrinsic reward and as such may focus students' attention on pleasing the teacher rather than on the intrinsic rewards or satisfactions that can be derived from their work. Even in the case of conduct, too much external guidance, even through praise, can make students overly dependent on teachers or other authority figures when they should be developing independent judgement and inner controls. (p. 272)

Brophy (1981a) indicates the following as appropriate occasions for praising children:

- Praise a child when the accomplishment is significant or when the child may not recognize fully the significance of the accomplishment. This means that teachers must avoid praising too often or too enthusiastically. Children generally know when their accomplishments or those of their peers merit praise. Teachers who praise indiscriminately undermine the value of praise.

FOCUS BOX 5–5, *continued*

- Use praise with children who respond well when praised. Young children, low-ability children, low-SES children, and children with a high need for social approval all respond well to praise (Cannella, 1984). It is important to remember, however, that children can become overly dependent on praise. Brophy (1981a) cautions that children should be encouraged to evaluate themselves.

Brophy (1981a) also makes recommendations about how teachers should praise children. The research indicates that **effective praise** should:

- give children specific information about the nature of their accomplishment so that they know what behaviors to repeat.
- link successful performance to effort and ability rather than to external factors (e.g., luck or ease of task) which the child cannot control.
- stress the value of the accomplishment for the child rather than pleasing the teacher.
- be given in response to genuine accomplishment.
- be offered privately and individually.
- be genuine (e.g., variety of statements used, natural language used, not overly emotional). This suggests teachers should avoid stereotypical praise statements such as "I like the way Katya is listening."

- Negate an incorrect response and probe to help the student develop a correct response. Students need to know when answers are incorrect, but the feedback should not be critical. For example, the teacher might say, "No, jump is not a noun." Then, the teacher should give clues, provide additional information, or rephrase the question to help guide the student toward a correct answer. The teacher might say, "Remember we said that a noun named a person, place, or thing. Look back at the sentence to find a person, place, or thing." Cazden (1986, p. 441) notes that the teacher's purpose here is to reformulate the questions so that the task becomes progressively less complex. After providing an opportunity for the student to correct an incorrect response, the teacher may find it necessary to provide the correct answer or move to another student. The difference between an effective and an ineffective teacher is that the effective teacher clearly communicates when responses are wrong and tries to help the student develop a correct response before moving to another student. If necessary, the teacher should reteach the skill or concept explaining how to reach the correct answer.
- If the student answers part of the question correctly, affirm the correct part and then probe, as suggested previously, to help the student correct the incorrect response.

STEP 5: MONITOR INDEPENDENT PRACTICE.   Independent practice assignments provide students with the opportunity to practice and apply skills and concepts learned during presentation and guided practice. When teachers are certain that students have mastered the skills presented in steps 1 to 4, they should present an independent practice assignment. Remember the vignette in which Ms. Gunther taught a lesson on nouns and verbs. In her lesson she moved very quickly through steps 1 to 4, and the students spent most of their time in independent practice. Effective teachers allocate time differently, with *at least 50 percent of the instructional time devoted to the development of skills and concepts using the strategies suggested in steps 1 to 4.* During guided practice, teachers determine whether students adequately understand skills and concepts, and then they assign independent practice to students, using seatwork and homework assignments.

In elementary grades, most independent practice exercises will be seatwork assignments. Selection of appropriate seatwork assignments is difficult and deserves careful attention. Appropriate assignments should be interesting and challenging, yet simple enough so that the students' success rate is almost 100 percent. Boring, repetitive assignments discourage student engagement and defeat the purpose of independent practice. Similarly, students gain little when they practice skills incorrectly. A pervasive problem in elementary teaching is that teachers assign practice exercises from workbooks and texts without adequately assessing their value or their difficulty.

As the students begin working, the teacher should circulate to monitor on-task behavior and success rate. If the lesson was taught well, and the practice exercise is interesting and appropriate, students should sustain involvement in the activity and their success rate should be almost 100 percent. Although teachers will provide individual corrective feedback at this time, the majority of their time should not be spent in reteaching. If many students require extended individual assistance, a repeat of whole-group instruction is necessary.

A second type of independent practice is homework that provides the opportunity for students to practice skills and concepts over an extended time period (**distributed practice**). Distributed practice enhances achievement; however, again the quality and difficulty of the practice exercise is important. Homework assignments, like seatwork assignments, should be short, varied, interesting, clearly related to skills and concepts developed in class, and simple enough that the students' success rate is almost 100 percent.

To ensure student accountability and to communicate that assignments are important, teachers should provide feedback to the students about the quality and correctness of all assignments. A good rule of thumb is that if teachers do not value the assignment enough to read it and give feedback (or guide the students through a self-correction session), then they should not waste the students' time by requiring them to complete it. It should be noted, however, that self-correction is a strategy that can easily be overused to the detriment of student achievement. Remember that good homework and seatwork assignments require a success rate of nearly 100 percent. If this is not the case, the assignments were poorly designed. Self-correction activities require that students spend class time reviewing material already mastered rather than learning new material. While some review is necessary, overuse of group self-correction provides unnecessary review and decreases student learning.

FOCUS BOX 5–6

Take a Moment to Reflect

Have you ever been required to complete work that you considered to be "busy work" or that was never returned to you? Think about that assignment and answer the following questions. Discuss your answers with your peers.

- What determines whether something is "busy work" or a valuable assignment?
- Why do teachers assign "busy work"?
- Is there a valid reason for using it in university classrooms? In elementary classrooms? If you answered these last two questions differently, explain the reasons behind your answers.
- Given what you know about elementary classrooms, is busy work inevitable? If so, how much is acceptable and what is the nature of acceptable busy work? If not, what are some productive alternatives to "busy work"?

STEP 6: REVIEW IMPORTANT LEARNINGS.   Regular review helps students retain knowledge and skills. Important learnings should be reviewed at the end of each week and month. Rosenshine (1987) notes that review is enhanced by periodic testing that encourages more conscientious efforts at review.

Summary of Active Teaching

Before you read our review of active teaching, you may want to assess your comprehension of the six steps of active teaching and compare the teacher effects model to your entering definition of good teaching.

The active teaching model involves the following six steps:

1. Help students see the purpose of the lesson.
   a. Review and check previous work (if appropriate).
   b. State the purpose of the lesson and its relationship to previous and future learning.
   c. Help students recall related information.
   d. Help students recognize relation of lesson to students' lives and goals.
2. Actively present skills and concepts.
   a. Organize information into series of small easy steps.
   b. Begin with an overview or an advance organizer.
   c. Provide an outline (if appropriate).
   d. Direct student attention to important points by reviewing or by using vivid examples or models.
   e. Repeat important points often.
   f. Present information enthusiastically.

3. Check student understanding.
   a. Assign and check practice problems (if appropriate).
   b. Ask questions to check student understanding.
      • Ask simple, low-level cognitive questions (80 percent should be answered correctly).
      • Ask high-level cognitive questions (if appropriate).
      • State questions clearly and one at a time.
      • Wait at least 3 seconds before calling on a student to respond.
      • Provide an opportunity for each student to respond.
      • Limit calling out by the students.
4. Provide regular and immediate feedback.
   a. Require response from students.
   b. Affirm correct answers.
   c. If praise is used, it should be specific, focused on academic content, and contingent.
   d. Negate incorrect responses and help students develop correct responses.
   e. Reteach if necessary.
5. Monitor independent practice.
   a. Devote no more than 50 percent of the instructional time to independent practice.
   b. Assign an appropriate task that is interesting and challenging (the success rate should be 100 percent).
   c. Circulate as students begin working.
6. Review important learnings. (Unless a lesson happens to be a weekly or monthly review, you will not observe this).

These six steps are accepted by many educators as defining the characteristics of effective teaching. Several states use these behaviors as criteria to assess the competence of beginning teachers. In Florida, for example, beginning teachers must demonstrate satisfactory performance on observation instruments based on teacher effects research during their first year of teaching. Other states use the Hunter System to train and evaluate teachers. The behavioral indicators included in both of these models are drawn from teacher effects research.

The wide acceptance of the active teaching model means it is very important for you to understand it and learn the behaviors involved. While some educators believe that following these steps assures effective teaching, we believe that appropriate application of active teaching requires more.

Constructivist Views of Active Teaching

To clarify the reasons why active teaching requires more than the six-step process, we describe the concerns some educators have about the model. Then we

FOCUS BOX 5–7

What Is Good Teaching Reconsidered

First, check your understanding of the teacher effects research. Complete the following self-assessment and then compare your answers to those of your peers. If you and your peers don't agree, look in the chapter to find supportive evidence for your answers.

Teacher Effects Research Self-Assessment*

Directions: Answer *true* (T) or *false* (F) to each question based on your understanding about the findings from the teacher effects research.

_____ 1. Teacher effects research was designed to determine how teachers can produce higher than expected gains in student achievement on standardized tests of academic achievement.

_____ 2. The only significant factor in research on student achievement is the socioeconomic level of the student body attending the school.

_____ 3. Students learn a subject to the extent that they spend time actively engaged in the study of that subject.

_____ 4. It is always best to increase the amount of time devoted to academics.

_____ 5. When a student successfully completes a worksheet, the teacher has concrete evidence that the student has mastered the relevant skills.

_____ 6. Individualized instruction is preferable to teacher-directed instruction when teaching basic skills.

_____ 7. Time spent in *independent* small groups is positively related to increased achievement in basic skills.

_____ 8. The most important, and most neglected, step in active teaching is the establishment of purpose.

_____ 9. Students are more on task when working with the teacher than when working alone.

_____ 10. In skill learning, independent practice is very important, so the teacher should limit instructional time to 30 percent of the class period.

_____ 11. For higher scores on standardized achievement tests in basic skills, teacher-directed learning is better than methods stressing student discovery.

_____ 12. Teachers should avoid using low-level cognitive questions.

_____ 13. To ensure a rapid instructional pace for lessons, a teacher should wait no longer than 2 seconds for a student to respond to a question.

_____ 14. Teacher praise is related to higher academic achievement.

_____ 15. All lessons should be taught within a framework that helps students understand the connection between current learning and previous learning.

_____ 16. Teachers should only call on student volunteers during recitation sessions, in order to avoid embarrassing low achievers.

*This self-assessment is an adaptation of a self-assessment developed by Professor Paul George at the University of Florida. We appreciate his willingness to allow us to adapt his work.

_____ 17. In order to build the self-esteem of students, it is important that teachers never tell students that their answers are wrong.

_____ 18. A major problem in elementary teaching is that teachers assign practice exercises from textbooks without assessing their value.

_____ 19. Active teaching describes characteristics of *good* teacher-centered instruction.

_____ 20. The practices derived from the teacher effects research define effective teaching.

Now, look back at the list of behaviors generated in the "What is Good Teaching?" activity (Focus Box 5–1). This list helps you identify your implicit assumptions about good teaching. Compare your original list of behaviors to the teaching behaviors recommended in the teacher effects research. Again, this will be most productive if you discuss your ideas with a group of your peers.

In making your comparisons, consider the following questions:

- What recommendations from the literature contradict your initial assumptions about effective teaching?

- Do you see any pattern to the differences you noted? Look for patterns within the answers of one individual and across the answers of all the members of your group.

- Are there any general assumptions about teaching and learning that might explain the differences you noted? Think back to your foundations courses and the assumptions that support a behavioral view of learning (based on research by Skinner) and a constructivist (or interactionist) view of learning (based on research by Piaget).

- Are you comfortable with the recommendations presented here? Why or why not?

Answer key:

1. T	6. F	11. T	16. F
2. F	7. F	12. F	17. F
3. T	8. T	13. F	18. T
4. F	9. T	14. F	19. T
5. F	10. F	15. T	20. F

suggest additional guidelines which we believe are necessary for appropriate application.

Psychologists hold different beliefs about how learning occurs. The concerns of many educators about active teaching are rooted in these different views. Behavioral psychologists believe that learning is transmitted by teachers to learners (**transmission model** of learning). They argue that the teacher's role is to break skills, concepts, and strategies down into their component subskills, develop a hierarchy of subskills, design an appropriate instructional sequence, and present information in small, easy steps with much redundancy and feedback about correctness. In contrast, many cognitive psychologists believe that learning is constructed by learners (**constructivist model** of learning). They argue that children learn by analyzing available data in order to detect patterns, forming and testing hypotheses, and integrating new knowledge with previous understandings. Many educators who hold a constructivist view of learning believe that the **traditional active teaching model** (i.e., the six-step model we described), which is a transmission model, is of limited use. Others believe active teaching does provide a useful model, but suggest additional guidelines which must be followed to facilitate student construction of knowledge. Let us use the work of some reading researchers to make this point clearer.

One Constructivist Response to Active Teaching[1]

Under active instruction, both high- and low-level cognitive skills are presented in small steps with much redundancy (Soar & Soar, 1983). Some reading researchers argue that active teaching is inappropriate for teaching reading because reading does not involve the sequential mastery of a hierarchy of skills. Instead, they believe reading is a highly complex, high-level cognitive task that must be presented as an integrated whole rather than simplified into steps and taught formally.

Researchers who have studied the learning of children who learn to read without instruction conclude that children construct their knowledge of reading by using available data to detect patterns and to generate and confirm hypotheses. They believe that sequentially organized, structured instruction in reading skills oversimplifies the process and may impede the children's mastery of reading in the broader sense (Douglass, 1978; Goodman, K. S., 1978; Hoskisson, 1979; Smith, 1977). Instead, these researchers recommend providing students with opportunities to interact with mature readers while engaged in small-group and independent reading and writing activities. In such indirect learning situations, children can construct and test generalizations.

Similarly, some mathematics educators argue that research on traditional active teaching is interesting but irrelevant because it is based on an assumption that the goal of mathematics is to increase children's test scores. While rote learning through presentation, demonstration, drill, and practice may improve test scores, these educators argue that such methods are unlikely to help children understand mathematical concepts and processes. This concern is supported by active teaching researchers who stress that the model is most appropriate for rote lessons, such as the memorization of facts. "If pupils were solving complex problems or engaged in creative production, a much lower degree of control would be appropriate" (Soar & Soar, 1983, p. 73). Math educators, such as Romberg and Carpenter (1986) argue that rote learning is too limited a goal for mathematics. They note that when the goal of instruction is understanding, active teaching research provides little assistance. As Romberg and Carpenter state:

[1]   An earlier version of these ideas appeared in Ross & Kyle (1987).

Most relevant studies have focused on improving traditional mathematics teaching by making it more efficient or effective. Because such studies are based on conceptions of mathematics and learning different [from those which stress the construction of knowledge], even their positive findings may be irrelevant or possibly detrimental. (1986, p. 860)

These educators argue that improvement on achievement tests is not a valid criterion for assessing instruction because tests tell us only what students can *do* and not what they *understand*. Because these educators are pursuing distinctly different goals than the researchers who advocate active teaching, they conclude that the traditional active teaching (TAT) model is of limited use.

The perspective offered by these researchers is supported by the work of cognitive psychologists who hold that children construct meaning from their experiences in the environment (Elkind, 1979; Piaget, 1969; Siegel, 1984; Vygotsky, 1978) and of brain researchers who note that the human brain constructs thoughts, concepts, and perceptions and must be challenged with complex tasks (Bussis, 1982; Levy, 1983; Tipps, 1981). Essentially, these researchers state that learning is discovered through interaction with the environment. This learning can be facilitated by a teacher who presents opportunities for discovery, but many aspects of complex tasks (e.g., learning to read or to think mathematically, or learning science or social studies concepts) cannot be structured sequentially and taught through methods, such as active teaching. From their perspective active teaching has little or no merit.

An Alternative View

While some constructivist educators argue that active teaching has little merit, others suggest that active teaching principles are important in teaching high-level cognitive skills. These educators are concerned that open-ended, discovery models may not meet the needs of low achievers. Doyle (1983) notes that high-achieving students seem to do well under indirect instruction that emphasizes the role of self-discovery and the invention of generalizations about reading. However, low-achieving students do less well and may invent inaccurate and dysfunctional generalizations.

For this reason, several researchers have investigated the role of active teaching in teaching the high-level processes that high-achieving readers use. For example, researchers have investigated ways to teach students how to draw inferences, to detect faulty arguments in reading passages, and to comprehend the structure of story grammar (Gersten & Carnine, 1986; Hansen & Pearson, 1983); how to monitor comprehension, to identify and use "fix-up" strategies, and to connect ideas in a passage with background knowledge (Paris, Oka, & DeBritto, 1983; Paris, Cross, & Lipson, 1984); how to answer comprehension questions (Raphael, 1982); and how to summarize, generate questions, clarify the meaning of reading passages, and make predictions during the reading process (Palincsar & Brown, 1984).

Research on teaching comprehension strategies through active teaching suggests that teachers must modify the traditional model in order to help students *construct* knowledge. It is important to note that the same general steps of the TAT model apply. However, from a constructivist perspective, the appropriate application of active teaching requires additional guidelines which change both the instructional emphasis and the basic instructional process. The addition of these guidelines provides a **constructivist interpretation of active teaching**.

Guidelines for a Constructivist Interpretation of Active Teaching

GUIDELINE 1: INSTRUCTIONAL EMPHASIS MUST BE PLACED ON THE DEVELOPMENT OF CONCEPTS, STRATEGIES, AND STUDENT THINKING.   We continue the example of reading instruction to make this clear. In reading, this guideline means that instruction must focus on the development of concepts (e.g., vocabulary concepts and concepts about print) and strategies for approaching text as opposed to the development of skills. Strategies are different from skills. Strategies are "thoughtful plans or operations readers use while involved in the reading process" (Routman, 1988, p. 40). Strategies require control and self-direction by the reader. Skills are the "learned procedures that the student has been repeatedly drilled on" (Routman, 1988, p. 40). Routman explained that:

> Strategies imply high-level thinking, integration, and self-direction; skills imply low-level thinking, isolation, and accurate rapid responses based on previous training. (1988, p. 40)

Research on the TAT model demonstrates that the method is effective in facilitating skill learning. However, skill learning is an inappropriate goal for reading instruction. To teach strategies, teachers must focus lessons on student thinking about when and why to use particular strategies. This means that in addition to teaching students how to draw inferences, detect faulty arguments in reading passages, assess their comprehension, and connect ideas in a reading passage with background knowledge, teachers also must help students understand when and why to do these things (McNeil, 1984; Paris et al., 1984).

From our perspective, this guideline about instructional emphasis is essential to the appropriate use of active teaching. Unfortunately, this guideline is not discussed in most of the literature on active teaching which stresses the multiple-step approach for structuring instruction. That is, most research details a *method* of teaching, but it does *not* specify the *content* of instruction. We are suggesting that appropriate application is dependent on selection of appropriate content and that this content *must* focus on development of concepts, strategies, and student thinking. From a constructivist perspective, TAT is a hollow procedure unlikely to result in lasting educational gain for students. Consider the following example:

> Ms. Kaplan is teaching a group of 28 fifth graders. The class has been studying fractions and are now beginning a lesson on adding and subtracting mixed fractions (i.e., dissimilar denominators).

Ms. Kaplan: For math today all you'll need is a pencil and a piece of paper. If you need pencil or paper, raise your hand. Nathan will pass out pencils, and Teena will pass out paper.

Ms. Kaplan begins the lesson by reminding the children that they have been studying fractions and by reviewing key terms (*numerator, denominator, equivalent fraction*). The children respond with memorized definitions of the terms.

Ms. Kaplan: I graded your papers and everyone is doing very well adding and subtracting fractions. Now we will learn something that is just a little bit harder.

Ms. Kaplan writes on the board: 1/4 + 1/8 = _____

Ms. Kaplan: Can we add these two fractions? George.

George: No, the bottom numbers aren't the same.

Ms. Kaplan: Does everyone agree? Michelle.

Michelle: Well, we can add them but we have to change them first.

Ms. Kaplan: Tell us what you mean; change them.

Michelle: Well they both have to be the same on the bottom. The, ah, denominator has to be the same to add them.

Ms. Kaplan: Excellent. You remembered that from fourth grade! Did everyone catch that? The denominators have to be the same to add them. So what would I do? Would I change them both to fourths? Sonya.

Sonya: Yeah, I guess.

Ms. Kaplan: Now look at that. Can you multiply 8 by something to get 4?

Sonya: No, you can't. Oh that's right you have to change to the big number.

Ms. Kaplan: So I know I have to change to eighths. Could I just change 1/4 to 3/8? Would that do it? Come on. I want to see everybody's hand. You all know this. Show me you are thinking. Wow! Look how many are ready to answer! Evangaline.

Evangaline: You have to make sure it's equal to 1/4, so you have to multiply 4 by 2 to get 8, so it would have to be 2/8.

Ms. Kaplan: Right. I'd say, "Can I multiply 8 by something to get 4?" [Class choruses, "No!"] Can I multiply 4 by something to get 8? Can somebody work this on the board to show us how you change 1/4 to 2/8? Thomas.

Thomas writes on the board: 1/4 x 2/2 = 2/8. After urging from Ms. Kaplan, he explains:

Thomas: You have to multiply the top number and the bottom number by the same number to get them equal and it has to be two because 4 times *2* is 8.

Ms. Kaplan checks the students' understanding of the procedures by having them work sample problems on individual slates she has made for this purpose. She puts problems on the board. The children work the problem on their slates and Ms. Kaplan checks each child's work visually, easily spotting those who have difficulty. If several students have made errors, Ms. Kaplan reteaches the procedure by asking a student to work a problem on the board. She then asks directed questions to review procedures for students who are having difficulty.

The lesson continues as Ms. Kaplan has students add the fractions now that they are stated in equivalent terms. Then the class works additional problems adding fractions, first on their slates and then in an independent practice exercise. As before, she reteaches as necessary by having students put problems on the board. At the end of the lesson, Ms. Kaplan reviews by having the children state relevant rules. She records these rules on a poster which she posts in the room. (An example of a rule is: To add or subtract fractions with unlike denominators, you must first convert the fractions so they have like denominators.)

Analysis: Ms. Kaplan follows many of the steps and principles of active teaching and, in fact, does many of them quite well. She begins with a review of previous learning; she organizes her instruction into small, easy steps; she emphasizes important points by asking students to explain the procedures used and to do demonstrations on the board; student interest is boosted by her fast pace and by the use of slates to maximize participation; she effectively uses practice problems and checks for individual understanding before assigning independent practice; she provides an opportunity for all students to participate (using the slates); she reinforces correct answers and lets children know when they have made errors; she reteaches when necessary; and she concludes with a review.

The problem in this lesson is not in the instructional procedures but in its actual content and focus. The lesson very skillfully teaches students to memorize procedures; however, there is no clear focus on concepts and student thinking (e.g., What does equivalent mean? Why do you multiply the numerator and denominator by the same number?) Put simply, this teacher failed to evaluate the quality of the content. That is, the lesson is designed to teach math procedures rather than mathematical thinking, concepts, and strategies.

GUIDELINE 2: INSTRUCTION MUST HELP STUDENTS UNDERSTAND THE PURPOSE OF A LESSON IN TERMS THAT ARE MEANINGFUL TO THEM.   The example of Ms. Kaplan's lesson also helps to clarify the importance of establishing a clear purpose for instruction. The first step in active teaching is to establish purpose for the lesson.

The TAT literature stresses the importance of review and connecting new learning to previous learning. Ms. Kaplan does review and does connect the lesson to past mathematics learning; however, she does not establish a purpose *in terms that are meaningful to the students* (e.g., "Why would we want to add fractions, anyway?")

A key point is that the teacher must *help* students see the purpose, not *tell* students the purpose. This distinction is important. *It is not enough to tell students why a particular skill or concept is important.* To place learning within a context of meaning, the students must believe that the skill has relevance to their lives and goals. Consider, for example, children who seldom observe adults reading and writing. Telling such children that they must practice a particular skill, so they can write better, or even more concretely, "so they can write notes to their friends," does not communicate purpose. Communicating purpose means that the teacher helps the children see that literacy has relevance to their lives, that there are things they want and like to do that involve and require literacy (Schieffelin & Cochran-Smith, 1984). The failure of teachers to establish these deeper purposes for learning contributes significantly to the failure of minority children in our schools (Schieffelin & Cochran-Smith, 1984; Van Fleet, 1983).

In our view, following the steps of traditional active teaching (TAT) without attention to these first two guidelines negates the value of the method. There is a danger that teachers, confronted with the dominant emphasis of texts and tests (in all subject areas) on low-level cognitive skills, will focus on the drill of facts, skills, and procedures, believing that they are increasing the students' time on task and therefore their achievement, knowledge, and literacy. Because many of the principles of active teaching focus on the **form of instruction** (i.e., the nature of effective teaching behaviors), teachers with an incomplete understanding of the research may fail to devote sufficient attention to the **quality of instructional tasks** (i.e., Does the lesson focus on important concepts and strategies? Is the lesson organized so that students understand the meaning of what they are doing? Does the lesson emphasize student thinking?).

This misunderstanding is common among teachers with whom we have worked, who report that a great deal of active teaching occurs in the schools. They base this conclusion on their observation of teachers who provide considerable lecture, drill, and practice on low-level facts and skills. Consider the following observation made by a preservice teacher.

> By teaching reading using [active teaching], I feel we are teaching our children how *not* to think. When I ask my students how they arrived at a particular answer, they usually change their minds. . . . Children's minds seem to have been programmed to take in basic facts and relay back answers. Somewhere along the line, they have ceased to be creative and they find problem solving nearly impossible.

Clearly, the problem discussed is an important one. However, appropriate use of active teaching should not result in programming children to "take in basic facts and relay back answers." In fact, the student was seeing an incomplete application of active teaching. This misunderstanding may be common because of the dominance of texts and workbooks in elementary instruction. For example, many reading researchers note that teachers spend far too much time on the independent drilling of reading skills and far too little time on reading for meaning and applying skills (Anderson, Hiebert, Scott, & Wilkinson, 1985; Cazden, 1978; Durkin, 1978-79; Strange, 1978).

The research on active teaching does not advocate increased use of drill and independent practice using worksheets and workbooks. In fact, the research indicates that teachers must spend more time actively presenting information, more time providing *teacher*-directed practice, more time structuring instruction to relate new information to past information, more time monitoring students' practice efforts, and more time selecting interesting and appropriate independent practice activities. However, Carbo (1987) notes that many teachers feel pressured to teach and keep detailed records of student progress on hundreds of skills because of district and state requirements, leaving little time for meaningful application of skills.

Considering the pressure to teach basic skills, the emphasis on skills in texts and on tests, and the use of beginning teacher assessment measures, which stress the behaviors of active teaching without a complementary focus on the nature of the instructional task, the potential for the inappropriate use of active teaching is great.

GUIDELINE 3: EMPHASIZE INTERACTION AND APPLICATION.   The first two guidelines clarify the purpose of active teaching (i.e., the development of student thinking and understanding). This third guideline changes the instructional focus of active teaching from almost singular concern about teacher behavior to concern about student thinking and understanding. This change requires that teachers provide opportunities for students to interact with the teacher and with peers so that the children can reveal and clarify their thinking. Additionally, instruction must provide multiple opportunities for students to test their knowledge. For example, these application opportunities help children learn when and why to use various reading comprehension strategies. Reading researchers studying the use of active teaching to teach comprehension strategies suggest four strategies which support this guideline:

- the use of small groups
- the use of discussion which encourages peer interaction and probes student thinking (i.e., to help students reveal how they think new knowledge is connected to and integrated with previous understandings)
- the use of high-interest learning materials
- the provision of increasingly more complex opportunities to apply concepts and strategies (Paris et al., 1983; 1984; Raphael, 1982; Palincsar & Brown, 1984).

Of course, not all strategies will apply to every lesson. For example, it is certainly possible to teach a large-group lesson that facilitates the construction of knowledge. The supporting strategies should be viewed as suggestions about ways to facilitate student interaction and provide students with opportunities to apply and test their learning.

Peer interaction encourages students to express their understandings.

GUIDELINE 4: USE COACHING AND SCAFFOLDING APPROPRIATELY.   Most teacher effects research focuses on methods to improve the achievement of low-achieving, low-SES students. In their studies of achievement, many researchers have noted that high-ability, highly motivated, low-anxious students and those with an internal locus of control perform better on achievement tests when the classroom is less structured and controlled than under active teaching (McFaul, 1983; Peterson, 1979; Soar & Soar, 1983). However, a misinterpretation of the research is that active teaching is *only* or *always* appropriate for low-achieving students. Low achievers would seem to profit more than high achievers from active teaching, but the model is appropriate for all children and other methods are required for all children.

However, if active teaching is to enhance achievement, the appropriate use of coaching and scaffolding is critical. Recall that the teacher coaches by offering suggestions, providing support (scaffolding), providing feedback, and designing new tasks to move the student closer to expert performance. To do this appropriately, the teacher must provide the minimum support necessary. Providing the minimum support necessary requires that the teacher be cautious about *overstructuring* and *overmonitoring*. Ignoring these cautions could lead to lower achievement by students. In fact, overstructuring and overmonitoring may explain why some studies have found that higher-achieving students perform less well when teachers use active teaching. While some researchers conclude that active teaching is inappropriate for higher-achieving students, a more valid conclusion is that inappropriate use of active teaching can diminish achievement for any student.

Caution 1: Avoid overstructuring. The teacher's level of control over learning can be too high (Berliner, 1984; Soar & Soar, 1983). When this happens, the teacher overstructures learning tasks and therefore spends longer on a task than is necessary. For example, one of our students remembers an English teacher who spent half the year teaching grammar rules despite the fact that everyone in this advanced section had mastered them. Devoting more time than necessary to one set of skills and concepts not only diminishes students' motivation for learning, but also decreases the amount of time available for additional learning. Whether teaching high or low achievers, teachers must be careful to avoid spending extensive time teaching, drilling, and practicing skills that students have already mastered or can master easily with minimal instruction.

This caution suggests that some high-achieving students may need very little active teaching because they are able to construct knowledge independent of instruction. Recall that much of the research indicating that children construct knowledge about reading was conducted with children who learned to read *before* they received instruction. Students who do not learn to read independent of instruction may require more direction and structure. However, whatever the achievement level of the child, the implication seems to be that teachers should provide the minimum structure necessary to support student learning.

Caution 2: Avoid overmonitoring. The teacher can monitor student success too closely. The TAT model suggests that teachers continually monitor the success of students and provide as much immediate feedback about the correctness of responses as possible. Some researchers have expressed concern that high levels of teacher monitoring may impede students' development of **self-monitoring** skills (i.e., the propensity and ability to assess whether one understands and to seek help if necessary). That is, if the teacher continually assesses and gives feedback about correctness, students will feel little need to assess their understanding independently. This ability to monitor one's own learning differentiates high achievers from low achievers.

The question is not whether teachers should provide help, but how they should determine when assistance is needed. Nelson-LeGall (1985) suggests that the most beneficial help is given when students request it. Other researchers believe that the ability to monitor one's learning efforts is so important that teachers should actively teach this strategy, especially to low achievers who are less likely to learn it independently. For example, Collins, Brown, and Newman (1989) stress that teachers should structure instruction so that students gradually take more responsibility for assessing their understanding. They note that an important part of active teaching is **fading** (i.e., the gradual removal of feedback and help so that students gain increasing experience with the skills of self-monitoring and self-correction). This is another way of suggesting that students need increasingly more complex opportunities to apply this strategy.

An Example of the Constructivist Interpretation of the Active Teaching Model (CAT)

What would instruction look like if you used the CAT model? The literature includes examples of the constructivist interpretation of active teaching. For example, you might look at the description of a sequence of mathematics lessons taught by Lampert (1986) or at the brief samples of the reciprocal teaching model in reading (see Chapter 4). Reading these lessons will help you understand the model better. To provide an immediate example, we include a lesson plan for an alternative version of the mathematics lesson taught by Ms. Kaplan.[2] As you read this lesson plan, evaluate whether the teacher is attending to each of the CAT guidelines.

Prior to this lesson, this mixed-ability group of fourth graders worked on addition and subtraction of fractions by creating and/or solving word problems that involved fractions. Up to this point, students have worked only with fractions with like denominators. The following introductory lesson plan is designed to prepare the children for a sequence of lessons on the addition and subtraction of fractions with unlike denominators. For this lesson, the children will work with partners.

Ms. Holbrook's Fraction Lesson Plan

Purpose: To help students discover how to add fractions with unlike denominators.

Grade Level: 4–5

Materials:

- Plastic bag packets for students containing four circles of different colors, divided into pieces of 1/2, 1/4, or 1/8. That is, each pair of students has a packet containing 1 whole green circle; 1 yellow circle cut in half; 1 red circle cut into fourths; 1 orange circle cut into eighths. Each piece in the packet is labeled with the appropriate numeral.

- Large versions of the same materials (with a magnet on each piece so it sticks to the chalkboard), organized into 4 whole circles, each of one color.

- Fraction circle chart for each partner pair.

Fraction Circle Chart

Directions: Make at least 6 different circles using the pieces in your packet. For each circle you make, record the number of red, orange, and yellow pieces you use.

	Red (1/4)	Orange (1/8)	Yellow (1/2)
Circle 1			
Circle 2			
Circle 3			
Circle 4			
Circle 5			
Circle 6			

Objectives:

1. Students will discover the relationship between different fractions.
2. Students will practice recording skills.
3. Children will be able to trade one fraction for an equivalent fraction.

---

[2]   This lesson plan was developed by a Jan Holbrook, a graduate intern at the University of Florida. We have included the lesson plan, instead of a transcript of the lesson, because the transcript is lengthy and we wanted to give a sense of how she developed the entire lesson.

4. Children will use "trading" as a concept to help them learn to add with unlike denominators.

Procedures:

1. Put the posterboard circles on the chalkboard. Explain that each child will receive a bag with smaller versions of these pieces. Distribute the bags.

2. Tell the children that they will work with their partners to explore the pieces for 5 minutes. First, they will make sure they have all the pieces by creating four complete circles.

3. Tell the children to create as many circles as possible, using their pieces and to record their circles on the chart, indicating the number of red (1/4), orange (1/8) and yellow (1/2) pieces used.

4. Distribute recording charts. After 5 minutes, ask students to share what they have discovered. Ask for specific examples of circles using a lot of colors.

5. Have some of the children re-create their examples using the large posterboard pieces so all can see. An example would be 1 red (1/4), 2 orange (2/8), and 1 yellow (1/2):

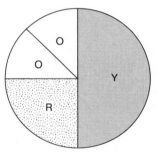

6. After several circles have been made, keep one on the board and ask, "What could I replace the orange with and still have a complete circle?" Ask the children how they know the answer and to prove it by demonstrating on the board. Repeat several times, asking children to share their observations about which fractions are equivalent. Be sure to use the term *equivalent* and to ask the children what it means.

7. Using a circle such as the one in Step 5, ask how much of the circle is orange. Then add more orange to the circle, and ask how much of the circle is now orange. Ask the students how they knew the answer. Have someone show how we could record this problem on the board (e.g., 1/8 + 1/8 + 1/8 + 1/8 = 4/8). Observe that each fraction has the same denominator.

8. Again using the circle in Step 5, ask the students, "What if we want to know how much of the circle is orange *and* red?" Have the children try this with their pieces. Then have volunteers share their solution process. Summarize what they did by noting that they are "trading" pieces that are equivalent so they can add fractions with like denominators. An example is:

   2/8 + 1/4   Trade 2/8 for 1/4, or trade 1/4 for 2/8.

9. Have a student volunteer to be a "banker" for you as you try to solve a problem. Put the following problem on the board:

   1/2 + 1/4 = ?

Put the pieces 1/2 (yellow) and 1/4 (red) on the board. Ask the students, "What could I trade with the banker so I would have an equivalent fraction that would give me fractions with like denominators that I could add?" Make the trade with the banker and add.

10. Have children work with a partner to solve fraction problems from their math text. Instruct one child to work the problems and tell the other child to serve as the banker. After they work several problems, they should exchange roles. As children work, circulate and ask children to explain why they did what they did.

FOCUS BOX 5–8

Practical Application Activities

Activity 1:   Analyze Ms. Holbrook's lesson plan using the guidelines suggested in the constructivist interpretation of active teaching. Were all of the guidelines followed? Can you think of ways to modify the lesson to include any that were omitted or to improve the lesson plan?

Activity 2:   Look back at the lesson taught by Ms. Gunther. In a small group, redesign the lesson using a constructivist interpretation of active teaching. Try to include all the steps of active teaching and the four guidelines. Make sure you devote serious attention to developing a purpose for the lesson. What is the purpose of this lesson? How can you redesign the lesson to make that purpose relevant and meaningful to students?*

Activity 3:   Tape-record yourself teaching a large- or small-group lesson based upon the constructivist interpretation of active teaching. Use the steps and guidelines to assess your expertise in using the model. After you have done this, meet with a small group of your peers who have done the same thing. In groups, listen to two lessons and answer the following questions:

- Evaluate the purpose and motivational quality of each lesson. (Does the lesson provide opportunities for children to apply their knowledge? Is the lesson interesting? Is it clearly related to the needs and interests of children? Is it taught with energy and enthusiasm?)

- Listen for evidence that the teacher is probing student thinking. (What opportunities are provided for students to share their thinking?)

- Listen for evidence of student learning. (What did they learn? How do you know?)

- Which parts of the constructivist modification are the most difficult to implement? Why?

- Which seem the easiest to implement? Why?

- What concerns do you have about the constructivist modification of active teaching? Explain.

*In using this activity with students in our classes, we have had several groups who have been unable to discern an intellectually valid purpose for teaching a lesson on the identification of nouns and verbs. We give them this hint: "In order for elementary children to talk about their writing, they must develop relevant vocabulary about different kinds of words (parts of speech) that are the tools of writing." Using this information see if you can communicate purpose in a way that will be meaningful to elementary children.

Summary Chart: Differences Between TAT and CAT

Both TAT (traditional active teaching) and CAT (constructivist active teaching) are based on the six-step model derived from teacher effects research. The following chart shows how the addition of the four guidelines for a constructivist interpretation of active teaching affects both the purpose and the instructional strategies involved in active teaching.

	TAT	CAT
Purpose		
Only instructional outcome is development of facts, skills, and procedures.	Possible	Impossible
Only instructional outcome is rote memorization.	Possible	Impossible
Instruction focuses on the development of strategies, concepts, and student thinking.	Possible	Required
Students learn when and why to use skills and strategies.	Possible	Required
Lessons are planned so that concepts, strategies, etc. are presented in terms and within the context of activities that are meaningful to the students.	Possible	Required
Strategies		
Guided practice enables teachers to determine little more than whether students can repeat what they have been taught.	Possible	Impossible
Guided practice is designed to include teacher-student and student-student interaction so that the teacher can probe student understanding of concepts and strategies.	Possible	Required
Lessons provide increasingly complex opportunities for students to apply and test their knowledge.	Possible	Required
Student-student interaction is encouraged.	Possible	Required
Teachers structure lessons so that they gradually remove feedback and help so students learn to be self-monitoring.	Possible	Required
Right answers alone (i.e., without articulation of reasoning) are accepted as evidence of learning.	Possible	Impossible
Students must articulate reasoning as well as correct answers.	Possible	Required

Concluding Thoughts About the Appropriate Use of Active Teaching

We have argued that the appropriate use of active teaching requires the combining of the six-step active teaching model (TAT) with the four guidelines developed for the constructivist interpretation of active teaching (CAT). Without the last four guidelines, the TAT model presents a limited view of teaching which focuses on defining teacher behavior without a complementary focus on student learning. The result is a limited model appropriate for rote learning that may lead to higher test scores but is unlikely to have a lasting impact on students. We are particularly concerned that routine application of the six steps may preclude low achievers from gaining academic independence and learning the "learning to learn" skills (e.g., asking if what they are learning makes sense, learning to identify important ideas within a lecture) to overcome learned helplessness. Additionally, the routine use of the steps does not provide an appropriate context for learning open-mindedness and reasoning skills that are necessary in a democratic society.

The addition of the four guidelines substantially changes the nature of the instruction provided by the six steps. The chart in Focus Box 5–9 clarifies the nature of these changes. The guidelines place primary emphasis on the purpose of instruction rather than on the nature of effective teacher behaviors. The guidelines stress student thinking, establishment of a meaningful purpose for instruction, the importance of interaction and application, and use of the minimum structure and help necessary to support student learning (i.e., coaching and scaffolding). These practices enable teachers to work collaboratively with students as they apply their knowledge, articulate their reasoning, and reveal their emerging ideas about how new knowledge is integrated with previous understandings. In contrast, the use of the steps without the supporting guidelines stresses teacher behaviors which enable teachers to present information and then determine whether the students have accurately received it. Our point is that the appropriate use of active teaching will help children construct learning. If this is to occur, teachers must use the guidelines as well as the six-step model. In our view, the use of active teaching without the four guidelines is inappropriate because it does not create conditions necessary for students to construct knowledge.

Even when using the constructivist interpretation of active teaching (CAT), it is important to remember that comprehensive learning of any subject requires multiple instructional methods. Active teaching is only one of many instructional strategies that effective teachers use. The research indicates that accomplishing goals such as the development of high-level cognitive skills, self-monitoring, creativity, and independence in learning requires that teachers develop a broad range of instructional strategies (e.g., cooperative learning strategies, strategies to foster thinking, whole-language strategies). No single set of teaching behaviors ensures effectiveness. Remember, the research does not tell us how to balance instructional time so that students develop academic skills and things such as curiosity, creativity, cooperation, and social interaction skills. Teachers must make decisions about what goals are worth achieving, what balance they will seek

FOCUS BOX 5–10

Take a Moment to Reflect

Pretend you are a teacher in a suburban, middle-class school. One-third of the children in your third-grade classroom have been selected for the gifted program. All but three of the children in your classroom scored at or above the 40th percentile on their standardized achievement tests taken at the end of the second grade. Your principal has just attended a workshop on active teaching and has announced that all teachers in the building must attend a similar workshop. To clarify what is meant by active teaching, the principal distributes the list of the six steps we have shared in this chapter. The list does not include the supporting guidelines we presented. In order to improve students' achievement, the principal wants all teachers to use active teaching (as defined by the 6 steps) as their dominant instructional strategy. He plans to observe to assess your competence using the model.

1. Will this model work to raise the achievement of children? Is this a sound educational policy or not? Is the implementation of this policy ethical? (*Note:* These three questions may sound familiar. They are the three questions reflective teachers use to guide their judgments about educational practice.)
2. Using the information presented in this chapter, develop a written response to the principal.
3. Would your response change if you were teaching a group of low-achieving children? If not, state why. If so, state how and why.
4. Would your response change if your principal suggested using both the six steps and the four guidelines necessary for a constructivist interpretation of active teaching? If so, state how and why.

---

among competing goals, and the appropriateness of various goals for various types of students. Active teaching is not a prescription for effective teaching. Active teaching is a model available for teachers to use if and when it is appropriate. Even when teachers decide the model is appropriate, it must be adapted to suit the teacher's goals, the characteristics of the particular children, and the teaching context.

Further Readings

Berliner, D. C. (1984). The half-full glass: A review of research on teaching. In P. L. Hosford (Ed.), *Using what we know about teaching* (pp. 51–77). Alexandria, VA: Association for Supervision and Curriculum Development.

Brophy, J. (1981). On praising effectively. *Elementary School Journal, 81* (5), 269–278.

Brophy, J., & Good, T. L. (1986). Teacher behavior and student achievement. In M. Wittrock (Ed.), *Third handbook of research on teaching* (pp. 328–375). New York: Macmillan.

Collins, A., Brown, J. S., & Newman, S. E. (1989). Cognitive apprenticeship: Teaching the craft of reading, writing and mathematics. In L. B. Resnick (Ed.), *Knowing and learning: issues for a cognitive science of instruction*. Hillsdale, NJ: Erlbaum.

Good, T. L. (1979). Teacher effectiveness in the elementary school. *Journal of Teacher Education*, *30*, 52–64.

Goodman, K. S. (1978). What is basic about reading? In E. W. Eisner (Ed.), *Reading, the arts and the creation of meaning* (pp. 55–90). Reston, VA: National Art Association.

McFaul, S. A. (1983). An examination of direct instruction. *Educational Leadership*, *40*, 67–69.

Peterson, P. L. (1979). Direct instruction: Effective for what and for whom? *Educational Leadership*, *37*, 46–48.

Romberg, T. A., & Carpenter, T. P. (1986). Research on teaching and learning mathematics: Two disciplines of scientific inquiry. In M. Wittrock (Ed.), *Third handbook of research on teaching* (pp. 850–873). New York: Macmillan.

Ross, D. D. & Kyle, D. W. (1987). Helping preservice teachers learn to use teacher effectiveness research. *Journal of Teacher Education*, *38*, 40–44.

Smith, F. (1977). Making sense of reading and of reading instruction. *Harvard Educational Review*, *47*, 386–395.

Webb, R. B, Ashton, P. T., & Andrews, S. D. (1983). The basic skills instructional system: A manual for improving the reading and language arts skills of low achieving students. *Florida Educational Research and Development Council Research Bulletin*, *17*, 1–33.

CHAPTER 6

Helping Students Develop Social and Interpersonal Skills

Ask elementary teachers to describe their students and you are likely to hear as much about students' social skills as about their academic competence:

- "Kirsten just doesn't realize how annoyed the other kids are by her constant goofing off."
- "Everyone wants to have Latonya as a partner."
- "Tony is so quiet. The kids like him, but they seem to ignore him when he tries to join their play, and he doesn't seem to know how to get their attention."
- "Paul is a charmer. You can tell that someday he's going to be a leader because he knows how to convince others to go along with his ideas."

Comments such as these highlight the importance of social skills in students' success.

In this chapter, we will explore the importance of social and interpersonal skills, the personal factors that can affect social acceptance, skills essential for good interpersonal relationships, ways in which classroom instruction can impede the development of such skills, and instructional strategies useful in helping children develop social competence. As in the previous chapters, the intent is to encourage you to be reflective and to connect your decisions to your aims.

Why Are Social Skills Important?

Why should teachers be concerned about helping children develop social competence? Let's begin by considering the importance of social skills.

Personal Benefits

As teachers, we want our students to become well-adjusted, knowledgeable, effective adults. A good predictor of such successful functioning is social competence in childhood (Asher, Renshaw, & Hymel, 1982; Michelson, Sugai, Wood, &

Kazdin, 1983; Rogers & Ross, 1986). According to Shultz, Florio, and Erickson, **social competence** means:

> all of the kinds of communicative knowledge that individual members of a cultural group need to possess to be able to interact with one another in ways that are both socially appropriate and strategically effective. (1982, p. 88)

Several researchers have looked at what happens to children who are *not* accepted by their peers. These children are more likely to become delinquent (Roff, Sells, & Golden, 1972) and have mental health problems (Cowen, Pederson, Babigian, Izzo, & Trost, 1973; Stengel, 1971). Michelson, Sugai, Wood, and Kazdin note:

> Social competency is of critical importance in both the present functioning and future development of the child. Social skills are not only important in regard to peer relations but also allow the child to assimilate social roles and norms. (1983, p. 2).

Although children who lack social competence in childhood are not necessarily destined for later problems, teachers should realize that such children may be more at risk than other children. Thus, they need more attention and assistance.

We have listed several problems that *may* later face children who lack social skills. But why can problems in childhood potentially lead to dysfunction in adulthood? Let's consider two types of children—the passive child and the aggressive child—and how their behavior can affect peer relationships. These two types of children are at different ends of the continuum in terms of interactions with others, but they are likely to develop similar problems in later life.

Think for a moment about children who are withdrawn, or isolated. Such children hesitate to express an opinion or to make a need known. They choose not to interact with others; as a result, they limit positive responses from their friends. The point is that interaction is reciprocal; how you behave affects the kind of response you get. Children who choose not to interact give and receive few socially rewarding responses, and are likely not to be perceived as popular. Over time, unpopular children tend to be the ones most likely to develop academic, emotional, and social problems.

Now think about children who are aggressive. These children may abuse others verbally or physically, tease, argue, or constantly fail to cooperate. They constantly interact with others, but in inappropriate ways. Rejected by peers, these children, too, have few opportunities for positive responses, and are likely to face the problems of the unpopular.

These examples of withdrawn children and aggressive children demonstrate that children who lack social competence critically need the help of their teachers and others. Their future functioning and happiness may depend upon it.

Societal Benefits

Schooling is one context for learning how to live in a democratic society. In Chapter 1, we stated that a democracy requires citizens who are dedicated to the worth and dignity of individuals, who recognize the need to balance individual

Teachers play a critical role in helping children who feel isolated become integrated into the classroom.

rights against societal rights, and who value and work toward the ideal of **equity** (e.g., assuring that each person has equal access to knowledge, and an equal opportunity to speak, be heard, and lead a self-determined life). Education for democracy requires that students feel connected to each other and to the society and that they learn to be compassionate, cooperative and responsible for the results of their actions (and society's) so that they are able to exhibit concern for the well-being of self and others (Goodman, 1992). Learning to be an effective member of the classroom community helps children learn how to function outside of the classroom. According to Corsaro:

> Socialization is not something that happens to children; it is a process in which children, in interaction with others, produce their own peer cultures and eventually come to reproduce and become members of the adult world. (1988, p. 24)

Schools help in this process, because the social interactions that occur there differ in important ways from family interactions (Corsaro, 1988). Within the family, interactions are based on emotional ties with a few people in familiar surroundings. These experiences play a necessary part in a child's initial social development, but they are insufficient for helping children develop all the skills necessary for functioning effectively in society. Schools can help to fill the gap. Children entering school confront the need to interact with a great number of people they do not know in a setting which is unfamiliar. Whether or not they learn to do this effectively has important consequences, not only for their success academically, but also for the success of our culture.

According to Johnson, Johnson, Holubec, and Roy, many students fail in this task, and much evidence exists to suggest that we currently face a societal crisis:

> A substantial number of children . . . feel isolated, disconnected from their parents and peers, unattached to school and career, without purpose and direction, and lacking any distinct impression of who and what kind of persons they are. (1984, p. 4)

These authors suggest that this inability to establish meaningful personal connections increases the likelihood that people will have little commitment to helping others or may have little remorse about doing harm to others. The following evidence quoted from Johnson et al. (1984, pp. 4–5) provides some alarming evidence of the societal impact of this inability:

- The dramatic increase . . . of the frequency with which juveniles are involved in serious crimes against property.
- The rise of more that 250 percent in the suicide rate among teenagers and 150 percent among children 5 to 14 years of age over the past 20 years.
- The presence of a permanent criminal underclass that is totally out of touch with the rest of society.

One implication drawn from this information is the importance for society, as well as for the individual, of focusing attention on helping children and youth acquire social competence.

Whether or not a child is accepted socially can depend, in part, on personal factors. While teachers cannot change these factors, they can design experiences which may mitigate their impact on social acceptance. Beyond these personal factors are important social skills teachers can help children acquire. In the following sections we address these two influences on children's development of social competence. Before reading further, complete the activity entitled "Who Are My Friends?" that is found in Focus Box 6–1.

What Personal Factors Affect Social Acceptance?

How children (and adults) respond to one another can depend on a number of factors. Clearly, the social skills of each person are important; however, as you probably figured out in doing the "Who Are My Friends?" activity, personal characteristics also can influence social acceptance (Asher, Oden, & Gottman, 1977). If you and your peers are like most people, you probably found that few of your friends have unusual names, most of them are attractive, and most are like you in terms of race and sex. Establishing a classroom community in which all children are accepted provides an environment in which children can learn to care about, accept responsibility for, and help each other. Before considering the social skills

FOCUS BOX 6–1

Who Are My Friends?

Directions: Make a list of the 10 (or fewer) people with whom you interact most often. As you do this:

- include only people who are friends (i.e., do not list relatives)
- include only people with whom you *voluntarily* do things twice a month or more
- exclude boyfriends, girlfriends, or spouses (i.e., we are looking for friendships, not dating relationships)

Assign each person on your list of names a number. Put a Y (yes) or an N (no) under each person's number on the following chart.

	1	2	3	4	5	6	7	8	9	10
Unusual name?										
Physically attractive?										
Same sex (as yours)?										
Same race (as yours)?										

Analysis

Use the chart to search for any patterns in the general characteristics of your friends and answer the following questions:

1. Compare your chart to that of three or four of your peers. Are there any patterns that are consistent for all of you? Why do you think those patterns exist?

2. Does anyone in your group have a decidedly different pattern related to some or all of the attributes? If so, try to figure out why these differences exist. Specifically, try to determine whether there are some particular experiences or life circumstances that have influenced this person's friendship patterns.

3. Compare your findings to the research reported in the section of the chapter on personal attributes that influence children's friendships. Do you see similarities and differences? Where you see differences, why do you think they exist?

---

children need to develop, let's look a little more closely at how personal characteristics influence peer acceptance or rejection.

In a review of literature on the social acceptance of children, Asher, Oden, and Gottman (1977) conclude that children's names, physical appearance, race, and sex influence their social acceptance. Although a child's name may seem rather insignificant, names apparently are important. Asher et al. (1977) cite studies by McDavid and Harari (1966) and Harari and McDavid (1973) that found that children with desirable names such as Sherri or Steven were more popular than their classmates with less common names such as Hugo and Hilda, and that teachers' evaluations of students' work were lower for this latter group. Children may behave differently when they meet children with unfamiliar names, and once this occurs, a cycle of interaction might be started (Asher et al., 1977).

Another factor is whether or not a child is considered to be physically attractive. Better-looking children are liked better by their peers *and* by adults, who according to a study by Dion (1972), tend to assume that attractive children will exhibit more positive social behaviors (Asher et al., 1977). Findings such as these raise important issues regarding the way children (and teachers) might tend to treat physically disabled classmates, often perceived to be less attractive and "different."

Race and sex also can account for children's responses to one another. Children tend to prefer children of the same race; however, they also make a considerable number of cross-race choices. When gender is the variable, its influence is much stronger than that of race (Asher et al., 1977). It appears, then, that children tend to choose children of the same sex and race in making friendship choices.

Whether or not children are accepted by their peers, are sought out and chosen to be friends, and have good experiences interacting with others depends on many factors, some of which we have already described. It is important to remember, however, that these factors *influence* but do not *determine* social acceptance. We are not suggesting that a physically disabled child with a very unusual name is destined for social interaction problems. Nevertheless, it is important to realize that children (and adults) are more comfortable with people who seem similar to themselves. Someone who is different in any way is likely to be less accepted. In our discussion of instructional strategies, we will suggest some ways to counter these perceptions of difference.

FOCUS BOX 6–2

Is It Important for Children to Make Cross-Sex Friendship Choices?

You might be wondering how important it is for children to make cross-sex friendships. Isn't this just developmental? When it's time for them to start dating, won't this just "take care of itself"? We believe that this is not just a developmental issue, and that the kinds of relationships established (or not established) can have an enduring effect on male-female relationships. The implicit message that children may receive is that boys and girls are not friends. Over time, this view may become sustained, as adolescents and then adults assume males and females may be dating partners but not friends.

By not providing opportunities for boys and girls to interact and to develop an understanding of common interests and abilities, teachers may be communicating that children's interests differ according to gender. Consequently, girls who are interested in science, math, or active sports and boys who are interested in literature, the arts, or less active games may have sanctions against them because their peers would be members of the opposite sex. Such experiences can exert subtle (and not so subtle) pressure to conform, and the ultimate effect can be interests never developed, possibilities never reached, and friendships never nurtured.

To this point, we have focused on the influence of children's personal characteristics. Now we turn our attention to the social skills children need in order to increase the likelihood of positive interactions with others.

What Social Skills Do Children Need?

Children in a democratic society need to develop compassion, cooperation, and the ability to accept responsibility for their actions. While lofty, these attributes are very vague. To help children develop social competence requires that teachers understand the component social skills that enable children to behave cooperatively and compassionately. To identify these skills, researchers have observed young children who are in the process of developing social competence. Let's look at what they have found. Later we will discuss why so much of this research has been done with young children and the implications of that fact.

Ability to Assess a Social Situation

According to Asher et al. (1977), "A child must learn to 'psych out' the environment to figure out what kinds of behavior will lead to acceptance or rejection" (p. 47). Many people have developed this ability. Whether we are new to a school's faculty, attending a cocktail party with our spouse's coworkers, or enrolled in a college class, we realize we have to "read" the situation. Although we probably do this without giving it much thought, we usually know when we have made a social gaffe, and we recognize quickly those people who just do not seem to be very perceptive about why their behavior is inappropriate.

What do children need to know and be able to do in order to initiate and sustain social interactions with others? Popular children are more likely to use specific strategies, such as suggesting a joint activity or joining others' activities. Unpopular children offer more vague suggestions such as smiling. In the following examples, we observe how two children attempt to enter a group. Note what seems to help or hinder each child.

Example 1
Dirk, Nathan, and Sabrina were working together to build a slide out of large hollow blocks. Nellie was nearby building an independent structure. When the slide was completed, Dirk selected an H-shaped block and used it as a raft to slide down the slide. Nathan also grabbed a raft, and Dirk called to Sabrina to get one, too. Nellie hoping to join their play, said, "I'll get in behind Sabrina." Dirk emphatically told her to get her own.

Nellie continued to try to join the play of the other children. . . . For example, she suggested they all build a house. This idea was emphatically rejected: "No way Jose! Not today!" She also went and told the teacher . . . and tried to use the teacher's authority. "The teacher says to let me on there." Finally, she went and got the teacher and successfully joined the play. However, when she sat on the slide refusing to go down, she was soon excluded from play again. (Ross & Rogers, 1982; pp. 26–27)

Example 2

Two girls, Jenny (4.0) and Betty (3.9), are playing around a sandbox in the outside courtyard of the school. . . . The girls are putting sand in pots, cupcake pans, bottles, and teapots. . . .

Another girl, Debbie (4.1), approaches and stands . . . observing the other two girls. Neither J nor B acknowledge her presence. . . . After watching for some time . . . D moves to the sandbox and reaches for a teapot in the sand. J takes the pot away from D and mumbles "No." D backs away and again stands . . . observing the activity of J and B. She then walks over next to B, who is filling the cupcake pan with sand. D watches B for just a few seconds, then says:

1. D–B: We're friends, right? We're friends, right, B? (B, not looking up at D and while continuing to place sand in the pan, says:)
2. B–D: Right.

(D now moves alongside B and takes a pot and spoon and begins putting sand in the pot.)

3. D–B: I'm making coffee.
4. B–D: I'm making cupcakes.
5. B–J: We're mothers, right, J?
6. J–B: Right.

(This now triadic episode continued for 20 more minutes until the teachers announced "clean up" time.) (Corsaro, 1979, pp. 320–321).

What do these examples tell us about the skills needed to assess a social scene? First, let's consider Nellie and her attempts to join her peers in play. One skill she lacked was the *ability to figure out the focus of an ongoing interaction and the interests of the children involved*. Her suggestion that they build a house showed a lack of awareness that the others were committed to building their slide. Furthermore, she failed to *predict how the other children might react* to her behavior. The sliding game played by the other children was frequently played in this classroom. Nellie should have realized that the children never shared a raft during this game and thus predicted their response to her strategy of getting in behind Sabrina. Finally, she refused to do what was an essential component of the activity—sliding down the slide. Thus, Nellie's inability to assess the focus of the play interactions, to predict the potential reactions of others to her behavior and to *select social strategies appropriate to the needs and interests of the other children* diminished her social effectiveness (Rogers & Ross, 1986, p. 11).

Unlike Nellie, Debbie in the second example was successful in joining her friends. According to Corsaro (1979), Debbie made her first attempts at entry by placing herself physically in the area and by behaving in a similar way to the behaviors of her friends. This exemplifies the use of a social strategy that is appropriate to the needs and interests of other children. Although unsuccessful, she tried again, this time referring to the friendship they shared. Noting no overt rebuff, she again behaved in a similar way and, this time, was allowed to join. Notice again, that Debbie's actions are consistent with the needs and interests of the other children. Based upon her observation of the ongoing play of the children, she initiated interaction consistent with their theme and actions and gained entry.

This example illustrates that in addition to being able to initiate interactions, children also *need to have a variety of other strategies to fall back on* if their peers at first reject them. This is especially important in light of the fact that rejection is a common experience (Corsaro, 1981; Harold, 1951).

Why might children have a difficult time joining other children? Corsaro (1988) explains that children simply want to continue their play without interruption. Children are not actively rejecting newcomers, but are acting to preserve the status quo, because they are productively and pleasantly involved. Establishing this sense of mutual (and at times exclusive) connection is part of the process of establishing a peer culture and, over time, realizing what it means to be a peer and a friend. But it may also mean that children in a well-functioning dyad or group may reject the play overtures of other peers. However, Corsaro (1981) points out that initial rejection does not necessarily mean permanent exclusion.

Corsaro (1979) notes that children who are eventually successful tend to approach the other children, observe them, and then behave in a similar way. By not disrupting the play, they increase the likelihood of being assimilated. Similarly, Putallaz and Gottman (1981) found that popular children, in their attempts to join ongoing play, took on the frame of reference of the play group, whereas unpopular children tended to call attention to themselves by being disagreeable, asking questions, or making comments about themselves or their feelings. While being able to assess a social situation is important in the development of social skills, this ability alone is insufficient; children also need to know how to interact in a prosocial way.

Ability to Interact in a Prosocial Way

Children need to know how to behave **prosocially**; that is, in ways which are viewed positively by others. They need to be *friendly, cooperative, approving, affectionate, and willing to share* (Asher, Renshaw, & Hymel, 1982). In the following illustration, we meet a young boy named Lester who demonstrates an inability to act prosocially. The scene shows Lester teasing a kindergarten classmate:

> As Marlene and Lester return to their seats after . . . snack, Lester quickly sits down in Marlene's seat. Marlene: "Get offa my seat. That's my chair." As Lester moves he says in a low, mocking voice: "Get offa my seat. Get offa my seat." Marlene: "You better stop." Lester continues with a smile: "Get offa my seat. Get offa my seat." Marlene is almost in tears: "That's not funny. You better stop." Lester continues. (Hatch, 1988, p.65)

In the language of Freed (1973), socially skilled children constantly give others "warm fuzzies" by acting in a positive, cooperative manner. When children give a warm fuzzy, they are likely to receive one in return. In contrast, socially unskilled children constantly give others "cold pricklies." These, too, tend to be returned. In the following vignette, Hatch helps us see what can happen to a child who lacks prosocial skills. The excerpt reminds us that the development of social skills deserves an important place in the elementary curriculum.

> Lester comes to the place where Sam and Steve are playing [with Lego blocks] and sits down on the edge of the group. He reaches across what they are building, picks up a piece from the box and adds it to their construction. Steve: "Don't." Sam: "You're breakin' it." (When Lester put the piece in, it separated another set of pieces). Frank comes and stands between Steve and Sam. Lester to Frank: "You can play." (We'll both join.) Frank looks to Sam to see if it's OK. (I don't see Sam's reaction but I see Frank sit down.) After Frank sits down, Sam says to Lester: "Only three can play." Steve: "Ya, only three. You have to leave." Sam: "I'll decide. Frank, what does your name start with?" Frank: "F." Sam: "Steve, what does your name start with?" Steve: "S." Sam: "My name starts with S. OK S's and F's can stay." Steve to Lester: "You gotta leave." Lester looks down but does not move. Steve repeats: "You gotta leave. Only three can play." Lester continues to look down and says nothing. Steve: "I'ma tell the teacher." (Hatch, 1988, pp. 67–68)

As the episode continues, Sam and Steve develop a series of criteria for group membership, each of which seems designed to exclude Lester. It is clear that Sam and Steve are determined to exclude Lester. It is equally clear that Lester ignores their efforts at rejection. At several points he tries to establish a connection by participating in their ongoing activities, a strategy which might have worked for another child but not for Lester (Hatch, 1988, pp. 67–68).

Even though Lester tried strategies which might have been successful, he experienced continued exclusion. A likely explanation is that Lester's previous interactions have shaped the children's perceptions. They now feel Lester is likely to cause problems, and they find ways to keep him away. The inability to behave in a prosocial way has set in motion a cycle of rejection, a cycle likely to result in devastating consequences as Lester grows up. In addition to being able to assess a social situation and to interact positively with others, children also need to know how to resolve conflicts.

Ability to Resolve Conflicts

Children are bound to have disagreements with their peers. These might have to do with sharing materials, deciding who's going to interact with whom, or resolving what the activity is going to be. Disagreements are unavoidable; what becomes important is how a child learns to deal with them.

During disagreements, some children are more likely to exhibit aggressive behaviors such as hitting. However, direct confrontation, especially aggressive confrontation, is likely to lead to rejection. Consequently, aggressive children need help in learning prosocial strategies for solving conflicts.

What kinds of strategies might be useful? Asher, Renshaw, and Geraci (1980) interviewed kindergarten children to elicit their suggestions about how children in two hypothetical situations should resolve their problems. In the first situation, a child tries to take a toy away from another child. In the second situation, two children watch television until one, the guest of the other, suddenly changes channels. The children interviewed suggested four strategies. One way of responding could be *direct but nonaggressive action*, "Take it back," or "Turn it back." Or, the children could *appeal to social conventions* such as pointing out that it is important to ask first, or that whoever has something first has priority. A third strategy would be to *compromise, take turns, or share*. Fourth, the affronted child could *appeal to the higher authority of parents or the teacher*.

> It appears, therefore, that children, by age five, already know that their rights can be defended in peer conflicts by direct action that is not overly aggressive, by persuasion through appeals to social conventions, by seeking a compromise through sharing, and by appealing to an authority. (Asher et al., 1982, p. 142)

Genishi and Di Paolo (1982) suggest that the arguments of preschoolers may help them to acquire important social understandings like how to assert them-

---

FOCUS BOX 6–3

Social Skills Checklist

In order to interact successfully with peers, a child must develop the following social skills:

1. Ability to assess a social situation (i.e., knowledge and skills necessary to enter a group and initiate and sustain social interactions with others)
   - Ability to figure out the focus of an ongoing activity and the interests of the children involved
   - Ability to predict how others might react to the child's actions
   - Ability to select social strategies appropriate to the needs and interests of the other children (e.g., child initiates and sustains interaction by using behavior that models or is at least consistent with the theme and actions of the other children)
   - Possession of a variety of strategies to fall back on in case of rejection
2. Ability to interact in a prosocial way
   - Adoption of a friendly, cooperative interactive style (i.e., friendly, cooperative, approving, affectionate, and willing to share)
   - Avoidance of actions that disrupt ongoing interactions and/or result in conflict
3. Ability to resolve conflicts
   - Knowledge of and ability to use appropriate strategies (i.e., taking direct but not aggressive action; appealing to social conventions; compromising, taking turns, or sharing; appealing to the higher authority of parents or the teacher)
   - Avoidance of direct confrontation

selves or to defend their status. Consequently, teachers might appropriately decide not to intervene unless the conflict becomes disruptive in order to allow the children the opportunity to learn from the experience.

So far, we have discussed why social and interpersonal skills are important and what skills seem to be necessary for children to acquire. As we noted, almost all of the available research on social development focuses on *young* children. It seems important to think about this. There is very little research about the social development of children who are elementary school age or older. Why?

The obvious explanation is that social development has typically been the focus of early childhood education. That is, there has been a societal view that children attend preschool to learn social skills; academic development comes later. It therefore makes sense that early childhood educators would conduct more research in the area of social development. However, this fact does not explain the lack of research focusing on older children. This lack suggests that, as a society, we place a low priority on learning social skills; or perhaps more accurately, we place such high priority on academic skills that we neglect the development of social skills. Mirroring the values in society, schools, too, place less emphasis on social development than on other goals. The unfortunate result is that children who do not learn good social interaction skills by age 5 or 6 may have few subsequent opportunities and little assistance in learning them.

How Do Elementary Classrooms Impede Development of Social Skills?

Although most elementary schools include the development of social skills on their lists of objectives, this part of the program tends to get less attention than other parts. One explanation is that other aims may seem more important. We noted that early childhood teachers place more emphasis on social development; however, even at this level, a shift has occurred toward emphasizing measurable academic skills. Moore (1981) notes that this shift began in the 1960s with Head Start programs. Concern about the academic failure of high-risk children led educators to increase the academic emphasis of their programs. While social skills were still stressed, Moore notes that they were not clearly described nor were they assessed:

> Program evaluators followed the lead of the program developers and relied on conventional measures of cognitive development, IQ tests, to document program effects. Little or no attention was given to the measurement of social gains. (1981, p. 105)

As we've noted previously, teachers tend to emphasize what will be tested. The failure to assess social skills suggests that they are not important. The emphasis on academics that Moore identified in preschool programs can easily be documented in the elementary curriculum. In Chapter 5 we discussed the teacher effects research focusing on increasing student achievement. These efforts have been translated into instructional practices that suggest, both implicitly and explicitly, that teachers should devote their attention to academics. This view is reinforced further as teachers realize what children will need to know "on the tests." Of course, the obvious result is that the development of social competence falls lower and lower on the educational agenda.

Another constraint that can impede social skill development is the type of activities typically used in a classroom. Social skill learning requires that children have time to work together, to talk, to work out problems, and to grow in their understanding of what it means to be an effective group member. These opportunities are not available in classrooms which stress teacher-directed lessons and independent seatwork. A pattern of teacher-dominated teaching exists in elementary classrooms that allows little room for the development of peer relationships.

A further constraint is the limited cross-race, cross-sex, and cross-ability interaction that tends to take place, largely due to decisions about classroom organization. Typical examples include seating children in ability groups, highlighting ability differences through differentiated work or through reward systems, and pitting girls against boys in competition (also lining up by sex and treating girls and boys differently in class). There may also be a failure to attend to the lack of significant cross-race, cross-sex and cross-ability group interaction.

About ability grouping in particular, Goodlad noted, "Organizing early elementary classes into instructional groups for reading and mathematics is about as common as a daily recess in schools (1984, p. 141)." Group membership tends to remain stable in large part because the work becomes increasingly differentiated making it difficult for a child in a lower group to catch up with a more advanced group. Thus, children tend to interact most often with those in their own groups. Since research indicates that a disproportionately large percentage of minority students comprise the lower-track groups, cross-race interaction decreases. Goodlad (1984) noted the apparent effects of ability grouping on the development of social relationships. He noted that students in high-track classes felt that others were friendly, felt included in class activities, and felt accepted and liked by their peers. In contrast,

> Students in low-track classes agreed the most strongly that other students were unfriendly to them and that they felt left out of class activities. They also reported the lowest levels of peer esteem and highest levels of discord in their classes. (Goodlad, 1984, p. 155).

These findings highlight the need for organizational changes in elementary classrooms.

Finally, social development will be constrained by teachers who either do not consider this aim important or lack knowledge about how to help children acquire such skills. Thus far, our discussion suggests that elementary teachers do little teaching of social skills. Yet, many teacher/child interactions are focused on

FOCUS BOX 6–4

Take a Moment to Reflect

Directions: Look at the following comments typically heard in elementary classrooms. For each one indicate whether, in your view, the teacher is providing instruction likely to help children develop social skills. When you think instruction is occurring, specify the social skill (using the social skills checklist in Focus Box 6–3) which is being taught and provide an explanation of how you think the skill(s) is being taught.

1. Don't take the clay tools from Carlos. You should share.
2. Fighting is not a way to solve your problem. Go sit in time-out and think about what you have done.
3. Do you think the other children like it when you just move in and take their things? Would you like that?
4. Angela, just wait a minute now! It's Melissa's turn to talk. You wait and raise your hand.

After you have completed this activity individually, share your ideas with your peers noting areas of agreement and disagreement.

related issues. In fact, many teachers report spending far too much time teaching social skills, so much that there is diminished time for academics. Perhaps more teaching occurs than the research suggests. Before reading further, complete the activity entitled "Take a Moment to Reflect" (see Focus Box 6–4).

Referring to Focus Box 6–4, what did you think about the teacher/child interactions in this activity? Clearly, these types of interactions occur often and are related to the development of social competence; however, none are likely to help a child develop social skills. In the examples, teachers tell a child what has been done wrong, but no instruction occurs. For example, the teacher does not help the target child learn the following: How do I learn to meet my own need for the clay tools without taking them from Carlos? How do I communicate angry feelings if I can't fight? How do I get other children to want to play with me? How do I develop the patience to wait my turn?

There is a big difference between reprimanding and teaching. The preceding comments assume the child knows the answers to the questions we posed and the problem is one of self-control. In fact, for many children the problem is that they do not know how to interact socially with other children. Neither a reminder, a reprimand, nor a consequence will help them adjust to the social demands of the classroom, because no one has taught them the necessary social skills. We hope that we have convinced you that the aim is one worthy of your attention. In the following section, we suggest some strategies that might be useful as you make your instructional decisions.

FOCUS BOX 6–5

Take a Moment to Reflect

Thus far in this chapter, we have presented several controversial ideas. It is important to examine *your* reactions to these ideas and to compare your reactions to those of your peers. If ideas are to be useful to you, you must determine how they fit with your entering ideas about teaching. Whether you accept or reject ideas presented in this chapter, it is important that you evaluate the evidence you use in making a judgment. Look at each of the following statements and decide whether you agree or disagree:

1. The development of social competence is as important—perhaps more important—than the mastery of academic content for elementary students.

2. All teachers would agree that social skills are important, but there is only so much a teacher can do. There isn't time for teachers to teach social *and* academic skills. Children should learn social skills at home. That is, parents should teach them; the teacher's role is to reinforce them.

3. Some typical practices of elementary teachers help to create social interaction problems among children in classrooms. Samples include:

   • ability grouping (particularly if teachers assign different work to children in different ability groups for large portions of the day)

   • lining children up in boys' and girls' lines

   • using terms like *boys and girls*, pitting boys against girls in competitions (e.g., I see all the boys are ready.)

Share your views with your colleagues. As you discuss your conclusions, focus on the following:

1. What evidence can you provide that your conclusion is a valid one? (*Note:* Evidence can come from this chapter, related readings, classroom experiences, or life experiences; however, it is important that you be explicit about the source and quality of your evidence.)

2. What additional evidence might you want to collect?

An Environment That Fosters the Development of Social Competence

Earlier in this chapter, we identified personal factors affecting social acceptance. We noted that, given the choice, children tend to interact with children of the same race and gender. Thus, these two factors, along with name and physical attractiveness, can account for a child's acceptance among peers. A first step in helping children develop higher levels of social competence is to create an environment that encourages children to accept one another and to value, rather than fear, diversity. What strategies can assist in overcoming some of these barriers?

Provide Consciousness-Raising Activities

One strategy is to increase children's awareness that choices of friends should not be based on surface differences. Although concepts such as racial or sex-role stereotyping may seem too complex for young children to comprehend, some teachers have found noncontroversial ways to help children begin to confront these important issues. For instance, Porro (1981) taught her primary-level children that certain ideas and practices were "old-fashioned" but now "we know better." It's "old-fashioned," for example, to think that only boys are strong enough to move furniture or that only girls should do housekeeping chores like cleaning the tables.

Given this approach to understanding, the children can look for examples of what's "old-fashioned." They can look for pictures in books that depict a limited range of occupational choices for women or minorities, or a lack of nurturing experiences for men. They also can look for patterns in their own play activities that reinforce the idea of boys being active and girls being passive. They can point out "old-fashioned" ways of doing things in the classroom, such as having competitions which pit boys against girls, or organizing children so that the same-gender or same-race nature of the grouping is apparent.

Of course, using this strategy requires that teachers feel comfortable with reminders that they are still making "old-fashioned" decisions! And it may require that teachers change some of their interaction patterns. For example, Porro (1981) experimented with strategies to encourage cross-sex friendship choices. Despite her efforts she found the girls staying in the classroom to do "housekeeping" tasks while the boys played games outside, until *she* moved outside the classroom to provide a model of a female who played such games.

Help Children See Beyond Differences to Similarities

Given guidance, children can learn that they have things in common with their peers, in spite of their differences. What strategies might be useful? One possibility would be to capitalize on children's interests as a basis for group instruction. Interest inventories can be used to organize the groups (see Focus Box 6–6). In this way, children can begin to discover connections they have with others in the classroom.

Another strategy is to encourage children to increase their circle of friends. For example, to encourage cross-sex interaction, Porro (1981) tried a "New Friends Club." After asking children to list some classmates they would like to know better, Porro paired children to play games (e.g., checkers, chess, Trouble) several times a week. Whenever possible, she created cross-sex pairs, and she praised *all* groups for their efforts to make new friends. She found that by creating an opportunity to interact and providing low-key reinforcement, children's cross-sex interactions began to increase throughout the school day. Obviously, this strategy could easily be adapted to facilitate all kinds of interactions among children.

Another strategy would be to create opportunities for all children to become "experts," highlighting various kinds of expertise—not just academic ability

Children can learn to look beyond differences to similarities.

(Asher et al., 1977). This communicates that everyone has special talents to share. In the elementary school that Dorene Ross' daughter attends, all teachers use "validation" activities, in order to help children attend to and publicly recognize the positive attributes of others. Pirkle (1982), a principal at an international school in Holland, initiated "validations" as a way to boost children's self-esteem while increasing a school's focus on communication processes. Here's how validations worked in Dorene's daughter's school.

Each Monday, every child received the name of a validation partner (a classroom peer). During the week, all children wrote a "validation" for their partners. Depending upon their ages and skills, the children wrote positive statements, drew pictures, and/or gathered small trinkets they thought a partner might enjoy. Children did validations at home so that they would have time to really think about their peers and do the assignment thoughtfully; however, in-class time was provided for children who forgot. On Friday, all children listened as each set of partners read their validations to each other; younger children often exchanged hugs. Initial validation partners were friends, but over time each child validated every other classmate. The result of this activity (and other activities which provided a prosocial climate) was that children became very knowledge-

FOCUS BOX 6–6

Sample Interest Inventory

Name: _____

Where do you live?

Do you have any brothers and sisters?

Do you have any pets? What kind? What are their names?

What do you want to be when you grow up?

What do you like to do after school?

What is your favorite toy or game?

What are your favorite foods?

What is your favorite color?

What kinds of books do you like best?

What's your very favorite book?

Do you have a favorite TV show?

Do you collect special things—like shells, stamps, or rocks?

What are some of your favorite things to do?

What are some places you have visited that you liked?

If you have some free time, what would be some things you would do?

This inventory was adapted from an interest inventory developed by undergraduate students enrolled in Dr. Jean Anne Clyde's language arts methods course at the University of Louisville.

able about the needs, interests, and special abilities of their peers and saw that each child made a special contribution to the class.

Another strategy is to create "special days" for each child. On these days, everyone tells or writes something they especially like about the "special" child. One way of doing this is to place words, phrases, or cutout pictures around the child's picture on a poster placed on the bulletin board. Another way is to have the children make special-day cards for the "special" child. One fourth-grade teacher we know does both activities. This teacher wraps the cards in wrapping paper decorated by the children. The "present" and the special-day poster become cherished possessions for each child. In this way, special days provide another way of communicating the importance of looking beyond differences and of realizing all children are special in some way.

A final, yet important strategy, is to help the children create a collective identity, a sense of themselves as a "group" rather than a collection of individuals. At some schools, this is begun with a class or school trip. The purpose is to foster **social bonding** (Goodman, 1992); that is, to help children perceive their connections to one another. Not all schools would allow such an activity, but any teacher can foster social bonding. For example, teachers might eat lunch in their rooms with their children for the first week of school to provide an opportunity for informal interactions and to help the children see their class as a unit. Children can create class books to communicate who they are and what they might contribute to the class. Additionally, the use of cooperative learning activities helps to reinforce the idea that all children have a responsibility to others as well as to themselves. We'll discuss cooperative learning more fully later in the chapter. As we write these suggestions, however, we recognize that teachers can do these things and still fail to create a collective identity. Creating an environment that fosters social acceptance requires more.

Analyze Your Actions and Interactions with Children

More important than any specific strategy is the attitude of the teacher. Unless a teacher's day-to-day interactions with students communicate recognition of the value of each child and an expectation that the children treat each other with compassion, the value of the suggested strategies will be minimal. Remember the discussions of student perceptions in Chapter 1 and of implicit curriculum in Chapter 3. The implicit messages sent through daily interactions with students are very powerful. Recall from Chapter 1 that children perceive differences in ability from patterns in the ways that teachers call on their peers (Weinstein, 1983). We have all heard comments by teachers that communicate subtly that certain members of the class are less valued. Consider the implicit message of each of the following incidents:

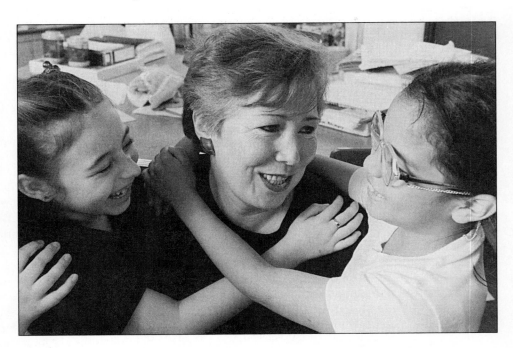

Teacher attitudes convey a sense of respect and value to children.

- Emanuel, Sally, and Theo are out of their seats and talking loudly, creating a disruption. Ms. Fischer says, "Sally what are you doing? This is not the kind of behavior I expect from *you!*"
- Everyone in Ms. Clift's class is ready for an art activity except Jan, who has no clay. Ms. Clift says impatiently and loudly, "I can't understand why you are keeping us waiting. How can you be so inconsiderate of your friends? They had other things to do but did they dawdle? No—they got ready. But now everyone has to wait because of you."

The impact of these two comments is obvious. Even teachers who work very hard to treat each child with respect occasionally will say things they wish could be taken back. The point here is that teachers must carefully monitor their interactions with children. Some teachers occasionally record themselves on audio- or videotape to try to see themselves as children might, to hear and see things they might otherwise miss. All reflective teachers mentally "play back" things said and not said to children to analyze the impact and to make commitments for "next time."

Use Instructional Strategies to Teach Social Competence

Creating a classroom environment that helps to remove barriers to social acceptance is a first step to creating a classroom community in which children can learn to be more compassionate and cooperative. However, many children lack the social skills that are necessary to interact positively with others. Teachers who are committed to helping children develop social competence must integrate into the normal routine of the classroom those strategies which help children learn social skills. We suggest four important strategies.

Assess the Social Competence and Acceptance of Children[1]

Previously we noted that teachers assess valued skills. Teachers who wish to help children become more socially competent should begin by observing children to assess their effectiveness in social situations. In this way, the teacher can identify those children who need help. For example, teachers should observe to identify passive and aggressive children. Also, teachers should be cognizant of children who overrely on an assertive/aggressive mode of interaction. Consider, for example, Dirk's interaction pattern.

> Dirk has a strong desire to be "the boss." Each time another child suggests an idea or states a desire, a disagreement occurs as Dirk reasserts his authority. . . . Dirk consistently gets his way, but the teacher notices many conflicts and disagreements centering around him. (Ross & Rogers, 1982, pp. 26–27)

---

[1] This section was modified, with permission, from "Encouraging Positive Social Interaction Among Young Children" by D. L. Rogers and D. D. Ross, 1986, *Young Children, 41*, pp. 12–17.

Overly assertive children demand their own way whatever the needs or desires of the other children. Leiter (1977) found that preschool children who are very demanding are likely to receive negative responses from peers. Similarly, Putallaz and Gottman (1981) found that unpopular children in primary grades were more likely to try to exert control over others.

Care should also be taken to identify children who always seem to say or do the wrong thing and thus are consistently excluded by their peers. Nellie, whom we met earlier, exemplifies this type of child.

> Few children seem to want to play with Nellie. She has great difficulty sustaining a play interaction. Her repeated attempts to enter the play of others are frequently rejected. When other children allow Nellie into their play, she is often excluded again within a few minutes. . . . By suggesting the wrong thing or by trying to alter the course of play inappropriately, she inadvertently alienates herself from the other children. (Ross & Rogers, 1982, p. 27)

Children like Nellie want to interact with others but do not have the skills necessary to enter an established group or to sustain interactions. Also of concern are social isolates. These children seldom initiate contact or respond to the overtures of peers; thus, they seldom interact with others.

It seems obvious that a teacher should observe children with problems. Less obvious, but equally important, is that the teacher observe children who are effective in social interactions. The social skills checklist (see Focus Box 6–3) is not enough to help a teacher know the kinds of strategies to suggest to a child having difficulty within the classroom. By observing competent children, teachers can identify strategies used by these children and then help children having difficulty learn to use more effective social negotiation strategies.

In addition to observing children, teachers may use sociometric measures to help identify differing levels of social acceptance in children. Sociometric measures validate observational data by providing additional information about the social status (acceptance) and social competence of children. As Vaughn and Waters pointed out, "Sociometric measures avoid the problems with assessing social competence from an adult's point of view by eliciting playmate preferences or nominations for each [child]" (1978, p. 276). They suggested that, although the variable measured by these procedures is popularity/unpopularity, social competence can be assumed to account for a child's popularity or unpopularity.

Asher, Singleton, Tinsley, and Hymel (1979) suggest the use of a sociometric measure which was found to be more reliable than the commonly used technique of asking children to nominate classmates they consider to be their most- or least-preferred playmates. (See TenBrink, 1974, pp. 182–187 for a description of the more common technique.) The sociometric measure developed by Asher et al. asks children to "assign pictures of each of their classmates to one of three faces according to how much they like to play with that person: a happy face, a neutral face, and a sad face" (1979, p. 444). Each child receives three scores: (a) the number of positive nominations, (b) the number of negative nominations, and (c) an average play rating (happy face = 3, neutral face = 2, sad face = 1). In using any sociometric procedure, teachers should stress that they are collecting information to help them work with the class better and that answers are not to be shared with friends. Information gained from sociometric measures and observation can be useful in deciding the most appropriate type of intervention for an individual child. What types of strategies might teachers use?

Provide Time for Peer Interaction With Minimal Adult Supervision[2]

Although children need adult guidance, they also need opportunities to interact with peers with minimal adult intervention. Charlesworth and Hartup (1967) confirmed this point in a study of social reinforcement among preschoolers. They found that positive peer social reinforcement was more likely to occur during play activities (e.g., block play, dramatic play) than during adult-structured or project-oriented activities (e.g., music, art, or table games). Rubin (1972) found a significant correlation between the frequency of children's contact with kindergarten peers and the development of empathy skills, which are an important element of social competence. These studies suggest that positive social interaction may be encouraged by providing young children with the opportunity to engage in such activities as block play, water and sand play, and dramatic play with limited adult intervention. For older children, the activities would be different but the principle remains the same. Loosely structured "project" activities, role-play activities, game periods, and recess can be used to provide time for children to practice social skills.

These kinds of peer interactions enable children to confront real social problems. Honig (1982) argued that children benefit from opportunities to provide sympathy and help to peers in real "situations of distress or misfortune." Similarly, Wilkinson and Dollaghan (1979) and Denzin (1977) stressed that peer interactions provide practice in situations where children get realistic feedback about the attitudes of others. In these situations, children continually try and discard behaviors and work toward developing their style and ability in social situations (Wilkinson & Dollaghan, 1979).

As they interact and experiment with social interaction strategies, children appear to be more likely to imitate and reinforce the positive social behavior of peers. Vaughn and Waters (1980) found that the behaviors of the most socially competent children are watched and imitated by their peers more often than the behaviors of less socially competent children. Similarly, children who played with altruistic peer models displayed significantly more altruism than those who did not have such models (Hartup & Coates, 1967). In addition, peer interaction encourages prosocial behavior because positive responses to children's prosocial behavior are reinforcing (Charlesworth & Hartup, 1967; Moore, 1981). Moore also stated that highly aggressive children receive negative reinforcement when they are resisted and avoided. Such peer interactions give aggressive children "the message that their companions would like them to change" (1981, p. 106).

---

[2]   This section was modified, with permission, from "Encouraging Positive Social Interaction Among Young Children" by D. L. Rogers and D. D. Ross, 1986, *Young Children, 41,* pp. 12–17.

Thus, peer interaction provides children with the impetus to change, the opportunity to observe and model competent behavior, and reinforcement for prosocial interactions.

To facilitate peer interaction, teachers must allocate time and space for activities with minimal adult supervision. When adults participate in or supervise an activity, the adult—not the children—controls the social interactions. Adults are able to anticipate potentially troublesome situations and structure the activity to avoid them. Consequently, interactions with adults do not create the same demands for social competence that interactions with children do. Interactions with children are interactions with equals and, thus, provide children realistic opportunities to resolve social problems. As Mead (1930) noted, individuals grow through conflict, through frustration, and through the confrontation of problems. Minimally supervised activities provide children with a context where such growth can occur, where they can test the validity and worth of their developing social skills and attitudes.

Play has long been stressed in early childhood education. There has been much less emphasis on play in elementary education. In fact, some suggest that elementary children should not waste school time in play activities. We want to be clear that we are not advocating a "play curriculum," nor are we suggesting that simply letting children play will teach them social skills. However, a curriculum in which all activities are structured by the teacher, the textbook, or an instructional activity limits children's opportunities to practice and learn social skills, and the teacher's opportunity to identify children who need help. Because there are many children who do not develop social skills before elementary school, these limitations seem very serious.

Intervene to Help Children Develop Social Skills[3]

Earlier we described several social skills children need to learn. These include such skills as the ability to assess what is happening in social situations, to interpret correctly the actions and needs of children in an ongoing group, to imagine possible courses of action and select the most appropriate one, to solve problems in a prosocial way, and to select an action that will be perceived positively by other children. Teachers can teach a variety of strategies to children in order to help them develop such skills.

Children need strategies that will help them assess an ongoing situation and interpret the needs and actions of others. Putallaz and Gottman (1981) suggested teaching children to ask questions as they approach an ongoing group. For example, children might ask, "What are you playing?" "What are the rules?" or "What are you making?" Once children are familiar with the group's intentions and direction, they are better able to integrate their desires into the group perspective. A similar, but less intrusive, strategy is for children to observe for a brief time before attempting to enter the peer group.

---

[3]   This section was modified, with permission, from "Encouraging Positive Social Interaction Among Young Children" by D. L. Rogers and D. D. Ross, 1986, *Young Children*, *41*, pp. 12–17.

Good communication skills also are required in order to interpret the needs and actions of peers (Asher, Oden, & Gottman, 1977; Gottman, Gonso, & Rasamussen, 1975). Communication skills enable the children to consider others' perspectives and make it less likely that children will be working at cross-purposes (Asher, et al., 1977). Schachter, Kirshner, Klips, Fredricks, and Sanders (1976) suggested that encouraging children to talk with adults about their problems, feelings, and desires improves their communication skills. For example, a teacher might help upset children clarify their feelings by saying, "You look very unhappy. Are you hurt? Are you angry? What made you so angry?" In studies of children's development of empathy, Hughes, Tingle, and Sawin (1981) and Hill (1983) supported this suggestion. They found that children who were asked to reflect about their feelings developed a greater understanding of the feelings of others. Similarly, Bryan (1975) reported that children who are encouraged to express themselves and who are able to seek help are more likely to offer assistance to others.

A logical next step is to encourage children to express desires, provide explanations, and conduct verbal arguments with other children. The key point is that teachers must help children talk about their feelings in order to increase their ability to understand one another. With guidance, children will get better at communication of feelings. It is important to note that this is a learned behavior. That is, children do not develop better communication skills simply by growing older. They have to be taught.

Children also need help in deciding which behaviors will be perceived positively by peers. Asher et al. (1977) supported the effectiveness of coaching to help children learn behaviors that would foster positive interactions. Coaching involves providing advice to children on how to have fun during play and then providing the opportunity to practice. For example, during the episode about Nellie presented earlier, the teacher might have called to her and suggested she try using a differently shaped block as a raft to join the play of the others. The teacher also might have told Nellie, "Everyone likes to slide down, so when it's your turn, slide down quickly. Then you'll get another turn very soon, and everyone will have fun."

Putallaz and Gottman (1981) advocated teaching children to cite rules or social norms during disagreements to justify their positions. This strategy, they found, was used by popular children. Other strategies to help children select appropriate behaviors are role playing and structured discussion (Krogh, 1982). Krogh found that both role playing and structured discussion were effective in helping children improve their **perspective-taking skills** (i.e., their ability to understand the feelings and needs of other children). Her findings indicated that both strategies helped children explore the possible consequences of alternative solutions to problems and, thus, improved their reasoning ability. By helping children understand how others might perceive their actions, these two strategies help children to distinguish appropriate and inappropriate behavior.

When problems occur during informal social interactions, teachers might guide children toward more appropriate behavior choices by using what Hill (1982) terms **reflective discipline**. Reflective discipline is a technique used to help children "reflect" on (i.e., think about) their feelings and the feelings and intentions of others. The teacher asks questions designed to provide children with information to increase their understanding of the consequences of their acts. For example, if Karla hit Evan with her backpack, the teacher might ask, "How do you think Evan felt when you hit him? Can you think of something you might have done to get him to give you your backpack without making him feel bad?"

While discipline strategies are useful, it can be beneficial to intervene before interaction problems become major conflicts. For children with poor communication skills, this may mean that teachers should offer support through their presence. For example, one teacher helped a child enter an ongoing play group by walking with the child to the group and saying to the group, "Sam has something he wants to say to you." The teacher's presence, support, and tacit approval of Sam's request to play were enough to encourage Sam to state his desires and to encourage the others to welcome him into their play. For other children, the teacher may need to provide verbal reasoning to help them negotiate social interactions (Asher et al., 1977). In the preceding example, the teacher might need to extend participation by suggesting appropriate reasoning and words: "Sam, tell Michael and Marsha that you want to play. Tell them you would like to play second base because they don't have anyone on second base." (*Note:* This coaching should be done privately.)

It is important to re-emphasize that the use of intervention strategies does not negate the need for interaction with minimal adult intervention. Intervention helps children learn the skills and attitudes necessary to negotiate social interactions effectively. Minimally supervised play provides the equally essential opportunity to practice these skills and to judge their effectiveness within a natural context.

Use Structured Classroom Groups

We have argued for activities which provide opportunities for peer interactions. However, much of the school day is devoted to structured activities. Carefully structured group activities can provide opportunities for students to learn social skills during the course of a regular classroom activity. As we noted earlier, grouping by ability—although a common characteristic of elementary classrooms—has a detrimental effect on the development of social competence. Additionally, ability groups and an emphasis on independent seatwork communicate that learning is an individual activity. While there clearly is a role for individual learning, citizens within a democracy also need to learn to develop responsibility for the well-being of others. This suggests that students need opportunities to work together and to develop a commitment to helping others learn. Accomplishing this requires that teachers develop alternatives to ability groups. However, teachers often struggle with how to organize a classroom differently. They wonder, "How can I make sure the advanced children are challenged, *and* make sure the slower children aren't lost?" "Do I just teach to the middle? If I do, won't I be ignoring the needs of the upper and lower groups?" "If I create mixed-ability groups, won't the faster students do all the work?"

"What about grading in a mixed-ability group?" "Do I use mixed-ability groups for *everything*?"

These important concerns of teachers are addressed in the writings of Johnson and Johnson (1987), Johnson et al. (1984), and Johnson, Johnson, and Holubec (1988a) about how to establish cooperative learning groups in the classroom. Although we draw heavily on the suggestions of these experts, we encourage you to examine these resources on your own, since the suggestions are explained in much more detail.

Strategies for establishing cooperative learning groups are not found in a prepackaged program. Johnson and Johnson provide clear but general guidelines which offer teachers information; however, these guidelines allow teachers to implement the strategies as appropriate for their students and situations. This idea is consistent with the theme of teachers as reflective decision-makers.

As a starting point, Johnson et al. clarify the **key attributes of cooperative learning**.

> The essence of cooperative learning is *positive interdependence*—students recognize that "we are in this together, sink or swim." In addition, cooperative learning situations are characterized by *individual accountability*, where every student is accountable for both learning the assigned material and helping other group members learn; *face-to-face interaction* among students; and students appropriately using *interpersonal and group skills*. (1984, p. 25)

To translate these ideas into practice, Johnson and Johnson (1987) offer several steps, which we will summarize. We also provide a sample cooperative learning lesson. Johnson and Johnson's steps to foster cooperative learning are as follows:

FORMULATE OBJECTIVES.   The teacher needs to select an academic objective and a collaborative skill objective for the lesson. Johnson and Johnson (1987) note that initial lessons may focus on simple collaboration skills such as helping children learn to take turns or use quiet voices. After some experience, students can learn other behaviors necessary for cooperation, such as:

1. having each member explain how to get the answer
2. asking each member to relate what is being learned to previous learnings
3. checking to make sure everyone in the group understands the material and agrees with the answers
4. encouraging everyone to participate
5. listening accurately to what other group members are saying
6. not changing your mind unless you are logically persuaded (majority rule does not promote learning)
7. criticizing ideas, not people (Johnson & Johnson, 1987, p. 55)

DECIDE GROUP SIZE, COMPOSITION, AND ROOM ARRANGEMENT.   Group size will depend on the task, the materials and time available, and the experience level of the students. It might be best to begin with groups of two or three. Then as the children become skilled, you can expand the group size—probably not beyond six children, though.

In deciding how to assign students, we recommend that teachers use mixed-ability groups as often as possible. In addition, mix nontask-oriented students with task-oriented students. Implicit in this suggestion is that teachers participate in deciding who works with whom. Student-selected groups tend to result in high achievers working with other high achievers, or single-sex or single-race groups. This is not to say that students should not have some voice. One strategy is to have students list three classmates they would like to work with, so that the teacher can select at least one. Or, students could "count off" according to how many the teacher indicates should be in each group.

Decisions about how long to keep the groups stable need to reflect the teacher's goals. For instance, it might be appropriate to keep a group together which initially has difficulty so they can learn how to resolve conflicts. On the other hand, it might be desirable to change groups often enough to give the students the experience of working with a wide range of students.

Decisions also must be made about the arrangement of the room in order to enhance the communication necessary for groups to function. Students in a group need to be close enough to make eye contact, hear each other, and see all materials.

PROMOTE INTERDEPENDENCE.   Interdependence can be promoted through materials or group roles. The teacher can give the group only one copy of the materials. In order to accomplish the task, the children must learn to share the materials. Or, the teacher might give different materials to each student in the group; then the students would need to synthesize the information. Or, the teacher might structure the materials in a tournament format to promote interdependence within the group as the students prepare to compete with other groups.

Another way to promote interdependence is to assign roles to group members. Johnson and Johnson suggest the following **cooperative group roles**:

> a **summarizer-checker** to make sure everyone in the group understands what is being learned; a **researcher-runner** to get needed materials for the group and communicate with the other groups and the teacher; a **recorder** to write down the group's decisions and edit the group's report; an **encourager** to reinforce members' contributions; and an **observer** to keep track of how well the group is collaborating. (Johnson & Johnson, 1987, p. 51)

Assigning roles fosters interdependence and provides a structure that teaches children the skills necessary for working cooperatively. It is important to note that only a highly experienced group would have members performing all of the roles. In early efforts at using cooperative groups, the teacher should assign only one or two roles. Which role or roles would be assigned would depend on the collaborative skills being taught.

Additionally, roles can be deliberately assigned to help children master particular skills, For example, a child who monopolizes the group might be assigned the role of observer. In this role, the child might be directed to note who contributes and how often. This would help increase the child's sensitivity to everyone's need to participate. Children who tend to push their own ideas and ignore those ideas of others might be assigned the role of summarizer-checker. In this role, children might be directed to make sure the specific ideas of each child are understood by all.

STRUCTURE POSITIVE GOAL INTERDEPENDENCE AND INDIVIDUAL ACCOUNTABILITY.   Teachers often express concern that in group work, some students might let others do the work. In cooperative groups, members encourage and help each other to learn; however, students also must understand that they are responsible for learning the material themselves. That is, students must truly become interdependent. They must accept responsibility for their own learning and work to insure that others learn it as well. If this is to occur, the teacher needs to structure the task to make cooperation necessary and then assess how each member is progressing. As noted earlier, the "sink-or-swim-together" idea is at the heart of cooperative learning. Johnson and Johnson (1987) recommend two strategies. First, teachers could ask the group to prepare a single product but stress individual accountability by asking one member of the group (selected at random) to explain the answers. Second, the teacher could stress group and individual accountability by providing group rewards. For example:

> Math lessons can be structured so that students work in cooperative learning groups, take a test individually, receive their individual score, and receive bonus points [or a reward like extra time at recess] on the basis of how many group members reach a preset level of excellence. (Johnson & Johnson, 1987, p. 318)

EXPLAIN THE ACADEMIC TASK, THE TARGETED COLLABORATIVE SKILL BEHAVIORS, AND THE CRITERIA FOR SUCCESS.   As in any lesson, teachers need to help students understand the academic purpose, connect the learning to previous experiences, clarify concepts and procedures, and check whether or not students understand what is expected. Teachers also must help children understand the collaborative skill objectives. It is very important that the teacher specify the behaviors expected of the children. As noted earlier, one way of highlighting these behaviors is to assign roles that focus on particular skills to be learned.

   In addition to helping children understand the purposes of the activity, teachers need to communicate the criteria for acceptable work. These criteria may, in some instances, be the same for all members and, in other instances, be different. Or, there may be criteria that the entire class must reach.

MONITOR, PROVIDE ASSISTANCE, INTERVENE.   Teacher observation is critical. Through observation, teachers can assess whether or not the students are completing the assignments and demonstrating collaboration skills. Based on the observations, the teacher can offer assistance to clarify the task or procedures and, when necessary, intervene to teach collaborative skills. Johnson and

FOCUS BOX 6–7

Group Process Checklist

The following checklist, developed using Johnson and Johnson (1987, pp. 151–153), provides a sample of what a teacher might consider in evaluating the cooperative process during group activities.

1. Prepare lists of collaborative skills to encourage in *all* students over an extended period of time.

2. Choose the two or three collaborative skills that will be observed in the lesson.

3. Develop a daily observation sheet.

4. Decide whether to observe all groups briefly or to observe one or two groups intensely. Asking a colleague to help observe may be useful. Plan how much time will be spent observing each group.

5. Use one observation sheet for each group. General rules for observing are:

   a. Each time a student uses a collaborative skill, place a tally mark in the appropriate box.

   b. Be alert for nonverbal messages, such as smiles, nods, pointing, eye contact, and so forth.

   c. Do not worry about recording everything, but observe as accurately and quickly as possible.

   d. Make notes on the back of the observation form if something takes place that should be shared with the group or class but does not fit into the categories being observed.

6. Keep the observation sheets to assess the growth of groups or individuals. One time-saving procedure is to use a single observation sheet per week and color code the days, so that Monday is red ink, Tuesday is blue ink, Wednesday is green ink, and so forth. This method allows teachers to assess weekly skill development at a glance. Another procedure is to transfer daily or weekly information to long-term record sheets.

From *Learning together and alone: Cooperative, competitive, and individualistic learning* by D.W. Johnson and R.T. Johnson (1987), 2nd ed., pp. 151–153, Englewood, NJ: Prentice-Hall.

Johnson (1987) offer a caution about intervening, however. It is best to wait for a while, giving the students the opportunity to solve problems for themselves.

PROVIDE CLOSURE.   The teacher needs to provide time for summarizing what has been learned. This information can be elicited from the students, and the teacher also might offer some synthesizing points.

EVALUATE STUDENT LEARNING AND GROUP FUNCTIONING.   Evaluation focuses on the outcomes of the assignment and on how well the group cooperated. According to Johnson and Johnson:

Processing the function of the group needs to be taken as seriously as accomplishing the task. . . . Teachers will want to have a structured agenda or checklist for the groups to work with during the processing, as inexperienced groups tend to say, "We did fine. Right? Right!" and not deal with any real issues. . . . Group processing should focus both on members' contributions to each others' learning and to the maintenance of effective working relationships among group members. . . . Problems in collaborating should be brought up and solved, and continuing emphasis should be placed on improving the effectiveness of the group members in collaborating with each other (1978, pp. 61–62).

SAMPLE COOPERATIVE LEARNING LESSON.   The following cooperative learning lesson was developed by Hildy Shanks from Hopkins, Minnesota. Her lesson is included in the book, *Advanced Cooperative Learning* (Johnson, Johnson, & Holubec, 1988a).

Planning a City Park

Subject Area: Math; Science

Grade Level: Intermediate

Lesson Summary: Students develop a plan for a city park, create a design, then prepare and present to the class a commercial to sell their park.

Instructional Objectives: Students will get practice in planning a large community project while staying within a maximum cost.

Materials:

The task	One per group
Materials and Cost Worksheet	One per group
16" x 20" piece of tagboard	One per group
Set of role cards	One per group

Time Required: Three class periods, each one week apart.

Decisions

Group Size: Four

Assignment to Groups: Teacher assigned, with one high-, two medium-, and one low-achieving student in each group.

Roles:

Accountant: Does the math computations and records the group's final report.

Architect: Lays out the park on the piece of tagboard.

Encourager: Makes sure every group member is participating.

Manager: Reads the instructions for the activity, reports the group's plan and its cost to the whole class at the end of the period, and leads the processing discussion for the group at the end of the second day.

Golden Valley Park: The Task

Golden Valley has decided to develop some of its land as an environmental park. Your engineering team has been asked to submit a proposal for the development of this land. The people of the town will do the work. Your team will plan what materials and equipment will be needed. The total cost of these materials and equipment must be $5,000 or less. Consider the following criteria when developing your plan:

Versatility
- Is the park suitable (meets the needs) for the elderly, the young, and the in-between?
- Can the park be used at night as well as during the day?
- Is the park useful in all seasons?
- Is there a wide range of activities available within the park?

Safety
- How safe is the design for young and old users?
- Are there any possible hazards?

Aesthetics
- Is the design pleasing?
- Would people of all ages enjoy the park?

Cost Effectiveness
- Was the money well spent?
- Is energy used efficiently in the park?

Innovation
- Is the design unusual?
- Are materials used in new and interesting ways?

Adapted from **S.P.A.C.E.S.**, Dale Seymour Publications, Palo Alto, California, 1982.

The Lesson

Instructional Task

Day 1:   Your task will be to build a park for the city of Golden Valley, Minnesota. You are to plan the design of the park, decide what you will have in it, and describe how it meets the criteria on the task sheet (see Golden Valley Park: The Task). All decisions must be made by consensus, which means that you all must agree. At the end of each session, put your work in the folder on my desk.

Cost of Materials and Equipment

	Cost	Unit	Quantity	Total Cost
Rope	$ 1	per 10 ft.		
Bricks	$ 1	each		
Sand	$ 1	cubic ft.		
Stepping stones	$ 5	each		
Plants and shrubs	$ 10	each		
Trash barrels	$ 10	each		
Benches (6' long)	$ 15	each		
Old telephone poles (10' long)	$ 25	each		
Wire fencing (6' high)	$ 30	per 10 running feet		
Asphalt pavement (4' wide)	$ 40	per 10 running feet		
Picnic tables with two benches	$ 50	each		
Community garden plot and seedlings	$ 50	10' × 10'		
Animals Small	$ 20	each		
Large	$ 100	each		
Drinking fountains	$ 75	each		
Pond	$ 100	each		
Playground equipment	$ 100	per item		
Bike racks	$ 150	each		
Barbeques	$ 150	each		
Street lights	$ 250	each		
Public telescope	$ 300	each		
Stage (20' square)	$ 300	each		
Bathrooms (one each, men and women)	$ 350	pair		
Bleachers (grandstand)	$ 750	each		
Bridge	$1000	each		
Other (list)	$			
	$			

Total cost: $ _____

Day 2:   Today you are to take your ideas for the playground and lay them out on a 16 x 20-inch piece of tagboard. Include somewhere in the park five trees, one hill, an outcropping of rocks, and one stream. You must decide where each natural feature goes. Keep the same roles you had last time. At the end of the class, the group manager will report your plan to the class. Then you will process how well you worked together.

Day 3:   Today your task is to (1) finish your plans for the park, (2) write a report explaining why your park has the design it has, (3) write a commercial to sell your park to the rest of the class, and (4) present your commercial to the class, with all group members participating in it. After that, we will vote as a class, using secret ballots, for which park is best and why.

Positive Interdependence

I want one plan from your group that you all agree upon, each of you must perform your roles to help the group get the task done, and you all must plan and take part in the commercial.

Individual Accountability

Each of you will be given a role which is essential to the group's work. In order to complete your park plan, every member has to fulfill his or her responsibility.

Criteria for Success

Your group is successful if you build a park plan which all members agree upon and which meets the cost requirement, if your written report is clear, and if your commercial is convincing.

Expected Behaviors

I expect to see you all working and helping, and all of you performing your assigned roles. If you have problems agreeing, try to solve those problems in your group.

Monitoring and Processing

Monitoring

Observe the groups during the lesson, giving advice and answering questions when needed. When you see students behaving skillfully, praise and reinforce the use of those skills. Also, collect information on students who use group skills effectively to report during the whole-class processing.

Intervening

If any groups have difficulties in working together or making decisions which they cannot solve, intervene to help them come to a satisfactory conclusion.

Processing

At the end of the second session, the Manager conducts a group discussion on what members did to work effectively with each other and what they can do to improve their working together. Each group's answers are written down and turned in with their work. Then, ask groups to report a few of their answers to the whole class, and report on the group skills you saw effectively used.

From *Advanced Cooperative Learning* (pp. 48–53) by D. W. Johnson, R. T. Johnson, & E. Holubec, 1988, Edina, MN: Interaction Book Company. Reprinted by permission.

FOCUS BOX 6–8

Practical Application Activity

Directions: Select three children in a classroom setting. Two should be children who have difficulty getting along with others. In selecting these two, try to select children who seem to have different problems. The third child should be a child who is popular and who seldom has disagreements with classmates.

1. Observe each child interacting with peers on at least three occasions. If at all possible, these should be times when minimal teacher supervision is provided. Use the social skills checklist (see Focus Box 6–3) and look for evidence of the use of each social skill for each child. Record *specific evidence* of the use of each skill (i.e., provide a concrete example of how it was used rather than simply checking the skill off).

2. For the two unpopular children, provide an explanation of the probable reasons for their difficulties. Include a discussion of possible personal factors as well as a discussion of each child's social skills.

3. Drawing on the strategies used by the popular child and on the instructional strategies suggested in this chapter, develop a 2-month plan for helping the two unpopular children become more socially competent. (We suggest you do this in outline format.)

Share your conclusions with a group of three or four of your peers. As your group discusses this activity, answer the following questions:

1. What are the similarities and differences among your children? That is, how did the children's problems differ and why?

2. What did you learn by observing a socially competent child?

3. Help each member of the group to consider additional instructional strategies to help the children become more socially competent.

Summary

The development of social and interpersonal skills has a legitimate place in the elementary curriculum. We have described the social skills children need, how classrooms can impede the development of those skills, and ways in which teachers can create classrooms in which children have the opportunity to develop social competence. As in previous chapters, we have encouraged you to consider these ideas as you clarify your aims and make instructional choices.

Comprehension Check

Directions: Check your comprehension of the major ideas presented in this chapter by answering the following questions.

- Why are social skills important?
- What do children need to know and be able to do if they are to be perceived as socially competent?
- Does the classroom environment of the classrooms with which you are most familiar support the development of social skills? (Support your answer with concrete evidence from the chapter and the classroom.)
- Which of the strategies presented in this chapter stand out to you as especially important? Why?
- Think of a child you know who has difficulty getting along with peers. Plan classroom intervention to help the child. Be sure to think of possible intervention at the classroom level as well as intervention with the child.

When you finish, compare your responses with those of your peers. Pay attention to similarities and differences in your answers, especially in your answers to the last two questions. Did some of you omit things that others considered important? What might this tell you about your understanding of instruction for the development of social competence?

Yes, These Look Like Good Ideas, but . . .

Whenever teachers encounter new ideas, they have to try to fit them within their current understandings about children, their knowledge of and beliefs about appropriate instructional strategies, their current knowledge base, and their specific teaching context. Because of this, you probably found yourself raising questions about the feasibility of the strategies for helping children develop social competence that we presented in this chapter. We suspect at times you found yourself thinking, "Yes, these look like good ideas, but . . . ?" Work with a small group of peers to raise and try to answer your questions about suggested strategies. The following questions may help to guide your thinking:

- What is your overall, "gut" reaction to the model? Does it look like something you might like to try? Why or why not?
- As you think about trying to implement the model, what concerns do you have?

- If you were to try to implement this model, what skills, abilities, and/or knowledge would you need to develop? How would you go about doing this?
- What contextual barriers do you see that might make implementation of this model difficult? How could you work around these contextual barriers?
- What are the implicit curriculum implications of this model? How do they fit with the aims you have identified as important for elementary education?

It is important to raise these kinds of questions and to explore the answers with your peers. Failure to confront these questions probably means you will not make any significant changes in your instruction.

Further Readings

Asher, S. R., Oden, S. L., & Gottman, J. M. (1977). Children's friendships in school settings. In L. Katz (Ed.), *Current topics in early childhood education, vol. 1* (pp. 33–61). Norwood, NJ: Ablex.

Denzin, N. K. (1977) *Childhood socialization*. San Francisco: Jossey-Bass Publishers.

Goodman, J. (1992). *Elementary schooling for critical democracy*. Albany, NY: State University of New York Press.

Honig, A. S. (1982). Research in review: Prosocial development in children. *Young Children, 37* (5), 51–62.

Johnson, D. W., & Johnson, R. T. (1987). *Learning together and alone: Cooperative, competitive, and individualistic learning* (2nd ed.). Englewood Cliffs, NJ: Prentice-Hall.

Johnson, D. W., Johnson, R. T., & Holubec, E. J. (1988a). *Advanced cooperative learning*. Edina, MN: Interaction Book Company.

Johnson, D. W., Johnson, R. T., & Holubec, E. (1988b). *Cooperation in the classroom*. Edina, MN: Interaction Book Company.

Johnson, D. W., Johnson, R. T., Holubec, E., & Roy, P. (1984). *Circles of learning: Cooperation in the classroom*. Alexandria, VA: Association for Supervision and Curriculum Development.

Rogers, D. L., & Ross, D. D. (1986). Encouraging positive social interaction among young children. *Young Children, 41*, 12–17.

Weinstein, R. S. (1983). Student perceptions of schooling. *Elementary School Journal, 83* (4), 287–312.

CHAPTER 7

Helping Students Become Good Thinkers

In recent years a flood of books and journal articles has highlighted the teaching of thinking. This attention is in great part the result of national reports which noted the lack of well-developed thinking skills in American youth. The same results have been reported across all subject areas, with particular concerns being raised in science, mathematics, and social studies areas. Many argue that in order to address the social and economic problems facing the nation and the world, to remain in step with constantly changing technology, and to contribute productively to the local and world community, citizens require the ability to think well. What does it mean to "think well"? In this chapter, we shall answer four main questions: What is good thinking? Why is good thinking an important educational aim? What is the current situation in schools? What can teachers do to help students become good thinkers?

What Is Good Thinking?

This is not an easy question to answer. As Resnick noted:

> Many candidate definitions are available. Philosophers promote critical thinking and logical reasoning skills, developmental psychologists point to metacognition, and cognitive scientists study cognitive strategies and heuristics. Educators advocate training in study skills and problem solving. (1987, p. 1)

Resnick's point is that different traditions (i.e., philosophy, developmental psychology, cognitive science, and education) approach the subject differently. Each has used its own assumptions, goals, and research methods, resulting in strikingly different definitions, studies, and recommendations for practice. It can be very confusing to sort through lists of "skills," "strategies," "basic processes," "complex processes," and "dispositions" all of which are claimed to define thinking. In this chapter we are not going to provide yet another lengthy list of the "pieces" of thinking. (Such lists are readily available; see, e.g., Costa, 1985; Marzano, Brandt, Hughes, Jones, Presseisen, Rankin, & Suhor, 1988; Morante & Ulesky,

FOCUS BOX 7–1

Take a Moment to Reflect

Before you read our definition of good thinking, consider your own definition. Think of people you know who you believe are good thinkers.

- What are these people like?
- What do they do that leads you to believe they are good thinkers?
- List as many specific characteristics of good thinking as you can.

As you read our definition, look for similarities and differences between it and your description of good thinkers.

1984.) Instead, we shall share with you our orientation to good thinking. Our orientation has much in common with the nature and purposes of reflection presented in Chapter 1.

Four Elements of Good Thinking

Because we find the lists of the pieces of thinking more confusing than helpful, we have synthesized a simpler set of elements that has clear application to teaching practice. These elements form a generic model of thinking that can be built into the teaching of different subject areas. The **four elements of good thinking** include dispositions, knowledge, critical and creative capacity, and metacognition.

Dispositions

Recent research suggests that the difference between good and poor thinkers is not a matter of skills but a matter of the tendency to *use* the skills they have. Clearly, the disposition to think plays an important role in an individual's thinking behavior. For example, Glatthorn and Baron note:

> Good thinkers are willing to think. . . . They value rationality, believing that thinking is useful for solving problems, reaching decisions, and making judgments. Poor thinkers, in contrast, need certainty, avoid thinking, must reach closure quickly, are impulsive, and rely too heavily on intuition. (1985, p. 51)

Similarly, Siegel describes the person possessing a "critical spirit" as one who has "a character which is inclined to seek, and to base judgment and action upon reasons; which rejects . . . arbitrariness; which is committed to the objective evaluation of relevant evidence" (1988, p. 39). Glatthorn and Barron and Siegel highlight **one disposition**, that of valuing thinking. People who value thinking are open to evidence, and committed to using evidence to make judgments and determine actions.

A **second disposition** focuses on the content of thinking. Good thinkers think about individual matters—personal, family, peer, and work-related concerns. However, they also think about broader social, political, and economic matters. They try to understand the world around them and to plan for the improvement of unacceptable conditions. For instance, even young children can be helped to examine the problems of pollution or homelessness in their community. With practice they can develop the disposition to think about and take action to improve conditions in the larger social sphere.

The **third disposition** is that of thinking collectively. Students can be helped to see that thinking can be a collaborative activity done for the purpose of improving the quality of life for all human beings.

While there are specific skills inherent in these dispositions, they represent a particular orientation to life. That is, good thinkers have a pervasive way of encountering their world. Research suggests that a person's dispositions toward thinking can be altered. We can think of good thinking as a habit that can be taught and learned (Resnick, 1987).

Good thinkers value collective thinking.

Knowledge

One of the debates in the thinking literature is whether thinking skills should be taught separately or in the context of traditional school subjects. Those who argue for teaching specific skills believe that general thinking skills apply across subject areas. Instruction on these skills should transfer to other contexts. People who support teaching thinking skills within the context of school subjects agree with Resnick who reports the following:

> Thinking is driven by and supported by knowledge, in the form of both specific facts and organizing principles. This knowledge . . . allows experts in any field to engage in more sophisticated thinking than people new to the field. (1987a, pp. 45–46)

In other words, the more you know and understand in a particular subject, the higher will be the quality of your thinking in that subject.

Certainly there are general thinking skills that apply across disciplines. Resnick calls these "**enabling skills** for learning and thinking" (1987a, p. 46). Many enabling skills are (or could be) built into instruction in any subject area. For instance, the ability to construct meaning and the ability to regulate one's own learning are aspects of good thinking which are stressed in the sciences and social sciences and as essential literacy skills. While instruction in general skills is useful (and will be discussed later in this chapter), instruction which builds knowledge of specific content is essential to good thinking.

Given the current tendency of teachers to rapidly "cover" material in texts and workbooks, it seems important to clarify what it means "to know." It is not enough to expose students to content, to pile up a load of facts and figures. If students are to become good thinkers, they must possess (and pursue the development of) well-integrated bodies of understandings (**knowledge**). O'Brien explained that "one's knowledge . . . resembles a fabric—a network of information, images, relationships, errors, hypotheses . . . and so forth" (1989, p. 362).

While it is possible for students to stockpile bits of information which they can reproduce on a test if the right question is asked, those bits are not knowledge but isolated pieces which float around in the head. Because these bits of knowledge are not anchored to other understandings, they are likely to drift out of reach. Resnick and Klopfer help to explain what it means **to possess knowledge** as opposed to lists of facts: "To know something is not just to have received information but also to have interpreted it and related it to other knowledge" (Resnick & Klopfer, 1989a, p. 4). Knowledge networks support and direct people's thinking. If students are to be good thinkers, they must have multiple opportunities to broaden and deepen these networks.

Critical and Creative Capacity

The phrases *critical thinking* and *creative thinking* are not easy to define. It has taken us a long time to reach an understanding of these aspects of thinking. Essentially, we have concluded that good thinking is both critical and creative.

We agree with Marzano, Brandt, Hughes, Jones, Presseisen, Rankin, and Suhor (1988) who wrote that critical and creative thinking cannot be described by listing a series of stages (p. 17). Instead, the terms *creative* and *critical* are "descriptions of the way [thinking] processes are carried out" (p. 32). In other words, when we think, we sometimes do so critically and creatively. Critical and creative thinking, then, are terms which describe the quality of thought. Good thinking has a critical and creative character.

Are we saying that good thinking must be critical and creative simultaneously? Aren't these opposite kinds of thinking? Actually it is a mistake to think of critical and creative thinking as opposites: "The two types of thinking are not opposites; they complement each other and even share many attributes. . . . school programs and practices should reflect the understanding that highly creative thinking is often highly critical and vice versa" (Marzano et al., 1988, pp. 17–18). Both are essential in the "production of valuable products" (Bailin, 1988, p. 61). Before we look at how critical and creative thinking work together, let's look at the features of each.

Critical and **creative thinking** share a number of the *features of higher-order thinking* (Resnick, 1987a). For instance, both are complex, effortful, and often yield multiple solutions. Both involve making judgments and imposing meaning on a body of information. Beyond these general characteristics, certain features of each kind of thinking may be noted.

Critical thinking is often thought of as "reasonable, reflective thinking that is focused on deciding what to believe or do" (Ennis, 1985, p. 54). Siegel emphasizes that a critical thinker "is *appropriately moved by reasons*" (1988, p. 32). By this Siegel means that the critical thinker "seeks reasons on which to base her assessments, judgments, and actions" (p. 33). This kind of thinker identifies questions, strives to analyze arguments carefully, seeks valid evidence, and draws sound conclusions.

There are several **components of creative thinking**:

1. attention to the nature of a problem and the purpose of a task
2. commitment to aesthetic qualities of scientific theories, mathematical systems, artistic works, and so forth
3. ability to reframe ideas
4. intrinsic motivation and locus of evaluation
5. inclination to work at the edge of one's competence (Marzano et al., 1988; Perkins, 1984)

The first component demonstrates the *importance of critical thinking to creativity*. In order to be creative, a person must clarify and evaluate the problematic situation. The second component highlights the *importance of knowledge to creative behavior*. The creative person knows enough to be able to move beyond knowing facts and rules associated with a topic to appreciating its intricacies, complexities, and special beauty. Knowledge of the topic is also helpful in reframing ideas, or shifting the problem so that it may be seen from another perspective. To do this the creative person draws upon deep knowledge of the subject to develop models, metaphors, or analogies to represent the idea. The fourth component—intrinsic motivation and locus of evaluation—refers to the importance of the creative person's drive, and trust in personal evaluation standards. This internal drive and self-trust is related to the fifth component, the inclination to work at the edge of one's competence. Creative people "maintain high standards, accept confusion, uncertainty, and the higher risks of failure as part of the processes, and learn to view failure as normal, even interesting, and challenging" (Perkins, 1984, p.19).

When reading about critical and creative thinking, you may have noticed similarities with reflective thinking. Recall that reflection is a cyclical process (plan-act-observe-make judgments) that is governed by certain attitudes (introspection, responsibility for decisions and actions, open-mindedness) and abilities (viewing from multiple perspectives, searching for alternative explanations, using adequate evidence to make and evaluate decisions). Critical and creative thinking are integral parts of reflection. Throughout the reflection cycle, the thinker balances the analytical, evidence-driven quality of critical thinking and the generative, reframing quality of creative thinking. Finding answers to questions requires the contributions of both kinds of thinking. Let's look closely at the way these kinds of thinking work together.

It is helpful when trying to grasp the connection between critical and creative aspects of good thinking to imagine a real-life episode. For instance, imagine that you are engaged in a debate about a controversial topic. You are determined that your friend will agree with you. So, you listen carefully to your friend's argument and point out flaws in reasoning. You assess your friend's arguments on the basis of reasons, but in order to do so effectively, you engage in creative thought. That is, you must do more than evaluate what your friend says. As Scriven wrote, "The very process of criticism necessarily involves the creative activity of generating new theories or hypotheses to explain phenomena that have seemed to other people to admit of only one explanation" (1976, p. 36). Good thinking, then, is both critical and creative.

We can also look at the convergence of critical and creative thinking by beginning with what on the surface appears to be a creative act. Bailin argues that creativity "involves skills deployed with imagination and imagination directed by skill. And it employs rational processes of thought which involve judgment, criticism and hence the possibility for evolution" (1988, p. 131). Imagine an artist creating a painting. While creating a painting seems to be a perfect example of creative thinking, the product is unlikely to be extraordinary unless the artist thinks critically about the project. The artist must make judgments about composition, color, materials, light, size, and so forth. Skill and knowledge about the visual arts enable the artist to produce something which others look at and call "creative." In other words, the artist exercises considerable skill, judgment, and knowledge in order to create.

Metacognition

The fourth component of good thinking is its metacognitive nature. **Metacognition** means being aware of one's thinking while performing tasks and

FOCUS BOX 7–2

Practical Application Activities

Activity 1:   What kinds of social, political, and economic topics can elementary students think about and take action toward understanding and remedying? List five topics which realistically could be addressed in an elementary classroom.

Activity 2:   Observe in an elementary classroom for one day. Make a list of each activity observed. For each activity or lesson, record the following:

- What happened during the lesson? (i.e., What did children do? What did the teacher do?)
- What assignments were the children asked to complete? (Obtain copies if possible)

Compare your observations with those of two or three of your peers by answering the following questions:

- Of the lessons that you observed, which ones seemed to promote the development of knowledge (i.e., well-integrated bodies of knowledge)? Support your answer with evidence.
- Which lessons seemed to simply "cover" isolated skills and facts? Support your answer with evidence.
- If the day you observed was typical of the instruction provided within this classroom, what conclusions would you draw about the importance of the development of thinking within this classroom?

Activity 3:   With a partner, select one of the following situations and explain how critical and creative thinking might operate together to produce an outstanding outcome:

- writing a movie review
- diagnosing a rare illness
- teaching a young child to sleep through the night
- preparing a gourmet meal

---

subsequently using this awareness to exert control over one's behavior. According to Flavell:

> Metacognition refers to one's knowledge concerning one's own cognitive processes and products or anything related to them. . . . For example, I am engaging in metacognition . . . if I notice that I am having more trouble learning A than B. . . . Metacognition refers, among other things, to the active monitoring and consequent regulation and orchestration of these processes . . . usually in the service of some concrete goal or objective. (1976, p. 232)

Metacognition, then involves knowledge and control (1) of self and (2) of one's cognitive processes which enable good thinkers to regulate, direct, and improve their cognitive activity and, consequently, the products of that activity (Paris & Winograd, 1990).

Knowledge and control of self encompass one's commitment to the task, attitudes toward learning, and awareness of attentional levels. People have the power to commit themselves to a task, to decide to work hard. Similarly, one's attitudes toward learning influence one's behavior. For example, individuals who have an *internal locus of control* (i.e., believing that they control their fate) are more likely to work hard and succeed than individuals who have an external locus of control (i.e., believing that outside forces control their lives). Finally, people can be aware of and control their attentional level. Tasks and events require different amounts of attention. Successful learners adjust their attention, giving more to important aspects of tasks and less to the trivial aspects.

The second aspect of metacognition is **knowledge and control of metacognitive processes**. As Marzano et al. (1988) have summarized, this aspect of metacognition includes three types of knowledge: (1) knowledge about the nature of the task, (2) knowledge of how to do the strategies necessary to accomplish the task, and (3) knowledge of when and why to use which strategies. In order to exert metacognitive control, learners must know *what* to do, *how* to do the necessary procedures, and *when* a procedure is appropriate for the specific situation at hand.

Knowledge and control of the metacognitive process also involves self-assessment, planning, and revision. Self-assessment takes place before, during, and after a task. *Before* doing a task, one asks questions such as: Have I done a task like this before? Do I understand what is expected? *During* the task, one asks: Did I get the main idea of that paragraph? Am I working toward accomplishing the goal? *After* the task, one asks: Did I do my best? Do I understand? Planning is related to self-assessment. Planning involves choosing strategies to meet specific goals formulated through self-assessment. (Remember, self-assessment takes place before, during, and after a task.) Revision occurs when self-assessment reveals that the strategies used were inadequate. Good thinkers continually self-assess and revise their plans as necessary. Not only are they active cognitively, but also they are aware of their cognitive activity and exercise control over it.

To summarize, we noted that good thinking requires the watchful, self-regulation known as metacognition. Certain dispositions are also necessary because having the skill to think well without the will to do so renders the skill worthless. Sound knowledge is essential because knowledge drives thinking. Good thinking incorporates critical and creative activity. Later in this chapter we shall discuss the implications of this definition of good thinking for teaching practice. First, however, we shall consider why thinking is an important educational aim.

Why Is Good Thinking an Important Educational Aim?

For years, helping students become good thinkers has been a valued educational aim. Perhaps the main reason this goal has topped the list of so many local, state, and national committees has to do with our political system. The survival of democracy depends on the contributions of its citizens. When the people stop participating, decision making gradually is assumed by the few rather than the many. What kind of participation is necessary? Well, simply obeying the law, while desirable, is not sufficient to ensure a healthy and productive democracy. Glaser observed that good citizenship within a democracy requires: "the attainment of a working understanding of our social, political, and economic arrangements and . . . the ability to think critically about issues concerning which there may be an honest difference of opinion" (1941, p. 5).

Recall the discussion of democratic ideals in Chapter 1. We explained that preparing future citizens entails more than instruction about political structures, voting, and individual rights. Citizenship also means commitment to working "towards the creation of a more compassionate, caring and socially just world" (Goodman, 1992, p. 226). Citizens must be good thinkers in order to examine the circumstances and conditions of people's lives and to work toward a good and just society. The importance of this issue is probably the reason that citizenship education has become a unifying thread for social studies education (Brophy, 1990).

Other reasons why this aim is important lie in the nature of our society. The movement from the industrial era into the information age has brought a tidal wave of information and new technologies. Successful participation in this kind of world requires good thinking. The National Science Board Commission on Pre-College Education in Mathematics, Science, and Technology has called for an expansion of the "basics" to include problem-solving and critical thinking so that people can understand and live productively in our technological world. Familiarity with subject matter cannot guarantee success when the **information half-life** (i.e., the period of time during which half of the information in a field becomes outdated) of certain fields is as short as 6 years (McTighe & Schollenberger, 1985).

According to McTighe and Schollenberger, "A different strategy is in order— one that emphasizes developing the life-long *learning* and *thinking* skills necessary to acquire and process information within an ever-expanding field of knowledge" (1985, p. 4). These skills involve the ability to locate, analyze, synthesize, and evaluate information.

Another aspect of our society which creates a demand for good thinkers is the increasing complexity of our problems. There are no simple answers to the problems of hunger, environmental collapse, and the nuclear arms race. As Webb and Sherman have argued, "We need a generalized intelligence . . . to see us through the pressing problems of our time. . . . Our future as a nation and as a species is bleak indeed" (1989, p. 376) if we fail to help *all* future citizens become good thinkers.

While there are social, political, and economic reasons to suggest good thinking as an educational aim, there are also important personal reasons. Siegel stated, "We seek to *empower* the student to control her destiny and to *create* her future, not submit to it" (1988, p. 57). Good thinkers are likely to be **empowered**. They will be able to take charge of their lives, to shape their futures in a manner satisfactory to them. Good thinkers are "liberated," in the sense that they are "free from the unwarranted and undesirable control of unjustified beliefs, insupportable attitudes, and paucity of abilities, which can prevent [them] from competently taking charge of [their own lives]" (Siegel, 1988, p. 58). In short, teachers who help students become good thinkers provide them the means to direct their life course.

A related rationale for promoting good thinking is derived from the belief that teachers "are morally obliged to treat students . . . with respect" (Siegel, 1988, p. 56). Siegel explains that treating students with respect includes "recognizing and honoring the student's right to question, to challenge, and to demand reasons and justifications for what is being taught" (p. 56). By this argument, teachers have a moral obligation to value and respect students' rights to have some control over their learning.

The reasons for making the promotion of good thinking an important educational aim range from the global to the personal. Together they provide a powerful rationale for infusing thinking into the curriculum. While many have given lip service to the importance of thinking, the degree to which this aim has been accomplished is another story. In the next section we will look at the current situation in schools and see why the generally agreed-upon aim of teaching for thinking is realized so infrequently.

What Is the Current Situation in Schools?

Goodlad's (1984) study of more than 1,000 elementary-, middle-, and high-school classrooms across the country is often used to provide a view of the nature of instruction in public school classrooms during the 1980s. Goodlad's research team reported that a "preoccupation with the lower intellectual processes" was found in all subject areas. Although all of the state educational documents stressed the development of thinking, Goodlad noted that the teachers focused on facts, skills, drill, and practice:

> Only rarely did we find evidence to suggest instruction likely to go much beyond mere possession of information to a level of understanding its implications and either applying it or exploring its possible applications. Nor did we see activities likely to arouse students' curiosity or to involve them in seeking solutions to some problem not already laid bare by teacher or textbook. (Goodlad, 1984, p. 236)

More intensive studies of a small number of classrooms have revealed a similar pattern. Johnson (1985) found isolated and intensely competitive seatwork to be the norm. Teachers delivered worksheets, students worked on their own to get as many answers right as possible, teachers graded the worksheets, and students moved on to the next one. Often students were chastised for helping one another. Durkin's (1978–79) term *mentioning* (i.e., saying just enough about a topic to enable students to complete an assignment) reflects the same pattern of teaching. Teachers very often are not teaching as much as they are whisking students across workbook pages. It is difficult to imagine how this kind of noninstruction could possibly cultivate good thinking. Critiques of science and social studies education stress similar patterns. For example, a National Science Foundation study reports that science teaching most often involves learning science content by rote from science texts (Brinckerhoff, 1989). Similarly, critics of social studies education report that too much emphasis is placed on textbooks and drill of isolated facts and skills (Brophy, 1990).

The results of assessments of students' ability to think indicate that the current curriculum has indeed failed to cultivate good thinking in many young people. For instance, while the majority of fourth, eighth, and eleventh graders could write informative compositions, only 20 to 25 percent could write analytically (Applebee, Langer, & Mullis, 1986). That is, most students were unable to provide evidence to support their positions or compare and contrast their positions with those of others. Findings are similar in the assessment of reading ability (The Reading Report Card, 1971–1984). While students perform well on basic reading tasks, many perform poorly on tasks requiring higher-level skills, such as analyzing and synthesizing unfamiliar material. This generalization also may be applied to math performance. Students of all ages have been found to handle straightforward calculations better than problems requiring reasoning (Carpenter, Corbitt, Kepner, Lindquist, & Reys, 1981).

Despite widespread agreement about the importance of thinking, many teachers still teach in ways that are inconsistent with this aim. Why? The answer lies in part in certain conditions of schooling, many of which we have discussed in earlier chapters. For instance, accountability and time pressures influence what teachers do and don't do in their classrooms. As Resnick and Klopfer point out, "With only a few exceptions, the tests now in place were not designed to support the Thinking Curriculum" (1989b, p. 209). Teachers perceive tremendous pressure to have their students perform well on criterion-referenced and standardized tests, and many perceive that "tests drive the curriculum." Much of what is covered in class can be traced directly to one test or another.

Time pressures are closely related to accountability. Teachers must cover an ever-increasing amount of information in a fixed time period. Each year it seems something new gets tacked on (e.g., economics, career education, safety, sex education). It's no wonder teachers neglect parts of the curriculum. Typically, they neglect those subjects on which students are not tested. If they do not have time for everything, teachers commonly neglect the subjects for which they are not held accountable.

Clearly, many teachers do not incorporate thinking into their curriculum because they believe there are too many other things to do. However, another reason thinking has been neglected is that teachers are not sure how to promote thinking. We think that certain kinds of instructional practices can help students become good thinkers. However, if these practices are to be effective, they must take place in an environment which supports and encourages good thinking. Before we describe the kind of instruction that can promote good thinking, we shall describe the kind of classroom climate in which good thinking is likely to thrive.

Classroom Climate

Classroom climate is the tone or feel of a classroom. The details of classroom life combine to create a distinct atmosphere: Does the classroom seem tense? caring? businesslike? chaotic? Classrooms conducive to good thinking could be characterized as "safe" and as evidencing a "spirit of inquiry."

Safety

Rogers (1961) believed psychological safety and freedom were necessary attributes of an environment conducive to good thinking. Marzano et al. explain, "We foster **psychological safety** when we accept people as being of unconditional worth, when we create an atmosphere of empathy and understanding rather than external evaluation. We foster **psychological freedom** when we permit the individual freedom of . . . expression" (1988, p. 31). Many communication techniques contribute to the psychological safety and freedom of a classroom (see the discussion on classroom management in Chapter 9). Ginott's (1971) sane messages, Gordon's (1970) language of acceptance, Dreikurs' (1968) emphasis on encouragement and the motives behind misbehavior, and Glasser's (1965) classroom meetings all contribute to the creation of a safe environment conducive to good thinking.

Ginott (1971) believed that adults' communication styles shape children's self-concepts. He advocated the use of **sane messages**, or comments that address a student's behavior rather than judge a student's character. He encouraged adults to speak respectfully to children and to avoid blaming, preaching, commanding, accusing, belittling, and threatening. Gordon (1970) promoted the use of techniques such as **passive listening, door openers,** and **active listening** to communicate to children that they are accepted. Gordon's three techniques are explained in Focus Box 7–3. He believed healthy development requires that children believe the adults in their environment accept them as they are. Gordon encouraged teachers to use "**I-messages**" in which teachers communicate their feelings to students and let students know that they trust children to use good judgment to modify their troublesome behavior (e.g., I feel frustrated when you all talk at once and I have to stop my lesson).

Dreikurs (1968) suggested that teachers determine the motivation behind children's misbehavior and provide continual encouragement. When the teacher understands a child's motives, the teacher and child can work collaboratively to solve problems. Dreikurs' strategies communicate respect, trust, and caring. When encouraged, a child develops confidence and inner strength. By helping students to recognize the motives behind their misbehavior, teachers help students develop self-understanding and self-discipline. Finally, Glasser (1965) suggested techniques such as class meetings to discuss problems. This kind of strategy focuses on making children responsible for their behavior. In class meetings, children also develop a sense of group responsibility; that is, they learn to consider the rights and responsibilities of all class members instead of focusing on personal preferences.

FOCUS BOX 7–3

Gordon's Communication Strategies*

Passive listening: Saying nothing while a speaker is talking can help the speaker feel accepted. Listening without questioning, challenging, or correcting can communicate that the listener is concerned about the speaker's feelings and wants to understand the speaker's point of view. Because this is not a conversation, the listener can devote total attention to trying to understand the speaker's concerns. This kind of nonjudgmental listening promotes communication in the future.

Active listening: By listening actively the listener "tries to understand what [the speaker] is feeling or what his message means. Then he puts his understanding into his own words . . . and feeds it back for the [speaker's] verification. The [listener] does not send a message of [his] own. . . . [He] feeds back only what [he] feels the [speaker's] message meant" (Gordon, p. 53). Once a speaker believes that listeners care about what he thinks or feels (and this acceptance can be communicated through passive listening), he may be ready to be listened to actively. The listener must attend closely to the speaker's words in order to interpret them and then verify the interpretation with the speaker. Active listening enables a listener and a speaker to construct mutual understanding of the speaker's perspective. Gordon warns against destructive responses to the speaker. These include ordering, warning, preaching, advising, lecturing, criticizing, praising, ridiculing, diagnosing, consoling, questioning, and distracting. These sorts of responses are destructive in that they carry the risk of "causing the [speaker] to stop talking, making him feel guilty or inadequate, reducing his self-esteem, producing defensiveness, triggering resentment, [and] making him feel unaccepted" (Gordon, p. 47).

Using door openers: When a speaker is reluctant to talk, the listener can send "invitations to say more" (Gordon, p. 47) by responding to students' comments in ways that do

---

One way to promote a climate of safety, then, is through caring, respectful communication. When students feel valued, they are likely to believe the classroom is a safe place. In such an environment they may feel free to question, to wonder, to step into uncertain territory. While it may seem obvious, it is worth adding that the safety of the classroom is enhanced when students know and trust one another. In the social skills chapter (Chapter 6) we discussed the importance of helping students get to know one another, developing a sense of groupness, and helping students feel a sense of school membership. Students are likely to feel safer when they feel connected to school and to their classmates.

A Spirit of Inquiry

Glatthorn and Baron assert, "The classroom where thinking is fostered is one where inquiry is valued" (1985, p. 52). Words such as *open, seeking,* and *challeng-*

not pass judgment. The simplest of these are the "noncommittal responses" (Gordon, p. 48) such as:

I see.	Really.
Oh.	You don't say.
Mm Hmmm.	No fooling.
How about that?	You did, huh.
Interesting.	Is that so!

Other door openers are more direct invitations for the speaker to say more:

Tell me about it.
I'd like to hear about it.
Tell me more.
I'd be interested in your point of view.
Would you like to talk about it?
Let's discuss it.
Let's hear what you have to say.
Tell me the whole story.
Sounds like you've got something to say about this.
This seems like something important to you.

When listeners use door openers, they keep their own thoughts and feelings out of the conversation, thereby conveying acceptance of and respect for the speaker and the speaker's thoughts and feelings. By encouraging the speaker to say more, the listener has a better chance of understanding the speaker's perspective.

Adapted from *P.E.T.: Parent Effectiveness Training* by T. Gordon, 1970, New York: Peter H. Wyden.

ing might capture the spirit of this classroom. Three guidelines can be followed to promote a **spirit of inquiry**. To help you envision implementation of the guidelines, we provide some practices that exemplify them.

First, the teacher must *value good thinking*. The teacher should talk about thinking and point out examples of good thinking by focusing on the *thinking* rather than the result (e.g., a correct answer). For example, students might identify and talk about examples of good thinking among fictional characters or people they know.

Second, the teacher should *direct discussions in ways that encourage good thinking*. Suggested practices include the following: (1) Emphasize asking questions and finding problems instead of providing correct answers. For instance, have students pose questions about subjects and then about the "answers" they discover through their study; that is, discourage students from accepting the first answer they find. (2) Slow the pace of discussion in order to provide time to think about the questions you pose and to pose questions to one another. (3) Encourage multidirectional communication by helping students listen to and respond to one another. Students could be required to summarize the preceding participant's comments before adding their own comments. They could also be required to clarify how their contribution is related. Teachers might also occasionally force themselves to remain quiet and avoid making eye contact with speakers. This practice encourages students to look at other students (Shor, 1980).

The third guideline is that teachers must *model good thinking*. Teacher modeling helps students identify what good thinkers do. We summarize three of the teacher behaviors which model good thinking for students (Marzano et al., 1988). (1) Teachers should stress diverse viewpoints in discussions. The teacher should model consideration of alternative solutions to problems and alternative interpretations of ideas and events. (2) Teacher should talk about how they make up their minds about a subject, stressing the importance of collecting evidence to support a position. This technique, often called a **"think-aloud"** enables the teachers to share their thinking with students. ("I've been using disposable dia-

FOCUS BOX 7–4

Practical Application Activities

Activity 1:   If possible spend a day observing in an elementary classroom. Otherwise, think about a classroom with which you are familiar.

1. Identify specific teacher behaviors that contribute to a climate of safety. List as many behaviors as you can, and indicate how they contribute to a climate of safety.

2. Can you also identify teaching practices which undermine the goal of establishing a safe climate? Again, be specific and indicate why you believe these practices undermine this goal.

3. If possible, indicate how students respond to these practices.

Activity 2:   In order to promote a spirit of inquiry, teachers incorporate practices such as those suggested in this chapter in their daily practice. To help you think about what this might mean, try the following:

1. First, make a list communicating what the suggested practices would look like in a small-group reading lesson.

2. Work with two or three peers to compare your lists and to critique them.

   • Did one or more of you omit important suggestions? Why?

   • Do any of the suggestions seem unrealistic or impractical? How could they be adapted?

pers, but I'm starting to wonder whether this is environmentally healthy. Disposables are so easy—but I don't want to contribute to our environmental problems. How can I find out whether using disposables is really an environmental hazard?") (3) Teachers should change their positions when the evidence warrants and be willing to admit mistakes. Similarly, it is important that teachers demonstrate a willingness to admit uncertainty. Teachers should let students know when they are unsure about something and share with them a possible course of action for gathering the necessary information. ("Are brontosaurus, apatosaurus, seizmosaurus, and ultrasaurus all different species of dinosaur? How could we find out?")

Notice how the four components of good thinking are represented in the suggestion that teachers model good thinking (Marzano et al., 1988). For example, critical and creative activity are apparent in the suggestions that teachers stress diverse viewpoints in discussions and that they stress the importance of collecting evidence to support a position. Do you also see evidence of the knowledge component? the dispositions component? the metacognition component? Look back over the other things the teacher can do to promote a spirit of inquiry in the classroom. Note evidence of each of the components of good thinking.

In safe classrooms where thinking is valued, students have opportunities to develop thinking skill. Remember, though, that developing the habit of good thinking is perhaps even more important than developing the skills. Just as reading skill is of little value to a person who never chooses to read, the ability to think well is useless if not coupled with the will to think. When teachers foster a spirit of inquiry, they may help shape students' dispositions for thinking.

Evaluation and the Classroom Climate

We have yet to say anything about how student evaluation is related to a classroom climate that supports good thinking. Teachers send mixed messages to students if they promote good thinking during lessons but test students for low-level recall of information (Barell, 1985). Students quickly come to see what is truly valued. If teachers value good thinking, they must incorporate it in tests and other evaluations of student work. While students' knowledge of facts can be checked through true/false, matching, and fill-in-the-blank questions, their ability to think about, integrate, and apply facts must be tapped through more elaborate oral, written, and artistic responses.

Now that we have established the general setting for fostering good thinking, we are ready to discuss the characteristics of teaching practices which promote good thinking. In describing a climate for instruction, we have already hinted at these characteristics. Completing the activity in Focus Box 7–5 may help you to clarify your entering thoughts about teaching for thinking before you begin to examine ours.

FOCUS BOX 7–5

Take a Moment to Reflect

Think of a lesson or activity you have observed that you believe promotes good thinking. What elements of the lesson promoted good thinking?

Then, think of a lesson or activity that did not promote good thinking. Why did it fail?

Compare your answers to those developed by one or more of your peers. Then do the following:

- List similarities and differences between the lessons/activities which seem to promote good thinking and those which do not.
- Draw tentative conclusions about how to promote and squelch good thinking.

What Can Teachers Do to Help Students Become Good Thinkers?

Teaching students to be good thinkers means that we want them to develop certain *dispositions*, add depth and breadth to their *knowledge* networks, develop their *critical and creative* capacities, and develop their *metacognitive ability*. As we consider practices which promote good thinking, keep these components of good thinking in mind as they help us to think clearly about what we hope to accomplish.

The model of instruction that we shall describe integrates the teaching of thinking with standard school subjects. This is important for several reasons. First, there is no time in the school day for another subject area. Second, research in all subjects suggests the importance of increased focus on thinking and reasoning skills to develop knowledge (as opposed to a collection of isolated facts). Third, isolating instruction for thinking from subject matter is probably not an effective approach to the development of thinking skills. As Resnick noted, "Cognitive research yields repeated demonstrations that specific content area knowledge plays a central role in reasoning, thinking, and learning of all kinds. . . . Such an understanding raises questions about the wisdom of attempting to develop thinking skills outside the context of specific knowledge domains" (1987, p. 18). Regular subject matter instruction can build enabling skills (i.e., skills which facilitate learning and thinking across many subject areas inside and outside of school). From the earliest grades, teachers can develop students' thinking abilities by teaching school subjects "in ways that engage mental elaboration and self-regulation" (Resnick & Klopfer, 1989, p. 4).

What kind of instruction promotes good thinking? Prawat (1989) suggested three general characteristics of good instruction. Prawat's framework describes the kind of instruction which helps learners construct knowledge. This framework is consistent with teaching practices described in earlier chapters. We are suggesting that Prawat's attributes of instruction are also helpful to teachers who hope to promote good thinking as we have defined it. Prawat argues that instruction that is (1) *focused and coherent*, (2) *interactive*, and (3) *analytic* helps learners construct knowledge. We think that Prawat's framework also can help students develop the other three components of good thinking: dispositions, critical and creative capacity, and metacognition.

Focused and Coherent Instruction

Focused and coherent instruction centers on key ideas and connections among ideas. **Focused instruction** provides thorough development of main ideas or concepts rather than covering masses of information. **Coherent instruction** builds connections between lessons and helps learners see these connections. When instruction is focused and coherent, learning experiences are woven together within and across school days. Key ideas receive thorough treatment and are not lost in a flood of unrelated content. When instruction is focused and coherent, it can promote all four components of good thinking. First, let's see what focused and coherent instruction looks like. Then let's see how this kind of instruction can promote thinking.

Even teachers pressured to implement multiple curricula can provide focused and coherent instruction. Some teachers organize instruction around themes

Focused and coherent activities promote conceptual development and good thinking.

(**thematic teaching**) in order to build connections across classroom activities. For example, a second-grade class might study whales for 3 weeks. Although technically part of the science curriculum, the topic is used to integrate experiences across the curriculum. The teacher's goals include wanting students to understand the role of whales in the ecological system and to value and respect this unique life form. To accomplish these goals the students engage in multiple activities across traditional subject areas and meet language, math, social studies, science, and art objectives. For example, students might construct a replica of the ecological environment necessary for survival of whales, write a letter to a senator explaining environmental hazards for whales, and/or prepare a chart demonstrating the amount of food required by a whale for a week.

It is important to note that a thematic unit does not necessarily provide focused and coherent instruction. That is, teachers can have students do lots of activities that are loosely connected to the topic "Whales," but fail to provide focused and coherent instruction. An obvious example would be asking students to do math problems on a sheet of paper shaped like a whale. Less obvious would be asking students to memorize a list of facts about whales or to learn spelling words related to whales. While either of these later activities could be useful if embedded within a meaningful activity such as those suggested previously, neither provides focus or coherence if presented as an isolated activity. It is essential that the teacher identify the key understandings to guide the development of learning experiences which help students develop these understandings. As students develop key understandings, they construct related skills and understandings from various subject areas. The teacher's goal is to probe the topic in enough depth and to maintain a clear connection across activities so that students understand how the pieces of their experiences fit together and are able to construct new knowledge and attitudes.

Key processes or concepts which are applicable in different contexts also can make the curriculum more coherent. For instance, processes such as estimating, hypothesizing, classifying, and observing are useful in many school and real-world activities. Rather than treating these processes as peculiar to a specific topic, teachers can help students recognize their role in other contexts. For example, students might consider the similarities and differences between the observations made by artists and those made by scientists. Students might brainstorm all the uses of classification in school subjects and in real life.

Similarly, concepts which are taught as part of one subject area can be used to interpret phenomena in multiple contexts. For instance, the concept of main idea, though typically addressed in the language arts curriculum, is relevant in all subject areas and in students' real-world experiences. The concept of "community" is relevant across subject areas, as is the concept of "balance." The point is that concepts and processes are understood more fully when applied in different contexts. By helping students make these connections, teachers make instruction focused and coherent.

Even simple workbook modifications can improve focus and coherence. For instance, we have seen teachers cluster all pages on a skill and allocate several days in a row to the skill rather than touching on it several times over the course of a few months. In this case, the skill receives thorough treatment, and the students have a prolonged rather than a fleeting opportunity to master it.

Carefully selecting children's literature to read to the class can also improve focus and coherence. Teachers can help students recognize concepts and use skills that are being developed in other contexts. For example, in *Alligator Cookies* by James Young, two children read a recipe and assemble the ingredients to make cookies. They are so intent on finding the key ingredient that they fail to observe carefully as they dash from place to place. In addition to being enjoyable, the book provides an opportunity to talk about observing, a skill typically reserved for science or art lessons. Other typical math and science concepts and skills can be related to the characters' experience preparing cookies. A common reading and math skill, sequencing, can be discussed in the context of following the recipe.

You may be wondering what focus and coherence would look like in a basic skills lesson, since elementary teachers spend so much time working in the areas of reading, writing, and mathematics. Essentially, in a focused and coherent lesson the teacher rejects "skill hopping" in favor of logically developed instruction grounded in real reading, writing, or mathematics activity. Also, the teacher refers to students' prior knowledge and experience in an effort to help them assimilate the new information and skills. The following reading lesson illustrates the fragmented, skill hopping that teachers should try to avoid:

> Mr. Gregory has students read the new vocabulary words in unison, and he repeats the word *magic* for them. Although all of the students did not say the words, he moves on to have them read the first page of the story aloud. He then asks the students the questions included in the teacher's manual. After the story, he directs them to three workbook pages. He asks them for examples of words with the initial "ch" sound, and then they complete one page together. For the other two pages, one of which deals with the new vocabulary and the other with finding details, the group does a sample item. The students finish the pages independently.

During this reading group, the students read vocabulary words, read each page and answer questions, complete a workbook page on the "ch" digraph, and receive directions for two more workbook pages. This lesson is not well-integrated; it is composed of a number of separate steps which the teacher does not help the students to connect. In focused and coherent reading instruction, the reading material serves to integrate the instruction. That is, all teacher and student activity centers on the text. Activity makes sense to students because it is carried out in the meaningful context of real reading. The following example of reading instruction illustrates focused and coherent instruction which takes place after the group has silently read a page of text. The teacher uses reciprocal teaching strategies to focus the lesson (Palincsar & Brown, 1984). From past modeling by the teacher, students have learned that they respond to a page by asking a potential test question on the passage, summarizing the content, clarifying any difficult parts, and predicting future content.

Mrs. Gregory:	Who would like to be the teacher? Okay, Mark?
Mark:	Do I do a question first?
Mrs. Gregory:	Sure, that's fine.
Mark:	Okay, um—Mr. Fig did what—um—um.
Mrs. Gregory:	What do you want to ask about, Mark?
Mark:	The magic.
Mrs. Gregory:	Can you start the question with the words, *What kind*?
Mark:	What kind of magic did Mr. Fig do?
Mrs. Gregory:	I think you've got it!
Nadia:	It was a good kind of magic. Happy magic.
Mark:	That's right. And now, the page was about um—Mr. Fig does happy magic in the afternoon.
Mrs. Gregory:	And how did you figure out such a good summary, Mark?
Mark:	Well, the important ideas are Mr. Fig and the magic in the afternoon. So, I just put them together in a sentence.
Sherrie:	And that it was *happy* magic, too.
Mrs. Gregory:	Okay, teacher, what's next?
Mark:	Well, there weren't any tricky parts on this page, so I guess I'll just do the prediction. [*He looks at the next page.*] It's a new story, so what should I do?
Mrs. Gregory:	Well, could you still make a prediction, using what you already know about Mr. Fig?
Mark:	Well, it's called "The Lost Mouse." It could be about Mr. Fig using magic to find the mouse.
Mrs. Gregory:	What do the rest of you think about that prediction?
Dwayne:	I think it's good because we just found out about the magic, so next we might find out how he uses the magic.
Josh:	Yeah, and on the cover he's with animals, so animals might be his friends.
Mrs. Gregory:	You mean if a mouse was lost, Mr. Fig would probably want to find it.
Josh:	Yeah, because it's his friend.

Several things make this lesson focused. First, all activity is focused on the story. Second, the teacher focuses on a small number of reading strategies—predicting, clarifying, summarizing, and self-questioning. Each of these strategies plays an important role in skilled reading and in skilled performance in other areas. The teacher makes the lesson coherent by prompting the students to draw on knowledge they already have to help them answer new questions. The teacher helps the students see that there are important connections between their experiences, their prior knowledge, and new understandings.

To summarize and extend what we have said, we offer the following practices that can improve the focus and coherence of instruction:

1. Always help students see how what they are currently studying is related to things they have already studied.

2. Sequence topics within and across subject areas so that they develop logically and reinforce each other. This may mean changing the order of topics in textbooks.

3. Identify the major ideas in each subject area and plan to spend more time on these than on the trivia. If you cover the trivia at all, it should be related to the major ideas so that students know where it fits in the larger scheme of things. Identifying major ideas is a project to undertake as a grade level team. It would be exciting if entire schools would identify major ideas in and across subject areas and provide focused and coherent instruction across grade levels!

4. Make review a regular part of your instruction. Help students piece together lessons to form coherent wholes.

5. Have students keep learning logs in which they make sense of what they are learning. In these logs students should address questions such as the following: What am I learning from these activities? What was the purpose of this lesson? What do I already know about this topic? What am I confused about? How does what I am learning in social studies relate to my science lessons? The questions should help students focus on main ideas and integrate understandings across lessons.

Now that we have described focused and coherent instruction, let's see how it promotes the four components of good thinking. Recall what we said about *knowledge* acquisition. Learners construct understandings as they act on and sort out experiences. If they are to develop their knowledge networks, learners need time and opportunities to build understanding. Quick tours across workbook pages do not enable students to develop knowledge. When instruction is focused and coherent, students are able to build conceptual knowledge which is at the heart of good thinking.

Focused and coherent instruction promotes the development of essential *dispositions* by fostering serious and thoughtful treatment of subject matter. Because the subject matter is examined thoroughly, students have opportunities to think about it individually, in small groups, with a partner, and as a whole class. Because students have time to think, they are more likely to develop positive attitudes toward thinking and an inclination to think than they might when they are rushed through a subject.

Did you notice the *critical and creative thinking* in Mrs. Gregory's reading lesson? Students made judgments and drew conclusions based on evidence and imposed meaning on a bunch of printed symbols. When teachers deal with key ideas in depth, they can encourage students to think critically and creatively about the ideas. This involves having them identify questions; analyze arguments; view ideas and problems from multiple perspectives; reframe ideas by placing them in a new light; seek evidence to support positions; and draw conclusions and generate solutions based on an understanding of the evidence and their goals. (Teachers should help students to see how their beliefs influence their thinking about decisions and solutions.) These critical and creative activities may take place together or a few at a time; they may be undertaken as a whole class, a small group, or as individuals; they may be exercised through writing, speaking and listening, the arts, or any combination of these modes of expression. The point is that focused and coherent instruction provides teachers with opportunities to stimulate and develop students' critical and creative capacity.

Focused and coherent instruction also facilitates *metacognitive growth*. While teachers work to help students develop key ideas, they also work to tune these students into their own learning. This means that teachers help the students to see what kinds of things they do or could do to learn. The students also learn what kinds of things may impede their learning. It is important for students to have knowledge, but it is also important that they understand how they learn so that they may gain control of themselves as learners. Specific techniques to promote metacognitive growth will be described later in the chapter.

When teachers focus on key ideas and the connections among ideas and experiences, they promote good thinking. This kind of instruction may have additional benefits. For example, it may help students understand the usefulness and applicability of what they sometimes view as isolated concepts and skills. Also, it may influence students' attitudes toward school learning by helping them see relationships across content areas and by giving them the time needed to acquire and be able to use new understandings. It may also be that skills learned in one subject will transfer to other subjects when teachers provide coherent instruction. While it is intuitively sensible that transfer will occur when teachers show their students how concepts and skills apply in different contexts, current research on transfer neither confirms nor denies this phenomenon. Further investigations of skill transfer must be done.

FOCUS BOX 7–6

Take a Moment to Reflect

Complete the following activities to help you think more about the nature of coherent and focused instruction.

Activity 1:   Look at each of the following concepts and think of several situations (i.e., subject areas or life situations) in which the concept could be applied:

- audience (typically taught as part of the composing process)
- fact versus opinion (typically taught in reading programs)
- fractions (typically taught in math programs)
- plant and animal adaptability (typically taught in science programs)
- pioneers (typically taught in social studies programs)

For one of the concepts, plan ways to help students apply the understanding in other contexts.

Activity 2:   Turn to Ms. Kaplan's math lesson that was described in Chapter 5. In a small group read the lesson and discuss whether or not it is focused and coherent, and explain why.

Interactive Instruction

The second characteristic of instruction which promotes good thinking is its interactive nature. The reading lesson we included to illustrate focused and coherent instruction also illustrates interactive instruction. By **interactive** we mean that there is sustained, verbal interaction between teacher and student and between student and student. This contrasts with the common classroom discourse pattern of question-answer-evaluation, in which the teacher asks a question, a student supplies an answer, and the teacher judges the correctness of the answer.

As Prawat (1989) explained, not much is known about how classroom interaction should be structured to develop student understanding and thinking. The methods of cognitive apprenticeship (Collins et al., 1989) which we described in the literacy chapter (Chapter 4) help clarify what interactive instruction can, but does not necessarily, look like:

1. **Modeling**—An expert models the process to be learned.
2. **Coaching and Scaffolding**—The expert provides suggestions, feedback, probes, clues, and whatever support (scaffolding) is necessary to help learners move toward expert performance.
3. **Articulation**—Learners explain the knowledge and reasoning used to do the task.
4. **Reflection**—Learners compare their efforts to those of an expert.
5. **Exploration**—Learners apply what they have learned independently in new contexts.

This interactive instructional model is well suited for the teaching and learning of those cognitive processes which are central to capable performance in reading, writing, and mathematics. In Chapter 4 we provided an example which illustrated the interactive (also collaborative) nature of the apprenticeship model. This model can be adapted to promote good thinking in all subject areas. Teachers could ask students to articulate their thinking, to compare their thinking to that of an expert (e.g., a teacher, a guest speaker, an encyclopedia, or a textbook), and to apply new understandings in unfamiliar contexts.

Prawat (1989) also writes about the central role of dialectical discussion in interactive instruction. **Dialectical discourse** describes a process in which knowledge is constructed through classroom dialogue; that is, ideas and opinions are articulated, compared, and contrasted in search of common understandings. Another way to think about it is that the participants negotiate understandings. The teacher serves as a moderator, having students clarify and expand their comments, question one another, and identify and synthesize important points. Shor (1980) notes that in this kind of discussion, student and teacher opinions are articulated and contrasted. The teacher plays important roles in the discussion, but does not dominate it. Shor describes the teacher's "broad spectrum of roles" like this:

> At times, the teacher may simply be a convenor. . . . In other circumstances, the
> teacher may be called upon to be a facilitator of a special study or project needed

> by the class. Still other functions are advocate for a perspective missing in the discussion or adversary to a line of thought or to a kind of oppressive behavior appearing in the discussion. The class may call upon the teacher to be a lecturer . . . which will propel the class across an impasse. On occasion, the teacher may serve as recorder of the sessions, whose minutes enable the class to examine its own learning process. Sometimes the teacher will need to be a mediator for divisive tendencies in the class, and at other times the teacher will be a clearing-house or librarian through which resource materials pass. (1980, p. 102)

In dialectical discourse the students take increasing responsibility for directing the course of their learning (Shor, 1980). While teachers occasionally play a high-profile role, their role is adjusted as the class pursues understanding. Similar to the scaffolding dimension of the cognitive apprenticeship model, the teacher provides only as much support and direction as the learners need—the goal being that learners assume responsibility for their intellectual development.

A final point about dialectical discussions comes from Prawat (1989). He suggests that teachers must establish "the norms of interaction that will govern how members of the group relate to one another" (p. 323). Students must know that they will not be ridiculed or penalized for participating in class discussion. The guidelines suggested for establishing a spirit of inquiry in a classroom will be useful in developing norms of interaction. Additionally, teachers might want assign roles to students. This strategy has been used extensively in cooperative learning research. Students could be assigned roles such as encourager, clarifier, note taker, or time keeper (see Chapter 6).

It may seem as though this kind of teacher-student interaction applies only to instances in which controversial topics are being debated. In fact, it is applicable to many common classroom situations. For instance, after reading a story, students can discuss some aspect of the story. In order to be dialectical, the discussion can be neither a question-and-answer period nor an opportunity for students to unload their opinions. The teacher should encourage students to resolve issues by listening and responding to one another. The same sort of discussion can take place when classroom social problems (e.g., persistent rule-breaking or other disruptive activity) arise.

There are additional practices a teacher can use to increase the amount and improve the quality of classroom interaction. Although we referred to these questioning strategies in Chapter 5, we review them here.

WAIT TIME.   Originally described by Rowe (1974), wait time refers to the time which elapses between asking a question and calling on a student to answer the question. When teachers wait from 3 to 5 seconds, they promote greater student participation and higher levels of thinking. Waiting 3 to 5 seconds provides time for students to consider the question and possible answers, and it encourages students to respond to each other.

CONSISTENCY AND EQUITY.   Classroom research has found that teachers interrupt some students more than others, provide more feedback to some students than others, provide cues and hints to some students and not to others, and ask more questions of some students than others (Good, 1987). Most teachers do not discriminate intentionally. Many call on some students less often and interrupt them more to try and protect them from the ridicule of classmates. Whatever their reasons, when teachers do not provide the same opportunity for growth to all students, they neglect their ethical and moral obligation as teachers. Students pick up messages from their teachers' behavior and quickly learn whom teachers view as capable and whom they see as incompetent. Furthermore, students who are not taught how to participate in discussions are not given the opportunity to progress; the same students who did not participate well in first grade will not participate well in fifth grade.

Rather than covering up students' difficulties, teachers should teach them how to answer questions. For instance, sometimes teachers need only to restate the question, perhaps more slowly. Paraphrasing the question, using simpler or fewer words, may also help a student understand what is being asked. Another technique is to simplify the question by focusing on one part of the original question. In this way, the student is helped to take one step at a time. The teacher can also teach students to be successful by helping them to recognize prior knowledge that can help them answer the question. It may also be valuable for teachers to model answering the question by doing a think-aloud. By sharing their thought processes, teachers demonstrate how one thinks through a question and formulates an answer. For students who lack experience answering questions or who lack confidence in their ability to answer classroom questions, a demonstration of a process to use to answer questions is more useful than giving the answer.

RESPONDING TO STUDENTS' COMMENTS.   The manner in which teachers respond to students' comments influences the level of student thinking (Wassermann, 1987). When teachers agree or disagree with students, offer general praise ("Great," "Very smart"), or cut them off ("That's it, you've got it," "Okay, okay, I get the idea"), they effectively close down student thinking. Such comments inhibit student thinking at the time they are made and may have the long-term effect of discouraging thought. Students quickly learn that there is no need or no time to think in this classroom. They may even learn that it is safer not to think.

By making comments which encourage students to continue to work on an idea, teachers promote higher-level thinking. Wassermann (1987) has summarized several categories of teacher responses that promote thinking. These include having students reflect on and analyze their own ideas, and posing questions that challenge their ideas. When students reflect on their own idea, they "examine the surface dimensions of an idea, . . . replay it in their head" (Wassermann, 1987, p. 464). Examples of teacher responses that require analysis include "asking for examples, asking for a summary, asking about inconsistencies, asking about assumptions underlying an idea, asking about alternatives, asking about ways to classify data, asking about ways to compare data, and asking what data support an idea" (p. 464). Challenging questions, which should be used carefully because they may frustrate students, include "asking the student to generate hypotheses, asking the student to interpret data, asking the student to make judgments and to specify criteria for those judgments, asking the student to apply principles to new situations, asking the student to make predictions, and asking the student to formulate ways to test predictions or hypotheses" (p. 464). Note that these kinds of responses have the potential to promote critical and creative thinking.

In this section of the chapter we pointed out that instruction which promotes thinking should be interactive. Let's consider how interactive instruction promotes each of the four components of good thinking.

Vygotsky (1978) explained that *knowledge* and cognition originate in interactions among individuals and then become internalized. That is, people can work out new understandings through group exploration and examination of ideas. The methods of cognitive apprenticeship further illuminate the role of interactive instruction in the construction of knowledge. By modeling, coaching, and scaffolding, teachers provide learners with the support needed to construct new understanding. By articulating, reflecting, and exploring, learners clarify and elaborate the new understanding. As learners verbalize their thoughts, they are forced to analyze, clarify, and modify their thinking. Hatano and Inagaki explain:

> In the process of trying to convince or teach other students, one has to verbalize or make explicit that which is known only implicitly. One must examine one's own comprehension in detail and thus become aware of any inadequacies, thus far unnoticed, in the coordination among those pieces of knowledge. (1987, p. 40)

Interactive instruction also fosters the development of essential *dispositions*. Resnick and Klopfer (1989a) state that the disposition to engage in thinking is socialized when students participate in communities that value thinking. When instruction is interactive and students are regularly engaged with a classroom full of peers who are busy making sense of ideas, they are likely to learn that good thinking is the norm of the classroom, that it is valued and expected. If good thinking can be socialized in this way, there is good reason for "basic skill and subject matter to be taught as occasions for thought, elaboration, and interpretation throughout school. It is a likely way, perhaps the only likely way, to shape dispositions for thinking" (Resnick & Klopfer, 1989a, p. 9). In addition, if teachers discuss a variety of topics, students can come to see that thinking is not only a school activity.

When instruction is interactive, teachers have multiple opportunities to move students toward *critical and creative thought*. Of course they can ask questions which promote critical and creative activity. In addition, in a social setting skilled thinkers model critical and creative thinking, thereby exposing novices to what is normally invisible. Learners have the opportunity to inspect, question, and experiment with cognitive activity to which they do not normally have access. In an interactive setting learners receive feedback on their ideas, conclusions, judgments, and so on. Feedback can help refine their ability to think critically and creatively.

Interactive instruction affords teachers opportunities to develop students' control of their thinking (*metacognition*). We already pointed out that interactions with others help students become more conscious of their own thinking. Increased awareness can lead learners to see the need for change and to gain control over their cognitive activity. This will not happen by magic. Teachers must take advantage of techniques such as the think-aloud to provide models of metacognitive activity for students. Additionally, teachers can make thinking a legitimate topic for discussion, so that students are not only thinking and talking, but talking about their thinking. In short, by making thinking a part of the instructional conversation, the teacher can open it up for individual and collective scrutiny.

In her review of programs which effectively teach thinking, Resnick (1987) noted that a common feature was their emphasis on social interaction. We have just described interactive instruction and its contribution to good thinking. Next we consider analytic instruction.

Analytic Instruction

The third characteristic of instruction for good thinking is its **analytic nature**. Prawat wrote, "The analysis or diagnosis of student learning occupies an absolutely key position . . . [and] should be the basis for instructional decision making" (1989, p. 8). When Prawat uses the term *diagnosis*, he does not mean the diagnosis of specific skill learning which is the common meaning of this term. Instead Prawat means making an analytic assessment of the understandings students construct as a result of instruction. For this reason, we use the term *analysis* rather than the term *diagnosis*. While it may seem obvious that teachers analyze student learning, it is often overlooked in classrooms where the emphasis is on covering material. Remember what we have said, however, about how knowledge is acquired. Learners construct understandings by using existing knowledge to interpret and integrate new information. Students' conceptions must be taken seriously because these conceptions determine how learning will proceed (Hewson & Hewson, 1988).

If students' conceptions are not in line with those of teachers, they can "lead to misinterpretation of new information or to a breakdown in the process of making sense and a reliance on rote memorization for coping with the demands of instruction" (Hewson & Hewson, 1988, p. 604). In other words, if new understandings can be reconciled with the learner's existing knowledge, "learning proceeds without difficulty. If, however, they cannot be reconciled, learning requires that existing conceptions be restructured or even exchanged for the new" (p. 605). Clearly, teachers must have insight into learners' entering conceptions in order to determine an appropriate course of action.

Researchers in all subject areas have stressed the importance of analysis. Research on student misconceptions has become especially important in science (Dreyfus, Jungwirth & Eliovitch, 1990; Tobin, Briscoe & Holman, 1990) and social studies (Brophy, 1990; National Commission on Social Studies in the

Schools, 1989). Researchers stress that instruction that ignores students' entering conceptions leads to an accumulation of facts rather than the development of knowledge. For example, Watson and Konicek (1990) describe a sequence of lessons on heat taught by Deb O'Brien to her fourth graders. While her students had memorized from previous lessons the various sources of heat, Ms. O'Brien discovered that from their everyday life experiences (e.g., "Put on your hat, it's cold outside"), her students also believed that sweaters, hats, and coats were sources of heat. Through questioning, Ms. O'Brien discovered this misconception and then worked with students to design and conduct a series of experiments to test their beliefs, leading the students to "a deeper understanding of heat."

The analytic feature of instruction refers to teachers' knowledge of their students. There is another way in which the analytic feature of instruction can be realized in the classroom: Teachers can help students develop an analytic orientation toward their own learning processes. We are thinking specifically of the metacognitive component of good thinking. Recall that metacognition refers to knowledge and control of self and cognitive processes. There are a number of things teachers can do to help students gain knowledge and control.

We have already discussed the importance of teacher modeling through *think-alouds*. Additionally, we described *learning logs* in our discussion of focused and coherent instruction. Encouraging students to share their questions, concerns,

When students write about their questions, concerns, and insights in learning logs, they gain control of their own learning.

insights, surprises, and confusions in logs helps them to focus on the cognitive processes they use to participate in learning tasks. A third strategy is to provide instruction in self-questioning. While some students do this naturally, many others fail to monitor themselves as they make their way through assignments. As noted in our discussion of the metacognitive element of good thinking, teachers can encourage students to ask themselves questions before they begin a task, while they work on the task, and after they have completed the task. Before beginning a task, students might ask, "Do I understand what is expected of me?" and "How should I go about completing this task in order to be successful?" While they work on tasks, students might ask themselves, "How am I doing?" or "Will this make sense to others who see it?" Upon completing the task, students might ask, "Did I accomplish what I hoped to accomplish?" and "What have I learned from doing this assignment?" Additionally, upon completion, teachers can have students rate their understanding—"I understand well"; "I sort of understand"; "I don't understand." Then the students can seek to identify the source of the comprehension difficulty, if one exists. Having determined the source of the difficulty, students are in a position to take corrective action (Bondy, 1984). These sorts of activities help students develop an analytic stance toward their thinking and learning which leads to increased self-knowledge and self-control.

The examples have shown that analytic instruction promotes good thinking. Although the clearest advantages of analytic instruction are in its contributions to the knowledge and metacognition components of good thinking, we believe this kind of instruction contributes to all four components.

In order to help learners construct *knowledge*, teachers need insight into learners' current understandings. Once teachers know what students understand, they can design experiences which help them modify, elaborate, or replace old understandings with new ones. It is important to note that interactive instruction, in which students actively articulate their understandings and thought processes, enables teachers to diagnose students' understandings.

By modeling their thought processes, teachers help students develop the *disposition* to think. Through think-alouds in which teachers model self-questioning about important issues, they communicate to students that thinking is a valuable activity.

The analysis of student understanding and subsequent decisions about instruction require *critical and creative thinking*. Teachers search for patterns in the students' behavior, generate several hypotheses to explain observed behavior, weigh evidence to help in drawing a conclusion, imagine lessons and experiences that might help students move toward desired understandings, think about the potential consequences of each, and settle on a plan of action. Teachers provide models of critical and creative thought when they share their thinking about these matters with their students.

The development of *metacognition* is an obvious by-product of analytic instruction. Not only do teachers diagnose student understanding and share their thoughts about this process; they also actively encourage students to become aware and take charge of their own thinking.

The three characteristics of teaching which promote good thinking are as follows: focused and coherent instruction, interactive instruction, and analytic instruction. We have shown how each of these characteristics can be applied to instruction in various subject areas in the elementary school. Our purpose in doing this was to demonstrate that "thinking" does not have to be tacked on to an already overloaded curriculum. Instead, the teaching of thinking is built into the traditional subject areas so that students develop skills which enable them to think successfully in many areas.

To emphasize this, let's consider again the example of science. The three features of instruction we have discussed clearly apply to science teaching: Instruction should be focused and coherent, interactive, and analytic. In his discussion of science instruction, Minstrell (1989) stressed the importance of restructuring students' knowledge as has been exemplified by Ms. O'Brien's lessons. Minstrell explained that restructuring knowledge can be accomplished by having teacher and students identify the students' existing understandings of the topic, clarifying those initial understandings through discussion, challenging those understandings with a demonstration or activity, clarifying the new understandings, and applying those understandings in multiple contexts over time. This kind of science instruction is *focused and coherent* because it stresses key ideas and the application of those ideas to contexts in and out of school; it is *interactive* because teachers and students work together to construct, coordinate, elaborate, and differentiate knowledge; it is *analytic* because it is based on students' understandings. When science is taught in this way, students acquire **generative knowledge**—"knowledge that can be used to interpret new situations, to solve problems, to think and reason, and to learn." This type of knowledge is essential if students are to be able to "learn easily and independently later on" (Resnick & Klopfer, 1989a, p. 5).

FOCUS BOX 7–7

Practical Application Activity

Choose one of the science concepts from the following list. Develop an introductory lesson to help students begin to develop this concept. Use Minstrell's guidelines as the framework for your lesson. Be specific about how you will accomplish each step (e.g., How will you identify students' existing understandings?).

- Friction is a force that slows down or stops motion.
- Sound comes from matter that moves back and forth, or vibrates.
- A body part or an activity that helps a living thing to survive is called an adaptation.
- Both the nose and the tongue are used to taste foods.

Choose a partner and use Minstrell's guidelines to critique each other's work.

So far we have focused on what teachers can do in their classrooms to promote the knowledge, dispositions, metacognitive skill, and critical and creative capacity which together define good thinking. Making any substantial curriculum change is difficult because it requires making adjustments in established routines to accommodate new methods. (Perhaps the most difficult part of the change process is the mental reprogramming it requires. Changing one's way of thinking about students and teaching requires conscious effort and constant attention, at least at the beginning.) Teachers can get some help by looking outside their classrooms, to their colleagues and to parents.

Outside Support

The school improvement literature stresses that significant changes in classrooms will come only with the commitment and combined efforts of teachers. Teachers who hope to make changes in their classrooms can gain support by joining with colleagues. Small groups of teachers or even informal meetings between two teachers can be helpful as teachers plan for and implement a change. When working together to build an emphasis on thinking into the curriculum, teachers might focus on topics such as these: currently used materials which work against the aim of promoting good thinking, strategies for modifying existing materials, the nature of teacher talk and its influence on student thinking, analysis of specific lessons for their potential impact on student thinking, or obstacles to good thinking (e.g., consider students, classroom, school, or home).

A peer support group might address how to involve parents in the thinking curriculum. As Barell pointed out, parents can become teachers' allies: "They can reinforce the thinking strategies teachers are working with during the day, thereby confronting students with not one but two settings in which they are challenged" to be good thinkers (1985, p. 39). Barell suggested several ways to communicate the teacher's expectations to parents and involve them in the development of the thinking curriculum:

1. Communicate your plan to engage children in a new program early on.

2. Meet with parents early on to provide information about the goals of the program and the changes you plan to implement. Share with parents the principles you will be keeping in mind to help you teach in a way that promotes good thinking. Help them translate these principles into specific practices they can use at home.

3. Ask for parents' advice about other ways to challenge students to be thinkers and for overcoming obstacles to good thinking.

4. Advise parents of difficulties as they arise and results of program implementation.

5. Ask parents to collect evidence of students' progress toward good thinking.

The support of colleagues and parents can provide much of the support a teacher needs to implement and sustain a thinking curriculum. Enthusiastic parents and a united faculty can even influence a skeptical administrator to adopt a thinking curriculum. Ideally, an entire school will adopt the practices of good thinking; in this sort of environment students become thinkers as they observe and practice good thinking day in and day out. Good thinking is expected and valued; it becomes a habit.

Summary

In this chapter we have argued that students' thinking will be improved most effectively by teaching them to think along with standard school subjects, despite the existence of many packaged programs designed to teach specific thinking skills. (See reviews by Costa, 1985; Nickerson, Perkins, & Smith, 1985; Resnick, 1987; Segal, Chipman, & Glaser, 1985.) Based on her review of the research which has been conducted on the effectiveness of a number of thinking skills programs, Resnick (1987) concluded that the small amount of research which is available is not particularly useful in determining program effectiveness. This is due to the fact that only a few studies have addressed the **question of transfer**: Do the newly acquired skills transfer to other parts of the curriculum or to out-of-school performance?

It appears that programs which embed thinking instruction in subject matter (e.g., the reciprocal teaching strategy in the area of reading) do lead to improved and transferable performance. Elementary school teachers have lots to do with lots of students in very little time. Therefore, we believe it is more realistic to expect teachers to adjust the mainline curriculum than to add on a new "subject area." Resnick (1987) mentions several other advantages to this approach. First, thinking is practiced and developed in the context of a knowledge base; that is, thinking is intimately related to knowledge of mathematics, or science, or to the construction of meaning in reading and composition. Second, students become familiar with the characteristic reasoning styles of different disciplines (i.e., what it means to think like a physical scientist, a mathematician, or a social scientist). Third, even if students do not attain thinking skill transfer, they will have gained knowledge of subject matter.

Although Resnick (1987) advocates joining thinking skill and subject matter instruction, she acknowledges that little is known about how to do this well. In this chapter, we presented some general principles to help you think about how to infuse thinking into the teaching of basic school subjects. We said that instruction should be *focused and coherent*, *interactive*, and *analytic*. This sort of instruction should take place in an inquiry-oriented, safe environment. Working with other teachers and with parents can facilitate the change process. In addition, keeping up with research on thinking provides new ideas to ponder and practices with which to experiment. Through teachers' efforts, commitment, and—most of all—their good thinking, students can develop thinking skills that will enable them to direct their futures and shape the future of our society.

FOCUS BOX 7–8

Practical Application Activity

Before beginning this activity, check your understanding of this chapter by completing the following open-ended sentences. You will need to write several sentences in order to complete each. Be sure to draw on the concepts from this chapter to help you.

1. Before I read this chapter, I believed that good thinking meant . . .
2. Before I read this chapter, I believed that a teacher taught students to be good thinkers by . . .
3. Having read and discussed this chapter, I have become aware that . . .
4. If I had to explain to my students' parents at Open House what I mean by good thinking, I would say (*brief and clear language is important!*) . . .
5. If I had to explain to my students' parents how I intend to help their children become better thinkers, I would say (*again, be brief and clear*) . . .

Once you have completed your sentences, work with a group of your peers to complete the following application activity:

List activities/lessons you have observed or conducted that promote good thinking as it is defined in this chapter. (List as many as you can but be brief in describing each one.) From your list select one activity that illustrates teaching for thinking as described in this chapter. For this activity do the following:

- Describe the activity in as much detail as you can.
- Explain what it is about the lesson that promotes good thinking. In order to do this, you must refer to the three characteristics of instruction (i.e., focused and coherent, interactive, and analytic) that were described in the chapter.
- Explain how the lesson contributes to the development of each of the four elements of good thinking (i.e., dispositions, knowledge, critical and creative capacity, and metacognition).

FOCUS BOX 7–9

Yes, These Look Like Good Ideas, but . . .

Whenever teachers encounter new ideas, they have to try to fit them within their current understandings about children, their knowledge of and beliefs about appropriate instructional strategies, their current knowledge base, and their specific teaching context. Because of this, you probably found yourself raising questions about the feasibility of the strategies for helping children develop into good thinkers. We suspect at times you found yourself thinking, "Yes, these look like good ideas, but . . . ?" Work with a small group of peers to raise and try to answer your questions about suggested strategies. The following questions may help to guide your thinking.

FOCUS BOX 7–9, *continued*

- What is your overall, "gut" reaction to the strategies? Do they look like things you might like to try? Why or why not?
- As you think about trying to implement the strategies, what concerns do you have?
- If you were to try to implement these strategies, what skills, abilities and/or knowledge would you need to develop? How would you go about doing this?
- What contextual barriers do you see that might make implementation of these strategies difficult? How could you work around these contextual barriers?
- What are the implicit curriculum implications of these strategies? How do they fit with the aims you have identified as important for elementary education?

It is important to raise these kinds of questions and to explore the answers with your peers. Failure to confront these questions probably means you will not make any significant changes in your instruction.

Further Readings

Bondy, E. (1984). Thinking about thinking: Encouraging children's use of metacognitive processes. *Childhood Education, 60*, 234–238.

Brophy, J. (1990). Teaching social studies for understanding and higher order applications. *Elementary School Journal, 90* (4), 351–417.

Dreyfus, A., Jungwirth, E., & Eliovitch, R. (1990). Applying the "cognitive conflict" strategy for conceptual change—Some implications, difficulties and problems. *Science Education, 74* (5), 555–569.

Flavell, J. H. (1976). Metacognitive aspects of problem solving. In L. B. Resnick (Ed.), *The nature of intelligence* (pp. 213–235). Hillsdale, NJ: Erlbaum.

Glatthorn, A. A., & Baron, J. (1985). The good thinker. In A. L. Costa (Ed.), *Developing minds* (pp. 49–53). Alexandria, VA: Association for Supervision and Curriculum Development.

Goodlad, J. I. (1984) *A place called school*. New York: McGraw-Hill.

Hewson, P. W., & Hewson, M. G. (1988). An appropriate conception of teaching science: A view from studies of science learning. *Science Education, 72*, 597–614.

Minstrell, J. A. (1989). Teaching science for understanding. In L. B. Resnick & L. E. Klopfer (Eds.), *Toward the thinking curriculum: Current cognitive research* (pp. 129–149). Alexandria, VA: Association for Supervision and Curriculum Development.

Paris, S. G., & Winograd, P. (1990). Metacognition in academic learning and instruction. In B. F. Jones (Ed.), *Dimensions of thinking and cognitive instruction*. Hillsdale, NJ: Erlbaum.

Prawat, R. S. (1989). Teaching for understanding: Three key attributes. *Teaching & Teacher Education, 5*, 315–328.

Resnick, L. B. (1987). *Education and learning to think*. Washington, DC: National Academy Press.

Resnick, L. B., & Klopfer, L. E. (1989). Toward the thinking curriculum: Concluding remarks. In L. B. Resnick & L. E. Klopfer (Eds.), *Toward the thinking curriculum: Current cognitive research* (pp. 206–211). Alexandria, VA: Association for Supervision and Curriculum Development.

Resnick, L. B., & Klopfer, L. E. (1989). Toward the thinking curriculum: An overview. In L. B. Resnick & L. E. Klopfer (Eds.), *Toward the thinking curriculum: Current cognitive research* (pp. 1–18). Alexandria, VA: Association for Supervision and Curriculum Development.

Tobin, K., Briscoe, C., & Holman, J. R. (1990). Overcoming constraints to effective elementary science teaching. *Science Education, 74* (5), 409–420.

CHAPTER 8

Engaging Students in an Empowering Curriculum

So far we have stressed that clarifying your educational aims helps you make decisions about what and how to teach. We have organized the book around aims that many teachers believe should guide children's elementary school experience. Thus far, we have discussed the development of literacy, social skills, and thinking. As we noted at the beginning of the book, one major aim for education, student empowerment, gives coherence to these other important aims. This chapter highlights issues and ideas related to student empowerment by (1) defining student empowerment, (2) summarizing the tools of empowerment, (3) defining educational engagement and discussing ways to promote it, and (4) presenting a synthesis of essential features of instruction.

A Definition of Empowerment

In recent years *empowerment* has become a buzzword in education circles. Many people talk about empowerment as if people share a common definition of the concept. In fact, there are multiple definitions of *empowerment*. Thus far, we have provided a general definition for the term. Now a clearer definition is necessary.

Simon (1989) reminds us that the literal meaning of **empower** is to give ability to, to permit, or enable. Ashcroft explains that "an **empowered person** [boldface added] . . . believe[s] in his or her ability/capability to act, and this belief would be accompanied by able/capable action" (1987, p. 143). The important question for educators is, "What do we want to empower students to do?" To say simply that we want to empower students remains a hollow aim.

We see *three main goals for student empowerment*. They are as follows:

1. Empower students to be eager and successful learners in and out of school.

2. Empower students to determine their futures and participate productively in society.

3. Empower students to play active roles in making society a better place for all human beings.

The first goal focuses on individual achievement. Cummins says, "Students who are empowered by their school experiences develop the ability, confidence, and motivation to succeed academically" (1986, p. 23). In addition, this goal involves helping students to be **lifelong learners**, people who have the skills and desire to direct their own learning in and out of school (Wigginton, 1989). As Cummins states, "Teachers that empower will aim to liberate students from instruction by encouraging them to become active generators of their knowledge" (1986, p. 27), rather than depending on an adult to tell them what they need to know.

The second and third goals of student empowerment focus on life outside of school. While meeting the second goal enables individuals "to make it in the real world" (Simon, 1989, p. 140), the third goal recognizes that adjusting to the real

An important dimension of empowerment is developing concern for the public good.

world is not enough. The third goal stresses helping students "to be able to define and shape, rather than simply serve in, the modern world" (Giroux, 1989, p. 183).

The three goals of empowerment differ in at least one important way. The first two goals focus on the individual's self-advancement. The third goal focuses on community and the individual's responsibility to the public good. As Goodman (1992) has explained, democratic living is based on the balance between individuality and community. "When the value of either individuality or community significantly supersedes the other, then the one which dominates distorts the democratic ideal" (p. 10). Americans tend to value **individualism** (i.e., personal goals, dreams, rights, and success) at the expense of concern for the public good. This suggests that teachers committed to fostering democratic values must help students to understand and develop commitment to community responsibility. The third goal of empowerment, then, is to prepare students to be active agents in making the world a better place for all human beings. This **critical citizenship** involves being caring and compassionate, accepting responsibility

FOCUS BOX 8–1

Take a Moment to Reflect

We have said that the values of individualism are more well ingrained in members of our society than the values of community. It is important to examine *your* reactions to this idea and to compare your reactions to those of your peers. If ideas are to be useful to you, you must determine how they fit with your entering ideas about educational aims and the nature of American society, and it is important that you evaluate the evidence you use in making a judgment.

Children come to school already oriented to self-advancement and competition. Do you think this is true? To help you develop an answer to this question, consider the following two questions:

- What experiences do young children have which teach them to "look out for number one"? What messages do adults and children receive which reinforce the values of individualism? Consider the media, government policies, and the structure of the workplace.

- What experiences do young children have which teach them that each individual has responsibility for the public good? What messages do adults and children receive which reinforce the values of community? Again, consider the media, government policies, and the structure of the workplace.

Share your views with your colleagues. As you discuss your conclusions, focus on the following:

- What evidence can you provide that your conclusion is valid? (*Note:* Evidence can come from this chapter, related readings, classroom experiences, or life experiences; it is important that you be explicit about the source and quality of your evidence.)

- What additional evidence might you want to collect?

for self and others, questioning assumptions about the "way things are," imagining alternatives, and working with others to bring about change.

If concern with self-determination and critical citizenship seem vaguely familiar to you, you have a good memory! We talked about the social responsiveness orientation to curriculum in Chapter 3. While advocates of this curriculum orientation view schools as responsible for empowering children to be productive members of society, they disagree about the purpose of this aim. Some see the purpose as assisting children to adapt to the society as it exists; others see the purpose as helping children challenge existing norms and help restructure society for the good of all people. In this chapter we suggest that both views are legitimate and should help teachers think about their curriculum and instruction practices.

In previous chapters, we described how teachers' long-term aims can easily get lost in immediate concerns about helping students perform well on tests or maintaining order in a class of 30 8-year-olds. Tests and order are very real parts of teachers' and students' lives. Nevertheless, decisions about how to approach such realities should be made in the context of long-term aims. What do we want for the students in elementary schools today? Certainly we want children to succeed as students. In addition, we want children to become active, productive citizens—people who can adjust to societal demands as well as "dream of new possibilities for human existence" (Fitzclarence & Giroux, 1984, p. 472). Accomplishing these broad aims is much more complicated than simply conveying subject matter to students. Teachers must help students develop empowering knowledge, skills, and attitudes. We have devoted whole chapters of this book to these tools of empowerment. In the next section of this chapter, we briefly summarize what we mean by empowering knowledge, skills, and attitudes.

FOCUS BOX 8–2

Synthesis Activity

In the "Tools of Empowerment" section of this chapter, we briefly summarize information about tools of empowerment that have been presented in detail in other chapters in the book. Reading this section will be a useful summary of the book, but you will learn more about empowerment if you try to "construct" this knowledge independently. To do this, try the following activity:

- Divide yourselves into groups of six.
- Have each person quickly review one of the following chapters (4, 5, 6, 7) to identify any tools of empowerment (i.e., things children need to know and/or be able to do) discussed in each chapter.
- Provide a rationale for your choices. That is, explain why you believe particular skills, knowledge, attitudes, or abilities are important for student empowerment.

Then read the section entitled "Tools of Empowerment." Focus Box 8–4 contains an activity designed to help you compare your conclusions to our discussion of the knowledge, skills, and attitudes necessary for empowerment.

The Tools of Empowerment

The tools that are necessary for student empowerment—knowledge, skills, and attitudes—are so closely interrelated that they become distorted when separated into independent categories. Nevertheless, we shall discuss them separately to clarify what each means. We shall also show how the categories are related.

Knowledge

When we say that **knowledge** is a tool for empowerment, we mean that students need thoroughly assimilated understandings as opposed to a storehouse of facts and procedures if they are to become productive, critical human beings. In Chapter 7, we discussed this view of knowledge at length. **Teaching for conceptual development** means helping students weave a complex tapestry of understandings about the world. Students can then draw on their understandings to help them interpret their experiences and their observations and to restructure aspects of their personal and social lives, when necessary. An example may clarify what we mean by thoroughly assimilated understandings.

One of our student teachers developed a unit on the invention process. In addition to studying inventors and their inventions, students focused on the process of invention. How did these people come to be inventors? How did they come upon their inventions? Had they invented other things? Were there similarities across their invention experiences? What were the similarities and differences across inventors? In addition to investigating famous inventors' experiences, students discussed and examined their own and their family members' experiences as inventors. Students were surprised and thrilled to find that inventions were not reserved for rich, famous adults! Through this unit, a class of third graders gained new insight into the invention process. They learned many facts about famous inventors and their inventions; but more important, in the long run, they constructed understandings about inventing and its role in their lives. All of the students came to the unit with some knowledge—most of it disorganized and vague—of the invention process. The unit activities helped them to make sense of invention as it applied to their lives.

Notice how our description of students' knowledge about invention was tied to the world outside of school. To develop sound understanding of concepts, students must answer the questions, "What does this mean in the context of my life?" and "How can I use this?" In other words, empowerment requires that students develop understandings which they can apply in their ongoing efforts to interpret, examine, and improve their lives. Knowledge which is not connected to students' lives is **dead knowledge** (e.g., learning names of inventors and the importance of their inventions). Cooperative students learn it so that they can pass tests. Resistant students see it as more evidence that school is a waste of time. For all students, dead knowledge emphasizes the boundaries between

FOCUS BOX 8–3

Practical Application Activity

Choose one of the following topics which is typically addressed in elementary classrooms:

- the northeastern region of the United States
- air
- sea life
- Plains Indians
- Thanksgiving
- seasons of the year
- explorers

For your topic, answer the following questions:

- What kinds of experiences would you provide for students to promote conceptual development tied to students' real worlds?
- How would these experiences serve the goal of critical citizenship as it is defined in this chapter?

Now work with a group of four or five peers who selected different topics and answer the following questions.

- Were some topics easier or harder to relate to students' worlds? Which ones? Why?
- Are there some topics that cannot be related to children's worlds? What might they be? Should teachers teach these topics? Why or why not?

school and life: There is school knowledge and there is real-life knowledge, and the two have little to do with one another.

Empowered students are actively involved in changing their world. Conceptual development tied to students' reality is at the heart of informed, intelligent action. This is an **expansive view of knowledge** rather than a restricted view of knowledge. In other words, what students are taught is not restricted to the objectives in a textbook or teacher's manual. While such objectives may provide a beginning, the teacher shapes the curriculum according to students' concerns and the aim of empowering them to be lifelong learners who can make the world a better place.

Skills

We have previously discussed the three interrelated categories of skills fundamental to empowerment: thinking, social living, and literacy. Critical thinking ability is stressed by many who write about the empowerment of learners (e.g., Giroux, 1988; Shor, 1980; Simon, 1989). These writers stress that students should learn to examine and question things that are usually taken for granted while also envisioning "versions of a world which is 'not yet'—in order to be able to alter the grounds upon which life is lived" (Simon, 1989, p. 140). In other words, empowered learners are good thinkers. As we discussed in Chapter 7, this means that they eagerly apply the analytical processes of critical thinking and the generative processes of creative thinking to sound knowledge of subject matter. In addition, they monitor and regulate their cognitive processes as they strive to accomplish tasks.

Interpersonal skills that are essential to social living are also fundamental to student empowerment. Simon (1989) argues that empowered people work collaboratively toward common goals. Being able to work as part of a team helps individuals to adjust to societal, family, and work structures and enables them to work with others to change inequitable and oppressive conditions. Specific social skills that help empower students were discussed in Chapter 6. These social skills include how to communicate feelings and opinions, how to resolve conflicts, and how to assess a situation and determine how to become part of a group. In addition to possessing social skills, empowered students see value in collective effort. They enjoy working with other people. Literacy is closely related to good thinking and skilled group work. Individuals must be able to examine and critique all kinds of texts. They must be able to express their understandings and judgments clearly and persuasively to others. Literacy encompasses fundamental sense-making processes in reading, writing, and mathematics as we have discussed previously. Examples of essential processes include drawing on relevant background knowledge, clarifying the purpose of the task and adjusting strategies to serve that purpose, and self-monitoring comprehension and performance.

Attitudes

As we mentioned before, valuing collective effort is fundamental to empowerment. Empowered students have positive attitudes about the ability and potential of the group as well as personal self-esteem. Confidence and courage enable students to forge ahead into unfamiliar territory knowing that they can achieve their goals. With confidence and courage students succeed in school tasks and make a difference in the world. They are not afraid to question, to experiment, to find a better way. They are empowered to take action because they believe in their ability to have an impact.

The knowledge, skills, and attitudes we have described enable students to take charge of their lives in and out of school and to take action to bring about positive change. Teachers who embrace the aim of student empowerment are faced with the challenge of shaping their curriculum and instruction so as to engage students in developing the tools of empowerment. Because educational engagement is both a widespread problem and a fundamental feature of an empowering school experience, we devote the next section to it.

FOCUS BOX 8–4

Take a Moment to Reflect

Compare your conclusions about the tools of empowerment (see Focus Box 8–2) to our discussion of the knowledge, skills, and attitudes necessary for empowerment by answering the following questions:

1. How does our description of the tools of empowerment compare to your list of knowledge, skills, and abilities you generated?

2. Do you think you were empowered by your elementary school experience?
   - What tools did you acquire?
   - What kinds of experiences contributed to your empowerment?
   - What tools did you fail to acquire and why?

3. Given all the things that elementary teachers have to do, how important do you think these tools for empowerment are? Provide a rationale for your answer.

Educational Engagement: A Key to Student Empowerment

Recent studies have shown that the problem of low engagement in schoolwork is widespread (Goodlad, 1984; Powell, Farrar, & Cohen, 1985; Sizer, 1984). While much of the research on educational disengagement has been done at the high-school level, many elementary teachers voice similar concerns. In fact, our teacher education students frequently choose the topic "Improving Student Motivation" for research papers. What exactly is educational engagement? According to Wehlage, Rutter, Smith, Lesko, and Fernandez, "**Educational engagement** refers to the psychological investment required to comprehend and master knowledge and skills explicitly taught in school" (1989, p. 177).[1]

Wehlage and his colleagues describe **levels of engagement**—students can simply do what they are asked, or they can demonstrate real interest in and commitment to school tasks. An important element of engagement is that it is not solely a student responsibility. "Engagement is the result of interaction between students, teachers and curriculum" (Wehlage et al., 1989, p. 177). A complex process, educational engagement is not synonymous with motivation or time on task because "promoting engagement requires attention to student characteristics, the tasks students are asked to perform, the school environment in which the work takes place, and the external environment that influences the student and the school itself" (p. 179). In other words, in order to engage students, teachers must examine multiple factors. Engaging students is not as simple as supplying rewards and punishments. If students are to be deeply engaged, teachers must look closely at

---

[1]   Wehlage et al.'s work was particularly helpful as we developed this section of the chapter.

To engage students with the curriculum, teachers must examine a variety of influential factors, such as students' values, interests, and expectations.

their own practices; the students' values, interests, and expectations; the classroom and school environment; and the culture of the students' home community. Educational engagement is a more multifaceted phenomenon than the engaged time referred to in our discussion of active teaching (see Chapter 5).

Three impediments to student engagement with the curriculum are as follows: (1) discontinuity between home and school, (2) narrow conception of learning used in school, and (3) lack of explicit and valued goals. While there are certainly other factors that lead to student disengagement (e.g., student mobility, family crises, substance abuse), these three have received considerable attention. Also, teachers have some control over these three impediments. It is important to note that these three factors overlap to some extent. In addition, these impediments to student engagement with the curriculum are also impediments to student empowerment.

Discontinuity Between Home and School

All students experience some degree of discontinuity between home and school due to the simple fact that life at home and life at school are not the same.

Saunders (1989) explains that all children enter school as outsiders. In order to be successful, they must gain knowledge of how things work in this new setting. They must learn new behaviors, such as raising their hand to get a turn to speak and standing in line. They also must learn new attitudes, such as patience and diligence, even in the face of unappealing tasks. As we discussed in Chapter 3, there are certain "facts of life" to which elementary students must adjust that shape their views of themselves and their roles as students (Jackson, 1968). These facts of life include the following: in classrooms students must live as members of a group, students are evaluated, and power is distributed unequally.

While all students experience some discontinuity between home life and school life, some students are able to adjust to the new routine and structure. However, others have difficulty adjusting to unfamiliar expectations. Schools are predominantly middle-class institutions, reflecting middle-class values. Many poor and minority students are not familiar with the language, skills, and attitudes taken for granted by members of mainstream American society. As a result, they can experience a kind of culture shock in school which Wehlage et al. (1989) call "**incongruence**." When students' views of themselves, their goals, and their futures do not fit with the activities and expectations of the school, there is incongruence. These students do not see school as useful or meaningful. Due to the conflict between the home and school cultures, students can quickly become disengaged. An excerpt from McLaren's (1989) diary can help us identify some examples of incongruence. Notice each part of the dialogue which causes your eyebrows to raise. Your surprise indicates that a *rule* has been broken. These **school rules** are the taken-for-granted norms of conduct, language use, and attitudes which operate in middle-class schools.

> After the class returned from gym, I asked them what improvements they'd like to see me make in the classroom.
>
> "You ain't gonna leave the room like that bitch had it?" Duke asked, cocking his head to one side.
>
> "What was wrong with the room?"
>
> "We didn't like the set-up!" he barked back. "We didn't like havin no spare time! It was always work." Levon stood up and walked to the back of the room, with a ruler stuck out of his open fly. "We wanna teacher with big boobs!"
>
> Marianne, one of my West Indian girls, rose out of her chair "We wants a black teacher!"
>
> "A black teacher with big boobs!" Levon cut in.
>
> "Naa!' someone else cried. "Who wants a fuzz-top for a teacher?" (McLaren, 1989, pp. 42–43)

You have probably noted a number of *school rules* that were broken in the vignette. The most striking ones relate to the use of what some people consider "foul" language and references to male and female anatomy. The students also break rules about what many people think of as racist remarks and addressing the teacher in a "respectful" manner. The interaction may seem more like a street shouting match than a classroom conversation. Levon provides us with additional insight into the incongruence between the students and the school when he tells his teacher that he wants more "spare time" in the classroom. Some readers might react in exasperation, "What does he think school is about, anyway?! Students are *supposed* to work in school!"

And this is exactly the point. Many students have not had access to the middle-class values which give structure to schools. These students are not *without culture*—they simply may not be familiar with the traditional middle-class culture of the school. Their behavior, while it may strike some readers as "uncivilized," has served them well in their home communities. If some of us were to spend time on Levon's turf, we would experience the incongruence he experiences when he enters our territory, the school. We are not implying that teachers should permit students to behave in any manner which is culturally comfortable. Rather, we are stressing that some students have trouble in school because the world of the school and the world they know outside of the school are markedly different. And, the world of the school often rejects the world of these students as inferior—as having no place in the classroom.

A number of researchers have studied cultural conflict and how it contributes to school difficulties (Boggs, 1985; Phillips, 1983; Trueba, 1988). An example of cultural conflict may help clarify the problems faced by many students. Tharp (1989) conducted research on Hawaiian and Navajo children at home and in school. One area of conflict is related to social organization. In most classrooms the teachers are the central figures, and students are expected to attend to teachers and comply with their directions. Tharp explains that Hawaiian children have difficulties with these expectations because they are at odds with the norms of their home cultures. Tharp summarizes Hawaiian and Navajo children's relationships to adults:

> Hawaiian society is in most settings age-graded, with children largely in association with children, adolescents with adolescents, and adults with adults. Children approach adults only with some form of prior permission or summons, and consequently do not closely monitor adult behavior. . . . Generally, Hawaiian children are much more peer-oriented than adult-oriented.
>
> Navajo adults are highly respectful of children's individuality and of children's sovereignty over their own persons. Any manipulation to control the behavior of others, including children, through such direct confrontational means as contingency management, is considered un-Navajo. . . . Navajo society is not age-graded, and children live in close association with generations of adults. (1989, p. 53)

You can see that Navajo children are more likely to adjust with ease to a teacher-oriented classroom than Hawaiian children. In fact, Tharp says that chaos is not uncommon in a classroom of Hawaiian children: "The first day of kindergarten, for example, is a considerable challenge to the teacher, who finds no children paying any attention to her instructions" (1989, p. 53). Navajo children, on the other hand, "visually track the teacher, and attend to slight clues as to her preferences" (p. 53).

Hawaiian and Navajo children both have difficulty with the large-group instructional format common in schools. Tharp explains the cultural orientations which are at the heart of these difficulties:

> Among Hawaiian children and adults . . . collaboration, cooperation and assisted performance are commonplace in everyday experience. As early as 5 years of age Hawaiian children learn domestic skills and routines and how to care for infants and toddlers. . . . Certainly peer groups are also a notable feature in Navajo culture, wherever living arrangements are conducive. The groups are formed of siblings, cousins and clan relatives. (1989, pp. 54–55)

Hawaiian and Navajo children prefer cooperation to competition and have high affiliation needs. Gilbert and Gay (1985) have made the same point about black children. While all three groups seem to prefer working in small peer groups to participating in whole-class lessons followed by individual assignments, differences among the cultures indicate that not any small group will do. Tharp says that in "Hawaii four to five students of mixed sex maximize peer interaction and assistance. . . . Among the Navajo this combination produced virtually no peer assistance. In Navajo the most effective independent groups were composed of two to three students of the same sex, working on the same task" (Tharp, 1989, p. 55).

These well-documented home-school cultural conflicts illustrate the tensions students may experience and the challenges teachers face. Teachers who do not understand students' behaviors may view students as disrespectful, annoying, disobedient, or stupid. As we said earlier, we are not suggesting that teachers should allow students to behave in any way which happens to be culturally comfortable. However, when students do not understand school expectations, or when they are reprimanded for behavior which has served them well in their home communities, they may respond by withdrawing from instructional activities. Thus, they become educationally disengaged.

Narrow Conception of Learning

The typical approach to teaching in school is another impediment to educational engagement. According to Wehlage et al., "the dominant learning process pursued in schools is too narrow in that it is highly abstract, verbal, sedentary, individualistic, competitive and controlled by others" (1989, p. 179). When we say that school learning is based in a **narrow conception of learning**, we mean two things. First, the instructional processes are based on a single view of teaching and learning. Essentially, this is the view that knowledge can be delivered by a teacher to a learner (see Chapters 1, 5, and 7). Sometimes this is modified so that a book is delivering the knowledge; nevertheless, the model remains one of transmission and absorption—someone or something transmits knowledge to a learner who is expected to absorb it. The second aspect of this narrow view of learning is that the outcomes of learning are overly narrow. In school students learn "school stuff," which often has little to do with "real world stuff." An excerpt from a case study of Travis, a third-grade student considered to be "at risk" by one of his teachers and not by the other (interesting!), illustrates the two aspects of the narrow view of learning in schools:

> Travis appeared to be one of those students to whom the typical process of schooling was not meaningful or motivating. He had a rich, full life with many social and real-life learning experiences outside of school. He had participated in many extended family activities, been treated in an adult manner, gone hunting and fishing with his grandfather, traveled with his grandparents, understood and handled some of life's complexities such as not having a father, and seemed to have an awareness and maturity about him that many other third grade children do not have.
>
> He seemed to find little relationship between school and real life. He found school boring and was not motivated by much of what was done in school. (Richardson, Casanova, Placier, & Guilfoyle, 1989, p. 238)

The following description illustrates Travis's behavior during a large-group presentation:

> The lesson focused on the "Words of the Day." As Ms. Jones wrote the words on the chalkboard, Travis gave no indication [of interest]. He talked to his neighbor, stared at the table and at other children, and did not look at the board. When Ms. Jones asked for volunteers to pronounce the words, Travis [did not raise his hand]. He scooted his chair back and forth from the table. When the lesson was concluded, Travis had not participated verbally nor had he been asked to participate. (Richardson et al., 1989, p. 236)

Travis readily admitted that he "didn't like school, couldn't think of anything that would make him like it and found it boring" (p. 235). His mother reported that "by the time he was two-years-old, he could do just about anything" (p. 232). Nevertheless, once he hit kindergarten the trouble started, and he was retained in second grade. Here is a boy who is bright, curious, and active outside of school but withdraws from most activities inside the classroom. His disaffection appears to be related to the narrowness of the instruction and curriculum he experiences in school.

Resnick (1987) helps us see the narrowness of school learning in her discussion of learning in and out of school. *School learning differs from out-of-school learning* in at least two important ways. First, school learning is individual while out-of-school learning is often social. That is, people often work together to solve problems outside of school. They share information and help each other to achieve a common goal. Second, school learning is most often assessed by having students answer questions. In the real world, there is a practical purpose for what is learned. Things are learned because they are valued or needed, and the test of the learning is the successful application of that learning.

What is the significance of the narrow conception of learning that dominates classrooms in our country? When students do not value the learning that is imposed on them, they feel no connection to it. Porro quotes from her conversations with a low-achieving high-school student:

> *Porro:*   What's going on in school?
>
> *Student:*   Nothing . . . it's boring . . . same thing every day . . . excitement level zero.

Porro:	So, you're trying to get through high school the easiest way possible?
Student:	Actually it'd be easier it we just did the work . . . the work's not so hard. I'd just rather not do it. (1985, p. 257)

This student, Bob, was one of a large group who found the work so senseless that they regularly risked failure and suspension rather than complete assignments. Because the content of the school curriculum is perceived as irrelevant by students like Travis and Bob, they become disengaged from school.

Lack of Explicit and Valued Goals

A third impediment to educational engagement is closely related to the previous two. If students are to be engaged, they must believe that what they are doing is somehow related to outcomes which they value. While the purpose of school tasks is often unclear even to middle-class students, many of these students have been primed to persevere. Middle-class students are likely to have some experience with the rewards of diligence in school. They are exposed to people who have been successful in school. They grow up hearing about the value of school and the importance of doing well. They probably have at least one parent who went to college and know other adults who have done the same. In middle-class families, working hard in school is the children's "job." These firmly ingrained attitudes about the value of school enable students to persevere in the face of what many students call "boring" tasks.

Many other students, however, do not grow up with an expectation of school success. They may have little exposure to people who believe that school can make a difference in one's life. In fact, many grow up believing that school is to be survived or perhaps escaped. These students do not have experience with college, do not know people who went to college, and do not hear talk about college in their homes. What do they have to gain from "boring" tasks?

Our point here is not that the school curriculum is only relevant for those children who plan to go to college. Rather, the point is that educational engagement requires that students see purpose in school tasks. Students must believe that their efforts are related to outcomes which they value. Simply telling students, "You'll need to know this for third grade," or "This will be important when you look for a job," may have little meaning for students. Teachers must have insights into students' values and understandings about the world and their futures in order to shape learning tasks which students view as purposeful, useful, and valuable.

Levin (1987) states that as many as 70 percent of U.S. students experience some degree of disengagement from school. Clearly, this problem is widespread. The three features of students' school experience that we described—discontinuity between home and school, narrow conception of learning, and lack of explicit and valued goals—are impediments to educational engagement. Each distances students from school, frustrates them, and causes them to drop out, mentally and/or physically. While these impediments are disturbing, they are also a source

Application Activity

Look back at the information we provided about Travis (see page 224). Analyze this information to look for evidence of all three impediments to educational engagement by answering the following questions:

- What evidence do you see of discontinuity between home and school?
- What evidence do you see of a narrow conception of learning?
- What evidence do you see of a lack of explicit and valued goals?

Having completed these questions, answer the following:

- What questions or concerns do you have about the three possible impediments to educational engagement?
- Do you think these are things the teacher can control? Provide evidence to support your answer.

of hope, because each is a factor over which the teacher has some control. Next we will look at teacher beliefs and practices that promote student engagement. Only through engagement do students have a chance of becoming empowered.

Promoting Educational Engagement

Kohl (1967) described his experience as a sixth-grade teacher in Harlem. Despite his enthusiasm and a degree from Columbia University's Teacher College, the students resisted Kohl's initial efforts; they were obedient at best, rebellious at worst. Few students displayed any signs of interest or enthusiasm in their school experience. In short, Kohl had not yet found ways to engage his students with the curriculum. Note his discouragement at the beginning of the year:

> I tried for the next six weeks to use the books assigned and teach the official curriculum. It was hopeless. The class went through the readers perfunctorily, refused to hear about modern America, and were relieved to do arithmetic—mechanical, uncharged—as long as nothing new was introduced. For most of the day the atmosphere in the room was stifling. The children were bored and restless, and I felt burdened by the inappropriateness of what I tried to teach. It was so dull that I thought as little as the children and began to despair. (Kohl, 1967, p. 26)

The impediments to educational engagement we described previously help explain the problems. First, Kohl's students experienced *discontinuity between home and school*. The real world of the students clashed with the culture of the school. Traditional school assignments were unimportant to Kohl's students, and the "official" school curriculum did not speak to the reality of their lives. In fact, for these students, the teacher and school may as well have been on another planet, so foreign were they to the students' realm of experience. Second, a *narrow conception of learning* existed in the school. These students had been learners for years. They may not have been considered successful *school* learners, but certainly they were learners; otherwise, they could not have survived to be sixth graders. In order to survive in a demanding environment, they had to learn many physical, cognitive, and language skills, some of which would have challenged the most clever of their teachers. However, in school the nature of learning was more limited, and teachers neither acknowledged nor valued the learning students brought with them to school. Third, there was a *lack of explicit and valued goals*. The carefully structured curriculum meant nothing to Kohl's students. A group of adults in a faraway place had determined this curriculum. These adults did not know this group of students. Because Kohl's students could not see how the curriculum related to their experiences, beliefs, or attitudes and because they did not value traditional school goals (e.g., getting an A on a test), they disengaged from the curriculum.

Van Fleet (1983) tells a similar story of well-meaning Yankee school teachers who traveled south to educate former slaves following the Civil War. Despite their enthusiasm, commitment, and modern teaching techniques, these teachers were unsuccessful with their students. Once again, the three impediments to engagement help explain what went wrong. (Can you apply the three impediments to the former slaves' school experience?) Van Fleet develops this example to introduce a concept which is at the heart of engaging students in the curriculum, and ultimately empowering them academically, socially, and politically. This is the concept of the teacher as a **cultural broker**. What does this mean?

You know what a broker is. A real estate broker is a person who links a consumer with a piece of property. The broker is the middle-person who helps negotiate the connection between the interested party and the desirable goal, a piece of property. A teacher can also be thought of as a broker. In the teacher's case, the brokering is related to a goal which we can refer to broadly as *culture*. To what does this word *culture* refer?

You may recall that we discussed the concept of culture in Chapter 2. In talking about the culture of teaching, we said that **culture** refers to the beliefs, knowledge, and behaviors that are shared by a particular group of people. Although teachers may not think of themselves in this way, they are in the business of enculturating students. As representatives of the mainstream culture, teachers work to make their students a part of that culture. They do this by teaching an array of values, attitudes, habits, ways of behaving, and even subject matter. While it may seem that subject matter belongs to everyone and is not "cultural knowledge," in fact it is. This is because some groups of people have determined over time the content that is to be transmitted to students in schools. This content is only a fraction of the knowledge that has been generated on this earth. If you were asked to do so, you could describe quite accurately the content of the elementary curriculum. Teachers, students, parents, administrators, and legislators tend to take for granted the kind of subject matter that is taught in school. Like the norms, values and attitudes teachers communicate to students, subject matter is part of the taken-for-granted culture.

Let us get back to the idea that teachers are linking agents who connect students with culture. We said earlier that the concept of the cultural broker is central to engaging students in the curriculum. What *conditions must be met if teachers are to be successful cultural brokers*? First, students must value what the teacher offers, a goal we implied in our discussion of the impediments to educational engagement. This idea is closely related to our point in Chapter 5 that teachers must help students see that school tasks have relevance to their immediate experience outside the classroom. Second, students must believe that they can achieve that which is set before them.

In order for these conditions to be met, teachers must develop knowledge of both the culture they offer students and the students' home cultures. This examination of cultures provides teachers with the insight they need to be able to help students value the school curriculum. Obviously, the Yankee schoolteachers lacked this cultural awareness. As a result, the teachers and students continued to operate according to their own culturally defined norms and values. While they all started out with good intentions—the teachers to teach and the students to learn—the teachers soon became frustrated as their students dropped out mentally and/or physically.

We suggest, then, four things that teachers can do to promote the educational engagement of students:

1. Examine the content of the school curriculum.
2. Become familiar with the culture of their students.
3. Help students to value what teachers offer.
4. Help students believe they can succeed.

Let's look at teaching practices in each category.

Examine the Content of the School Curriculum

Recall from Chapter 3 that when we use the word *curriculum*, we mean all of the lessons students learn in school. Some of these lessons are related to subject matter, and others are related to personal and social attitudes, values, expectations, and rules of conduct. Teachers teach these powerful lessons to students through the content of instruction and through their instructional practices (**implicit curriculum**). While on the surface it may appear that teachers are merely teaching subject matter and attempting to maintain an orderly classroom, a closer look reveals implicit learnings. Consider the following vignette from a fifth-grade class:

Mr. Guthrie: Please put away your spelling work and get out your social studies homework from last night. You'll have time to finish the spelling assignment later, but we have to get the social studies checked now.

Mr. Guthrie:	[Shouts over the scuffle of papers and books.] Let's be snappy. We have exactly 20 minutes before music, and I want to check all of the questions. [He looks around.] I see some of you have gotten the spiral notebooks for your social studies work, as I asked you to. That's very good. You'll be able to keep everything together. The rest of you need to remember to get that notebook. On Monday I'll start taking off points if you don't have your notebook. Okay, who's ready with number one?
Terrence:	[Calls out.] I got it.
Mr. Guthrie:	I'm looking for hands. Ryan? Go ahead and remember to read the question.
Ryan:	Why do you think that the President must have more qualifications for office than members of Congress?
Mr. Guthrie:	Good reading.
Ryan:	He has the most important job in the whole country.
Mr. Guthrie:	That's exactly right, Ryan. Any other ideas? [No hands go up. Then Jasmine tentatively raises her hand.]
Mr. Guthrie:	Jasmine? You want to add something?
Jasmine:	Well, I was just thinking that Ryan said "*He* has the most important job," but it could be a *she*, too.
Mr. Guthrie:	Oh, so he did. Well, that's a thought, isn't it? Anybody have anything to say about that? No? Okay, well we do need to move along. Sheila, you go next.
Sheila:	Why does the United States need local and state governments in addition to a national government? Uh, because the national government can't do everything.

[A number of hands instantly shoot up.]

Mr. Guthrie:	Dina?
Dina:	The United States needs local and state governments in addition to a national government to satisfy the different needs of each community.
Mr. Guthrie:	Nice, that's just how the book explains it. Did you catch your problem, Sheila?
A few students:	It wasn't a complete sentence.
Mr. Guthrie:	Right. We don't start a sentence with "Because."

This "lesson" is similar to Ms. Gunther's nouns and verbs lesson we critiqued in Chapter 5. The teacher, Mr. Guthrie, focuses on quickly "covering" the material, allows little student input, and stresses the accuracy of answers. What is the content of Mr. Guthrie's curriculum? Some might say that he's teaching social studies. But what is he teaching about social studies and about other things, for that matter? Think about the manner in which he deals with the content, the United States system of government. He had the students read a passage and answer several questions for homework. He calls on students who raise their hands to read the question and the answer (which must be a complete sentence). You may have noticed that the session focused on accuracy; the teacher praised accurate reading of the question, answers which matched the content of the chapter and the use of complete sentences. When Jasmine raised a question about Ryan's answer, Mr. Guthrie acknowledged the question but did not promote dialogue about it. What does this kind of experience teach students about the subject matter, about learning, about themselves, and about school?

It is possible that with repeated experiences of this type, students could learn a number of pieces of information about the structure of the U.S. government. Students may also learn certain things about knowledge and learning. They may learn that school books are the source of knowledge, or perhaps, that when they are in school, school books are the only legitimate sources of knowledge. From this kind of experience, students may learn that in school, learning is a solitary activity most often requiring a form of printed material and a writing implement. They may come to see that classroom learning is very different from what counts in the real world; in school, being able to retrieve information from books and present it according to certain rules (e.g., raising one's hand and using complete sentences) is essential if one is to be viewed favorably.

We haven't said anything yet about the attitudes and values implicit in this brief vignette. Did you notice several references to time? Mr. Guthrie told the students when it was time to shift activities. They were expected to move quickly and efficiently. Typically, in classrooms, time and knowledge are fragmented, broken into pieces which are managed within carefully defined segments. Spelling is from 8:15 until 8:45, and social studies is squeezed in before music. Adherence to a strict timetable is the norm in many classrooms. Related to efficiency, students who had their spiral notebooks received Mr. Guthrie's approval, while those without the notebook were warned of the consequences. Losing points, at least in the teacher's view, is not desirable because points determine an individual's grade or scholastic "value." Implicit here are school beliefs about how to be organized, compliance with authority, the value of uniformity (i.e., everyone must be organized in the same way), and a message about how one's worth is determined and measured. Additional values are communicated in practices such as requiring that students raise their hands, read the question and the answer, and answer in a complete sentence. The teacher clearly communicates to students that "this is how we do things in school."

Our point is that the school curriculum is full of lessons about subject matter, values, attitudes, beliefs, and norms of conduct. Teachers teach much more than subject matter. They teach ways of thinking about self, school, and society. Some of these ways of thinking are consistent with middle-class values and, as a result, are familiar to many students. For instance, norms about being "well-organized," using formal sentence structures, and using time efficiently are likely to be familiar to many students. (Do you think there might be some gender differences in students' response to these norms?) To other students, school expectations are unfamiliar. If students do not know how to or can see no reason to comply with school expectations, they become disengaged. This problem is not unique to poor and minority students. Although middle-class students may cope with school expectations, they also can be disempowered by these expectations. Recall our earlier summary of the tools of empowerment. It does not appear that Mr.

Practical Application Activity

Choose a typical part of the day in a classroom in which you teach or have observed. This might be sharing time, reading group, "free" time, spelling bee, current events—any piece of the school day will do. Analyze this event for the expectations implicit in it. That is, what must students be able to do in order to participate successfully in this event? Consider the norms of conduct, attitudes, values, and beliefs implicit in the event. You might want to look back at our analysis of Mr. Guthrie's social studies lesson as a guide.

Are there aspects of this event that need adjustment if students in this classroom are to be empowered? What are specific ways in which the event could be modified? What might be the results of these modifications?

Guthrie is providing opportunities for students to develop the knowledge, skills, and attitudes that are likely to empower them.

Teachers who want to promote the educational engagement of all of their students need to look more closely at what they expect of their students. What are the lessons implicit in the form and content of the curriculum? What are the many personal, social, physical, and academic skills students must demonstrate in order to be successful in this classroom? Teachers should become aware of their expectations and of the range of cultural knowledge they expect students to master. Once they are aware of the many dimensions of the curriculum, they can take steps to alter those which do not serve the aim of empowering students. In addition to this analysis, teachers must begin to examine their students' values, attitudes, expectations, and rules of conduct and look for the points of congruence and incongruence between them and the school curriculum.

Become Familiar With Students' Culture

It seems obvious to say that the Yankee schoolteachers would have been more successful had they become familiar with the culture of the former slaves. However, it is only in recent years that educators have begun to understand the power of culture to promote and impede educational engagement. As we have noted, one source of the problem lies in the conflicts between the culture and language of students and those of the school. Another source of the problem lies in the history of some cultural groups.

Ogbu (1985) explains that some minority groups have more difficulty adjusting to school values than others due to their historical treatment in the larger society. For instance, black Americans who have been denied access to good education have come to distrust the schools and the white people who run them. Similarly, Blacks' experiences with limited opportunities in the job market inevitably influence their attitudes toward school. In response to their historical treatment by the dominant cultural group, many black Americans see themselves "not just as *different* from the dominant group but in most respects as *opposed* to their 'white oppressors'" (Ogbu, 1985, p. 866). Children learn this **cultural antagonism** from the adults in their community. Teachers see this antagonism in students' resistance or hostility to teachers' expectations.

In order to protect their sense of collective identity as a cultural group, the minority persons develop certain ways of behaving (i.e. walking, talking, dressing) which separate them from "white people's ways." Being successful in school is likely to be regarded as "acting white" (Fordham & Ogbu, 1986) and is therefore a risky move for many black students. This kind of behavior is perceived as a threat to the collective identity and security of the group and is therefore subject to intense peer pressure.

The experience of oppressed minorities—blacks, Hispanics, and Native Americans in this country—suggests that engaging them in the school curriculum may be considerably more complicated than simply becoming aware of their cultures. Many years of "traumatic social history" (Comer, 1989) have shaped their cultures and are not easily erased. Nevertheless, insight into students' cultures helps teachers who want to reach out to students and get them interested in school.

What can teachers do to gain insight into their students' home cultures? Certainly it is an enormous task to learn about an unfamiliar culture. Anthropologists sometimes spend their entire lives studying a single cultural group! What do teachers really need to know about students if they hope to engage them in the school curriculum? As McDiarmid suggests, "Teachers need to know how school knowledge is valued in their learners' cultures . . . and which knowledge, skills, and commitments are valued in the learners' culture. . . . Teachers [also] need to know about students' prior knowledge of and experience with the subject matter" (1989, pp. 20–21). With these kinds of insights teachers can help students tune in to the curriculum. But how does a teacher gain this insight?

McDiarmid's answer is deceptively simple. He says: "If teachers are to discover what their learners understand, value and are curious about, they must create opportunities for learners to talk about these things" (p. 21). By giving students opportunities to communicate what they know and care about, teachers can find out who these students are and how they see the world. However, developing this knowledge takes more than one or two "All About Me" activities. It requires building opportunities for sharing, self-expression, and dialogue into the fabric of the curriculum. More and more teachers are attempting this through the use of such techniques as student autobiographies and dialogue or response journals. (*Note:* Although writing response journals is frequently considered a language arts activity, many teachers have begun using them to initiate dialogue about the meaning of curricular content in any area of the curriculum. Both of these writing activities [i.e. student autobiographies and response journals] take place over a long period of time. Both activities help students to get to know themselves as well as help teachers and students get to know each other.)

Additionally, teachers must increase student expression by viewing students as an integral part of all lessons. As we have discussed in several chapters, **collaborative instruction** involves students and teacher in a mutual endeavor to construct understanding. Only by understanding students' views can teachers hope to link students to new understandings.

It sounds easy to incorporate the students' voices into instruction. However, it is difficult for many teachers to do so because of pressure to cover the material, to move students along. It is quicker to cover the material if the teacher just tells the students what they need to know. We've seen this happen in our own classes. What we've noticed, however, is that when we just tell students what we think they need to know, the class is lifeless. We feel like performers rather than teachers, and we don't know what our students are thinking or what sense they're making of our carefully constructed lectures. Although it is more challenging to orchestrate many voices, we think it is more satisfying to teacher and students than a teacher monologue.

Teachers can gain insight into students' values, attitudes, understandings, and expectations by letting students take part in the curriculum. Similarly, by observing students in the classroom, the library, the corridors, the cafeteria, and on the playground, teachers can learn a lot about their manner of encountering the world. Regarding the importance of teachers observing their students Kohl wrote:

> Observing children at play and mischief is an invaluable source of knowledge about them—about leaders and groups, fear, courage, warmth, isolation. Teachers consider the children's gym or free play time their free time . . . and usually turn their backs on the children when they have most to learn from them. (1967, p. 23)

Careful observation can provide insight into students' rules of conduct, values, and beliefs. Having gained this insight the teacher is in a better position to shape curriculum and instruction so that it speaks to the students' real world.

Help Students Value What the Teacher Offers

A third task for teachers who hope to engage students is to help students to value the curriculum. The first two tasks we discussed—examining the content of the curriculum and becoming familiar with students' cultures—are, of course, essential in order to accomplish the third task. In addition, teachers can (1) draw on what is known about how learning occurs in the real world to shape in-school learning experiences and (2) help students feel that they are a part of the school community.

MODEL IN-SCHOOL LEARNING EXPERIENCES AFTER OUT-OF-SCHOOL LEARNING EXPERIENCES.   We noted earlier that both the purpose and the nature of learning look different in school and out of school. When learning takes place outside of school, there is a practical purpose which drives the learner. For example, we taught ourselves to use the Word Perfect word-processing program while writing this book. Although we were not enthusiastic about learning to use computers before writing this book, doing so made computer literacy essential. While learning a word-processing program was not a valued goal in the abstract, in the context of producing a collaboratively written textbook it became a *highly valued goal*.

To continue with the Word Perfect example, the manner in which we learned to use the program exemplifies the discussion of learning in and out of school. Learning to use Word Perfect was a *social experience*. Although we each spent time studying the Word Perfect manual and certainly we each spent time independently at our machines, we also spent a lot of time consulting with one another and with friends who were Word Perfect "experts." People showed us what to do, and we gave one another advice about tricks we were learning along the way.

Another critical element of learning to use Word Perfect was the amount of practice in which we engaged. It has taken a lot of time for us to feel comfortable with this program. This is not because the program is especially tricky or that we are especially slow learners. It often takes a lot of time and *a lot of practice* to really know how to do something—to understand and know how to apply what one has learned.

Another aspect of learning to use Word Perfect is relevant to our discussion on the manner in which the learning is evaluated by learners. As Wehlage et al. have said, "The '*test*' for most out-of-school learning *is successful application* in a practical setting" (1989, p. 183). We have engaged in self-evaluation as we have struggled to get the computer to do what we want it to do. We quickly find out whether we "know the material" when we see what happens when we press this key or that! We also have provided feedback to one another when we have traded discs to work on each other's writing (e.g., Dorene Ross to Buffy Bondy, "I think you need to learn about the indent key.")

These aspects of learning—purposefulness, social nature, lengthy practice periods, and opportunities for self-evaluation and feedback from others—are not often found in today's classrooms. In-school learning tends to be for unknown or contrived purposes and individualistic in nature. Students typically have a brief period of time to practice before moving on to something new, and the practice itself is of a superficial nature. Evaluation is conducted by teachers and usually entails having students provide answers to questions. Wehlage et al. explain that "competence displayed by correctly answering teacher questions is so restricted that it seems unimportant to the present or future of many students. They feel no personal ownership of the knowledge school requires them to learn" (1989, p. 183).

How can teachers help students feel "personal ownership" of school knowledge, thereby helping them to value the curriculum? We list five suggestions that we feel help students value the school curriculum:

1. Be sure that students see a purpose for learning. In order to accomplish this, teachers must see the world through the eyes of their students. They must structure lessons in ways that enable students to recognize personal meaning in school tasks and to see the connections between new activities and things they already know and value. Creating instructional problems out of students' life experiences is one strategy that is often suggested.

2. Allow students to have some control over the activities they do in school. Give them some choices in what they will do and how they will do it.

3. Have students work with partners or in small groups. More experienced or knowledgeable students can serve as "experts," just as happens in "real life."

4. Use the **apprenticeship model** as outlined in the literacy chapter. Recall that this model is based on learning in real-world contexts. It involves the processes of modeling expert behavior, providing coaching and scaffolding to support the learner's efforts, having learners articulate the processes used to perform the new behavior, having learners compare their efforts to those of an expert (*reflection*), and having learners apply the new knowledge or processes independently (*exploration*). These application experiences should be meaningful to the learners; learners should understand what their efforts will produce.

5. Have students examine their own learning. They can engage in ongoing self-evaluation by keeping learning logs (see Chapter 7), being responsible for group progress reports, and participating in class discussions about questions, concerns, and next steps. Students can be made responsible for identifying their own strengths, weaknesses, and goals for improvement.

An example of a long-range project in Kohl's (1967) classroom illustrates a number of these suggestions.[2] Kohl describes the origins of the language study curriculum in his classroom:

> One day Ralph cursed at Michael and unexpectedly things came together for me. Michael was reading and stumbled several times. Ralph scornfully called out, "What's the matter, psyches, going to pieces again?" The class broke up and I jumped on the word "psyches."
>
> "Ralph, what does *psyches* mean?"
>
> An embarrassed silence. "Do you know how to spell it?"
>
> Alvin volunteered. "S-i-k-e-s."
>
> "Where do you think the word came from? Why did everybody laugh when you said it, Ralph?"
>
> "You know, Mr. Kohl, it mean, like crazy or something."
>
> "Why? How do words get to mean what they do?"
>
> Samuel looked up at me and said: "Mr. Kohl, now you're asking questions like Alvin. There aren't any answers, you know that."
>
> "But there are. Sometimes by asking Alvin's kind of questions you discover the most unexpected things. Look."
>
> I wrote Psyche, then Cupid, on the blackboard. "That's how psyche is spelled. It looks strange in English, but the word doesn't come from English. It's Greek. There's a letter in the Greek alphabet that comes out psi in English. This is the way psyche looks in Greek. . . ."
>
> [Kohl then told the Greek myth about Psyche and shared with the children the large number of words coming from Cupid and Psyche.]
>
> Leaping ahead, Alvin shouted: "You mean words change? People didn't always speak this way? Then how come the reader says there's a right way to talk and a wrong way?"

[2]   From *Thirty-Six Children* by Herbert Kohl. Copyright © 1967 by Herbert Kohl. Used by permission of New American Library, a division of Penguin Books USA, Inc.

"There's a right way now, and that only means that's how most people would like to talk now, and how people write now."

Charles jumped out of his desk and spoke for the first time during the year.

"You mean one day the way we talk—you know, with words like cool and dig and sound—may be all right?"

"Uh huh. Language is alive, it's always changing, only sometimes it changes so slowly that we can't tell."

"Mr. Kohl, can't we study the language we're talking about instead of spelling and grammar? They won't be any good when language changes anyway."

We could and did. That day we began what had to be called for my conservative plan book "vocabulary," and "an enrichment activity." Actually it was the study of language and myth, of the origins and history of words, of their changing uses and functions in human life. (Kohl, 1967, pp. 33–35)

Kohl then describes how language study flowed into social studies, with the students branching off into projects of their own choosing. For example, one child studied Greek architecture and created a model of the Parthenon. Two others used a chemistry book to create an erupting volcano.

Teachers can help students value what the school has to offer them by letting the real world into the classroom. All students—even those considered *at risk*, unmotivated, or underachieving—are learners. In certain contexts, "unmotivated" students are motivated learners, and "underachievers" are high achievers. So-called *at risk* students pass all kinds of physical, social, and cognitive tests daily. The problem is not that some students cannot or do not want to learn. The problem is that the kind of teaching they encounter and the kind of material they are offered seem senseless to them. When learners value what is offered and are given opportunities to learn in ways that involve and challenge them, they are likely to become engaged in the curriculum.

DEVELOP STUDENTS' SENSE OF SCHOOL MEMBERSHIP.   Another way to help students value school learning is to develop their sense of belonging to the school community. Wehlage et al. (1989) have identified school membership as one of students' "basic, common deep-seated needs" (1989, p. 113). Essentially, **school membership** refers to students' belief that they belong at the school, that they are accept-

---

FOCUS BOX 8–7

Application Activity

Look back at the five suggestions for helping students value the school curriculum (see pages 234–235).

- Analyze the vignette from Kohl's book for examples of these practices.
- Summarize what you see as the critical features of his teaching practice.
- Which of these teaching practices seem most difficult to you? Why?

ed and supported by peers and adults, and that people are willing to help them with their personal and academic needs. Wehlage et al. point out that when students believe that they are accepted and cared for as individuals, they reciprocate by conforming to school expectations and participating in school activities.

According to Wehlage et al., promoting school membership requires that teachers be strongly committed to student success. While it seems that we should be able to assume this commitment, Wehlage et al. found that some high schools actually withheld it:

> Students with certain personal or background characteristics may be seen as unworthy or at least very unlikely to benefit from teachers' efforts; these students are viewed as "damaged," and cannot benefit from school. (1989, p. 121)

Although the Wehlage et al. research was done in high schools, we believe their findings are relevant to elementary teachers. Even in elementary schools, teachers make judgments about students based on family background. When teachers view students as unable to be helped, they cease to reach out to those students. Students respond by withdrawing from school, sometimes quietly and passively and other times aggressively and violently. In schools where teachers did demonstrate their commitment to all students, students responded with "(1) behaviors that [were] positive and respectful toward adults and peers; and (2) educational engagement" (Wehlage et al. 1989, p. 120).

Students who feel they belong to a classroom community are likely to become engaged in the curriculum of that classroom.

Wehlage et al. describe school membership as "the foundation for other goals involving academic achievement and outcomes concerning personal and social development into productive adults" (1989, p. 133). That is, warm personal relations between teachers and students help students feel accepted and help them achieve. In her study of successful teachers of fourth- through sixth-grade black students, Ladson-Billings concluded that "successful teaching of black students is as much about relationships as it is about pedagogy per se" and that "without the relationship, there is no real teaching and learning and those relationships must be renewed and renegotiated throughout the school year" (1990, p. 24).

In Chapter 6, we described teaching strategies relevant to this discussion. In that chapter, we described the kind of classroom environment that supports the development of prosocial behavior and attitudes. Essentially, we said that the classroom should be a place in which all students feel accepted. Strategies that contribute to an environment of acceptance are also likely to contribute to students' sense of school membership. The following strategies, discussed in detail in Chapter 6, are useful: help students to value human diversity, help students to recognize the similarities among human beings, help students to expand their circle of friends, help the class create a collective identity, encourage students to share their special talents with the class, and recognize the unique qualities of each student by celebrating "special days." In this chapter, we have discussed two principles important in helping students to value the school curriculum: modeling in-school learning experiences after out-of-school learning experiences and developing students' sense of school membership. These principles help students to see the sense in school activities and to care about what happens in school. The final practice which is important in fostering student engagement is helping students believe that they can be successful at the tasks which the teacher presents.

Help Students Believe They Can Succeed

Teachers' beliefs about the likelihood of student success influence students' beliefs. We discussed the construct of teachers' sense of efficacy in Chapter 1. This idea is helpful in illuminating the relationship between teachers' beliefs, their classroom effort and practices, and student outcomes (Ashton & Webb, 1986).

> Teachers with a strong sense of **efficacy** [boldface added] believe that they are capable of having a positive effect on student performance. They choose challenging activities and are motivated to try harder when obstacles confront them. (Ashton & Webb, 1986, p. 3)

Two studies by the Rand Corporation (Armor, Conry-Oseguera, Cox, King, McDonnell, Pascal, Pauly, & Zellman, 1976; Berman, McLaughlin, Bass, Pauly, & Zellman, 1977) provide evidence that teachers' sense of efficacy affects both teacher and student performance. Clearly, teachers' beliefs about students' abilities and their own teaching abilities make a difference in classroom practices and the messages communicated to students.

Wehlage et al. (1989) describe four beliefs that teachers must possess in order to reach out to students, to help them believe they can be successful, and to engage them in the curriculum. These include:

> Teachers accept personal accountability for student success; they believe in practicing an extended teacher role [beyond simply conveying subject matter]; they accept the need to be persistent with students who are not ideal pupils; they express a sense of optimism that all students can learn if one builds upon their strengths rather than their weaknesses. (Wehlage et al., 1989, p. 135)

Essentially, Wehlage et. al., are saying that a high sense of efficacy is a prerequisite for helping students believe they can succeed. Another way to look at it is that teachers must believe they can succeed with students if they are going to be able to convince students that they can be successful.

Bredemeier (1988) reached similar conclusions in a study of effective teachers of inner-city high-school students. These teachers recognized the factors that contributed to students' low aspirations and lack of engagement in school but denied that students' academic fates were sealed. They believed that all students could be successful and were determined to bring about that success. What else can teachers do? Some clues are available in the literature on teacher expectations.

Good (1987) has summarized the research on the nature and impact of teacher expectations. To help students believe they can succeed, teachers must be attentive to the expectations they communicate to students. It is easy for teachers to say, "I want to help all of my students to succeed," but to communicate through their classroom practices that they do not expect much from certain students. Good lists *classroom practices which communicate low expectations* to students:

- giving students less time to answer a question and accepting and using students' ideas less often
- supplying the answer or calling on someone else instead of providing clues or rephrasing a question
- praising incorrect answers and providing excessive teacher sympathy
- criticizing students more for incorrect answers
- praising students less, calling on them less, interacting with them less, providing less eye contact and other nonverbal communication
- seating students far from the teacher

Weinstein (1983) reports that students notice which students are treated in what manner, and that they use their observations as they formulate perceptions of self and peers. Good also reports that certain *general teacher practices communicate low expectations*. These include emphasizing rules and procedures, dominating the classroom, closely monitoring students, attending to minor details, maintaining a slow instructional pace, omitting discussion of the meaningfulness of topics studied, giving students inappropriate tasks, and maintaining a barren physical environment. These practices communicate low expectations to whole groups or classes of students.

Good (1987) recommends that teachers examine their practices to gain insight into the kinds of expectations they are communicating to particular students, groups of students, or to entire classes. Often teachers believe there are good reasons for using some of these practices. For instance, teachers say, "I don't call on him because I don't want him to be embarrassed when he gives the wrong answer," or "I have to keep the reins in tight because these students need structure." We are not suggesting that there is no validity to these practices; but we want teachers to become aware of what they are doing rather than acting based on taken-for-granted assumptions about what certain students need. With the best intentions, teachers can communicate to students that they will never amount to much.

Good's recommendations for raising teacher expectations are similar to the practices that foster educational engagement. For instance, he talks about attending to students' ideas and interests and encouraging students to be active self-evaluators. He suggests designing lessons that actively involve students and providing opportunities for meaningful application of new concepts and skills. By increasing students' responsibility for learning, teachers communicate that students can succeed.

We have just discussed the nature of, impediments to, and means of achieving student engagement. Students must be engaged with the school curriculum if they are to become empowered academically, socially, economically, and politically. Next we will summarize essential features of instruction for student empowerment. These features, drawn from our discussion of student engagement and from the other chapters of this book, will help you pull together the main ideas in this book.

Synthesis of Features of Instruction for Student Empowerment

You have no doubt noticed that certain concepts recur throughout this book. Indeed, as we have written about curriculum and instruction, we have been guided by themes that define the nature of teaching for student empowerment. Here we summarize what we see as essential characteristics of instruction. You will notice that we have drawn heavily on Prawat's (1989) attributes of instruction for understanding (see Chapter 7). We have also drawn on a constructivist orientation to teaching and learning and on ethics of care and equity (see Chapter 1).

CARING.   As we stressed in our discussion of helping students develop a sense of school membership, teachers who wish to empower students must care about them and be committed to helping them succeed. Teachers must reach out to students, treat them with respect, and help them participate actively in school life. In addition, they model the qualities of care and compassion that students must learn if they are to become caring human beings, a part of the broad aim of student empowerment.

EQUITY.   Teachers must work to assure that all students have equal access to knowledge. This is easier said than done in schools where ability grouping, tracking, and pull-out programs are the norm. Often teachers say that these programs are helpful to students because they enable teachers to individualize instruction. Many educational researchers would argue, however, that these practices in reality function "as a 'ranking' system that legitimizes differences based on race, gender, and social power and locks students into positions of limited opportunity" (McLaren, 1989, p. 9). Oakes (1985) explains that low-track students, who are likely to be from poor and minority backgrounds, are hardest hit by school tracking that denies them access to the kinds of experiences that could empower them. Instruction for student empowerment is equitable in that it provides access to the knowledge, skills, and attitudes essential for empowerment to all students rather than to those deemed "ready" for it.

FOCUSED INSTRUCTION.   Focused instruction thoroughly develops several main ideas or skills rather than superficially covering many. Rather than skipping lightly across multiple, disconnected pieces of information, the teacher identifies key ideas and helps students develop a sound grasp of these.

COHERENT INSTRUCTION.   Coherent instruction helps students to see the connections across parts of a lesson and across lessons. The teacher helps students integrate experiences and build an elaborate network of understandings that they can use to interpret new experiences and solve new problems.

ANALYTIC INSTRUCTION.   Teachers must create many opportunities to observe and examine students' thinking and understandings. While many teachers fail to attend to students' ideas and explanations during instruction (Smith & Neale, 1989), this kind of information is essential because it provides teachers with a window into students' cognitions. Once teachers know "where students are" conceptually, they can make better decisions about how to move the students toward the desired understandings.

MEANINGFUL INSTRUCTION.   In many chapters, we have stressed the importance of grounding instruction in the real worlds of students. We say "worlds" instead of "world" intentionally. As discussed in this chapter, students do not necessarily share the same frame of reference—with the school or with one another. If they are to value what the school offers, they must see it as relevant to their lives.

COLLABORATIVE INSTRUCTION.   In this book, we have used the words *interactive*, *reciprocal*, and *collaborative* to describe instruction. These terms refer to the idea that learning involves ongoing negotiation among the members of a learning community. "Teaching," then, is not something teachers do to a group of students. Instead "learning" takes place among a community of students, one of whom traditionally has been called "teacher." While the teacher may possess some kinds of knowledge that the students do not have, the teacher must be a student of students in order to help them come to share that knowledge.

CRITICAL INSTRUCTION.   Instruction that is critical promotes student examination of taken-for-granted features of their lives. Rather than assuming that all is right with the world and that students should simply learn and adjust to the status quo, we suggest that teachers model and encourage a questioning attitude that helps students wonder about why things are as they are.

An example might help to clarify what instruction incorporating these characteristics would look like. A student in Buffy Bondy's Elementary Curriculum class, Meddie Bidwell, created a unit on the Jamestown colony for fifth graders. Meddie had only 45 minutes per day to work with students on unit activities. To make the topic real and important to her students (*meaningful instruction*), she identified key understandings about human behavior and community life which are embedded in the Jamestown story and which apply to human activity across time (*focused instruction*). Here are her three key understandings: (1) The survival of a community depends on the participation of individual members. (2) A conflict in values, like the clash between the Powhatan Indians and the Jamestown colonists, often results in a misunderstanding between the parties and may have devastating results such as death or war. (3) Preplanning and careful thought is essential to the successful execution of an activity. The first two understandings offer the potential for *critical instruction* because they suggest a close examination of often unexamined parts of students' lives, the concept of community and personal values.

The key ideas which Meddie wanted all students to construct directed her lesson planning. In all lessons Meddie tied the seventeenth century to the twentieth century to help students recognize the present-day significance of the Jamestown story (*coherent* and *meaningful instruction*). For example, students compared and contrasted responsibilities of Jamestown children with their own. Students examined children's responsibilities to the family, the school, the city, the country, and to other people. They examined problems faced by the Jamestown colonists, considered how some problems could have been prevented, and designed solutions to problems. Students did the same sort of activity aimed at problems in the school community (*critical instruction*). Most of these activities involved discussion and consensus-seeking in small, heterogeneous groups which Meddie monitored and participated in when necessary to move the group beyond an impasse. Groups then shared their conclusions during whole-class discussion (*collaborative, diagnostic, caring*, and *equitable instruction*).

In Meddie's unit, social studies and language arts activities merged as students pursued projects that made sense in terms of their everyday realities. Students learned facts about Jamestown in a meaningful context. Also, they developed key ideas that apply across time and help them to understand and perhaps participate more productively in community life.

This kind of instruction engages students and helps them develop the tools of empowerment. While teachers cannot organize all of their instruction in this way, especially given the constraints within which many teachers work, they can take steps in this direction. You might, for instance, identify important concepts from your social studies, science, language, and math curricula as a grade level team

FOCUS BOX 8–8

Application Activity

Look back at the brief description of the "inventions" unit (see p. 216) and at the eight features of instruction which we have just described.

- Look for evidence of the eight features of instruction which we have described in the "inventions" unit.

- For any feature which is not represented, plan additional experiences related to the unit theme. In other words, be sure that *your* description of the "inventions" unit incorporates all eight features of instruction for student empowerment.

and distribute responsibility for unit planning across teachers. If a colleague handed you a general plan for a unit on "machines," "water," or "space exploration," you would be well on your way to having a set of lessons appropriate for your class.

Meddie's unit illustrates the characteristics of instruction for student empowerment. There is one more feature of her teaching that enabled her to implement these essential characteristics. Can you guess? Meddie is a highly reflective teacher. Clear about her goals, she engaged in ongoing examination of her instruction and students' responses to it. She used students' oral and written feedback as evidence to help her determine if and when to shift her original plans. Her teaching consisted of ongoing cycles of planning, acting, observing, and reflecting. Meddie had the tools necessary to empower her students.

Summary

In this chapter, we asked the questions, "What is the ultimate aim of teachers who work with elementary school students?" and "What teaching practices help teachers accomplish this aim?" In answer to the first question we discussed the notion of empowerment for lifelong learning, self-determination, and critical citizenship. In answer to the second question, we discussed the concept of student engagement which is central to accomplishing all educational aims, and we summarized and illustrated the characteristics of instruction for student empowerment. While we addressed the problems faced by students who are culturally different from mainstream, middle-class American students, we believe that educational engagement and student empowerment are relevant for all kinds of school children. We invite you to take on the challenge of engaging all of your students in a curriculum designed to empower for school success, self-determination, and critical citizenship. Your students' individual futures and the future of our planet depend on your efforts.

FOCUS BOX 8–9

Yes, These Look Like Good Ideas, but . . .

Whenever teachers encounter new ideas, they have to try to fit them within their current understandings about children, their knowledge of and beliefs about appropriate instructional strategies, their current knowledge base, and their specific teaching context. Because of this, you probably found yourself raising questions about the feasibility of the alternative practices we have suggested. We suspect at times you found yourself thinking, "Yes, these look like good ideas, but . . .?" Work with a small group of peers to raise and try to answer your questions about the strategies suggested in this chapter. The following questions may help to guide your thinking:

- What is your overall, "gut" reaction to the ideas? Do they look like strategies you might like to try? Why or why not?
- As you think about trying to implement the strategies, what concerns do you have?
- If you were to try to implement these strategies, what skills, abilities, and/or knowledge would you need to develop? How would you go about doing this?
- What contextual barriers do you see that might make implementation of these strategies difficult? How could you work around these contextual barriers? (*Note:* By **contextual barriers**, we mean circumstances specific to your teaching situation. For example, you may teach or student teach in a school where teachers are required to "cover" every unit in the social studies text. Or you may teach in a team-teaching situation where teachers are expected to cover the same content within the same time frame.)
- What are the implicit curriculum implications of these strategies? How do they fit with the aims you have identified as important for elementary education?

It is important to raise these kinds of questions and to explore the answers with your peers. Failure to confront these questions probably means you will not make the significant changes necessary to empower students.

Further Readings

Fordham, S., & Ogbu, J. (1986). Black students' school success: Coping with the burden of "acting white." *The Urban Review, 18* (3), 1–31.

Good, T. L. (1987). Two decades of research on teacher expectations: Findings and future directions. *Journal of Teacher Education, 38* (4), 32–47.

Goodman, J. (1992). *Elementary schooling for critical democracy.* Albany, NY: State University of New York Press.

Kohl, H. (1967). *36 children.* New York: The New American Library.

Ladson–Billings, G. (1990, April). Making a little magic: Teachers talk about successful teaching strategies for black children. Paper presented at the annual meeting of the American Educational Research Association, Boston, MA.

McDiarmid, G. W. (1989, February). What do teachers need to know about cultural diversity: Restoring subject matter to the picture. Paper presented at the Policy Conference of the National Center for Research on Teacher Education, Washington, DC.

Oakes, J. (1985). *Keeping track: How schools structure inequality*. New Haven: Yale University Press.

Ogbu, J. (1985). Research currents: Cultural–ecological influences on minority school learning. *Language Arts, 62*, 860–869.

Resnick, L. (1987). Learning in and out of school. *Educational Researcher, 16* (9), 13–20.

Richardson, V., Casanova, U., Placier, P., & Guilfoyle, K. (1989). *School children at risk*. Philadelphia: The Falmer Press.

Trueba, H. T. (1988). Culturally–based explanations of minority students' academic achievement. *Anthropology and Education Quarterly, 19*, 270–287.

Wehlage, G. G., Rutter, R. A., Smith, G. A., Lesko, N., & Fernandez, R. R. (1989). *Reducing the risk: Schools as communities of support*. Philadelphia: The Falmer Press.

Weinstein, R. L. (1983). Student perceptions of schooling. *The Elementary School Journal, 83*, 287–312.

CHAPTER 9

Empowering Students by Teaching Self-Discipline

What are your biggest concerns about teaching? One is likely to be classroom management; in fact, Gallup polls (1986) indicate that this aspect of teaching is the primary concern of students, teachers, parents, and school administrators—and with good reason. Goodlad (1984) reported that instruction consumes only about 50 percent of the school day, while behavior control consumes nearly 40 percent of the day (Goodlad, 1984).

Classroom management can present several problems for teachers. School administrators noticing a noisy room may not look further to determine the nature of the noise and may form opinions of the teacher's competence. Supervisors are likely to spend more time in a noisy room. Of course, this attention may be helpful to the teacher, but it also may add considerable stress to an already stressful life. Also, this attention may cause the teacher to devote more time and attention to issues of order and control than to issues of student learning.

We do not mean to suggest that classroom management problems lie in the imaginations of supervisors or that supervisors are apt to bother more than help teachers! Certainly, teachers have real difficulties with classroom management; however, we also are concerned that inappropriate emphasis on order and control through power, punishments, and/or fear can impede teachers' abilities to achieve other important educational aims. Learning cannot occur within a chaotic environment, and we believe strongly that classroom order is essential. However, classroom order is a means to an end, not an end in itself. Classroom management strategies, like other *instructional* strategies must be determined within the context of the teacher's aims for education. Strategies that "work" to keep children quiet and on task but undermine the aim of empowering students are problematic for teachers who accept empowerment as the principal aim of education. We will begin with a discussion of educational aims and ask you to clarify your aims by completing the self-assessment in Focus Box 9–1.

FOCUS BOX 9–1

What Are Your Aims? A Self-Assessment

Directions: Answer the following two questions working alone or with a group of your peers.

1. Think about an orderly *class*. List all the characteristics that come to mind.
2. Think about a self-disciplined *child*. List all the characteristics that come to mind.

Now look at your two lists and answer the following questions:

1. Are the characteristics you listed similar? Why or why not? What are the implications of any differences?
2. What is the difference between discipline and *self*-discipline? Are there different defining characteristics for these two terms?

Educational Aims: A Basis for Thinking About Classroom Management

In this book, we have stressed that the principal aim of teachers within a democratic society is to empower students to be active, critical citizens. Recall that this broad aim of **student empowerment** has three related subgoals: the ability (1) to succeed as a learner, (2) to determine one's path through life, and (3) to participate actively and critically as a citizen in a democracy. These subgoals represent social values associated with individualism and community; the first two focus on individual self-advancement, and the third stresses a community orientation in which individuals value the public good and their responsibility to members of the community. In Chapter 6, we noted that schooling is an important context for socializing children to learn how to participate in community life. Classroom management strategies, then, must be viewed as a means to socialize students so that they develop the self-discipline necessary for socially responsible action as a democratic citizen. (Because the issues involved in the development of *self-discipline* and *responsibility* are integrally linked, you will notice that we use the terms almost interchangeably.)

Looking back at the self-assessment you just completed may help to clarify this point. Typically, teachers note that an orderly class is one in which the children do their work, turn things in on time, follow directions, follow class rules, and so on. In contrast, teachers describe self-disciplined children as those who respect the rights and needs of others, have good social skills, accept responsibility for the consequences of their actions, are able to get along cooperatively with peers, are able to control their emotions and actions, and are able to secure positive attention from others. The contrast between these two sets of characteristics is significant.

The first set of characteristics implies that discipline is a means to get work done efficiently within a classroom. The second set implies that discipline provides *instruction* that enables each child to develop social tools essential for self-discipline.

What Does Self-Discipline for Responsible Action Mean?

Stensrud and Stensrud define **self-discipline** as entailing "the ability to comply appropriately with authority and to withstand the pressures of authorities to coerce compliance when it is inappropriate given one's personal value system" (1981, p. 163). This definition includes two of the **four elements of self-discipline for responsible action.** First, self-discipline involves *the ability to follow some socially derived principles of behavior.* Wayson (1985) says that existing within a society requires that humans develop and comply with **norms** (i.e., rules or guidelines) for behavior. That is, no true form of *self*-discipline exists, because the needs of others constrain each individual. Within a classroom, as within society, rules and procedures are necessary, and people must comply with them.

A second element is that the individual must have the *inclination to act responsibly* (Duke & Jones, 1985). Children must not only comply with group norms but must choose to act responsibly, because they have incorporated those norms as a part of an internal value structure that guides action (Benson, 1987; Wayson, 1985). That is, children develop the capacity to make reasoned choices that match the social norms of the group.

A third element is the *ability to make judgments about appropriate action within alternative contexts.* Wayson (1985) notes that the norms for appropriate behavior change dependent on one's context. Yelling across the room may be appropriate (even desirable) in the gymnasium, but inappropriate within the classroom. This ability involves more than being able to memorize and follow different rules in different settings. It means being able to recognize the different social constraints and possibilities of different settings and to make judgments about appropriate behavior.

A fourth element is the *"ability to act contrary to a norm when it violates a higher ethic"* (Wayson, 1985, p. 228). This criterion discriminates self-discipline from obedience. Power and Kohlberg (1986) point out that the essence of morality is making "thoughtful decisions about values which may be in conflict" (p. 16). To resolve such conflicts requires the ability to reason, the courage to stand by one's ethical commitments, and the ability to balance individual and community needs. Wayson (1985) sees this criterion as a critical factor in the development of social responsibility as opposed to obedience.

Lessons From Classroom Management Research

Brophy (1985) notes that most research on classroom management focuses on how to control behavior rather than on how to promote self-discipline. We can understand this by mentally dividing teachers into three groups (Table 9–1).

Table 9–1   Classroom Management Styles

Effective teachers		Ineffective teachers
Group 1	**Group 2**	**Group 3**
Aim: develop self-discipline and social responsibility	Aim: classroom order	Aim: classroom order
Successful in establishing order	Successful in establishing order	Unable to establish order
Prevent problems	Prevent problems	Unable to prevent problems
Children on task	Children on task	Children off task
Children develop all four elements of self-discipline	Children develop first element of self-discipline	No elements of self-discipline are developed

Group 1 teachers establish classroom order in ways that foster the development of self-discipline and help children develop all four of the abilities previously described. *Group 2* teachers maintain orderly classrooms by skillfully using their authority as teachers to prevent management problems and keep students on task. These teachers help children develop the first ability that we described. *Group 3* teachers are not able to establish effective classroom order.

Most researchers investigating classroom management have studied the differences between effective teachers (Groups 1 and 2) and ineffective teachers (Group 3). However, researchers have not investigated the characteristics that differentiate teachers who emphasize self-discipline and, thus, develop all four characteristics of self-discipline (Group 1) from those who emphasize order and, therefore, only develop one element of self-discipline (Group 2). In this section, we will present those characteristics that all good classroom managers possess. In the remainder of the chapter, we will identify the characteristics and strategies that differentiate teachers who foster self-discipline (Group 1) from teachers who simply secure appropriate behavior from children (Group 2).

Kounin (1970) conducted the first systematic inquiry into effective classroom management practices. After two decades of classroom research on discipline and group management techniques, Kounin found few differences in the way effective and ineffective managers handled misbehaving students. However, he did identify a number of *teacher behaviors that contributed to the smooth functioning of classrooms* and, thus, prevented many classroom disruptions from occurring: These teaching behaviors are as follows:

1. **Withitness:** Teachers who are "with it" are able to stop misbehavior before it escalates. These teachers appear to know who is doing what at all times; seem to have "eyes in the back of their heads"; intervene immediately after spotting a potentially disruptive activity; keep interventions subtle, simple, and private. "Withitness" requires that the teacher be watchful, monitoring the behavior of the entire class even when working with individual students or small groups.

2. **Overlapping:** Related to withitness, overlapping refers to conducting more than one activity simultaneously. Teachers who can do this are more likely to maintain a calm and orderly atmosphere and to establish themselves as a strong presence in the classroom.

3. **Smoothness and momentum:** Related to each other, these concepts refer to the pace within and between activities. The important points for the teacher to keep in mind are avoiding student confusion and waiting time. Teachers must anticipate students' concerns and questions, and think through the lesson and the transition ahead of time. Chaos can result during poorly planned periods of time when students do not know what they are expected to do.

4. **Group alerting:** This concept refers to focusing the group's attention on the activity at hand. The good manager uses signals (e.g., a tone bell, songs, or fingerplays) to get the group's attention and other techniques to maintain their attention. Many teachers vary their voice tone and quality as well as pitch and speed. When questioning students, teachers can alert the group by alternating between calling for individual and group responses. When calling on individuals, teachers ask the question before saying the students' names, thereby encouraging all students to listen to and think about the question. Another way to alert the group is to have students react to one another's comments or answers.

5. **Avoiding satiation:** When students get too much of something, they feel bored and may turn their attention elsewhere. Teachers can avoid satiation by providing progress, challenge, and variety. Students who believe they are making progress are less likely to become satiated. Enthusiastic teachers who challenge students with statements such as, "We're really going to have to think about this one, but I know we can do it," prevent satiation. In order to capture students' interest and attention, teachers must be genuinely enthusiastic and positive when they make challenging statements. Finally, teachers can avoid satiating students by building variety into their lessons and the school day. Within lessons, teachers can use a variety of materials, formats (e.g., whole-class, small-group, partners, lectures, learning stations), and levels of thinking. During the day the same principle should be applied.

Evertson, Emmer and their colleagues built upon the work begun by Kounin and have identified specific practices used by effective classroom managers. We have drawn on their work to present **four guidelines for effective classroom management** (Evertson & Emmer, 1982; Evertson, Emmer, Clements, Sanford, & Worsham, 1984; Sanford & Emmer, 1988). Each guideline includes specific strategies for implementation.

Guideline 1: Set Expectations for Student Behavior

Effective teachers spend time before their students even arrive for the first day of school, thinking about and developing expectations for appropriate student behavior. **Expectations** may be thought of as either routines or rules. **Routines** specify behavior in a particular area, such as how pencils are to be sharpened or what students are to do after they complete seatwork. **Rules** prescribe general classroom behavior, such as how one is to treat other individuals in the room or the manner in which one is to complete assignments.

How do teachers know what routines to add to their list? Your observations and experience in classrooms can help you identify those routines that are important to you. Sanford and Emmer (1988) suggest teachers consider **routines in five areas:**

1. administrative routines (e.g., taking roll, collecting lunch money, distributing school notices)

2. procedures for student talk and movement (e.g., How do students get a turn to talk? Is talking and movement allowed during seatwork? during large-group lessons?)

3. procedures for managing student work (e.g., where students place completed papers)

4. procedures for student use of equipment and supplies

5. procedures for group work (procedures for students working with the teacher and those working independently)

Look at the vignette in Focus Box 9–2 to see if you can identify specific areas of classroom life that need to be routinized, if students and teacher are to live together happily and productively.

FOCUS BOX 9–2

Classroom Vignette

Directions: Read the following vignette and list any places where the lack of clearly established routines and procedures contributes to disruptive or inappropriate behavior by students. After you compile your list, share it with a group of peers to compare your observations. Then make a list of the routines you would establish in order to ensure that small-group work will proceed smoothly. The routines should state specifically the behavior expected of students.

[Mr. Garcia sits at the reading group table.]

Mr. Garcia: I'd like to have the Jets up here, please.

[Several students look up from their seatwork and quickly look back to it. Mr. Garcia turns the pages in his teacher's manual, scanning each one. He marks several places with a pencil. Then he looks up.]

Mr. Garcia: Jets? Come on, let's go.

[Although several students shift in their seats, no one gets up.]

Mr. Garcia: Jeremy? Maurice? Come on! Sheila? Let's go.

Maurice: Oooh, I just wanna finish this page.

Mr. Garcia: It's time for reading group now. Let's go.

FOCUS BOX 9–2, *continued*

[Grumbling, five students slowly move toward the reading table.]

Mr. Garcia: First let's look at those skilpak pages you did for homework.

Maurice: Oh-oh.

Mr. Garcia: What's the problem, Maurice?

Maurice: I forgot my skilpak.

Sheila: Me, too.

Mr. Garcia: Well, go back to your seats and get them. You know you need skilpaks for reading group!

[Laura stands up and turns toward the door.]

Mr. Garcia: Laura, what are you doing?

Laura: Well, I have to go to the bathroom.

Mr. Garcia: Not during reading group you aren't. You'll have to wait.

[Maurice and Sheila return to the table.]

Mr. Garcia: Okay, now on page 34, who can read the first sentence?

[Maurice and Micah call out: I can! I can do it!]

Maurice: I want to do it.

Mr. Garcia: That's not the way to get a turn! Can someone raise a hand? Okay, Sheila?

[A student, Gerald, is standing next to Mr. Garcia, tapping his arm with a pencil.]

Gerald: Mr. Garcia? Mr. Garcia? I need help.

Mr. Garcia: What is it, Gerald?

Gerald: Well, I don't know how to do this page.

Mr. Garcia: Gerald, I'm in the middle of a reading group. You'll have to wait.

Gerald: But I've finished all the other pages. This is my last one.

Mr. Garcia: I'm sure you can find something else to do until I can help you. Now sit down.

[Maurice and Micah are pinching one another and Laura is gazing out the window.]

Maurice: Hey, he's pinching me!

Mr. Garcia: Cut it out. Now, where were we?

Sheila: It's my turn to read.

Mr. Garcia: Go ahead, Sheila. Oh, wait a minute. Hey, Stephanie, what are you doing?

Stephanie: I'm all finished.

Mr. Garcia: Yes, but I don't think Shannon is finished, is she? Don't bother her.

The reading group in the vignette (see Focus Box 9–2) is having trouble getting underway. The trouble spots are all related to poorly established routines. The students do not come to group when they are called; they do not bring their materials; Laura attempts to leave for the bathroom; Maurice and Micah fight over who will answer the first question; Gerald interrupts the group to get help from the teacher; Stephanie, who has finished her seatwork, wanders the room,

Students can design posters and bulletin boards to illustrate important classroom rules and themes.

bothering classmates. All of these incidents demand Mr. Garcia's attention and draw him away from the instructional task.

A teacher must orchestrate hundreds of details of classroom life in order to make the most of instructional time. Mr. Garcia and his students were trapped by these details and, thus, were frustrated because things never seemed to go smoothly.

Rules are the general guidelines for classroom life. By what general principles do you want your students to operate? There is no one right answer here; your choice of rules reflects your values. Teachers should keep in mind that for rules to be effective in guiding students' behavior, they should be stated clearly and positively and confined to a small number. Students will have difficulty keeping track of a long list of rules. In addition, too many rules may promote an atmosphere of repression and student resentment.

Sometimes teachers develop themes, such as family, community, safety, and responsibility, as a way to help students think about how to behave in the classroom. From the first day of school these teachers talk about the meaning of these words and the specific behaviors that promote them, as well as examples of behaviors that detract from the theme. Rules fall naturally under a theme. For instance, if the classroom theme is "We are a community," a rule might be, "We help one another." If the theme is "We are responsible people," a rule might be, "We complete all assignments to the best of our ability." The important point to remember about classroom rules is that they should refer to significant as opposed to trivial behavior. Rules should capture the spirit of your classroom—the values by which you want to teach and learn.

Guideline 2: Teach Classroom Rules and Routines

Effective teachers begin teaching classroom rules and routines from the moment students enter the room on the first day of school. These teachers recognize the importance of spending the first few weeks of school establishing their expectations. The students' first experience on the first day of school is especially important because it sets the tone for the school year. What happens when students arrive at the classroom? What is the first thing the class does as a whole? As you read the incidents in Focus Box 9–3, think about what students might learn from each.

Students entering any classroom quickly form an impression of the teacher—his or her style, personality, and expectations of students. In addition, students' emotions are aroused—they feel relieved, confused, frightened, or happy.

The tone of the classrooms in Focus Box 9–3 varies from calm and orderly to frantic. While the first two teachers are ready to greet students and move them smoothly into a clearly defined activity, Miss Langer appears to be behind schedule. When she is finally ready to talk to the students, the first topic of conversa-

FOCUS BOX 9–3

The First Day of School

Directions: Read the brief descriptions of the beginning of the school day on the first day of class in three classrooms. Make a list of the expectations students in these classrooms are formulating based on their first experiences of the school year. What kinds of lessons do students learn in these first few minutes of school?

Second-Grade Class

Students entering this second-grade class find Ms. Nichols right inside the door. She greets all students cheerfully and directs them to put their belongings in the cubby with their name on it, choose a book from the classroom library, and sit at the desk with their name on it. She says she will be talking to them again once all of the children have arrived.

Third Grade-Class

In Mr. Gedney's third-grade classroom, there is music playing as students arrive on the first day of school. He greets arriving students and tells them to read the directions on the chalkboard. These directions tell students they may investigate the materials located on the blue rug until he calls for everyone's attention.

Fifth-Grade Class

Miss Langer hurries around the room finishing last-minute preparations as students enter her room. She repeatedly calls out, "Sit down, just sit down, and I'll be with you in a minute." Breathless, she moves to the front of the room and says to the class, "Now, there are a few rules we have to discuss first."

tion is classroom rules. While rules are an important topic to discuss, they do not have to be the very first topic of a new school year. Miss Langer may unintentionally create an oppressive and even hostile atmosphere by focusing on the rules before she has even said hello to her new students.

Students' expectations of their teacher and classroom life will also vary based on initial experiences. We can imagine Mr. Gedney's students may begin to sense his trust in them and the importance he places on responsible, independent action. These students may also feel curious about what they will be doing with these interesting materials. Ms. Nichols' students might get a sense that people and things in this classroom have a special place where they belong. They might also get the feeling that their teacher cares for them and will take care of them. What kind of expectations might Miss Langer's students begin to form?

In these first few minutes of the new school year, teachers are already teaching, and students are already learning. Lessons may include such concepts as, "School is fun," "My teacher cares about me," "There is a lot of neat stuff in here for us," "This teacher is going to boss us around just like the teacher I had last year," "This classroom is a safe place," and "I don't know what's expected of me in here." Although students may not be conscious of these lessons, they do take shape early on and influence the students' behavior. Wise teachers will consider what lessons they want to teach, and plan their actions to clearly communicate their expectations. Although there is no one right way to teach one's expectations, several strategies are useful.

PLAN TIME TO DISCUSS CLASSROOM RULES.   While teachers should avoid setting an oppressive tone in the classroom, they should set aside time during the first day of school to discuss rules, defining precisely what each means and how it is associated with specific actions. For instance, a typical rule is "We respect one another." What exactly does one do to show respect to another person? What kinds of actions break this rule? To demonstrate that they have a clear understanding of the rule, students can make up examples of actions that adhere to the rule and actions that break the rule. Students can perform skits, make posters, and generate lists of incidents to illustrate behavior that follows and breaks this rule.

TEACH ROUTINES SYSTEMATICALLY AS A LEARNING OBJECTIVE.   Not only must teachers introduce rules but they must *teach* the routines students should know to function successfully in the classroom. Note that we have emphasized the word *teach* to highlight its importance. Effective teachers recognize that their role is to *teach* appropriate behavior rather than to control by punishing inappropriate behavior.

Evertson and Emmer (1982) explain that the **elements of lessons about routines** are the same steps that define active teaching of academic content: purpose, demonstration, guided practice, feedback, and review. This means that the teacher tells the class (or helps the children construct) the purpose of the routine, demonstrates how it is to proceed, provides practice opportunities for students, gives feedback on their performance, and reviews the procedures several times in the future.

TEACH ROUTINES AS THEY ARE NEEDED.   You will likely want students to master a large number of routines; however, students do not need to know all of the routines on the first day of school. In fact, covering too many routines may only confuse students and make them wish they had stayed home. Which routines should be established right away? The answer will depend on your particular setting, but probably routines related to the use of the bathroom, lining up, getting students' attention, and turning in completed assignments would have high priority. Others, such as those related to small-group work, can wait until you are ready to meet with small groups. You will need several weeks to teach all classroom routines.

BUILD INTO LESSON PLANS TIME FOR TEACHING ROUTINES.   This strategy obviously is related to the last one. A teacher can plan an interesting, creative activity for students, but have the activity flop, because the students were not adequately prepared to succeed. We see this happen often with small-group activities and learning centers. In order for students to work productively in any activity format, they must be taught the routines they need to be successful. For instance, how many students are permitted to be in the learning center at one time? At what times during the day are students permitted to be there? How long may students stay at a center? What do students do with work completed at a center? How do students indicate that they have completed a center assignment? Introducing a new teaching-learning format must include time to teach students how to negotiate the activity.

PROVIDE FOR PRACTICE AND REVIEW OF NEW PROCEDURES.   During the first few weeks of school it is important to take time to practice and review the routines and rules you have established. The success of the academic program rests on the foundation of classroom management built at the beginning of the year.

Two more strategies are useful in establishing a well-managed classroom. Both refer to the kind of academic activities in which students engage at the beginning of the school year.

AT THE BEGINNING OF THE YEAR INVOLVE STUDENTS IN EASY TASKS AND PROMOTE A HIGH RATE OF SUCCESS.   When students know how to do an assignment, they are less likely to be disruptive than they might be if confused about what to do. Also, students who can successfully complete an assignment feel confident and optimistic about future challenges. Teachers who enable students to be successful promote a positive classroom atmosphere. In addition, when the academic task is easy, the students are able to focus on using the new rules and routines properly.

AT THE BEGINNING OF THE YEAR USE WHOLE-CLASS FORMATS AND SIMPLE PROCEDURES.   The purpose of this practice is to minimize student confusion so that new procedures receive the attention they require. Whole-class activities, conducted by the teacher, are less demanding of students than activities in which students operate independently. Simple procedures offer fewer opportunities for students to forget what is expected and to get into trouble. The classroom will be more orderly and peaceful when students know exactly what to do and how to do it.

The majority of instruction about classroom rules and routines will occur during the first few weeks of school. However, whenever teachers introduce a new routine, or when they introduce a new student to the routines of the classroom, they will need to return to the strategies discussed. In addition to establishing and teaching routines and procedures for appropriate behavior, teachers must also spend time at the beginning of the year establishing expectations for student academic performance. While these practices are especially important during the first few weeks, they will be used throughout the school year.

Guideline 3: Teach Expectations for Academic Performance

When students believe that they are responsible for their behavior and for doing their academic work to the best of their ability, they are less likely to present management problems in the classroom. What can a teacher do to encourage student accountability? Some useful strategies, many of which are discussed by Evertson et al. (1984), are described.

CLEARLY COMMUNICATE EXPECTATIONS FOR STUDENT PERFORMANCE ON ASSIGNMENTS.   Teachers must think ahead of time about how students should complete a particular assignment and then precisely communicate these expectations to the students to avoid confusion that can lead to disaster. When giving assignments, teachers should ask themselves, "What are the students going to be confused about? What questions will they have?" Clear directions lessen the chance of confusion, frustration, and disruption.

MONITOR STUDENT WORK.   Teachers have two reasons for monitoring students as they work independently—(1) to see whether they are being successful with the assignment or require additional instruction or assistance, and (2) to solve potential problems. In other words, teachers practice *withitness*. The students should know that teachers are aware of what the students are doing and should feel confident that they can do the work expected of them. No one gains when students do an entire assignment incorrectly, or sit frustrated and miserable because they have no idea what to do. Additionally, teachers who monitor student work are able to determine when greater variety is necessary within independent assignments. When teachers monitor student progress and behavior, intervening when necessary to ensure student success and interest, they promote student independence and responsibility.

CHECK STUDENTS' WORK AND PROVIDE FEEDBACK.   Students learn to be responsible for their work when the teacher regularly checks assignments and provides feedback to students about their performance. Student interest in and motivation to complete assignments are likely to falter if they know the teacher does not look at their work. However, when students know that the teacher will review their work and provide constructive feedback, they are apt to take the work more seriously and assume responsibility for its careful completion.

GIVE CLEAR INSTRUCTIONS.   Teachers can help students to be responsible for their work by providing clear directions for students to follow. When formulating directions, teachers must consider several points. First, teachers must ask themselves what problems or confusions the students are likely to have and help them avoid likely mistakes (**hurdle lessons).** This step becomes easier as teachers come to know their students and the materials, and as they gain experience teaching certain concepts and using certain activities.

Another step in giving clear instruction is to choose words carefully, thinking ahead of time about exactly how to present a lesson or assignment to students. Too many words confuse students; too few words may do the same. Teachers should use words that communicate precisely what students are expected to do. We once observed a teacher explain to her first graders how to indicate the right answers on a test. She kept repeating that they should "bubble in" the right answer. Finally one student raised her hand and asked, "What bubbles are you talking about?"

Clear and specific instructions, however, do not preclude teachers from supporting student creativity; rather, they provide the framework within which students can create. Consider, for example, the difference between the following two sets of directions for a creative spelling assignment.

> *Direction Set 1:* Write a story using all of your vocabulary words.

> *Direction Set 2:* Write a story using any seven of your vocabulary words. The words you choose may be used more than once in the story. This story may be written on any kind of paper, but it must be written in cursive. Somewhere in the story, there must be a reptile—any reptile you want, but it must appear in the story. It's pretty hard to tell a story in only a couple of sentences, so you should have at least 10 sentences in this story. Does anyone see some vocabulary words that seem to go together in some way? Any ideas for stories based on these words?

The first set of instructions lacks clarity and does not communicate the teacher's expectations. These instructions might leave students confused about expected length of the story, whether it has to be written in cursive, whether it can have illustrations, and whether vocabulary words may be used more than once. In the second set of directions, clear, precise language gives students the information they need to complete the assignment independently and successfully. The instructions provide students with the support they need to feel confident about handling the assignment without stifling their creativity. Also, when teachers add a little twist to a typical assignment ("there must be a reptile") and help students think about how to approach an assignment ("Does anyone see some vocabulary words that seem to go together in some way?"), they boost student motivation and confidence.

When giving instructions, teachers should also monitor student comprehension by asking them questions along the way. After explaining the second set of directions, the teacher might ask, "Will it be okay to write your story on the typewriter?" "What will happen if you use nine of the vocabulary words in your story?" "What am I likely to say if you write your story on newsprint?" "What do you think I will say to you if you turn in a story that has two sentences in it?" By asking these questions, the teacher stresses to students that they are accountable for following instructions and completing the assignment correctly.

To summarize what we have said about giving clear instructions, *teachers can do at least three things to give instructions that promote student accountability.* Teachers should anticipate confusions students are likely to have and present assignments in order to minimize these problems, use clear, precise language so that students know what is expected of them, and check student understanding of instructions by asking questions during and after they are given.

USE DESCRIPTIVE RATHER THAN JUDGMENTAL LANGUAGE.   An example will clarify the difference between descriptive and judgmental language (Cangelosi, 1988). Suppose the students referred to in the preceding example have all completed and turned in stories using their vocabulary words. The teacher could return the students' papers and say, "You did a great job on these." This feedback is **judgmental** in that it evaluates or judges the students' stories. The teacher could also say, "These stories are great, because you really used your imaginations to weave in the vocabulary words so they made sense. You also took the time to develop the stories so they have interesting plots." This feedback is **descriptive,** because it tells students what they did that resulted in successful performance. When students receive descriptive feedback, they gain information about what they can do to demonstrate appropriate behavior and be successful in the future. Students will feel good when the teacher tells them they did a great job; they will know how to do a great job in the future if the teacher provides descriptive information.

When teachers set expectations for student behavior, teach classroom rules and routines, and establish and teach expectations for academic performance, they minimize the occurrence of inappropriate behavior. In addition, effective teachers clearly communicate and follow-through with consequences for inappropriate behavior.

Guideline 4: Use Consequences for Inappropriate Behavior

While *consequence* seems to have a negative connotation, the word actually refers to any event that immediately follows a given behavior. Thus, a consequence can be either positive or negative.

USE POSITIVE CONSEQUENCES FOR APPROPRIATE BEHAVIOR.   Evertson and Emmer (1982) stress the importance of establishing positive consequences early in the school year when students are becoming familiar with the teacher's expectations. This does not mean that teachers should toss M&M's to students who correctly follow rules and routines. Teachers can reinforce appropriate behavior through nonverbal and verbal means. Nods, smiles, thumbs up, and pats on the back all communicate to students that a job has been done well. Particularly for students beyond second grade, private consequences like these are more effective than public displays, which tend to embarrass students.

When used correctly, positive verbal consequences **(praise)** can also be effective in reinforcing appropriate student behavior. When delivering praise, teachers should remember that the frequency of praise does not correlate with student outcomes (Brophy, 1981b). In other words, praising students often for their behavior does not guarantee that the desired behavior will be maintained. Remember from Chapter 5 that the research on praise indicates that the teacher should focus on the development of self-monitoring and self-control of behavior rather than simply rewarding students for being obedient. Teachers should use descriptive language ("You walked to the front of the line so calmly and quietly") rather than judgmental language ("Great job"), because the former gives the student more information on which to base future actions. The teachers' comments should communicate to students that they have control over their behavior and the ability to be successful now and in the future.

USE RETEACHING AND LOGICAL CONSEQUENCES FOR PROCEDURAL VIOLATIONS.   When thinking about negative consequences, teachers should distinguish between consequences for procedural violations (not following routines correctly) and consequences for major rule violations. Teachers should not ignore students who fail to carry out routines properly. The focus, however, should be on *reteaching* the student what is expected rather than punishment. Evertson and Emmer (1982) recommend that the teacher follow several steps:

1. Ask the students to stop what they are doing.

2. Make sure the students know what they are supposed to do. If they know, have them perform it correctly.

3. If the students do not know what is expected, reteach the routine.

4. For those students who resist the teacher's direction, Evertson and Emmer recommend that the teacher deliver a **logical consequence.** This is an event which is logically connected to the misbehavior. For instance, if the student refuses to line up correctly, the student will be last to leave the classroom. If students continue to talk too loudly to friends, they will not be permitted to work with those friends for the remainder of the work period. Logical consequences help students to see the connection between their behavior and the results of their behavior. Also, logical consequences encourage students to work to avoid them in the future.

RESERVE PENALTIES FOR MAJOR RULE VIOLATIONS.   According to Evertson et al. (1984), penalties should be reserved for major rule violations. A **penalty** is a punishment for an offense; however, some penalties are inappropriate and ineffective. All research on classroom management and socialization of children indicates that harsh punishments (e.g., spanking, use of derisive language) are inappropriate. McDaniel (1980) summarized research that demonstrated the disadvantages of using **severe punishments** (i.e., strong aversive stimuli) for dealing with student misbehavior. While applying a punishment may temporarily extinguish the misbehavior, the long-term consequences of observing and experiencing punish-

FOCUS BOX 9–4

Practical Application Activities

Directions: In our discussion on consequences, we have stressed the importance of using appropriate praise and logical consequences. Using both of these strategies can be difficult until you gain some experience. Practice these two strategies by doing the following two activities individually.

Activity 1: Practicing Effective Praise

Effective praise uses descriptive language to help students develop confidence in their ability to be successful. What would you say to praise students in the following situations?

- Margie has gotten 100 percent for the first time on a spelling test.
- Three boys worked quietly together on a math assignment.
- Sam put the proper heading on all of his assignments.
- The whole class read quietly while the teacher spoke to a visitor.

Activity 2: Practicing Logical Consequences

Make up logical consequences for the following student behaviors:

- Jeremy does not clean up the chess game with which he played during free time.
- Two children argue over the glue and end up spilling it all over the table.
- Charlotte wrote her story so quickly that it is illegible.
- Dwayne and Carol do not come and line up when they hear the teacher blow the whistle on the playground.

Compare the praise statements and logical consequences you developed with those developed by four or five of your peers. As you look at them try to determine if some are better than others and why. Be prepared to justify your choice of the best praise statements and best examples of logical consequences.

---

ments make the temporary benefits less desirable. For instance, children who observe punishing adults learn to behave similarly. In addition, individuals who are punished tend to be fearful of and hostile toward their punishers. Fear and hostility are emotions that make both cooperation and learning unlikely.

So what are appropriate penalties? Penalties might include such things as losing privileges or going to a time-out area. Penalties such as these can include a teaching function by helping students learn to confront their misbehavior and seek alternatives. For example, Glasser (1965) suggests that a student who breaks a rule be required to answer three questions: "What did I do?" "Why was this a problem?" "What could I do next time so as not to cause this problem?" The teacher and student then develop a plan for resolving the problem. Pay particular attention to the way these questions are phrased. Glasser does not suggest asking, "Did you do this?" which forces a child to confess or to lie. Nor does he suggest asking, "Why did you do it?" Instead, the questions encourage the child to confront the behavior and design an alternative.

Summary of Guidelines from Classroom Management Research

As is apparent, teachers can learn a great deal about effective classroom management from research conducted in this area. Focus Box 9–5 includes a summary of the guidelines and strategies we have reviewed. The importance of these guidelines should not be underestimated. Teachers who establish orderly classrooms use these guidelines; teachers whose classrooms are chaotic fail to use them or do not use them consistently. However, as we noted at the beginning of this chapter, a well-managed classroom is not an end in itself but is a means to

FOCUS BOX 9–5

Lessons from Classroom Management Research: Guidelines and Strategies

1. Set expectations for student behavior
   - Specify expectations for classroom rules
   - Specify expectations for classroom routines
2. Teach classroom rules and routines
   - Plan time to discuss classroom rules
   - Teach routines as systematically as any other learning objective
   - Teach routines as they are needed by students to negotiate the classroom setting
   - Build into lesson plans time for teaching routines
   - Provide for practice and review of new procedures
   - At the beginning of the year, involve students in easy tasks and promote a high rate of success
   - At the beginning of the year use whole-class formats and simple procedures
3. Set and teach expectations for student academic performance
   - Clearly communicate expectations for student performance on assignments
   - Monitor student work
   - Check students' work and provide feedback
   - Give clear instructions
   - Use descriptive, rather than judgmental, language
4. Use consequences for inappropriate behavior
   - Use positive consequences to help teach appropriate behavior
   - Use reteaching and logical consequences for procedural violations
   - Reserve penalties for major rule violations

achieve important educational aims (i.e., aims that foster the self-sufficiency and empowerment of students). The guidelines we have reviewed thus far enable teachers to teach *one* of the four abilities required for students to develop self-discipline for social responsibility, the ability to follow socially derived principles of behavior. Other guidelines are necessary, however, if teachers wish to help children develop the other three abilities required for self-discipline: the inclination to act responsibly, the ability to make judgments about appropriate action within alternative contexts, and the ability to act contrary to a norm when it violates a higher ethic. Teachers who seek to empower their students will need additional practices.

The Importance of Teacher Reflection

It is easy to assume that classroom management problems are the result of poorly communicated expectations, a failure to reinforce appropriate behavior, or a failure to establish and enforce consequences for inappropriate behavior. In fact, assertive discipline, a very popular approach to classroom management is based on this very assumption (Canter & Canter, 1976). However, student misbehavior may have other sources and may require much more comprehensive solutions. Recall, for example, the case in Chapter 1 of a student who was not completing assignments. One teacher assumed the problem was the child's lack of "stick-to-it-iveness" (a management problem) and another considered whether class assignments were too routine and lacked connection to the "real" tasks involved in reading (a curriculum problem). Also, student misbehavior may be more evident when students feel alienated or rejected.

Reflective teachers seek the broadest possible definition of any classroom management problem by trying to see the classroom from the students' perspectives. Reflective teachers continually seek alternative explanations for classroom occurrences by trying to determine the potential sources of classroom management problems. Although we have discussed these issues in previous chapters, a brief review is provided here to highlight the importance of meaningful curriculum and students' feelings of belonging in helping students become self-disciplined.

Assess Whether Problems May Be Rooted in Inappropriate Curriculum

The research on classroom management identifies a clear connection between curriculum and management (Brophy, 1985); however, in our view, the research underemphasizes the significance of this connection. In working with teachers and student teachers, we have repeatedly found the most serious classroom management problems in classrooms where the curriculum can best be described as a meaningless blur of dittos, boardwork, and workbook pages emphasizing the drill and practice of isolated skills and fragmented pieces of knowledge. Despite the fact that this type of curriculum has no inherent meaning for children, many will comply with teacher directions because their parents have communicated to

What About Assertive Discipline? Is This the Answer?

Assertive discipline is a packaged classroom management approach that has swept this country. Developed by Canter and Canter (1976) the approach is based in a view that no student has the right to prevent the teacher from teaching or any other student from learning. Canter and Canter, who claim a high success rate, recommend that teachers establish and assertively maintain classroom rules by communicating expectations, reinforcing positive behavior, and applying negative consequences consistently and with increasing severity. Other researchers question the validity of the Canters' claims (Render, Padilla, & Krank, 1989). However, even if the claims are true, assertive discipline is a management program that enables teachers to force children to comply with the teacher's will. If the empowerment of children is an important aim for education within a democratic society, this management program must be viewed as unacceptable. We have the following concerns:

> Teachers are not encouraged to examine the curriculum, the social context of the classroom, or their own practices to determine how they might be contributing to classroom management problems within the classroom.
>
> Teachers are not encouraged to provide a rationale for classroom rules and routines (or even to reflect and determine whether the rules are reasonable and just).
>
> The program does not encourage teachers to see things from children's perspectives or to consider the rights or needs of children.
>
> Behavior is monitored, rewarded, or punished by teachers. Children are not encouraged to develop responsibility for their own behavior.
>
> Children are told that they make "choices" about their behavior. In reality, children have only one choice—to comply with teachers or to be punished. This is not the kind of choice that fosters self-discipline.

Assertive discipline fosters unquestioning obedience to authority, a lesson that is inconsistent with democratic principles. Render et al. conclude their review of assertive discipline with a strong statement:

> If further reminding is needed of the dangers of compliance with and obedience to authority, we suggest consideration of the extremes to which the Nazi party could go supported by people trained to do what they were told and to follow orders. Never can we risk becoming a nation prepared to follow a directive from one person in a position of authority without the right and obligation to question the implications of that directive. (1989, p. 627)

them that school is important and that they should do as the teacher says. Others, who have not been as well socialized into middle-class values, resist, and teachers find it necessary to bribe or coerce them into compliance.

Curriculum problems are pervasive across all areas of the curriculum (see Chapters 4, 5, 7, and 8). Limited curriculum not only diminishes students' opportunities to learn academic concepts, skills, and abilities, but also diminishes children's willingness to cooperate with teachers, thus creating classroom management problems. As Glasser (1985) has noted, teachers must help children see that doing their work and following the rules will help them gain something that they want. If this is to occur, he stresses that "what students, especially young students, learn must be satisfying at the time it is taught" (Glasser, 1985, p. 244).

In Chapter 8, we synthesized eight characteristics of instruction that empower students to interact meaningfully with the curriculum. Here we rephrase six of these eight characteristics as questions.[1] We suggest that teachers with classroom management problems ask these *questions to determine whether their problems may be rooted in inappropriate curriculum:*

1. Do all students have **equal access** to knowledge? Is the nature and quality of content and instruction provided different for low as opposed to high achievers?

2. Is instruction **focused?** Do lessons and assignments touch lightly upon multiple, disconnected pieces of information and skills, or do they help students identify key ideas and develop a sound grasp of these?

3. Is instruction **coherent?** Does instruction help students to see the connections across parts of a lesson and across lessons?

4. Is instruction **analytic?** Does the teacher create many opportunities to examine students' thinking and understandings during lessons? Do assignments assess understanding as opposed to skill or fact mastery?

5. Is instruction **meaningful?** Is instruction grounded in the real worlds of students? Does the teacher help students see the curriculum as relevant to their lives?

6. Is instruction **collaborative?** Do discussions and assignments provide students with a significant role in the teaching/learning process? Do the teachers and students jointly develop understandings, or do teachers expect students to passively absorb teacher-transmitted information?

Assess the Classroom Environment

In Chapter 6, we noted that teachers help children develop social competence by creating an environment in which all children feel accepted by the teacher and their peers. In Chapter 8, we noted that children are more likely to engage in school activities when they feel people within the school care about, support, and accept them. That is, a **sense of belonging** leads students to accept more responsibility for themselves and their classmates and fosters cooperative action. Wayson explains it this way:

> Because learning is largely a social process, students need to feel a sense of belonging to, contributing to, and benefitting from a social agency before they see any need for or *feel* any reward from accepting the norms governing behavior within the group. (1985, p. 228)

---

[1]   In developing these questions, we omitted characteristic one (caring) because it is discussed in more detail in the next section. We also omitted the eighth characteristic (critical instruction). While this characteristic is important to student empowerment, it is possible to have a meaningful curriculum that is not critical.

Working collaboratively with peers promotes the development of peer acceptance and group identity.

Unfortunately, many students feel they do not belong in today's classrooms. Lasley notes that, "American schools are filled with students who are seldom acknowledged and are given few opportunities to participate" (1985, p. 250).

Teachers who have many classroom management problems should question themselves to determine whether they are actively fostering the development of group identity and peer acceptance. To determine this, teachers ask themselves whether they are helping students to value human diversity, to recognize the similarities among human beings, to expand their circle of friends, to create a collective identity, to share their special talents with the class, and to recognize the unique qualities of each student. All of these practices can help students feel like welcome members of the school community. For more specific information about how to create a feeling of belonging, see Chapter 6.

Socialization Strategies

We wish that we could tell you that if you have an empowering and meaningful curriculum and you use strategies to help all children feel they belong within your classroom, you would have no classroom management problems. In fact, this was the message communicated to Dorene Ross during her teacher education program. She discovered on her first day of teaching that it simply isn't true. She still remembers her feelings of panic and helplessness when one of her third graders stood up (after a "marvelous" description of the wonderful activities planned for the first hour of the day) and said, "You can't tell me what to do, you bitch!" Despite the importance of curriculum and social bonding, and no matter how well you attend to them, you *will* have classroom management problems. There are **two reasons for classroom management problems:**

1. Many children have not been taught (by parents and/or teachers) the skills and abilities necessary for self-discipline and orderly group life.

2. You are working with children. Even if parents and former teachers have been skillful at facilitating the development of self-discipline, *all* elementary children are still in the process of learning these abilities and are dependent on adults for instruction.

This means that all elementary teachers are responsible for the **socialization** of children (i.e., teaching children to participate responsibly in group life); although, of course, they share this responsibility with other adults in children's lives. Our definition of **self-discipline** means students must develop the ability to:

- follow socially derived principles of behavior

- act responsibly

- make judgments about appropriate action within alternative contexts

- act contrary to a norm that violates a higher ethic

Notice that the last three abilities require students to make **judgments about action based on internal standards.** In order for students to develop this internal framework, they must *construct* moral principles to guide their future decisions and actions. Adding the following guidelines to those derived from the classroom management research of Kounin and Evertson and Emmer enables teachers to empower students to construct moral principles and practice responsible decision making.

Always Provide a Rationale for Rules, Routines, and Procedures

In a review of research on successful socialization practices, Brophy (1985) notes that parents of well-socialized children set standards and expect children to cooperate, but they do not expect immediate and unquestioning obedience. Successful parents recognize that children do not automatically construct internal standards for action by learning to comply with rules established by adults. To help their children construct a moral philosophy, parents share the values used to determine rules and procedures. Seeing that rules are based in values such as caring for others, fairness, honesty, or justice helps children evaluate their own behavior and that of others, even when a rule for behavior has not been specified.

One way that teachers do this is by stating the rationale for their rules and procedures. For example:

I'm always concerned about pushing, but I'm especially concerned around the water fountain where someone could get a tooth knocked out.

The rationale behind rules can (and should) be communicated in other ways too, however. Many children's books deal with value issues. Discussing the underlying values and how they might be applicable within "our classroom" helps children understand the classroom value structure. Current events activities can help children see that these same values guide the action of all members of our society. For example, the teacher might use a story about a child who saves a younger child from an attack by a dog by shielding the younger child with her body. This news story could help children recognize the importance of caring for others, especially those who are younger or more dependent. For older children, a story about local racial conflict might be used to raise issues about the need to balance individual rights against the rights of the society.

Additionally, **decision stories** (i.e., stories in which two important values conflict) can help children grapple with difficult value decisions. Schuncke and Krogh (1983) present multiple examples of decision stories appropriate for elementary children; they also discuss how role playing might be used to facilitate children's thinking.

Allow Students to Make Important Decisions in the Classroom

Duke and Jones (1985) note that teachers often talk about wanting students to act responsibly but seldom give them significant opportunities to practice responsibility. A study of 12 middle-school teachers (Cornbleth & Korth, 1984) found that the majority defined student responsibility as "doing assigned work." This seems more like the definition of **compliance** (i.e., doing what you are told to do) than responsibility. Pepper and Henry (1985) note that democracy is based on principles of **shared decision making.** In a classroom, this means that the teacher shares with students the power to make as many decisions as possible. Benson (1987) echoes the idea that children must learn how to use power. He stresses that involving children in significant decisions communicates that teachers respect students and their abilities. This atmosphere of mutual respect contributes to children's feelings of "belonging." How can teachers provide such opportunities?

INVOLVE STUDENTS IN DEVELOPING CLASSROOM RULES.   From the classroom management research, you know that you must have clear expectations about classroom rules and procedures and that these must be communicated to students. However, *cooperative* construction of rules helps children feel that they are a part of the class; helps create a sense of "ownership" of classroom rules, thereby making cooperation more likely; and provides opportunities to discuss the rationale behind rules so that values as well as rules will be stressed. Remember, the values that guide classrooms are the same values that guide most kinds of group experiences. Children are familiar with these values and almost always generate rules which match those that teachers might have developed. Note that constructing rules with children does not relieve you of the obligation to determine your expectations ahead of time. Students are very good at generating lists of rules, but they will need your help to distill guiding principles for classroom action.

While most rules would be developed before problems occur, children might also be involved in analyzing past events and constructing solutions to avoid problems in the future. For example, Goodman (1992) shares an example in which a child complains that other children threw stones at her and her friends on the playground before school. Goodman reports that Jim, the teacher, led a group meeting in which the children developed a rule to govern their behavior:

> Several kids suggested that there should be a rule against throwing things at each other. Jim said that he thought this might be a good idea, but "Aren't there some things that it might be fun and also *safe* to throw at each other?" The kids then started naming objects that it might be fun to throw at each other such as water, feathers or confetti. Jim suggested that maybe the rule should state that kids should not throw anything that could possibly hurt other people. The kids agreed, and Jim asked, "But what if someone doesn't want anything thrown at them even if it's safe?" Nearly every child unanimously called out that "he [the victim] should tell him [the thrower] to *stop,* and then he [the thrower] should." (1992, p. 107)

This teacher guided the children during rule-making discussions by helping them to extend their thinking, to see the implications of their rules, and to think about possible situations for application that might not occur to them. The teacher, thus, protects the safety of all the children, helps them avoid an overly restrictive rule, and encourages them to think about the rights of an individual whatever the group rule.

In addition to generating rules, students should have opportunities to discuss why rules are necessary or why particular rules are important. Some teachers conduct special activities to demonstrate the importance of rules. For example, one teacher divided the class into small groups and gave each group except one the rules they needed to play a card game. While all proceeded smoothly within the groups that had received the rules, chaos quickly broke out in the rule-less group. The teacher then led a discussion about what had happened. The teacher asked how the students with and without rules felt about the activity, each other, and the teacher; and why rules might be necessary for groups of people. In addition to discussing rules in general, students need opportunities to think about the rationale behind specific rules. Why should we always try our best? Why should we cooperate with one another? Students who understand the significance of rules are likely to assimilate those rules and use them to negotiate and interpret classroom life.

INVOLVE STUDENTS IN DEVELOPING AND/OR REVISING CLASSROOM ROUTINES.   Teachers should involve children in the development of routines for the same reasons children should be involved in the development of rules. An example might help you see how a teacher can involve the children.

Ms. Correa's fourth graders are going to attend their first assembly of the school year. She knows her students will be excited to be in the large auditorium, to see their friends from other classes, to try out the new seats, and to watch the performance on the stage. Of course, she wants them to enjoy the experience, but she also is well aware that some of the students may get a bit carried away. She decides to spend the last 15 minutes before the assembly developing some routines for action in an assembly. She begins her lesson with a story.

> As I mentioned this morning, we're going to an assembly today to see a play put on by high-school students. We read a few parts of the play this morning, and I know you will enjoy it. Thinking about going to the play reminds me of my experience at the movie this weekend. I went to see "Batman and Robin." I was excited to see the movie, but I didn't enjoy it very much. Before the movie started, the people behind me were yelling across the theater to some of their friends. They were so loud! Then when the movie started, they talked to each other and booed and cheered. I couldn't even hear some parts of the movie. I left thinking there should be some rules for going to movies!

Following her story, she guided a discussion with the following questions:

What did the people behind me do that bothered me?

Why was that bothersome?

Why were they doing that? Don't they have a right to enjoy themselves? Should I have been annoyed? (Here the teacher is helping the students see the importance of balancing the needs of all individuals within a group.)

If the movie did set rules, what rules would help here?

Why do you think the assembly made me think of my movie experience? (Here the teacher is helping the students make the transition to the current situation.)

Which of the movie rules would be applicable for us? Would any need to be changed and why? Do we need any others and why?

Note that our guideline mentions development and *revision* of routines. If children are to believe that teachers respect them and feel that they have power within the classroom, they must be allowed to question and suggest revisions within classroom routines. For example, students in Mr. Bressio's room may believe that the requirement that they sign out on the blackboard to go to the bathroom is too public and embarrasses them. Yet, Mr. Bressio may feel that he needs to know where each student is at all times. Also, he wants a way to ensure that only one student goes to the bathroom at a time. Both the teacher and the students have legitimate concerns here. Through negotiation, they might decide that students must take a bathroom pass from the teacher's desk and put their name on a list. The students return the pass and cross out their name upon return. This procedure is more private but still meets the teacher's needs. More importantly, being able to ask for review of a classroom routine gives students the power to affect their lives in the classroom.

WHENEVER POSSIBLE, USE CLASSROOM ROUTINES THAT PROVIDE OPPORTUNITIES TO MAKE CHOICES.   Don't underestimate the power of everyday classroom routines to teach values to children. These routines are as value-laden as any lesson the teacher teaches. For example, the children might learn whether the teacher trusts them or whether they have power within the classroom. Because the "trivial" events are experienced with such frequency, the values they carry tend to be especially well learned, another instance of the significance of learning constructed through the *implicit curriculum*. An example may help clarify what we mean.

Sharpening students' pencils is a small but important classroom task. The teacher who wishes to find a routine for this task has many options, such as the following:

- The teacher allows students to use the electric pencil sharpener whenever their pencils need to be sharpened.
- The teacher forbids all students to use the electric pencil sharpener because it is expensive and insists on doing all pencil sharpening.
- The teacher asks one student to sharpen everyone's pencils once in the morning and once after lunch.
- The teacher has one student at each cluster of desks responsible for sharpening the group's pencils.
- The teacher allows one student at a time to sharpen a pencil, except during large-group lessons.

Many other possibilities exist. How is a teacher to decide which to choose? The decision should be guided by the teacher's aim of empowering students. If the teacher wants to promote self-discipline and responsibility, options that enable the children to make decisions and exercise responsibility are more desirable. Of course, some students will make irresponsible choices. We'll talk about how to handle this in the next section.

View Inappropriate Behavior as an Opportunity for Collaborative Problem Solving

According to classroom management research, inappropriate behavior should be used as an opportunity to teach appropriate behavior. Guidelines for responding to inappropriate behavior progress from asking the student to stop to using logical consequences. In many cases, this is exactly what the teacher should do, making sure to stress the rationale behind the classroom rule or procedure and to remind the student of group agreements where appropriate. However, at other times the problem is disruptive enough or serious enough or recurs often enough than the teacher determines one or more children have not learned the underlying classroom values. In such situations, teachers must not only stress appropriate behavior but also must teach problem-solving strategies and classroom values. Stensrud and Stensrud state:

> By giving students the right to participate in the making of decisions that affect
> their lives, we encourage the learning of self-discipline and cooperation. A
> central distinction between coercive structures and self-disciplining ones is that
> the latter is based on cooperative goal structures. (1981, p. 165)

Just as we have stressed in earlier chapters that *teacher-student collaboration* is
important for academic learning, in this chapter, we are suggesting strategies
that will enable teachers to work *with* students to help them learn to direct their
own behavior. This is difficult, time-consuming work, but we must remember that
the teaching of self-discipline is as much a part of the teacher's role as the teaching of science or reading. Far too many teachers believe that their role is to teach
subject matter to students who are ready and willing to learn. The teacher's role
is much broader—to empower students to participate actively within a democracy. Thus, the teaching of self-discipline is worthy of teachers' efforts.

GOOD COMMUNICATION PROVIDES A BASIS FOR COLLABORATION.   Working collaboratively means that the teacher must understand the child's perspective and help
each child understand the perspectives of the teacher and those of other children. Specific practices that help people see through the eyes of others have
been described by advocates of a "human relations model" (McDaniel, 1980) of
discipline. Ginott (1971), Gordon (1970), and Dreikurs (1968) have recommended practices to help teachers understand students' perspectives, particularly when
those students are behaving in ways deemed inappropriate according to school
or classroom expectations. Teachers must not only practice good communication
strategies but also *teach them to their students.* Practices that have primarily been
advocated for teacher use in managing student behavior can be learned and used
by all members of the classroom community.

One way to understand another person's point of view is to listen carefully to
what the person has to say. Gordon (1970) has described three techniques teachers can use to communicate their acceptance of students, thereby facilitating
communication (see Focus Box 7–3, p. 188). We advocate that all members of the
classroom (including the teacher) learn to use Gordon's listening techniques—
passive listening, active listening, and **using door openers,** as ways of communicating respect for one another and gaining insight into other perspectives.

Facilitating communication is also enhanced when all members of the classroom work to support the self-esteem of all classroom members. This has been
the focus of Ginott's writings about adult-child interactions (1965, 1969, 1971).
Ginott states that adults shape children's self-concept by the way they communicate. Children's comments to other children have a similar impact. Just as teachers should teach children to use Gordon's communication strategies, teachers
should also teach children how to communicate in ways that support the self-
esteem of their classmates. Ginott describes two kinds of messages adults send to
children: sane and insane messages. To build students' self-concepts, teachers
must be self-disciplined to use sane messages when correcting misbehavior. What
makes a message sane? What makes a message insane? Let's take a look.

Imagine that two students whisper and giggle while their teacher explains to
the class how to do an assignment. The teacher might say, "You two are being

incredibly rude to me and to your classmates. I expect better manners from you. I guess I just can't trust you to sit together and behave properly." On the other hand, the teacher might say, "When I give instructions to the class, everyone must be quiet and listen to me." In the first comment the teacher judges the students' characters—they are told that they are rude and untrustworthy. According to Ginott, **insane messages** that blame, preach, command, accuse, belittle, and threaten can damage children's self-concepts. A **sane message** addresses the situation rather than the children's character. When students receive sane messages from the teacher and from their peers, they are able to "appraise the situation, consider what is right and wrong, and decide how they feel about themselves" (Charles, 1985, p. 50).

Another way to see through the eyes of others is to try to understand why people act as they do. We encourage teachers and students to develop compassionate and caring attitudes toward members of their communities. When a community member behaves in a way that upsets other members of the group, the offending person is often ostracized in some way. Empowered human beings are socially responsible. They seek to help group members; in doing so, they strengthen the efficacy of the group. At the same time, persons who have disrupted the group must come to see that they do not operate in a vacuum. They have a responsibility to fellow group members. Note that this is different from saying that children must be taught to obey the rules; we are saying that efforts can be made to teach them to think in a socially responsible way.

Dreikurs' (1968) **four motives of misbehavior** can be helpful to students and teachers who seek to understand the behavior of group members. The four motives are attention getting, power seeking, revenge seeking, and displaying inadequacy. Each motive is briefly explained:

- *Attention getting:* People who do not get the recognition they desire may resort to seeking attention through misbehaving. In order to feel accepted, they demand attention by breaking rules and otherwise acting inappropriately.

- *Power seeking:* People who try to engage others in arguments and confrontations are looking for power. These people believe that the only way to get what they want is by challenging others.

- *Revenge seeking:* People who try to hurt others may be seeking revenge for feeling hurt. While they may appear to be tough, these people are actually discouraged because they have failed to gain status through other means.

- *Displaying inadequacy:* People who feel like failures may "play stupid" to avoid any challenges to their already shaky self-esteem. These people do not interact with others or participate in community activities.

This kind of information about the motives of behavior should not be the private domain of teachers. Students can become more caring and group-oriented if they understand their own behavior and that of others. When such information is shared, people's behavior (including the teacher's!) becomes a group concern rather than the teacher's responsibility. Dreikurs (1968) advises asking these questions of the "offending" person:

1. Could it be that you want me to pay attention to you?
2. Could it be that you want to prove that nobody can make you do anything?
3. Could it be that you want to hurt me or others?
4. Could it be that you want me to believe you are not capable?

These questions are helpful in opening up communication. When an understanding of the person's motives is reached, group members can work collaboratively to solve the problem. The intervention should focus on teaching persons to be responsible for themselves and to their fellow human beings. This can be done in part through class meetings or private conversations which we shall discuss later. Dreikurs' suggestions for helping solve these problems are described in Focus Box 9–7.

CLASS MEETINGS PROVIDE OPPORTUNITIES FOR COLLABORATIVE PROBLEM SOLVING.   Many problems confronted in classrooms are group problems. We provided an example in which one group of students threw rocks at another group. Other examples of group problems are things such as failure to take care of class property, bickering and disrespect to classmates, and noisy behavior in communal areas of the school (halls, cafeteria, library). At the heart of a model for teaching self-discipline and responsibility is what Glasser (1965) calls the **classroom meeting,** a large-group session at which problems are presented and solutions are proposed and considered. Our earlier descriptions of group generation and revision of classroom rules and routines provide glimpses of class meetings.

The classroom meeting is an expression of democracy in action. It is a cooperative venture embodying respect, responsibility, and concern for the group. The purpose of the meeting is to explore problems and consider solutions. The teacher stays in the background, helping students to participate and clarify their attitudes. Students must focus on problems and solutions. They may not blame or punish. Glasser believes that the meeting should be a regular part of the curriculum, like math or social studies. Power and Kohlberg (1986) note that classroom meetings provide an important opportunity for students to raise issues important to them and to help establish procedures and rules that influence their lives. As such, these meetings provide strong instruction about democratic principles and procedures (much stronger than lessons about the formal structure of American government). However, Power and Kohlberg stress that teachers must not underestimate the importance of their role. They stress that teachers must "be willing to speak up strongly as advocates of justice and community in the democratic meetings" (1986, p. 17). Remember (from our rock-throwing example) how Jim, the teacher, encouraged his children to consider the rights of those who'd like to throw safe things, and the rights of children who do not want things thrown at them. He is an example of a teacher who guided children to create just rules and procedures based in community values.

Gordon's (1970) **"no-lose method" problem-solving approach** specifies steps that can be used during class meetings to resolve conflicts. When the group works

FOCUS BOX 9–7

How Does Understanding the Source of the Problem Help With the Solution?

Dreikurs recommends the following steps to help people who have problems with attention, power, revenge, or inadequacy.

Solutions for attention-getting behavior: Ignore the attention-demanding behavior and give attention for prosocial behavior. If the attention-demanding behavior is too serious to ignore, give attention in ways that are not rewarding. For instance, make eye contact and look sternly at the person but do not engage in conversation.

Solutions for power-seeking behavior: Avoid power struggles by withdrawing from them. A teacher often reacts to a student challenge by asserting authority: "I'm not doing this stupid homework!" "Oh, yes you will, unless you'd like to miss recess for the next week." While the teacher might win the battle, the student is likely to resent the teacher's actions, and the battle soon becomes a war. Dreikurs recommends that the teacher help the student recognize and use legitimate power in the classroom. For instance, in the above situation, the teacher might say, "Could you tell me some things I might do so you won't think the homework is so stupid?"

Solutions for revenge-seeking behavior: While the group may dislike the mean and tough-acting revenge seekers, they can help such students most by being kind and caring. Revenge seekers believe that no one likes them and that they are unworthy of being liked. The group can give such students opportunities to display strengths, thereby receiving attention and status for socially responsible behavior.

Solutions for displaying inadequacy: These students work to avoid the attention of others and can succeed in getting lost in the crowd. Classroom members must offer encouragement to these students so they can begin to see themselves as capable. By "encouraging" students, Dreikurs means providing feedback and assistance which helps students develop a sense of efficacy. Dreikurs provides examples of encouragement such as letting students know you have faith in their abilities, helping students learn from mistakes, emphasizing students' strengths, and encouraging student effort and improvement rather than requiring perfection. Dreikurs' advice about encouraging students is supported by research on praising students. This research indicates that the teacher should focus on the development of student self-monitoring and self-control of behavior rather than simply rewarding students for being obedient. Teachers should use descriptive language ("You walked to the front of the line so quietly") rather than judgmental language ("Great job"), because the former gives the student more information on which to base future actions and communicates to students that they have control over their behavior and the ability to be successful now and in the future.

on a problem together, all participants are winners. Gordon identifies six steps (1970, p. 237):

1. identifying and defining the conflict
2. generating possible alternative solutions

3. evaluating the alternative solutions

4. deciding on the best acceptable solutions

5. working out ways of implementing the solution

6. following up to evaluate how it worked

For these steps to be successful, group members must concentrate on using passive and active listening as well as door openers. Speakers must work to describe feelings and actions rather than judging, criticizing, and blaming. In other words, the no-lose method rests on mutual respect and shared power. The nature of the communication among group members is as important as following the six steps. Gordon (1970) would say that a **"language of acceptance"** is essential. This is a nonjudgmental, inviting kind of language that opens people up to share their feelings. Unaccepting language "closes people up, makes them feel defensive, produces discomfort, makes them afraid to talk or to take a look at themselves" (p. 32).

We want to add an important concept to the discussion of the class meeting, the concept of "voice." **Voice** refers to the unique means individuals use "to make [themselves] understood and listened to, and to define [themselves] as active participants in the world" (Giroux & McLaren, 1986. p. 235). While the dominant voice of the classroom has traditionally been a white, middle-class voice, the members of the classroom community have multiple voices "shaped by personal history and distinctive lived engagement with the surrounding culture" (Giroux & McLaren, 1986, p. 235). Teachers who hope to facilitate classroom dialogue will respect and nurture the voices in their classrooms. Students' experiences will be viewed as worthy of discussion and examination and students' lives, concerns, and beliefs about the world will be viewed as legitimate content for dialogue and reflection. By incorporating students' voices into class meetings, teachers communicate the values of equity, respect, and caring that are essential to constructing empowering interpersonal dynamics.

What is the significance of facilitating dialogue among classroom members? When students' voices are respected and their active participation is encouraged, the stratification between teachers and students (and among students) is reduced. In other words, through dialogue power is shared. Students become engaged in the examination of problems and the deliberations involved in the decision-making process. Students are no longer in the role of receiving and obeying someone else's mandates. They participate in the dialogue that shapes classroom policy and practice. It is important to remember, as Goodman reminds us, that the "purpose of gaining power . . . is to care for (be responsive to the needs of) others as much as to care for oneself" (1992, p. 119). That is, teachers share power with students as a means of teaching them how to use power for the public good.

COLLABORATIVE PLANNING AND EVALUATION IS THE KEY TO SOLVING INDIVIDUAL PROBLEMS.   We hope that you find many of the ideas that we have presented to be appealing, but we also suspect you are skeptical about how these ideas might

Through collaborative planning and evaluation, teachers can help students make choices that benefit the individual and the group.

work with individual children within your classroom. You might be thinking about children who:

- are easily angered and get so angry that you must physically protect other children.
- seem incapable of sitting still for a 15-minute group lesson and wander during independent activities.
- seem to require constant individual attention, come to you 15 or 20 times for "help" each morning, do no work unless you are directly watching, and entertain themselves by disrupting others when you are not.

You may have 6 out of 28 children who have these problems or others like them. How do you help these children? How do you protect the learning environment for the other children? How do you maintain your own sanity?

Glasser (1965) believes that teachers must help students to make good, rather than bad, choices. **Good choices** serve the interests of both the individual and the group. Before talking about Glasser's approach, we want to stress the importance of teaching social skills. Many classroom management problems are rooted in children's inability to work and play cooperatively with their peers. Part of helping children to gain self-control requires that they learn to cooperatively resolve conflicts. In Chapter 6, we noted that this ability is grounded in the abilities to perceive the perspective of others and to avoid direct confrontation, and in knowledge of and ability to use appropriate social interaction strategies.

Children who lack these social skills will be unable to "will" themselves into peaceful existence with classmates. Their problem is as much rooted in lack of social skills as in lack of self-control. To help children develop social competence, we suggested that you use the following strategies: assess the social competence and acceptance of children, provide time for peer interaction with minimal adult supervision, intervene to help children develop social skills, and use structured classroom groups to foster social acceptance and development. Refer to Chapter 6 for more specific suggestions.

At the same time that children are working to develop better social skills, they should be working with the teacher to solve specific problems. In his **responsibility training model,** Glasser (1965) described steps for teachers to follow when students behave in ways which cause problems for the group:

- The teacher first has the students confront their actions directly ("What are you doing?").
- Then the teacher has the students evaluate the behavior ("Is that helping you or the class?").
- Finally the teacher has the students identify suitable alternatives ("What could you do that would help?").

The thrust of these questions is that students are responsible for their behavior choices and that this responsibility must take into account the needs of the group. Pepper & Henry (1985) stress that alternatives should be generated collaboratively by the teacher and the student and that the agreement must be acceptable to both. Within this agreement the teacher and student should specify consequences for future inappropriate behavior, and the teacher is responsible for following through with consequences (or reteaching/renegotiation).

In determining consequences, teachers and students may look to logical consequences. In cases of more serious problems, they may develop a contract that specifies external reinforcement for positive behavior or they may rely on penalties. Although the use of **external reinforcers** (e.g., prizes, candy) is not a practice we recommend enthusiastically, it is important to acknowledge that *some* children have had so little successful experience that they do not know how it feels to work cooperatively with others. External rewards can provide transitional motivation for those children who have little or no internal motivation to cooperate. Once they begin to experience success and some of the intrinsic benefits of cooperation, external reinforcement should be discontinued. If many of the children seem to lack internal motivation to cooperate, the teacher should examine critically the curriculum and the classroom environment before turning to external reinforcement.

We have seen teachers modify Glasser's technique to make it a written exercise. Disruptive students go to a time-out place where they write answers to questions similar to those suggested by Glasser. Very young children, who cannot write, draw pictures to answer the key questions. Later in the day the teacher and student go over the paper together, focusing on alternatives to the troublesome behavior. Whether the questions are spoken or written, at the heart of this responsibility model is teacher/student collaborative efforts to help the student succeed.

In conclusion, we note that some children have great difficulty controlling their impulses; that is, they often act without thinking and their actions get them into trouble. After a while, such students come to view "being in trouble" as the normal course of events at school. The purpose of the strategies we suggest, and of Glasser's model in particular, is to work with students to help them become less impulsive and to take control over their behavior. We are not in any way suggesting that students be allowed to disrupt the learning environment. In other words, there will be times when the teacher simply has to require the student to conform to classroom expectations. The difference between our model and a model that stresses obedience is that these requirements will be based in class-generated expectations, and consequences for the individual will be based in agreements made collaboratively with the teacher. In this way, the underlying rationale for classroom expectations is repeatedly taught. However, until students internalize the value structure, the teacher will have to help them live within its boundaries.

FOCUS BOX 9–8

Strategies for the Development of Self-Discipline

1. Assess the curriculum to determine whether problems may be rooted in inappropriate curriculum.
   - Do all students have equal access to knowledge?
   - Is instruction focused?
   - Is instruction coherent?
   - Is instruction analytic?
   - Is instruction meaningful?
   - Is instruction collaborative?
2. Assess the classroom environment to determine whether you are actively fostering the development of group identity and peer acceptance.
3. Always provide a rationale for rules, routines, and procedures.
4. Give students opportunities to make important decisions in the classroom.
   - Involve students in developing classroom rules.
   - Involve students in developing and/or revising classroom routines.
   - Whenever possible, use classroom routines that provide opportunities to make choices.
5. View inappropriate behavior as an opportunity for collaborative problem solving.
   - Good communication provides a basis for collaboration.
   - Class meetings provide opportunities for collaborative problem solving.
   - Collaborative planning and evaluation is the key to solving individual problems.

Take a Moment To Reflect

Directions: Look at Focus Box 9–5 and Focus Box 9–8, which summarize the guidelines for classroom management. Focus Box 9–5 summarizes the guidelines from classroom management research, and Focus Box 9–8 summarizes guidelines for helping children develop self-discipline. With a group of your peers compare and contrast the two sets of guidelines by answering the following questions.

1. What, in your view, are the critical differences between the two sets of guidelines?
2. Look at each list of guidelines and think about the implicit curriculum lessons that might be learned. What similarities and/or differences do you see in possible implicit curriculum learnings?
3. Do any of the recommendations from either list contradict your initial assumptions about effective classroom management? In thinking about this consider the following questions:

    • Do you see any pattern to the contradictions you noted? Look for patterns within the answers of one individual. As a group, look for patterns within the answers of the group as a whole.

    • Are there any general assumptions about teaching and learning that might explain the differences you noted? Think back to your foundations courses and the differences and the assumptions that support a transmission view of learning and a constructivist (or interactionist) view of learning (Piaget).

Rethinking Classroom Management and Discipline

We noted at the beginning of this chapter that classroom management is the primary concern of students, teachers, parents, and school administrators. Certainly, figuring out how to design a classroom to allow 30 human beings to live peacefully and productively together is no small task. We recognize teachers' concerns and agree that serious consideration must be given to the means by which order and harmony will be achieved.

Our main point has been that decisions about how classroom life is to be lived should be grounded in the teacher's *educational* aims. There is no one "best way" to organize classroom life. Decisions about what is "best" and "effective" must be based on the teachers' visions: What do teachers hope students will learn through their classroom experiences? We have advocated the aim of student empowerment that we defined as entailing individual and community values. Because our society stresses values associated with the advancement of the individual, we have argued that teachers can create the balance required for democratic living by promoting values of community. Traditionally, classrooms have been organized according to authoritarian power relations. Teachers have laid out their expectations, and students have complied. Students who fail to obey receive a predetermined punishment. Under these conditions, students may work quietly and stay in their seats, but what do they learn about themselves, other students, adults, and society? Do they learn **values of community** (e.g., compassion, equality, responsibility) by participating in a stratified system in which they have little power and control? We think not.

We are not suggesting that teachers and students are "equals" in the classroom. We believe that teachers have legitimate authority that they should use "to teach [children] how to live according to community values" (Goodman, 1992, p. 104). They do this by creating routines, rules, and practices that help students become responsible for themselves and to others. While the teacher may be seen as having the "master plan," students play a central role in the construction of group life through ongoing dialogue with members of the group.

We have suggested ways for teachers to help children develop self-discipline by reviewing the guidelines generated by classroom management research and by suggesting the need for five additional guidelines:

1. Assess the curriculum to determine whether problems may be rooted in inappropriate curriculum.

2. Assess the classroom environment to determine whether you are actively fostering the development of group identity and peer acceptance.

3. Always provide a rationale for rules, routines, and procedures.

4. Give students opportunities to make important decisions in the classroom.

5. View inappropriate behavior as an opportunity for collaborative problem solving.

In our discussion of these classroom practices, we are trying to shift the emphasis away from controlling students' behavior to teaching students how to be responsible members of a community. It is through their relations with others that students learn important lessons about how to live in a community. We believe teachers should take responsibility for deliberately shaping classroom relations to promote students' sense of social responsibility and facilitate student empowerment.

However, we also recognize that this is a very difficult task. In Chapter 1 we introduced the idea of **teaching as dilemma management** (Lampert, 1985). By this we mean that many teaching problems have no clear, "best" solution. As a result, teachers manage the dilemma by selecting the most acceptable or least undesirable solution but continue to mentally debate the underlying issues and to search for a better resolution. A teacher we know has said that classroom management is the area in which she most often finds herself balancing conflicting aims. She notes that she never feels "settled" about her classroom management decisions. We believe this is true because there is an inherent tension between the need for an orderly environment and the need to provide children with enough freedom to help them develop responsibility. This teacher's comments suggest that a key indicator of reflective teachers may well be whether issues related to the development of self-discipline haunt them. They certainly have haunted us as we worked on this chapter. The fact that this chapter was the most difficult one for us to write seems indicative of the challenges of classroom management and magnitude of the dilemmas for teachers who wish to empower students.

Practice Application Activities

Directions: Draw on the guidelines presented throughout this chapter to propose solutions for each of the classroom management problems described below. These problem descriptions have been adapted from descriptions written by graduate interns at the University of Florida. They are written from the teacher's perspective. As you develop ideas for solutions remember to tackle each problem in terms of (1) immediate action you might take, and (2) long-term actions you might take.

Problem 1: Small Group

Background: I teach a reading group of fifth graders who are on a second-grade reading level. These six children impede their own learning by constantly degrading one another. For example, Ken cannot sit next to Aaron because they provoke each other to fight. Jake cannot sit next to Tina because he teases her provocatively. Prevonka tries to sit next to me because she seems to need a protector. If anyone says a cross word to her, she wilts. Micah and Adrianna are nonreaders and need to sit next to me for instructional support. Micah seems afraid to talk and won't participate. Adrianna likes to participate and constantly raises her hand but then stares at me blankly when I call on her. The rest of the members of the group participate when they are "in the mood."

The problem: As the children are called to group and begin sitting in our reading circle, some decide that others are sitting in the "wrong" seats. They begin yelling—"Get out!" "You can't sit there!" "Ms. Kerry don't let him sit next to me!" "I won't sit next to you, you stink!" I finally get them seated, but they continue to make faces at one another and kick each other under the table. It is clear to me that today is going to be like every other day—a continual struggle to get them to attend and to stop bothering each other so I can *try* to teach the reading group.

Problem 2: Large Group

Background: I team teach with two other kindergarten teachers. Our classes are in an open-space pod. Although we have moveable walls between our classes, it is very easy to hear through the walls. Every day after lunch the children in all three classes are expected to return to their rooms, get their mats, and rest for 30 minutes.

The problem: Many of the children do not want to rest (and *that* is a major understatement!). They talk, sit up, disrupt their neighbors, and start tattling on one another (just to have a chance to walk up to me instead of lying down). They also use the bathroom continuously. Rest time has ended up being a hated time for me and the children. They don't want to be quiet and stay still. I spend my entire time saying, "Lie down, lie down,"

"_____, move your mat somewhere else," "If you are not quiet you will not be able to watch the video after rest time." I feel more like a sheriff than a teacher, but I also feel I have to keep the kids quiet or I'll disturb the other teachers.

Problem 3: Individual

Background: This problem actually involves two second-grade children. I guess most problems do. Joshua is a responsible child. He is caring and conscientious and takes classroom responsibilities seriously. Monica is relatively new to our room. She has been with us for about 3 weeks. She comes from a very low-SES home and is relatively nonverbal. Joshua and Monica sit next to each other.

The problem: Yesterday, as we lined up for lunch, Joshua seemed very upset. When I asked what was wrong, he told me he did not have his lunch money. He did not seem sure whether he had lost it or if his mother had forgotten to give it to him. I lent him the money and forgot about it. Today, as we lined up for lunch, Joshua began to cry. He said he did not have lunch money again, and he guessed he had lost it again. He was very upset. He does not usually lose things. At that point, I remembered that Monica had proudly showed me her "quarters from home" earlier that morning. I began to wonder if Joshua had "lost" his money.

After school today, Joshua's mother called to tell me that she had been sending Joshua's money and putting it in the pocket of his backpack as had been her habit since the beginning of school. She suggested that someone might have taken his money. I guess I have a real problem to confront tomorrow.

After you have proposed your solutions, work with a group of two or three peers to critique your work:

- Evaluate the solutions proposed by each person using the guidelines presented in the chapter.
- Were some guidelines omitted by one or more members of the group? Why might this be?
- Do some guidelines seem more difficult (or less realistic) than others? How could they be adapted to make them more feasible?
- As a group, generate two or three other problems that you have confronted as a teacher or seen in a classroom. How would you solve these problems?

FOCUS BOX 9–11

Yes, These Look Like Good Ideas, but . . .

Whenever teachers encounter new ideas, they have to try to fit them within their current understandings about children, their knowledge of and beliefs about appropriate instructional strategies, their current knowledge base, and their specific teaching context. Because of this, you probably found yourself raising questions about the feasibility of the practices about classroom management we have suggested. We suspect at times you found yourself thinking, "Yes, these look like good ideas, but . . .?" Work with a small group of peers to raise and try to answer your questions about the strategies suggested in this chapter (particularly in the second half of the chapter). The following questions may help to guide your thinking:

- What is your overall, "gut" reaction to the ideas? Do they look like strategies you might like to try? Why or why not?

- As you think about trying to implement the strategies, what concerns do you have?

- If you were to try to implement these strategies, what skills, abilities, and/or knowledge would you need to develop? How would you go about doing this?

- What contextual barriers do you see that might make implementation of these strategies difficult? How could you work around these contextual barriers? (*Note:* By **contextual barriers**, we mean circumstances specific to your teaching situation. For example, you may teach or student teach in a school where teachers are required to use a particular management program or you may teach in a team-teaching situation where teachers are expected to use similar classroom management strategies.)

- What are the implicit curriculum implications of these strategies? How do they fit with the aims you have identified as important for elementary education?

It is important to raise these kinds of questions and to explore the answers with your peers. Failure to confront these questions probably means you will not make the significant changes necessary to empower students.

Further Readings

Brophy, J. (1985). Classroom management as instruction: Socializing self-guidance in students. *Theory Into Practice, 24* (1), 233–240.

Dreikurs, R. (1968). *Psychology in the classroom* (2nd ed.). New York: Harper & Row.

Evertson, C. M., & Emmer, E. T. (1982). Preventive classroom management. In D. L. Duke (Ed.), *Helping teachers manage classrooms* (pp. 2–31). Alexandria, VA: Association for Supervision and Curriculum Development.

Evertson, C. M., Emmer, E. T., Clements, B. S., Sanford, J. P., & Worsham, M. E. (1984). *Classroom management for elementary teachers.* Englewood Cliffs, NJ: Prentice-Hall.

Ginott, H. (1971). *Teacher and child.* New York: Macmillan.

Glasser, W. (1965). *Schools without failure.* New York: Harper & Row.

Glasser, W. (1985). Discipline has never been the problem and isn't the problem now. *Theory Into Practice, 24* (1), 241–246.

Goodman, J. (1992). *Elementary schooling for critical democracy.* Albany, NY: State University of New York Press.

Gordon, T. (1970). *P.E.T.: Parent effectiveness training.* New York: Peter H. Wyden.

McDaniel, T. (1980). Alternatives to punishment. *Phi Delta Kappan, 61* (7), 455–458.

Render, G. F., Padilla, J. N. M. & Krank, H. M. (1989). Assertive discipline: A critical review and analysis. *Teachers' College Record, 90* (4), 607–630.

Schuncke, G. M. & Krogh, S. L. (1983). *Helping children choose.* Glenview, IL: Scott, Foresman & Co.

PART 3

Maximizing Professional Autonomy

By now, we're sure you have recognized a fundamental **is/ought** dichotomy that exists in this book. That is, we have provided many descriptions of "typical" instruction in classrooms, and we have noted the multitude of problems associated with those practices. For example, because of common instructional patterns many children fail to perceive school learning as a personally meaningful activity; fail to develop depth of understanding in various content areas; do not trust their ability to reason and make sense; believe they lack the capacity to learn; fail to develop self-esteem, self-discipline, and motivation; and do not develop sufficient social skills to relate well to others.

We also have provided suggestions of alternative practices that would avoid the problems associated with traditional instruction. These are not hypothetical alternatives. All of the strategies we presented are used successfully by many teachers in elementary classrooms. However, we also must acknowledge that they are not "typical." If they were, the problems associated with typical elementary instruction would not exist. A question that should be haunting you is, WHY? Why do traditional teaching patterns persist despite pervasive evidence that they are not effective in helping us reach goals that most elementary teachers believe are important?

In Chapter 2, we discussed the culture(s) of teaching and how culture influences what teachers do. We cannot regard the persistence of traditional practice as idiosyncratic coincidence. Something about the circumstances of teaching encourages teachers to make particular decisions. Unless we accept the view that teachers have little commitment to children, and lack knowledge about good teaching practice (which we do not), we must conclude that traditional teaching practice persists because it is functional within the culture of schools. As

Rosenholtz has noted, teachers learn how to behave in schools as a part of working in schools:

> People come to define their workday realities . . . through the communications people have with, or the observations they make of, others. Thus teachers learn through everyday interactions how to name and classify things, and in that process learn how they are expected to behave with reference to those things. In this way, teachers define the nature of their work, their sentiments toward their work, the substance of their work. (1989a, p.3)

Critiques of schooling and its impact on teachers and children provide several compelling reasons for the persistence of traditional instruction. Based upon a review of this literature, Goodman (1987a; 1988a) offers the following explanations:

- In our **patriarchal society** (i.e., society marked by supremacy of men and dependence of women), teaching traditionally has been defined as "women's work." Because of this, teaching is a low-status profession, teachers' perspectives are not valued, teachers are viewed as people who need to be managed, and teachers are allowed little professional autonomy (Apple, 1986; Belenky, Clinchy, Goldberger, & Tarule, 1986; Rallis, 1988). By **autonomy** we mean the right to assume significant authority for making professional decisions.

- In the hope of increasing efficiency, schools adopted a technical, bureaucratic organizational structure from industry. This has lead to centralized decision making and the adoption of standardized procedures, and in the process has lowered teachers' work commitment and autonomy (Goodman, 1987a). In addition, the goals of organizational efficiency have taken precedence over educational goals (McNeil, 1988a).

- The introduction of prepackaged curricula reduces teaching to a technical, managerial task. The longer teachers use such programs, the more their teaching skills atrophy. Apple (1986) calls this the **deskilling** of teachers. The influence of these programs and tests cannot be underestimated. Goodman (1992) argues that their use is so pervasive that teachers no longer question them and do not recognize them as controlling forces. That programs and tests have become well ingrained in the "taken for granted reality" of schooling is perhaps the strongest control of all.

Hatton (1987) and Giroux (1989) argue that teachers' perceptions about and practices within schools are determined almost exclusively by the working conditions within schools. Further, they argue that changes in teaching are unlikely without substantial changes in the organizational context of schools and society. While we agree that many changes are necessary in the way schools are structured, we do not accept this deterministic view. We are more inclined to agree with Grant and Sleeter who suggest that working conditions are *a* major influence on teachers but not *the* major influence.

> Teachers, like all social actors, are neither totally free nor totally determined. . . . Present constraints make some courses of action difficult or impossible and

others likely, but allow room for choice. Past experiences also limit what one is likely to choose and strengthen the "sense" of a narrow range of choices. But neither completely determines a person's actions. (1987, p. 62)

The tremendous range in the quality of teaching practices convinces us that these practices are not determined by the structural characteristics of schools. As we noted in Chapter 2, the culture of teaching does influence the choices that teachers make, and we support the work of educators striving to change the organizational characteristics of schools and society. However, we believe there are things teachers can do to increase their power within schools. In Part 3 of this book, we will present strategies to help you gain and maintain the power to implement your professional ideas.

In Chapter 10, we will review the characteristics of school environments that support the professional growth of teachers. We also will present ideas about how to select a school environment with these characteristics. In Chapter 11, we will suggest strategies for working within any school environment to establish a collaborative community of colleagues and to maximize teachers' collective professional power and autonomy. In Chapter 12, we will present strategies useful in self-evaluation and in the documentation of a teacher's effectiveness. These strategies will help teachers to articulate their knowledge as practitioners (i.e., knowledge about the impact and effectiveness of their practices). Teachers who are able to articulate the reasons for and evidence supporting their decisions are more likely to be given the autonomy for putting their ideas into practice. Thus, in Chapter 12, reflective self-evaluation is presented as a critical link in achieving that autonomy.

CHAPTER 10

Selecting a Professional Environment

A variety of factors influence whether a teacher is more or less likely to be reflective about practice (see Chapter 2). Said simply and obviously: Schools differ, and the experience of teaching differs dependent on the teaching context. Consider the comments of two beginning teachers:[1]

> Teachers don't work together at my school. . . . I don't think my principal values teachers working together . . . although they do help each other with resources.

> At my school we do grade-level planning and meet at each other's houses. . . . Cooperation hasn't been a problem. I also get a lot of feedback about my teaching. . . .

Both of these beginning teachers *survived* their first year of teaching and were judged successful by their principals. However, their opportunities for professional growth, for collaborative interaction, and for **professional autonomy** (i.e., the right to assume significant authority for making professional decisions) were not the same. How important is the choice of a school in which to teach? How do you recognize a good school?

Does It Matter Where You Teach?

The answer to this question is yes, Yes, YES!!! Although all teachers recognize this fact, it is easy to forget when they begin searching for a job. The importance of securing a job, *any* job, often becomes so important that the nature of the teaching environment is never considered. However, the selection of a teaching environment for the first year of teaching is probably the most important professional decision any teacher makes.

Success or failure in the first year of teaching has a significant impact on teachers' careers, often determining whether they remain in the profession (Johnston & Ryan, 1983). Additionally, many teachers who stay in the profession

---

[1] These quotations are from field notes of teachers' comments at the Beginning Teachers' Conference at the University of Florida, February 1988.

fail to develop or grow professionally after the first year (Ryan, 1979). That is, they become **disempowered.** To illustrate this point, consider the experiences of one first-year teacher (Kilgore, Ross & Zbikowski, 1990).

The Case of Lisa: Teaching in a Disempowering Context[2]

Lisa taught in a homogeneously grouped third grade in an inner-city school in a large urban district. The class consisted mostly of low-achieving, low-SES black students. Lisa chose to discuss the instructional and management problems that she encountered. Lisa described her students as,

> difficult to teach. . . . There is nothing to work with. . . . My kids don't care. They just want to go outside and fight. [Their parents] don't care. They are not interested. They are drop-outs from high school. The students have a bad home environment: drugs, violence and alcohol. They don't have any good role models; they don't have any support.

In many respects, Lisa felt powerless to effect any change in the children.

> I have only a limited amount of time with them; the pressure from home and from their friends is not to change, not to change their speech, their language, their attitude, their behavior. . . . I expected these low-SES kids to be slow learners but I did not expect them to have the attitudes they had . . . the disrespect.

During her first year of teaching, Lisa developed the view that these children were unteachable and her major focus became maintaining discipline. She reported that she became much stricter than she had expected to be because any attempts at creative activities were disruptive.

> I gave them constant structure. No creativity. . . . They had seatwork and dittos every day. They had to be in their seats, in their place.

In addition to using paperwork, Lisa maintained order by using a system of rewards and punishments based on assertive discipline (Canter, 1979).

Lisa saw herself as virtually powerless to effect any meaningful changes in the educational lives of her children. She said,

> These kids are more powerful than any adults in the building. . . . I learned that their problems were a lot more than being slow learners. When a kid looks you in the face and says, "I don't care. I don't care if you call my mother. I don't care if you send me to the office," there's not much you can do.

Lisa characterized her students as incapable of being taught and herself as incapable of teaching them.

---

[2]   This example is reprinted with permission from "Understanding the Teaching Perspectives of First Year Teachers" by K. Kilgore, D. D. Ross, & J. Zbikowski, 1990, *Journal of Teacher Education,* Volume 41, Number 1, pp. 23–38.

Lisa's description, interpretation and assessment of her situation show little evidence of reflection. Although she did search for solutions to her problems with control, by the conclusion of the year she had abdicated her responsibility for student learning by blaming students for their school failure. What factors within the environment and within Lisa contributed to this?

Lisa believed she lacked support for dealing with her problems. She felt her peers and the administration were also ineffective:

> The principal and assistant principal did not have much power. They had no effect on the students' behavior. This is a school-wide problem.

Although Lisa characterized her fellow teachers as willing to help, she did not believe them capable of assisting her.

Lisa saw the entire school staff as victims in the situation, rather than as active agents who could initiate change. As a result, she concluded the children were not teachable. The other teachers and staff reinforced that viewpoint rather than encouraging her to develop alternatives. In such an environment, Lisa was unable to sustain a reflective attitude.

Learning From the Case

The description of Lisa's first year of teaching is from a study of the experiences of six beginning teachers who finished their preservice teacher education program committed to providing high-quality education for children. These teachers had successfully completed a student-teaching internship (Kilgore et al., 1990). During their first year of teaching, four of these teachers were able to maintain a reflective approach to teaching. Two, one of whom was Lisa, were not. Clearly, the fact that the majority of Lisa's students were low-achieving minority students was one factor in the difficulties she encountered.

However, other beginning teachers maintain a reflective approach and their commitment to students when teaching low-achieving, minority students. One Florida graduate was assigned to teach sixth-grade, low-achieving, problem children in a large school in an urban district. In 1989, she reported at the Florida Beginning Teacher Conference that she found this to be empowering rather than disempowering. Because no one else had been successful with the children, she felt she had more freedom to experiment and to be different. As a result, she reported that the children responded well to her and were excited about learning. Also, her principal thought she was doing a great job. The nature of the student population, then, is not the key factor in determining whether a school will support the professional growth of teachers. In some schools at-risk students are taught successfully, and teachers have opportunities for growth and reflection (Bredemeier, 1988).

We included Lisa's case to illustrate the profound impact of first-year experiences upon the professional development of teachers. In one year, Lisa abandoned her commitment to children. To preserve her self-esteem, she concluded that her children were unteachable, a conclusion that would have appalled her just one year earlier.

While teaching context may be slightly less important for experienced teachers, it is still critical. For example, Hayes and Ross (1989) report the experiences of Jennifer, an experienced kindergarten teacher who moved into a very controlling teaching environment. Despite a strong knowledge base, a coherent belief structure, previous experience with her instructional strategies, and a strong external support system, Jennifer's experiences caused a high level of self-doubt and great dissatisfaction with teaching. She often considered leaving the field and, although once committed to the importance of teacher reflection, began to question its value.

Research on **effective schools** (i.e., schools in which children score higher than expected scores on standardized tests of achievement), on the characteristics and effects of differing educational leadership styles, and on the influence of school context on job commitment provides additional evidence of the importance of school **context** (environment). These studies indicate that school context influences teachers' morale, self-esteem, and commitment; the nature of the curriculum provided and levels of student achievement; the growth or decline in teachers' professional knowledge; and the levels of teacher stress, burn-out, and frustration (Frymier, 1987; McNeil, 1988a, b, c; Rosenholtz, 1989a). Whether you are an experienced teacher seeking a transfer or moving to a new community, or a beginning teacher seeking your first professional job, the school where you teach will play a major role in enhancing or limiting your professional growth. How does one find a positive school context? Before you read the next section, you may want to clarify your entering ideas by completing the activity in Focus Box 10–1.

FOCUS BOX 10–1

Take a Moment to Reflect

Before you read our discussion of the factors that support or constrain teacher development, try to determine your entering ideas about the relevant factors. First, think about a school context with which you are familiar. Now, clarify your thinking by answering the following:

- Do you think this context supports or constrains teachers' growth and development?
- List as many specific factors as you can that contribute to the professional environment of the school.

After you read the section entitled "Selecting a Context That Stimulates Professional Growth" compare the ideas we developed with your entering ideas. Have any of your ideas changed? How and why?

Selecting a Context That Stimulates Professional Growth

To find a positive school context, you must first have a picture of the kind of environment you are seeking. We've just told you of Jennifer's experiences in a controlling or disempowering school environment. After her experiences at Northside Elementary, Jennifer sought and obtained a job at Canter Elementary, a **professionally supportive or empowering context** (i.e., a school environment that encourages the professional growth of teachers). What is it about Canter that made it such a good place to teach? Here's what Jennifer said:

> At Canter I feel I'm part of a professional team. The respect the principal has for teachers was communicated from our very first meeting. During the interview the principal asked me lots of questions about my beliefs and my goals. . . . he was trying to determine if my goals matched the school's goals [e.g., meeting the needs of the whole child] . . . because teachers are given so much autonomy at Canter. . . .
>
> It's not that we don't work together. . . . Teachers spend a lot of time talking about what they do at Canter and trying to decide how to do it better . . . you are respected and trusted to make professional decisions.

Jennifer's comments reveal many of the characteristics of growth-enhancing environments. Many of these characteristics were explained in Chapter 2.

Characteristics of Positive School Contexts

GOAL FOCUS.   A key characteristic of any successful organization is a strong sense of shared purpose (Peters & Waterman, 1982). Although goals may be stated in a variety of ways (e.g., "meeting the needs of the whole child," "helping children do their best academically and personally"), Leithwood and Montgomery (1982) stress that the dominant goals must be to promote the cognitive growth and happiness of students. *Happiness* is as important as achievement. Good schools are purposeful, but they are also places that children and teachers enjoy.

Principals in schools with clear goals behave in ways that make it more likely that goals will be accomplished. For example, they provide necessary resources and reasonable teaching assignments, protect instructional time (i.e., eliminate unnecessary tasks), and provide teachers with feedback related to school goals (Leithwood & Montgomery, 1982; Rosenholtz, Bassler, & Hoover-Dempsey, 1986). All of these actions make it more likely teachers will accomplish their goals and, therefore, develop professional satisfaction, efficacy, and self-esteem.

NORMS OF COLLEGIAL INTERACTION AND EXPERIMENTATION.   In good schools, teachers talk to each other and to administrators about teaching **(professional collegiality)**. As a result of their interactions, they develop or learn about new ideas to try in their classrooms **(experimentation)** (Lieberman, 1988b; Little, 1982; Maeroff, 1988b; Rosenholtz, 1989b). An essential component of profes-

Collaborative relations among colleagues is a key characteristic of effective schools.

sional growth is the willingness to take risks, to try something new, and evaluate what happens. Collaboration with peers provides a context that supports risk taking and provides encouragement for the effort required to teach well (Veal, Clift, & Holland, 1989; Wildman & Niles, 1987).

SHARED DECISION MAKING AND RESPECT FOR TEACHERS' PROFESSIONAL AUTONOMY.   It is not a contradiction to say that good schools stress shared goals, teacher collaboration, and respect for the teachers' professional autonomy. In good schools, administrators communicate respect for teachers' professional knowledge and judgment by involving them in decisions about practice (Frymier, 1987; Goodman, 1988a; Rosenholtz, 1989b). In empowering schools there is a "significant and meaningful distribution of authority" (Goodman, 1992); teachers and administrators collaboratively share authority over decisions (i.e., **shared decision making).** In a study of teacher efficacy in different middle-school contexts, the following was found:

> The sense of commitment and involvement that distinguished middle school teachers from the more resigned junior high school teachers in our study seemed to be tied to the greater role middle school teachers played in decision-making. (Ashton & Webb, 1986, p. 171).

PARENT INVOLVEMENT.   In good schools, parent involvement is high, and this is true whatever the SES of the student population served by the schools (Mortimore & Sammons, 1987; Rosenholtz, 1989b). In fact, teachers experience more success teaching low-SES students when parents are involved, so parent involvement is particularly important in low-SES schools. Rosenholtz (1989b) notes that lack of parental involvement often breeds distrust between parents and teachers and leads teachers to blame parents for the learning problems of their children, thus lowering teacher's sense of efficacy.

> The more teachers complain about difficult parents and children, of course, the stronger their conviction that their potential for classroom success lies outside their control. (Rosenholtz, 1989b, p. 435)

SUMMARY.   Teachers seeking professionally enhancing environments are looking for schools characterized by goal focus, norms of collegiality and experimentation, shared decision making and respect for teachers' professional autonomy, and high levels of parental involvement. Such schools do exist. In fact, the literature on school effectiveness and the characteristics of effective educational leaders suggest that all schools should provide such environments. However, empowering school environments are not pervasive enough that teachers can accept a job and feel confident the environment will foster professional growth. Consequently, teachers need strategies for discreetly assessing the professional quality of a school environment.

General Guidelines for Assessing Professional Environments

Let's assume that you have some choice about where you teach.[3] Of course, some teachers have no choice; however, with teacher shortages in many areas of the country, many beginning and experienced teachers report having multiple job offers. Additionally, many teachers work in areas accessible to two or more school districts. While it may be inconvenient to drive a long distance to work, the chance to teach in an empowering environment should be worth some inconvenience, if you are serious about your commitment to teaching.

Gaining information about school contexts will be easier if you are familiar with a school district. Teachers talking about their jobs or parents talking about their children's experiences in a school will reveal important information about the character of schools within the district. By listening carefully, teachers desiring transfers or beginning teachers returning to their home districts will be able to determine where they want to teach.

If you are moving into a new area, which is common, gaining information about school contexts is more difficult. If you are fortunate enough to interview

---

[3] If you have no choice, acquiring information about different teaching contexts may still be useful. For example, you may identify schools to which you would like to transfer after "serving your time," and you may identify individuals who could provide professional support as you struggle with a difficult teaching context. We will talk more about support groups in Chapter 11.

for your position while school is still in session, we encourage you to refer to Bullough (1989) for some excellent suggestions about assessing a school context. Bullough encourages prospective teachers to visit classrooms and the faculty lounge; to attend a faculty meeting; to observe the physical environment and atmosphere of the school; and to interview teachers about support for new teachers, about resources provided for instruction, and about the way decisions are made in the school.

While we believe Bullough's suggestions are good, they seem unrealistic to us. We know very few teachers who were hired before July, and even fewer who were able to talk to anyone besides the principal as part of the interview process. The reality of securing jobs in teaching is that most teachers make their decision based upon information gained during one or more interviews with the principal. Often the principal does most of the question asking (or talking) during the interview process. Nevertheless, you can learn a significant amount of information during an interview if you have planned a few key questions to ask, and if you know how to interpret the answers.

Key Interview Questions

When you interview for a teaching position, the principal will direct the course of the interview.[4] You will be asked many questions and should be as honest and straightforward as possible in providing answers. You may be nervous because the principal is making judgments about you and your potential as a teacher at that school. Unfortunately, you probably will not know the criteria being used to judge you. However, keep in mind that you also are making judgments. Remember that the principal, most frequently, is the dominant influence on the professional climate within a school. As you interview, try to make a judgment about the nature of that climate and the leadership characteristics of the principal. Is this an environment likely to enhance your professional growth? Is this a principal with whom you would like to work?

In order to make judgments, you must listen carefully as the principal asks questions. Notice whether the principal uses the interview to ask questions or to communicate expectations and routine procedures (Hayes & Ross, 1989). A principal who uses the interview to communicate expectations is more likely to expect teachers to follow rules than to exercise professional judgment. A principal who indicates interest in your values and beliefs and who talks about the school's philosophy and goals is more likely to respect the professional judgment of teachers.

During the interview, you will probably be asked if you have any questions. (If you are not asked, this could be a clue that your ideas and opinions are not valued.) At this point, you should ask *one or two* questions that you feel will help you make your decision. Which questions you ask will be determined by what has

---

4   You may have a district-level screening interview prior to your interview with one or more
    principals in the district. This section is designed to guide your actions during an interview with a
    principal, not during a screening interview.

happened in the first part of the interview. Asking a question that has already been answered would make you seem inattentive. Similarly, there is no point in asking questions if you have already determined that this is not the job for you.

It is not possible to ask enough questions to gain information about all aspects of the school context. We are providing questions related to professional autonomy and parent involvement. Information about these two key aspects of the environment should help you make your decision. Notice the way the questions have been phrased. It must not seem like you are interviewing the principal, though that is, in fact, what you are doing. You must seem to be trying to learn more about the school as if you have already decided to teach there and you want to gain information that will help you do a better job.

QUESTIONS RELATED TO PROFESSIONAL AUTONOMY.   Asking one or more of the following questions will help you assess the principal's beliefs about allowing teachers professional autonomy:

1. Could you tell me a little about the other (third)-grade teachers with whom I would work? What are their classrooms like? Do they plan together?

2. What curriculum resource materials are available for teachers? Are there requirements or guidelines about how they should be used?

3. Do you use a particular model of discipline or classroom management? How do new teachers learn about it? Has it been effective for all the children?

When the principal answers, listen carefully. A principal who creates an empowering school climate will be able to speak knowledgeably about the teachers, curriculum, and management procedures used in the school. It is not a good sign if a principal stresses uniformity in answering questions. This might be communicated by comments such as:

• Oh, yes, my teachers plan together. I like them to be together in what they do. I like the same work to go home with each child, so we can avoid parent complaints.

• We all use this basal program. Teachers are given guidelines about when to complete each unit so everyone stays together.

• All my teachers are the same.

• This discipline approach is great. It works in every classroom, with every child.

A principal who fails to acknowledge the distinctiveness of teachers and children is unlikely to respect the autonomy of teachers. Conversely, a principal who speaks knowledgeably and proudly of the distinctive accomplishments and curriculum adaptations of the teachers is one who respects the professional knowledge and discretion of teachers.

The answers to these questions also may provide you with information about the nature of collegial interaction among teachers. Notice whether the principal tends to talk about individual teachers or about pairs and groups of teachers,

Parents can provide many types of valuable service for a school.

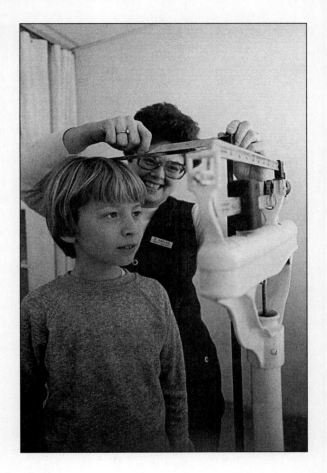

especially when answering the question about teachers who teach at the same grade level you would be hired to teach.

QUESTIONS ABOUT PARENT INVOLVEMENT.   The following set of questions may be useful:

> Tell me a little more about the school population. From where in the district do your children come? Do you have many parents involved with the school? What kinds of things do they do?

You will be hoping to hear the principal say that parents are highly involved. To know if this is the kind of involvement indicative of effective schools, you must probe further, however, for most principals will say that parents are involved. The question is not whether *some* parents are involved but whether the school is able to involve a large percentage of parents. Principals in high-involvement

FOCUS BOX 10–2

Take a Moment to Reflect

In this chapter we have presented several controversial ideas. It is important to examine *your* reactions to these ideas and to compare your reactions to those of your peers. As we have emphasized throughout this book, if ideas are to be useful to you, you must determine how they fit with your entering ideas about teaching. Whether you accept or reject ideas presented in this chapter, it is important that you evaluate the evidence you use in making a judgment. Look at each of the following ideas and decide what you think:

• The first year of teaching has a significant impact on your teaching career.

• Lisa's teaching context was probably a highly significant negative experience on her professional development.

• Teachers who complain about low parent involvement probably have low efficacy.

• You should interview the principal during a job interview.

Share your views with your colleagues. As you discuss your conclusions focus on the following:

1. What evidence can you provide that your conclusion is a valid one?
2. What additional evidence might you want to collect?

schools are likely to describe active strategies they have used to involve parents, such as lending parents educational games, writing parent newsletters, scheduling parent workshops, and asking parents to read to their children (Epstein, 1987). Principals of low-involvement schools are likely to say, "Some of our parents just don't have the time or don't seem to care." Principals who blame parents for not participating rather than seeking ways to reach out to them are limiting the educational potential of a substantial portion of the school population. Students in these schools are less likely to be successful learners and, therefore, teachers are less likely to feel professionally successful (Rosenholtz, 1989b).

These questions will be useful in helping you find a professionally enhancing teaching context. However, there are few perfect teaching contexts, and you may not be able to get a job in the school you most desire. Additionally, teachers are not helpless victims of their teaching contexts. Teachers' beliefs, interpretations of events, knowledge, social skills, energy, and motivation also influence the role they play within a school context (Goodman, 1987b; 1988b; Grant & Sleeter, 1987). Within the same school context, one teacher may feel powerless to implement professional beliefs, while another may find ways to "work the system" and create opportunities for the exercise of professional autonomy. In the next chapter, we will present strategies that will help you maximize your professional autonomy within the constraints of your particular teaching context.

Further Readings

Frymier, J. (1987). Bureaucracy and the neutering of teachers. *Phi Delta Kappan, 69*, (1), 9–14.

Hayes, L. F., & Ross, D. D. (1989). Trust versus control: The impact of school leadership on teacher reflection. *International Journal of Qualitative Studies in Education, 2* (4), 335–350.

Kilgore, K., Ross, D. D., & Zbikowski, J. (1990). Understanding the teaching perspectives of first year teachers. *Journal of Teacher Education, 41*, (1) 23–38.

Lieberman, A. (1988). Teachers and principals: Turf, tension and new tasks. *Phi Delta Kappan, 69*, (9), 648–653.

Little, J. W. (1982). Norms of collegiality and experimentation: Workplace conditions of school success. *American Educational Research Journal, 19* (3), 325–340.

Mortimore, P., & Sammons, P. (1987). New evidence on effective elementary schools. *Educational Leadership, 45* (1), 4-8.

Rosenholtz, S. J. (1989a). *Teachers' workplace.* New York: Longman.

Rosenholtz, S. J. (1989b). Workplace conditions that affect teacher quality and commitment: Implications for teacher induction programs. *Elementary School Journal, 89* (4), 421–439.

Veal, M. L., Clift, R., & Holland, P. (1989). School contexts that encourage reflection: Teacher perceptions. *International Journal of Qualitative Studies in Education, 2* (4), 315–334.

Wildman, T. M., & Niles, J. A. (1987). Reflective teachers: tensions between abstractions and realities. *Journal of Teacher Education, 38*(1), 25–31.

CHAPTER 11

Working Within the Social System of the School

> In the politics of everyday life, people are required to be in a position to use influence, to "own" their power, or to suffer the consequences of their unwillingness or inability to do so. Yet there is a great deal of reluctance about its use. (Gross, 1985, p. 137)

Schools and Micropolitics

This chapter is about power and acquiring and using power. This statement may make you a little uneasy. Teachers want to be professionally autonomous, but acquiring power sounds so aggressive, so calculating. As a friend of ours said, "Oh, I know all about power. Most of the time it comes in on wires from above, and if you play with it too much you'll get burned." This comment communicates the feelings many of us have. Power is held by people above us, and the pursuit of power is dangerous. To be called "power hungry" is not a compliment! We tend to perceive power as coercive control over others.

However, according to the dictionary, **power** can also mean to possess influence, to take action within one's sphere of authority, to act to produce an effect, or to be able to withstand pressure. You may feel more comfortable with these definitions. Within any organization, and schools are no exception, differences of opinion exist. As decisions are made, some individuals will have more influence than others; their opinions will be heard and acted upon. Others will not be heard, even if their opinions are grounded solidly in the professional knowledge base. Some individuals will seem to be immune from administrative edicts, and others will feel constrained by them. For example, one teacher said of a colleague:

> I don't know why or how it happened but Ms. _____ who everyone says is "super teacher" has some special dispensation. . . . She doesn't have to follow the same policies the rest of the teachers have to follow.

If you want to make professional decisions and have the autonomy to act upon those decisions, you want to be powerful (Gross, 1985). Wanting to be powerful means you must become politically aware. You must know how to recognize and use **micropolitical strategies** that are necessary to exercise power within an organization.

Throughout this book we have suggested strategies to help you empower students. We defined this broad aim of **student empowerment** as the ability to succeed as a learner, to determine one's path through life, and to participate actively and critically as a citizen in a democracy. In this chapter, we suggest strategies that will empower you within the social system of a school so that you will be able to serve as an advocate for children and implement alternative practices that might enable you to reach the kinds of educational and ethical goals we have discussed previously. Accomplishing these purposes *requires* that you work collaboratively with other teachers. If teachers were to use micropolitical strategies to manipulate others and acquire individual power, they would be unlikely to foster collaborative action among teachers. The manipulation of others would undermine the broader effort to empower children to learn and to function productively within a democratic society (Goodman, 1992). As you read about micropolitics, we urge you to keep in mind that power is not an end in itself; rather, it is a means to foster collaborative interaction among teachers and to pursue important educational and ethical goals for children. In short, we encourage teachers to pursue the development of collective power rather than individual power-grabbing. Having said this, let's find out what micropolitics is and its influence in schools.

What Is Micropolitics?

If you asked how decisions are made within a particular school and school system, you might be told about curriculum committees, textbook committees, advisory councils, research reports, administrative edicts, and team planning meetings. You would be told the formal, procedural mechanisms the organization uses to convey that a rational decision-making process exists. While these procedures do play some role, they are far from the whole story about how decisions are made. The complex web of personal and professional relationships within a school also influences decision making (Ball, 1987). For example, some committees are more powerful than other committees. Who is put on these committees and why? The task assigned to a committee shapes some decisions. (e.g., The task to select a textbook for science presumes a textbook will be used and precludes making a decision not to use a text.) Who defines the tasks? These political considerations shape the nature of decisions within organizations. It is naive to think that these political decisions are fortuitous. They are planned. As Ball states:

> Decision making is not an abstract rational process which can be plotted on an organizational chart; it is a political process, it is the stuff of micro-political activity. (1987, p. 26)

Before we continue in this chapter by defining micropolitics, we'd like to make a cautionary statement. The study of the micropolitics of schooling is relatively new, yet highly important. Only a handful of empirical studies exists, mostly con-

FOCUS BOX 11–1

Researchers Speak Out on the Professional Environment for Teaching

Directions: In Chapter 2 we discussed the culture of teaching and the way culture influences what a teacher may or may not do. Read the views of these researchers and identify common factors that influence the actions of teachers. Can you provide any examples from your personal and professional experiences that are consistent with the perspectives of these researchers? Have you had experiences that contradict their perspectives? What is your reaction to their description of the professional environment of teaching? Compare your reaction with those of your peers.

Sykes

The implicit message of many public policies directed at teachers is clear; "We don't trust you; we have little confidence in your competence; we are going to scrutinize you carefully and, wherever possible, constrain your discretionary behavior with rules, prescriptions, systems, technology, and administration." (Sykes, 1983, p. 92)

Maeroff

Few other professionals or aspiring professionals spend their workday with children. Few others must deal with a constituency—parents, taxpayers, school board members, lawmakers—all of whom have been through the process and think they know something about it. Few others work a full time job that many outsiders view as part-time employment because of the vacation schedule. Few others must attend to so much busy work that is not intrinsic to the main task. (Maeroff, 1988a, p. 21)

Being a schoolteacher is having so much to do and so little time to do it that keeping up with knowledge is a luxury. Even the most dedicated teacher finds that trying to stay abreast of subject matter is like paddling upstream on a fast moving river. (Maeroff, 1988a, p. 36)

---

ducted in Britain. The most comprehensive empirical work in this area has been done by Stephen Ball (1987). While we used several sources to develop this section, Ball's writing about the micropolitics of schooling is significant because of its depth, its comprehensiveness, and because he is exploring such a new area. His work shaped our thinking, and even where he is not cited, his influence is felt.

Although the organizational context of schooling is slightly different in Britain, the discussion of micropolitics is not unique to British schools. Micropolitics exists in all schools, and the research and theoretical work are useful for understanding the political context of schooling. However, no rules for action exist, only suggestions that may help you to understand the political life of your school and to take a more active role within that context.

Micropolitics occurs within an organization, as opposed to within the society at large (**macropolitics**). Hoyle defines micropolitics as the strategies used by groups and individuals in an organization "to use their resources of authority and influence to further their interests" (1986, p. 126). (The interests that reflective teachers work to further should be the interests of children within a demo-

Goodman

While the education establishment has been eager to apply an industrial organization to the management of school labor in an effort to increase "productivity" it has failed to recognize the well documented, negative effects (e.g., loss of workers' innate talents, loyalty, pride) of this managerial style. (Goodman, 1987a, p. 8)

McNeil

When teachers see administrators emphasizing compliance with rules and procedures, rather than long-term educational goals, teachers begin to structure their courses in ways that will elicit minimum participation from their students. . . . And when the complicated and often unpredictable task of educating students is less valued than having quiet halls and finishing paperwork on time, teachers try to create in their own classrooms the same kind of efficiencies by which they are judged in the running of their schools. . . . A vicious cycle of lowering expectations and of minimum participation is set up as teachers enact in their classrooms controls similar to those they perceive to be operating in the school. (McNeil, 1988b, p. 433)

Rallis

Although teachers are not exclusively women and administrators are not exclusively men, the arguments against allotting more responsibility to teachers have a sexist ring. Administrators tend to view teachers as feminine, as needing care and guidance, as not capable of taking care of themselves. (Rallis, 1988, p. 645)

---

cratic society.) Therefore, the field of micropolitics provides insight into how *power struggles* are resolved in schools and other organizations.

Perhaps this makes sense, but perhaps you don't see power struggles within your school. In fact, this is true most of the time. Most conflicts in schools remain hidden or "subterranean," a dominant reason why traditional practice tends to persist in schools (Lacey, 1977). Burbules suggests thinking of **power as the "status quo"** and notes that it is

> difficult to make problematic, to defy, or to rally popular opposition against; it [power] is implicit and latent in the common sense, ordinary way of things . . . it limits without expressly forbidding. (1988, p. 103)

Part of understanding micropolitics is to understand how this **latent power** (i.e., power vested in the status quo) operates.

What factors within the culture of teaching might influence the actions of teachers in ways that encourage traditional instructional practice? Focus Box 11–1 presents the perspectives of some educational researchers.

How Do Schools Preserve the Status Quo?

The **bureaucratic structure** of schools is one way control is exercised over teachers. In a bureaucracy, individuals at higher levels of the hierarchy receive status, privileges, and the power to set policy and impose regulations that individuals at lower levels are expected to follow (Burbules, 1988). This type of organization undermines the status and autonomy of teachers who are on the lower rungs of the bureaucratic ladder (Simpson & Simpson, 1969). This means that many teachers believe they must accept and comply with traditional practices because "that's the way the system works" or "that's what I was hired to do."

Teachers have not always been regulated as they are in today's schools. Schools have not always been organized bureaucratically, and at one time, teachers held much greater professional status and autonomy (Goodman, 1987a). Elsbree (1939) reports that colonial teachers, who were mostly male, possessed almost unlimited professional autonomy. However, as more and more women entered the profession, the status of teaching declined. Goodman notes:

> Underneath the rhetoric of women as the natural and superior guardians of children was an unspoken belief that these young women could not be trusted in the same way as their previous male colleagues. The leaders of most communities simply did not believe that young, female teachers could make significant decisions regarding their lives either inside or outside of school. (1987a, p. 11)

Historically, control over teachers has been exercised by male school board members, central office administrators, and principals. The **patriarchal** (i.e., social organization marked by supremacy of the male) nature of the profession is changing; however, the bureaucratic structure and the lowered professional status of teachers remain and constrain. Many teachers believe they must conform with administrative expectations, even when they believe the resultant practices are not in the best interests of the children.

However, schools are not tightly structured bureaucracies with strict policies and procedures and close supervision of employees to assure compliance. Instead, schools can be characterized as **"loosely coupled" systems** (Weick, 1976) with little direct supervision and often few *procedural mandates*. Ball (1987) notes that in a loosely coupled system, policy is "open to interpretation," and many administrators or individual teachers can negotiate special arrangements or exceptions. Given this fact, why do teachers perceive a lack of power and autonomy?

One reason is that instructional materials provide **technical control** over teachers. Giving teachers "teacher-proof" materials tells teachers that certain decisions are beyond their control, and that they are not trusted to make responsible professional decisions. Another reason is that *taken-for-granted assumptions* **(ideology)** about schooling and teachers' and administrators' roles shape teachers' ideas about their role. Remember that everyday experiences are the strongest influence on how teachers define their work (Rosenholtz, 1989a). Tradition is powerful. The status quo continues because it is the status quo. After working in the "system" for a while, many teachers believe, "It's always been this way, and it always will," so they no longer question the system or seek to exercise professional autonomy.

Informal interactions with colleagues help teachers to assess the micropolitical structure of the school.

This means that on the surface few conflicts occur within a school or school system. However, bubbling under the surface are conflicting interests and beliefs. Hoyle (1986) notes that areas of conflicting interest can revolve around such things as age differences (the young turks versus the old guard),[1] different attitudes toward change or issues, or friendship patterns. Consider, for example, this comment made by a beginning teacher about conflicting interests within her school:

> In my school there is a split between progressive and conservative teachers (young and old). . . . Older teachers want more control. They don't like field trips and are more test conscious. They do less fun stuff. During lunch we avoid talking about professional stuff like the plague. (Comment made at Florida Beginning Teacher conference, 1988)

Ball (1987) notes that this type of generational conflict described is common within schools, because new teachers frequently have more knowledge of the latest research and newest ideas about curricular innovations. These new ideas may challenge the existing **norms of practice** (i.e., standards of acceptable practice) within the school. In turn, older colleagues may critique novices for lack of knowledge of "the system" or for not living up to standards of appropriate practice. In this way, the two groups seek to discredit each other, and "resolve" the conflict by pretending it does not exist.

---

[1] While the difference between these two groups often is based upon age, it is important to note that whether one is a "young turk" or an "old guard" can be a philosophical as well as a generational issue.

FOCUS BOX 11–2

Take a Moment to Reflect

Traditional practice persists in schools for the following reasons:

1. Schools are organized hierarchically, and teachers hold low-status positions within the bureaucracy.
2. Teachers are not given the autonomy to make professional judgments because teaching is a predominantly female profession.
3. Instructional materials exert technical control over the actions of teachers.
4. Teachers do not question many "taken-for-granted assumptions" about the nature of teaching.

Answer the following questions:

- Can you provide any examples from your personal and professional experiences that are consistent with the preceding assertions?
- Have you had experiences that contradict these assertions?
- Have you any knowledge of a school in which innovative practice is the norm? What forces encourage innovative practice?
- What are your current beliefs about the reasons traditional practice persists in schools? Compare your beliefs with those of your peers.

In order to develop professional power, you must find ways to resolve such conflicts in ways that preserve your autonomy to act and foster collaboration with colleagues. This means resolving conflicts without open confrontation. Ball (1987) stresses that direct confrontation is doomed to failure and demonstrates a lack of "micropolitical competence." What kinds of strategies can you use to exert political influence competently?

Strategies for Gaining Professional Power[2]

Micropolitics is about subtle influence, not about the confrontational exercise of power. **Skillful micropolitical action** involves developing relationships with others and "is a skill of judgement and coalition-building rather than a matter of position" (Ball, 1987, p. 246). So how do you play this game?

---

[2]   The remainder of this chapter is adapted from Bondy, E., & Ross, D. D. (in press). Micropolitical compentence: A key to developing professional autonomy and changing the status quo. *The Clearing House*. Reprinted with permission of the Helen Dwight Reid Educational Foundation. Published by Heldref Publications, 1319 18th Street, N.W., Washington, D.C. 20036-1802.

Develop an Understanding of the Micropolitical Context

In Chapter 6, you learned that socially competent children assess a social situation before taking any action. By doing this, they can join an ongoing activity without disrupting it and suggest a new activity that is likely to be well received by their peers. This same social sense will serve you well as you enter a new teaching environment. Learning the informal (micropolitical) structure of a new school is difficult, because new teachers lack knowledge of their school's formal policies and procedures, informal history, social customs, implicit values, and hidden agendas (Johnston, 1985).

To learn this informal structure, you must spend time listening and observing. The social dynamics of the faculty lounge or work room often mirror those of the entire school (Ball, 1987). A teacher reported to us that at her grade level, one teacher held the power and set the tone for the rest.

> At lunch, everyone would sit and chat but when _____ stood up, everyone stood up. I quickly learned that I was violating some kind of "rule" by delaying even a minute after this signal was given.

Through observation in the faculty lounge, during faculty meetings, in the hall and cafeteria, and in the office you can learn which teachers hold informal positions of power, what conversational and professional topics are acceptable or unacceptable, what informal networks exist, and which teachers are more or less "like you" in terms of their personal and professional interests.

Additionally, informal talk is necessary for learning about formal matters (Ball, 1987). **Organizational stories** communicate the character of the organization and help one to predict the organizational response to an event. For example, a common story in schools tells teachers whether the principal is supportive. Although the story can be told in a variety of ways, it always has three characters: the principal, the teacher, and an angry parent. The parent complains about some action taken by a teacher, and the principal reacts. Like many organizational stories, this one has a positive and a negative version (Martin, Feldman, Hatch, & Sitkin, 1983). In the positive version, the principal listens to the parent, asserts that the teacher is competent and reasonable, and perhaps promises to investigate the matter. In the negative version, the principal listens to the parent, communicates that the situation will "be resolved" and calls the teacher "on the carpet." Such stories convey and reinforce the existing organizational culture (Mumby, 1987).

Informal talk is also one of the primary ways of communicating information and conducting business in schools (Ball, 1987). The following examples are illustrative:

- Mary, new to Storybook School, learns which reports are due when by hearing teachers talk about doing them in the teachers' lounge.

- Two third-grade teachers meet in a classroom after school, "plotting" to get one of the two of them "elected" as grade-level chair for next year.

FOCUS BOX 11–3

Take a Moment to Reflect

Directions: Informal interactions in the faculty lounge and around the rest of the school will help you assess the school's social and political environment. Read the comments below and write what they suggest about the environment of a school and the kinds of actions that might be politically competent within that context. Compare your perceptions with those of your peers.

Teacher 1

I noticed that some teachers never go into the faculty lounge. I started going in at lunchtime, but all of the teachers there complained about children all the time. After about a month, I just stopped going.

Teacher 2

Mrs. _____, our grade-level chairman, is always telling us that the curriculum specialist says we have to do this and we have to do that. No one challenges her or talks back or hardly talks at all. But behind her back everyone talks about her and makes fun of her. They say she follows the administrative line, because she's trying to become a curriculum specialist. They complain that her "directives" keep them from doing things they think would be good for the children. But they always do what she says.

Teacher 3

At faculty meetings, all the teachers sit with other teachers who teach at their grade level, except for the black teachers. They all sit together.

Teacher 4

We have "shared decision making" in our school. The principal brings a problem to a faculty meeting and suggests a solution. Then he opens the floor for discussion; nobody says anything except to say what a great solution he has. Then we have a "democratic" vote and adopt his solution. No one suggests an alternative. Even if two alternatives are presented, and that is rare, he makes it really clear which one he favors. And we'd better vote for it.

Teacher 5

The curriculum specialist has rigid rules about testing and what has to be done when. She doesn't seem to like anything that deviates from the text, nothing creative, nothing fun. But the weird thing is that there are about five teachers who just seem to ignore her. They do really neat things with their children. Sometimes their testing is done late. They just don't seem to follow the rules, and she never says anything to them. But, wow, I was late with some testing once. She really came down on me!

- Two teachers who develop a pattern of meeting on Sunday afternoon to plan together and make materials will sometimes make extras for a colleague just "in case she wants to use them." While others tease them about being "compulsive," they also are very attentive when either teacher speaks at grade-level meetings.

FOCUS BOX 11–4

What About Gossip?

Gossip and rumor are powerful forms of social control. Ball (1987) states that gossip serves the following functions:

- It provides a way to test ideas informally to find out reactions before publicly endorsing them.
- It reinforces basic divisions within a group (e.g., dividing traditional and more innovative teachers) and reflects basic rivalries.
- It helps to preserve the morale and unity within subgroups.
- It provides a way to maintain the status quo and a way to undermine people or their policies without public confrontation.

Listening to gossip can help you assess the micropolitical allegiances within a faculty. It can be a form of harmless entertainment, but it can also intensify rivalries and conflict. In entering a new environment, remember that gossip to which you attend and particularly gossip you share (if any) communicates emergent allegiances and can alienate you from others. Be careful here!

- Karen takes a few minutes each day to chat with the school secretaries and occasionally brings them plates of cookies, fruit, or cheese and crackers. Some teachers complain about shortages of supplies, not hearing about upcoming deadlines, and not receiving phone messages. Karen never has these problems.

Common sense suggests that people consult with their friends about both personal and professional matters. Informal social relations within a school influence the flow of information and patterns of influence (Ball, 1987). If you are friends with the curriculum specialist, you are more likely to influence each other, or at least respect one another's opinions. If you are friendly with the custodians, they are less likely to complain about the mess your kids make during art activities.

Additionally, within any organization one or more persons always knows *the scoop*. "Information is a source of power in the organization, and the person 'in the know' may be sought after and favorably perceived by colleagues" (Ball, 1987, p. 220). It is important, then, to identify and develop friendly relations with good sources and to make sure that your own information is reliable and comprehensive as a way of increasing your own influence.

Use Effective Communication Skills

Do you remember the teacher from Chapter 1 who drew her whole curriculum from textbooks despite her belief that this curriculum was not the most appropriate for her children? She said she did this because she felt pressured by her principal who expected this type of curriculum. Yet, her principal stated that he did not dictate curricular decisions because he trusted the professional judgments of his teachers (Ross, 1978).

How can such radically different perceptions of expectations occur, and why do they persist? Maeroff (1988b) suggests that lack of communication or poor communication leads to misunderstandings between teachers and administrators and is a major reason why teachers lack access to power. Similar miscommunications may occur among teachers, keeping them from perceiving their common interests or from accepting different orientations to practice.

A *key assumption behind good communication* is that confrontations are a signal of misunderstanding or differences in perception (Murphy, 1988). Clarifying such differences is important for individual reasons such as getting others to view you positively, getting them to accept your viewpoint as valid, gaining their respect, and convincing them to grant you professional autonomy. However, clarification of differences is also important for the cohesive functioning of the group. Communication enables others to understand and accept your views; it also must enable you to understand and accept the views of others and to work collaboratively toward common purposes. The real **purpose of communication** is not to manipulate others so you can get your way (even if you believe your way is what is best for children) but to negotiate with others so that real understanding results and mutual respect and professional collaboration is more likely.

In Chapter 9, you read about Gordon's human relations model of discipline. Because this model is based upon communication theory, many of the same principles and strategies are used: learning to see the world from the perspective of others; mastering the techniques involved in active listening, the use of "door openers and I-messages"; and avoiding language patterns that provoke hostility or defensiveness (e.g., blaming, criticizing). These specific strategies can be useful in communicating with adults in the school context; however, differences between communicating with adults and communicating with children exist because of differences in the authority relationships. We suggest two basic (though not simple) principles to guide your communications with adults in the school context. These principles and the strategies you can use to implement them are derived from writings about business and personal communication (Bradley & Baird, 1983; Carnegie, 1981; Murphy, 1988; Okun, 1977; Rogers & Farson, 1977).

PRINCIPLE 1: USE ACTIVE LISTENING TO GAIN AN UNDERSTANDING OF THE OTHER PERSON'S PERSPECTIVE.   When someone disagrees with us or confronts us, our initial reaction is to argue, to justify our actions, to criticize or blame the other person. These reactions are natural, but they are not productive. Key words to remember in such a situation are: *People will respect me, if I respect them. People will listen to me, if I listen to them.*

To earn the respect of others, you must communicate that you are sincerely interested in the ideas of other people, that you want to try to understand their perspective, and that you see their perspective as a valid interpretation of the world. People's actions are always reasonable if viewed from their perspective.

Active listening helps diffuse angry confrontations.

You may not understand that perspective, initially. Once you understand it, you may not share it, but you must accept it as valid for that person and you must communicate to the person that you care what they think and how they feel. Listening often will solve a problem without requiring any other action (Carnegie, 1981). If the other persons feel they have been listened to, the problem may no longer seem important.

Whether you are talking to your principal, a curriculum specialist, another teacher, a spouse, a friend, or a parent, the following strategies will help you to understand the other person's perspective.

- Listen actively. Passively allowing the other person to "vent" is not enough. Using the kinds of opening statements suggested in Chapter 9 invite the person to share a personal perspective **(active listening).**

- Listen for the total meaning of a statement. Remember that any communication has two components: content and feeling. The emotional component causes dissonance in people's relationships. Respond to the feelings first. Reflect them back to make sure you understand them. Acknowledge them as valid feelings. (e.g., "So you are concerned that the county reading specialist will jump on you if I don't follow these guidelines exactly, and you're worried parents will start flooding your office with calls because my curriculum is different than everyone else's. I guess I'd be concerned about that too, if I were in your shoes.")

- If you are wrong, admit it and sympathize with the other person's point of view. (e.g., "I've really messed this up, haven't I? These test results are past due, and I've put you in a bind. I just didn't realize when they were due. I am really sorry. I don't blame you for being upset.") Obviously, you cannot continually make mistakes and expect to be forgiven, but we all make them occasionally. Admitting them diffuses the other person's anger.

- Let the other person do most of the talking. Don't try to present your viewpoint or defend your position. Listening makes the other person feel that personal concerns and perspective have received attention.

PRINCIPLE 2: PRESENT YOUR IDEAS IN TERMS OF THE OTHER PERSON'S PERSPECTIVE.   To gain acceptance of our ideas, our goal is to "find some means of stimulating [our idea] in his or her thoughts" (Bradley & Baird, 1983, p. 88). This quote makes it sound like you are trying to manipulate your colleagues into doing things your way. However, this is not the intent. It's important to avoid manipulation because the likely result is that your colleagues will learn to view your ideas and actions with suspicion. This is the antithesis of collaborative action. To foster improved communication and work toward collaborative action, your *goal in presenting your ideas* is to help the other person understand your perspective and ideas. If you have developed an understanding of the other person's perspective, you are in a position to couch your own thoughts and ideas in terms that match this perspective and thus enable the other person to understand. That is, your goal is to allow people to accept your view, without negating their views.[3] The following strategies are important:

- Do your homework. Try to determine the other person's probable perspective and the potential roadblocks before you initiate a conversation. Seek out a person who is a good information source, who already has power in the school, and/or who has good social and communication skills. Get advice about how to approach the person and the issue. (You may remember this strategy from your adolescent years. You would talk to your siblings or your peers to try to figure out how to get your Mom or Dad to understand your *desperate* need for the car, and you would wait for just the right moment to present your case. This is exactly the same strategy.)

- As you listen, look for areas of agreement. Emphasize these so the person starts out agreeing with you rather than disagreeing with you. (e.g., "Oh I think you are so right. Children have to develop competence in the subskills of reading, or they are at a tremendous disadvantage in life.")

- Fill in any gaps in the other person's information. For example, a colleague may think that because you use process writing, you do not teach writing

---

[3]   When we say "accept," we mean that the person will accept your ideas as valid, not that the person will adopt your ideas or practices.

skills. You might diffuse these concerns by stressing how important you think skills are in writing. You might also help the other teacher to see that you both teach many of the same lessons but organize and sequence them differently.

- Offer your idea casually and let the other person draw the conclusions. Invite the other person to help develop the idea. (e.g., "I can see your point. Parents who don't know anything about process writing might think their children are not learning skills at all and might complain to the principal or the school board. We'd all be in hot water—unless there's a way to help the parents understand.")

- Appeal to the other person's best motives. If another teacher is trying to subvert your efforts to implement a whole-language approach in reading, assume that the teacher's motivation is concern about children's learning. Do not assume that the teacher is concerned about not knowing or not wanting to learn the new approach. When you appeal to people's best motives, they are more likely to agree with you, because they want to perceive themselves in a positive light.

The importance of good communication skills cannot be overemphasized. Without them, your ability to gain and maintain power in ways that foster cooperation and collaboration will be severely limited. Unfortunately, good communication is not simple. You may have to change communication patterns you have developed over your lifetime. Practicing with friends and family is a good way to begin, and many of these strategies are relatively simple to use. However, over time, old and ineffective communication patterns will tend to recur. If other people argue with you and react negatively to you, you probably need to renew your acquaintance with these basic techniques.

Use Strategies of Political Resistance

We have suggested many alternatives to traditional practices in the elementary school. Most of you will teach or are teaching in classrooms where traditional practice is pervasive and where you may be discouraged from trying alternatives. Blase (1988) and Ball (1987) both note that principals not only seem to favor traditional practice, but many actively discourage alternatives even if they are supported by solid research evidence. This creates a real dilemma. You may be in a position where you face administrative or collegial opposition to practices that you believe are in the best interests of children.

Several studies have demonstrated how teachers react to this kind of dilemma by using different strategies of political resistance (e.g., Blase, 1988; Goodman, 1988b; Lacey, 1977). The terminology used by researchers varies, but the basic strategies they describe are similar. In this discussion, we are drawing on Goodman (1988b) who describes five distinct strategies used by student teachers trying to implement a reflective approach:

- **Overt compliance:** Teachers conform to the expectations of others. Sometimes this involves a change in the beliefs of the teacher. At other times, it may reflect a lack of necessary instructional competence or a belief that there is no alternative.

- **Critical compliance:** Teachers conform to expectations but retain beliefs that contradict their practices. They are critical of their practices and suggest that they will change them in time.

- **Accommodative resistance:** In general, the teachers conform to expectations but supplement the curriculum with small incidental activities.

- **Resistant alteration:** Teachers make significant alterations in the traditional curriculum to make it more meaningful to students. For example, Goodman describes a teacher who used the workbook on only two days of the week and used alternative materials for reading group lessons on the other three days.

- **Transformative action:** The teachers replace traditional curriculum with personally developed curriculum. An example would be a teacher-developed unit that required students to develop knowledge (i.e., observe, make hypotheses, draw conclusions). This strategy was much more common in science and social studies than in basic skill areas.

Goodman (1988b) stresses that 9 of the 10 teachers he studied used all of these strategies at one time or another. Awareness of these alternatives may help you to use them more deliberately, to decide when you can actively resist ("do battle") and when that would not be wise. Given a particular context, overt compliance may be essential at times for survival (Ball, 1987; Bullough, 1989); at other times compliance might be easier, but transformative activity is possible. To maximize your professional power, you must make judgments about when each type of strategy might be appropriate.

Actively Participate in Professional Networks

> It's the teacher's disease. You have to talk about it all the time, get someone to listen, tell you were right. . . . It's a wonder we still have any friends isn't it? But I couldn't manage without them. (Nias, 1985, p. 185)

Maintaining commitment to one's professional values and goals, often requires the support of fellow teachers (Goodman, 1987b; Maeroff, 1988b); this support is called **networking.** Although some teachers think the best way to achieve autonomy is to close their door and do as they please, others find it hard to work in isolation. Others discover, as did Kerry, a beginning teacher, that professional power only comes through "informed involvement" with one's colleagues (Bullough, 1989).

Many teachers need some kind of support from teachers within their school. This type of support is usually informal and can involve as few as two teachers who share a common perception of their role as teachers (Hayes & Ross, 1989; Nias, 1985). A "within school" support group that is organized around educational values (as opposed to social relationships) can be a powerful force within a school (Ball, 1987; Bradley & Baird, 1983; Nias, 1985).

Networking with other teachers provides support that promotes professional autonomy.

Unfortunately, not all teachers are able to find supportive colleagues within their school building. In fact, in some schools the majority of teachers are unwilling to talk about their difficulties or to consider experimenting with new strategies. You are unlikely to gain support for taking risks from these teachers. In this case, you must search for ways to connect with other teachers. The following suggestions derived from the literature and from teachers' experiences may be useful:

- Seek out teachers who share your ideas and interests at staff development activities (Bullough, 1989).

- Enroll in coursework and establish connections with fellow teacher/students (Nias, 1985).

- Maintain telephone or written contact with colleagues from your preservice teacher education program (Kilgore, Ross & Zbikowski, 1990; Nias, 1985).

- Look for support in books or from friends, family, or former teachers (Nias, 1985).

- Join organized networks of teachers such as TAWL (Teachers Applying Whole Language),[4] or your local chapter of the Association for Childhood Education, or the Association for the Education of Young Children.

- Become involved in your local teacher's union (Goodman, 1987b; Nias, 1985).

[4]   TAWL is a grass-roots organization of whole-language teachers. If you are unable to locate a local organization, you can contact the umbrella organization to find the closest branch or to get information about starting one in your area. The address is:

Teachers Applying Whole Language
c/o Debra Goodman
20020 Renfrew, Detroit, Michigan 48221

Draw on Parent Involvement as a Source of Support

Blase (1988) reported that teachers believed administrators were very responsive to parents, particularly to their concerns. The teachers in Blase's study felt that parental pressure limited their professional autonomy; however, teachers who are able to marshall strong parental support have a power base that can increase their autonomy. For example, Epstein (1987) found that when teachers foster high levels of parent involvement, parents were more likely to recognize the efforts of the teachers and to understand what their child was being taught. Also, parents rated these teachers higher in teaching ability and interpersonal skills than teachers who did not foster this involvement. High levels of parental involvement are associated with higher teacher efficacy and higher levels of student achievement (Epstein, 1987; Rosenholtz, 1989b). In other words, teachers with high parent involvement are more effective teachers. Also, effective teachers are in a much stronger position to request and be granted professional autonomy than others.

Unfortunately, research suggests that many teachers fail to involve or even inform parents. For example, from a questionnaire study of 1,269 parents, Epstein (1986) found that fewer than 30 percent of parents reported ever receiving a request from a teacher that provided specific suggestions about what to do. Yet, over 80 percent of the parents stated that they would be willing to spend more time helping their children if they knew what to do. Perhaps even more telling of the problems existing in communication between parents and teachers is the fact that 36.5 percent of the parents reported never receiving a handwritten note from a teacher, and 59.5 percent reported never receiving a phone call.

Teacher and administrative attitudes are one factor contributing to the poor relationships between parents and teachers:

> Studies indicate that the majority of teachers and principals see the ideal relationship with parents as one in which parents *support* teacher practices and the school in general, *carry out* requests but *do not* interfere with plans and decisions. (Ost, 1988, p. 168)

These attitudes suggest an element of distrust in parent/teacher interactions that interferes with the development of the cooperative relationships necessary to benefit the educational growth of children (Ost, 1988). This is particularly true of the relationships between teachers and low-income and minority parents (Menacker, Hurwitz, & Weldon, 1988; Ost, 1988).

While some educators argue that single parents and low-income, minority parents have too many other life pressures to become involved in the education of their children, Epstein (1986, 1987) found that teachers who work to involve parents were able to do so regardless of the parents' marital status or income level. It seems particularly important for teachers to involve low-income, minority parents because of the positive impact on student achievement and student attitudes toward school (Epstein, 1987). As we have noted, teachers who are supported by parents and who produce high achievement in children (especially children whom other teachers have difficulty teaching) are more likely to be granted professional autonomy.

The following practices are suggested to involve even those parents who are not typically thought to be helpful.

1. Improve home/school communication by suggesting that parents check with the child frequently for messages; writing individualized letters and newsletters in clear, understandable language; phoning parents regularly, especially parents who cannot read; using home visits or mail to communicate with parents if the child is an unreliable carrier (Epstein, 1987; Stafford, 1987).
2. Use guidelines for effective communication (see pages 311–315 and Chapter 9) in communications with parents (Margolis & Brannigan, 1986).

FOCUS BOX 11–5

Guidelines for Conducting Effective Parent-Teacher Conferences

No matter how many I do, I will always approach some conferences apprehensively. . . . Even parents whose kids give them fits can react very defensively if you suggest their child has a problem. Conferences are just (long pause) REALLY hard, but SO important. (third-grade experienced teacher)

Parent conferences *are* hard for most teachers. Parent conferences involve communicating with other adults about *their* children, and most parents care a great deal about their children (although they may not demonstrate it in the same way you might). Feelings such as love, anger, concern, or fear may impede communication and may keep some parents away. After repeated negative experiences, some parents refuse to attend conferences to learn what is "wrong" with their children.

The same effective communication strategies used with children and adults within the school are important in communicating with parents. Let's review these principles:

Principle 1: Use active listening to gain an understanding of the other person's perspective.   Several common problems with parent conferences diminish the teacher's opportunities to understand parent perspectives. Teachers tend to contact parents only when problems occur (Moles, 1987) and to assume the role of expert in the conference (Elksnin & Elksnin, 1989). Both tendencies mean teachers do most of the talking during conferences and are therefore unlikely to learn a parent's perspective. By scheduling conferences early in the year before problems have surfaced, you can encourage parents to share their knowledge of, hopes for, and concerns about their children, thus communicating that you will listen and that you value their insights. In all conferences, the following effective communication strategies are important:

- Listen actively.
- Listen for the total meaning of a statement (Try to hear the parents' feelings and concerns).
- Admit errors and sympathize with the parent's views.
- Let the parent do most of the talking (You have data about the child, but parents also are "experts").

FOCUS BOX 11–5, *continued*

Principle 2: Present your ideas in terms of the other person's perspective.   An effective plan to foster the educational accomplishments of children requires involving parents. Children benefit when their parents actively collaborate in their education (Epstein, 1987), yet many parents, especially young and/or low-income parents, lack needed knowledge and skills (Menacker, Hurwitz, & Weldon, 1988). Once you understand the parent's perspective, you are in a position to use your educational expertise to offer encouragement and support likely to be accepted by the parent. This requires that you do the following:

- Do your homework. (Learn as much as possible about the parent's perspective and come to the conference prepared with specific data about the educational accomplishments and school behavior of the child.)
- As you listen, look for and emphasize areas of agreement. (Help the parent to see that you have common goals and that you see common strengths in the child.)
- Fill in any gaps in the parent's information. (This may be information about the child that the parent does not have or about child-rearing practices the parent might try to support the child's learning. Ask if these ideas make sense in terms of the parent's knowledge about the child.)
- Offer your idea casually and let the parent draw conclusions. (e.g., "I've known several children who have improved greatly in school when their parents have read to them for 15 minutes a night. Would a strategy like that work into your schedule?")
- Appeal to the parent's best motives. (Focus on the parent's hopes and dreams for the child.)

In addition to using good communication strategies, a few other suggestions will help you establish productive conferences:

- Create a comfortable setting for the conference, someplace other than the classroom with soft, noninstitutional furniture. If such a setting is not available, try to create an informal setting within your classroom by drawing two chairs of similar size together (do *not* sit behind your desk), offering a soft drink, and greeting the parent warmly at the door.
- Help to put the parent at ease by beginning the conference informally. Begin with topics of common interest to establish a common bond (e.g., weather, recipes, sports, current local news, current school news).
- Summarize the essential points of the conference and plan a time to evaluate future educational progress of the child (e.g. "I think we've talked about a number of good suggestions here today. Let's see, I've agreed to find a big buddy for Clarice who will read to her twice a week, and you've agreed to read to her every night for 15 minutes. I really think this is going to help, but I know finding time every day is going to be hard with your busy schedule. Why don't I call you in two weeks to see how things are going and to let you know if Clarice's work and interest are improving?").

3. Make specific suggestions of home-learning activities (Epstein, 1987; Moles, 1987). Epstein (1986) reports that teachers who are effective in securing parent involvement make the following suggestions to parents:

   - Sign homework assignments.
   - Work on spelling and math drills.
   - Help with a worksheet assignment.
   - Ask the child about school regularly.
   - Use everyday objects to teach the child. (Teachers suggested what objects to use and how to use them.)
   - Play games to teach the child. (Teachers sent home game materials and directions.)
   - Visit the classroom.
   - Take the child to the library.

4. Devise alternative strategies for involving parents in classroom activities. Many parents are unable to assist with field trips or classroom parties or to work regularly as classroom volunteers. However, these parents can become a recognized part of the classroom by doing such things as sending ingredients for cooking activities; making classroom games; sending in old magazines, newspapers, or "junk" for art activities; or cutting out objects or letters for classroom displays. Parent involvement will be more visible to children, if you recognize parents' contributions during classroom activities. Parents will be reinforced for participation, if you send notes of appreciation or "awards" for classroom service.

FOCUS BOX 11–6

Practical Application Activities

Getting parents involved takes thought and effort. In large part it is dependent on your ability to take the perspective of each parent and invite involvement in ways that fit the parents' perspectives and abilities. Try one or both of the following activities to stretch your thinking about ways to involve parents. Working with a group of peers will increase the value of these activities.

Activity 1

Write a parent newsletter that communicates what you have done in your classroom (or in the classroom where you are student teaching) during the last two to four weeks. Use language that is clear and simple. Include at least five suggestions for home activities to reinforce classroom instruction.

   Ask a colleague or a group of colleagues to critique what you have done. They may find the following criteria useful:

FOCUS BOX 11–6, *continued*

- Is the language clear and simple?
- Is the length of the newsletter appropriate?
- Is the major focus of classroom instruction over the designated period clear?
- Are the suggested activities appropriate? Clearly explained? Simple enough for home application?

Activity 2

Write a hypothetical letter that you might use at the beginning of the year to introduce yourself to parents. In the letter try to include a welcome, a brief statement of what you want to try to accomplish with the children this year, an invitation for parent participation and some suggested ways parents might participate, and any procedural information you think parents might need.

Try to do all this in clear and simple language and in one page or less. Then draft a parent response form on which parents can indicate their preferred types of parent involvement.

Ask a colleague or group of colleagues to critique what you have done. The following criteria may be useful:

- Is the language clear and simple?
- Is the tone of the letter warm and inviting?
- Are parents presented with a variety of ways to participate? Is it clear that all types of participation are welcome and considered important?
- Is the response form clear and easy to use?

Don't Forget the Importance of Public Relations

One role of a principal is to defend and enhance the image of the school (Ball, 1987). In terms of creating an image, the local media can work for a school or against it. Teachers can help to build the positive image of a school by communicating with local media when they do something unusual and exciting. For example, the music teacher at the preschool attended by Dorene Ross' daughter worked with the children to help them write a song. Because she felt preschool children have little idea how the tapes and records they enjoy so much are made, she made arrangements with a local recording studio to enable the children to record "their" song and receive a tape of the recording.

A phone call to the local paper sparked the newspaper's interest, and a reporter was sent to cover the "event." The day after the recording, the paper included a brief story and a photo. Education editors of newspapers and of local television stations are interested in covering interesting and innovative practices by teachers. By informing them when you are planning such activities, you not only enhance your image with parents and with the principal but you also enhance the image of the school. Obviously, this is not a practice to use often; but it can be effective in increasing other people's perceptions that you are a competent and highly professional teacher.

FOCUS BOX 11–7

Take a Moment to Reflect

In this chapter we have presented several controversial ideas. It is important to examine *your* reactions to these ideas and to compare your reactions to those of your peers. As we have emphasized throughout the book, if ideas are to be useful to you, you must determine how they fit with your entering ideas about teaching. Whether you accept or reject ideas presented in this chapter, it is important that you evaluate the evidence you use in making a judgment. Look at each of the following ideas and decide what you think:

- If you want to make professional decisions and have the autonomy to act upon those decisions, you want to be powerful.
- Decision making is influenced by the complex web of personal and professional relationships existing within a school.
- It is appropriate, even desirable, that teachers use their resources of authority and influence to further their interests. (Make sure you define teachers' interests.)
- Gaining professional respect and autonomy requires teachers do more listening than talking. Arguing for your position is counterproductive.
- The ideas presented in this chapter could be viewed as manipulative and dishonest rather than professional.

Share your views with your colleagues. As you discuss your conclusions, focus on the following:

1. What evidence can you provide that your conclusion is a valid one?
2. What additional evidence might you want to collect?

FOCUS BOX 11–8

Practical Application Activity

Before trying the activity, check your understanding of each of the six micropolitical strategies by answering the following about each strategy:

- What is the purpose for using this strategy?
- What are some important practical tips for using it?
- Can you provide examples from your experience about how this strategy works or might work?

Share your answers with a group of peers.

Work with a group of four or five peers. Select one situation for each. Use as many of the ideas from this chapter as you think apply, state your dilemma, role-play your solution, and explain which ideas from the chapter you used. In addition to your role play, you might want to share ideas for long-range solutions.

FOCUS BOX 11–8, *continued*

Situation 1

During your first year of teaching, two of your priorities are using a problem-solving approach in mathematics and science and helping your students accept and appreciate diversity in others. Nathan's parents have expressed concern about not enough drill, worksheets, or tests. He is saying school is "fun"! You schedule a parent conference.

Situation 2

You are a first-year teacher attending teacher-planning days in August. The principal tells you about the positive results of an assertive discipline program adopted last year by the whole school. You do not agree with assertive discipline.

Situation 3

You are a fourth-year teacher new to a school and very excited about starting a whole-language program. One of the other teachers in your grade level mentions that she and the previous teacher used to group students by ability between the two classes for reading instruction. This made it easier to cover the material in the basal reading series. (After role-playing, consider the following: Would your solution change if you were a first-year teacher? How and why?)

Present your role-play(s) to another group of students. When you observe the role-play of another group, use the ideas in the chapter to suggest additional ideas they might try.

Our thanks to Dr. Paula DeHart, the University of Florida, who developed these hypothetical situations and agreed to let us use them.

Summary

We have presented six strategies that you might use to gain and maintain professional power within any school context: (1) developing an understanding of the micropolitical context before attempting to assert influence within an organization; (2) developing and using effective communication skills; (3) using strategies of political resistance deliberately; (4) actively participating in professional networks, consisting of informal and formal support groups; (5) drawing on parent involvement as a source of support; and (6) serving as your own public relations agent. Which strategies are most productive for you will depend on your personality, your current social interaction and communication skills, and your current teaching context. Additionally, as you negotiate your role with your school, keep in mind that your aims are to foster collaborative action among teachers and to help children develop the skills and abilities necessary for full participation within a democratic society.

FOCUS BOX 11–9

Yes, These Look Like Good Ideas, but . . .

In evaluating the suggestions made in this chapter, it is important to try to fit the new ideas in with your current understandings about schools and the role of teachers within schools. Because of this, we encourage you to actively confront your questions about the feasibility of our suggestions. Work with a small group of peers to raise and try to answer your questions about the strategies presented in this chapter. The following questions may help to guide your thinking.

- What is your overall, "gut" reaction to the suggestions? Do they look like strategies you might be able to use? Which ones seem more or less possible? Why?
- As you think about trying to use the strategies, what concerns do you have?
- Are there any skills, abilities, and/or knowledge you feel you would need to develop to use the strategies effectively? How would you go about doing this?
- What contextual barriers do you see that might make the use of these strategies difficult? How could you work around these contextual barriers?

It is important to raise these kinds of questions and to explore the answers with your peers if you are to develop your capacity to be treated as an autonomous professional.

Further Readings

Ball, S. J. (1987). *The micro-politics of the school: Towards a theory of school organization.* New York: Methuen.

Blase, J. J. (1988). The everyday political perspective of teachers: Vulnerability and conservatism. *International Journal of Qualitative Studies in Education, 1* (2), 125–142.

Bullough, R., Jr. (1989). *First year teacher: A case study.* New York: Teachers College Press.

Carnegie, D. (1981). *How to win friends and influence people.* New York: Simon & Schuster.

Epstein, J. L. (1986). Parents' reactions to teacher practices of parent involvement. *Elementary School Journal, 86* (3), 277–294.

Goodman, J. (1988). The political tactics and teaching strategies of reflective, active preservice teachers. *Elementary School Journal, 89* (1), 23–41.

Hayes, L. F., & Ross, D. D. (1989). Trust versus control: The impact of school leadership on teacher reflection. *International Journal of Qualitative Studies in Education, 2* (4), 335–350.

Kilgore, K., Ross, D. D., & Zbikowski, J. (1990). Understanding the teaching perspectives of first year teachers. *Journal of Teacher Education, 41* (1), 28–38.

Rosenholtz, S. J. (1989b). Workplace conditions that affect teacher quality and commitment: Implications for teacher induction programs. *Elementary School Journal, 89* (4), 421–439.

CHAPTER 12

Reflective Self-Evaluation and Professional Autonomy

At the beginning of this book, we set out to help you become a more reflective teacher, and we hope we have provided guidance toward that goal. In this chapter, we review the cycle of reflective teaching and then describe how reflective self-evaluation can help teachers maximize their professional autonomy.

A Review of the Cycle of Reflective Teaching

Before reading *our* review, think about *your* understanding of reflective teaching and why it is important. Spend the next few minutes with some of your peers and share your perceptions based on how you've made sense of the last eleven chapters. Looking at the diagram of the cycle may help to refresh your memory (see Figure 12–1). Do you find that you and your peers have the same understandings? If not, what are the differences, and what might account for them?

We hope you recalled that *planning* is the important first stage of the reflective process and involves *defining the problem* and *searching for the most desirable solution*. Problem recognition and definition become easier when you increase your appreciation system and when you interact with other teachers regarding problems they are confronting. This book is one source for identifying possible problems. Throughout our discussions, we have posed dilemmas for you to consider, such as the limited attention given in schools to children's development of social competence and what we need to do in order to empower at-risk students. These and other understandings have become a part of your professional knowledge (appreciation system) and, thus, a basis for identifying problems and considering possible solutions and the potential consequences of each. Once identified, the problem becomes the focus for the reflective process.

In that process, the teacher *acts* by implementing the planned action, *observes* what happens, and *reflects* on the desirability of the intended and unintended consequences. Although this process can be systematic, reflection can be more fluid than the explanation sounds. As a systematic process, reflective self-evaluation

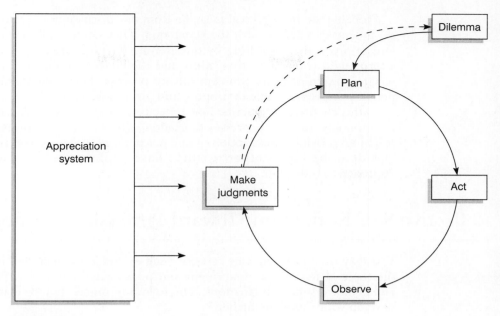

Figure 12–1

can be defined as **action research,** or "research undertaken by practitioners in order that they may improve their practices" (Corey, 1954, p. 375). The essential characteristics of action research include the following (Noffke & Zeichner, 1987):

1. It is conducted in a field setting by participants in the field.
2. Problems of practice selected by the practitioner are studied.
3. Much of the data collection and analysis are done by the practitioner.

Although we draw heavily from the literature on action research in our discussion of reflective self-evaluation, we also provide several illustrations of a less formal application of reflective self-evaluation.

In addition to the cycle of reflective teaching, we also want you to remember our earlier points about the attitudes and abilities needed by reflective teachers. Such teachers need to be introspective, willing to take responsibility for decisions, and open-minded. It is not enough to be able to explain what the reflective process is or even to argue its merits; teachers must have attitudes that are compatible with the process in order to incorporate reflection as a natural and continuing part of their teaching styles. Additionally, teachers need to have the ability to view situations from multiple perspectives, to search for alternative explanations for classroom events, and to use adequate evidence to evaluate a decision in terms of practical, educational, and ethical criteria. Recall that we stressed that using the model and all the rest of the attitudes and abilities required of reflective teachers is insufficient unless the teacher evaluates practice in terms of educational and ethical, as well as practical, criteria.

Probably the most critical message from our discussion is that reflective teachers are never satisfied with the status quo. They continually seek to understand and improve their teaching by questioning existing practices and considering alternatives in terms of their aims and their ethical commitments. They view teaching as an ongoing problem-solving process. They view themselves as competent professionals able to propose and justify solutions.

In this chapter, we describe how reflective self-evaluation relates to professional autonomy, present processes to guide teachers' initial attempts to study their teaching, provide a description of one teacher's experiences with action research, and describe topics other teachers have explored using a more informal approach to reflection.

Reflective Self-Evaluation: Toward Professional Autonomy

You may be wondering why reflective self-evaluation is included in a section on the topic of teacher empowerment and professional autonomy. We assume you already have some explanations. The following points, however, might help you develop your rationale further.

Action Research Leads to the Creation of Knowledge

According to Garrison, "since knowledge, and the ability to obtain it, is power, the legitimization of practitioner-knowledge would lead to the empowerment of teachers" (1988, p. 501). Garrison offers a contemporary reminder that, since its origin in the early 1950s (Corey, 1953; 1954), action research has been a teacher empowerment movement. Key to this discussion of action research has been advocacy for practitioner-generated knowledge—what Argyris (1982) calls "theories of action"— as legitimate. According to Cochran-Smith and Lytle, "As the body of teacher research accumulates, it will undoubtedly prompt reexamination of many current assumptions about children, learning, and classroom processes" (1990, p. 8).

Action Research Leads to the Transformation of Teaching

Teachers involved with action research view it as a powerful factor in increasing their understanding and transformation of teaching. Goswami and Stillman cite numerous effects for teachers who conduct research as a regular component of their teaching. For example,

1. Their teaching is transformed in important ways: they become theorists, articulating their intentions, testing their assumptions, and finding connections with practice.

2. Their perceptions of themselves as writers and teachers are transformed. They step up their use of resources; they form networks; and they become more active professionally.

3. They become rich resources who can provide the profession with information it simply doesn't have. . . .

4. They become critical, responsive readers and users of current research . . . more authoritative in their assessment of curricula, methods, and materials. . . . (1987, preface)

Similar points have been made by Lasky (1978), McCutcheon (1981), Williams, Neff, and Finklestein (1981), Ruddick (1985), Whitford (1984), and Noffke and Zeichner (1987). The important message of these writers is that if you are going to be empowered, you must be able to convey to others why you do what you do. In other words, evidence about what your students have learned enables you to justify practices others might question. That justification is likely to give you the autonomy to continue making decisions you believe to be most appropriate for students.

Action Research Cultivates the Attitudes of Reflection

Action research helps teachers learn to be introspective (Parsons, 1983), to consider alternatives (Dewey, 1933; Goodman, 1984, Oja & Pine, 1984), and to recognize, through the data that *they* have collected, errors they might have made and changes they need to implement (Hovda & Kyle, 1984; Ross, 1984). These attitudes of being open-minded about change and responsible for one's decisions help teachers develop as self-reliant professionals who can trust themselves to make judgments.

Throughout this text, we have reiterated the importance of teachers making informed decisions. We suggested that teachers who are able to articulate the reasons for and evidence supporting their decisions are more likely to be given the autonomy for putting their ideas into practice. As the previous points illustrate, reflective self-evaluation is the critical link in achieving that autonomy.

Reflective Self-Evaluation: Suggested Processes

As we noted, reflective self-evaluation is not as linear as a description of "suggested processes" might imply. However, reflective self-evaluation is a more systematic activity than what many teachers mean when they describe themselves as reflective. Many teachers believe reflection is essential and consider themselves to be reflective. However, these teachers typically mean that they "take school home with them," and that they "never stop thinking about the kids." As you'll recall from Chapter 1, reflective practitioners do much more than think. Reflection requires thinking about practice *and* the collection of evidence about the effects of decisions *and* evaluation of those effects in terms of practical, educational, and ethical criteria. The collection of evidence is not an optional part of the process; it is a key to honest self-evaluation. How does reflective self-evaluation begin?

Plan: What's a Good Question? What's a Reasonable Solution?

The very notion of evaluation suggests that questions about the value and results of *someone's* decisions need to be answered, and for reflective teachers, these questions focus on their own teaching. The problem that initiates the reflective process provides the source of questions for self-evaluation.

For instance, you will soon read about a teacher who identified a problem about teaching writing in her kindergarten classroom. Emerging from this problem were critical questions for her to answer (e.g., "What happens when children have the chance to write in any way that makes sense to them, even if it's scribbling?" "How do children interact with one another about their writing?" and "What's the relationship between children's drawing and children's writing?") in order to understand the consequences of her decisions and to feel confident about continuing such practices in the future.

In Chapter 1, we cautioned against defining a problem too narrowly. Remember the teacher who observed Jayne dawdling and defined the problem as Jayne's need for greater self-discipline. This narrow definition then led to a narrow solution of using tokens to manage Jayne's behavior. By broadening the definition of the problem, however, the teacher might also broaden the range of possible solutions. Many of the issues raised throughout this book, such as developing students' conceptual understanding in various disciplines and empowering students for critical citizenship, provide a basis for broadening problem definition.

During initial experiences with reflective self-evaluation, teachers tend to focus on "what works" rather than on how or why something happens (Goodman, 1984). "What works" questions lead to *yes* and *no* responses with little opportunity for exploring possible explanations. Ross (1987b, p. 143) shares the following example of a "what works" question, "Will using a contract system encourage students to complete their morning work?" and suggests how it can be refocused, "How can a teacher motivate the nonmotivated student to complete morning work?" This last question provides the opportunity for the teacher to consider many reasons why the students might not be completing their work and then to consider the effects of different solutions. Continued effort on the part of teachers to broaden their appreciation systems will help them develop more *why* and *how* questions, thus expanding the exploratory nature of their reflective self-evaluations.

In defining initial questions, however, it is also important to remember that other questions may become significant later in the self-evaluation process. For instance, a teacher interested in the effects of cooperative learning activities might initially pose questions related to academic achievement. However, after observing the children, the teacher might begin to raise questions about the development of social interaction skills.

Once a teacher has determined questions related to the problem, several sources can be helpful in identifying ideas for problem resolution. Perhaps some strategies suggested in teacher education courses have not been tried yet. Strategies suggested in professional journals might be appropriate. Other

Discussions with colleagues can help clarify dilemmas and identify strategies to implement.

sources might include staff development opportunities or suggestions from colleagues.

Whatever the source of ideas, it is important for the teacher to consider the potential consequences of each one. For instance, a teacher who determines that students have little grasp of historical events might use simulations so that the experience of people in the past (such as the arrival of immigrants to Ellis Island) becomes more real. In implementing this solution, the teacher needs to consider how well the goal was accomplished as well as any unintended consequences. For example, the teacher might find that this approach motivates most children to search through available texts for historical information that will enable them to understand and portray the historical experience but that a small number of children are intimidated and withdraw from class discussions and particularly from enactment activities.

Act and Observe: Where Are the Data?

Implementing the plan is the next stage. As the plan is implemented, the teacher engages in a continuous process of gathering **data** (information) and making adjustments as needed. Keep in mind the notion of *action* research—as the teacher collects information, it is used as the basis for future action. For teachers who must make day-to-day (and sometimes moment-to-moment) adjustments, the future arrives quickly.

Practical Application Activity

Suppose a teacher decides that simulation activities might be an appropriate way to engage students and increase their understanding of historical issues, events, and experiences. The teacher divides students into groups and provides parameters for the activity. For instance, the teacher wants each student to participate in each phase of the simulation—doing research, writing a script, creating props and costumes, and enacting the simulation. The teacher makes this requirement to insure greater likelihood that all of the children will have access to the knowledge rather than some doing the research while others paint scenery.

What if the teacher realizes that the intention of having all children participate equally has *un*intentionally resulted in some children being intimidated by the "performance" of the simulation? How could the teacher be responsive to this concern that some of the children have and still accomplish the goals of the activity? Develop a suggested response to this dilemma and then discuss your ideas with your peers. Once finished, read and discuss the two suggestions offered.

Solution 1

The teacher might give the same simulation starter to four or five small groups of children (about three children in each group) who do research and then generate ideas for a script, characters, scenery, and props. In this way, all the children participate in ideas regarding each aspect of the activity. Generating these ideas in these groups helps children commit to some specific plans that they will have to negotiate with other children. Having to serve as an advocate for their ideas is another way for children to "own" their own knowledge. Each group nominates a "writer," an "actor," and a "scenery and props maker." All the writers meet and take their ideas to a script-writing committee. Once they have met and identified general themes, the scenery committee begins meeting to discuss what's needed and begins work. (The group may need to do additional research.) The "actor" committee reviews the draft of the script and suggests changes based on their sense of the people they are playing, making suggestions to make it more real. (Again, this may require more research.) In this solution, all the children have had involvement with ideas throughout the activity, but the ones intimidated by the performance can focus their attention on one of the other tasks.

Solution 2

The acting could be done with puppets behind a puppet stage, which is often much less intimidating to reserved children than "real" role playing.

Questions for Discussion

1. How do the preceding solutions compare with the ones you and your peers developed?

2. What are potential advantages and disadvantages of the two solutions suggested?

Teachers engaged in reflective self-evaluation need some systematic way to collect information about children's learning. This requires looking in new ways at the typical "stuff" of classroom life. Children's work, questions, and interactions, for instance, become sources of information that can help teachers understand the effects of their decisions.

What information to collect and how to collect it depend on the questions asked. For example, suppose Mr. Widden has become concerned that his students tend to "memorize" science content rather than develop depth of knowledge, interest, and commitment. He begins with a broad question about how he can help children become more involved in learning science. As an "action" step, Mr. Widden decides to alter his current, text-based approach. He begins by designing a number of high-interest activities to help the children learn more about endangered animal species. He wants the children to learn about the relationship between people and animals, the relationship between the environment and living things, the role of zoos in the preservation of endangered species, and the role individuals might play. Mr. Widden also wants children to develop a greater understanding about how people's and animals' needs may conflict and the reasons why some people are less concerned about endangered species than others. In teaching the unit, the teacher not only wants the children to develop knowledge but also a greater awareness of their responsibility to the environment and to other species.

To assess the impact of his changes, Mr. Widden might ask, "How has children's knowledge changed? What do they see as the critical problems related to this topic? What do they suggest as possible solutions? In what ways have they demonstrated respect and responsibility for the environment and other species?"

To answer these questions, the teacher would need to gather information in a variety of ways, such as:

- examining children's reports (e.g., reports on specific animals; position papers supporting or arguing against protection of animals; class book on endangered animals; "reaction" journals kept by children; research logs recording the results of experiments about the impact of the environment on animal life)

- examining the content of children's projects (e.g., posters on endangered animals, child-created bulletin boards; plays written and performed by the children; debates on the pros and cons of protection of endangered animals; child-created endangered species game)

- tape-recording class sessions (or discussions during a field trip) or keeping notes in a journal in order to assess the children's understanding and their problem-solving suggestions

- examining pictures taken by children during the zoo visit to determine what they considered to be important about the trip (i.e., prior to the trip, the teacher would designate four to six children as "picture takers" assigned to take pictures representing what they learned on the trip)[1]

[1]   This may sound unrealistic, but we know several teachers who have accumulated five or more used cameras by asking for donations from parents and/or by finding "deals" at garage sales.

- interviewing five or six children who represent different initial perspectives or different achievement levels to assess children's responses to the unit

You may have noticed that these "data collection" ideas are also curriculum ideas in many cases. That is, teachers can collect information by drawing on some or all of the activities children do as part of the unit. It is important that the ways of gathering information fit naturally into teachers' classroom activities. Since their primary responsibility is instruction, teachers don't have extended periods of time to set aside for making observational notes, interviewing children, and so on, the way an outside evaluator might. Teachers need to depend upon what is readily available to them as a source of information for self-evaluation. Some possible sources include audiotapes, videotapes,[2] photographs, questionnaires, portfolios of student work, checklists, test scores, interviews (both teacher- and student-conducted), planbooks, entries in journals or diaries, teachers' guides and other curriculum materials, and school-wide memos and policy statements.

Reflect and Recycle: What Does It Mean? What Happens Now?

Teachers who engage in reflective self-evaluation soon find themselves inundated with information—journals full of entries, stacks of students' portfolios, or transcripts of taped class sessions—or maybe a little of all of these. Some of this **data** (information) will be **quantitative** (i.e., things you can count and measure such as test scores) and some will be **qualitative** (i.e., things you cannot count and measure such as interview data, students' projects, and notes on class discussions). The kind of data you collect will depend on your questions. Almost all teachers collect various kinds of qualitative data as a part of ongoing classroom activities; many teachers also collect some quantitative data to help them answer their questions. Making sense of the meaning of the data can seem a bit overwhelming, but a few guidelines can help.

AS YOU REVIEW DATA, KEEP YOUR QUESTIONS CLEARLY IN MIND.   It is very important to return often to the *how* and *why* questions posed at the beginning of your self-evaluation cycle. This provides a useful starting point that can then be extended by addressing other questions that might have become important during implementation. By sustaining this kind of focused look at the data, what is significant becomes more obvious.

CREATE CHARTS AND GRAPHS TO MAKE QUANTITATIVE DATA COMPREHENSIBLE.   A chart or graph makes data visible and thus more comprehensible. It is important to note, however, that there often is more than one way to record quantitative

---

[2]   We feel a word of caution is necessary here. It sounds easy to collect audio- and videotaped data. And in many cases it is. However, it is *very* time-consuming to transcribe and/or review this data; and unless the teacher transcribes the data or takes notes based upon a careful review, the data are useless. At times these methods of data collection are very valuable. In deciding to use them, however, think carefully about your time.

data on charts and graphs. For example, one teacher wanted to alter her mathematics instruction to include more collaborative instruction (as described in Chapter 4) and more emphasis on student thinking and problem solving.[3] Additionally, she wanted to teach students in heterogeneous rather than achievement-based groups. She hoped that her efforts would improve students' attitudes toward and success with problem solving. To assess the latter she tested students on their problem-solving abilities at four different times. In trying to make sense of their scores, she charted her data in three ways. First she made a chart showing change in total group scores from Time 1 to Time 4. Second, she used her previous math achievement group structure to divide the students' scores into three groups; then she charted the changes for each group from Time 1 to Time 4. Third, she made individual charts for the six students who showed the least improvement. By looking at the same data in different ways, the teacher was able to look at class progress, similarities and differences in the progress made by children of different achievement levels, and similarities and differences in the records of children who continued to have difficulty with problem-solving activities. Notice that by looking at her data—very simple classroom data by the way—in several ways she demonstrated that she was interested in broader questions than whether her strategy "worked." Her analysis enabled her to move beyond this question to questions about whether the methods influenced different children in different ways and to begin to explore some potential reasons why.

REVIEW QUALITATIVE DATA TO SEARCH FOR REGULARITIES (AND EXCEPTIONS). Analysis of qualitative data requires the teacher/researcher to read and reread the data (e.g., notes on class interactions, student assignments, notes on individual discussions or interviews with students) to try to identify categories. For example, the teacher might identify:

- kinds of reasons students give for learning to read (as indicators of students' purposes for reading)
- ways students participate in class (as indicators of increased motivation and involvement)
- ways that students try to get teacher attention (as a way to explain students' actions)
- ways that students show empathy toward one another (as evidence that children are developing social interaction skills)

Let's look more specifically at how one teacher used qualitative data analysis to help him address his self-evaluation questions.[4] Mr. Springer asked the question, "How can I help my students learn to evaluate their own work and progress?

---

[3] This sample study is an adapted composite of studies conducted by three students in an action research course at the University of Florida during Spring 1990.

[4] This example is adapted from a study done by a student within an action research course at the University of Louisville.

What happens when I change my role from the one who evaluates to the one who helps them evaluate?" Mr. Springer kept notes on his conferences with students, recording students' initial responses—their questions, concerns, and the criteria they first identified for evaluating their work—and then how these conversations changed over time. He also kept copies of student work to provide evidence of how the students progressed based on the areas *they* identified as needing attention. He made observation notes of any comments that were associated with giving the students more ownership of the evaluation process.

In analyzing these data, Mr. Springer made categories of the types of concerns students initially expressed and the kinds of comments they made after experiencing the process for awhile. He also found evidence of the criteria students identified as important in their efforts to improve, and he identified emergent effects of increasing opportunities for students' self-evaluation. Mr. Springer discovered far more than "self-evaluation works." His extensive data enabled him to conclude that students are capable of making judgments about the quality of their work, of posing ways in which they might improve their performance, and of determining when they have accomplished their goals. For a teacher who aims to increase students' capacities for critical thinking, these are significant insights.

EVALUATE AS AN ONGOING PROCESS.   One implication of "action" research is that the information teachers collect becomes a part of their decision making; that is, they *act* on it right away. For instance, if the teacher implementing the unit on endangered species realizes from children's comments that they have multiple and conflicting views about the meaning of the term *endangered,* he must use that information immediately to plan further instruction. Similarly, if the children begin to glibly propose "easy" solutions that fail to recognize the complexity of environmental problems and the importance of confronting conflicting interests in efforts to resolve them, the teacher must use that information to plan additional activities.

By realizing that self-evaluation is ongoing, teachers can then examine information in manageable amounts as it is collected. However, it is also important to realize that information accumulated over time is necessary for answering some questions, such as the question raised previously about how students develop their ability to engage in self-evaluation.

COLLABORATE/SHARE WITH COLLEAGUES.   In trying to make sense of the information they collect, teachers might find the questions and perspective of a colleague helpful in facilitating reflection and in providing a different way of thinking about their actions. For instance, a colleague could ask: "What do you know now that you didn't know before? *How* do you know what you know? What evidence might convince me that the solutions to your problem were beneficial?" A colleague may help by challenging some of your entering assumptions and encouraging you to redefine your problem or your resolution strategies. For example, suppose you have been concerned about the increasing number of conflicts between students and have decided to use a token system to reward students who are helpful and considerate to one another. You want to see whether, as a result of this system, student conflicts decline. During discussion of your problem and suggested solutions, a colleague might ask you to explore reasons that might account for the increase in conflicts—changes in student-grouping arrangements, types of activities students work on together—and possible unintended consequences of using tokens. As a result of these discussions, you might decide to refocus your study to consider what might account for conflicts among students and, once identified, what strategies seem to enable students to learn how to resolve those conflicts.

Of course, reflective self-evaluation mostly affects the individual teacher, leading to increased awareness and understanding of the consequences of decisions and, thus, modifying the teacher's appreciation system. These are significant effects that, in and of themselves, make the process worthwhile. However, if teachers have opportunities to share the results of their self-evaluations, more far-reaching effects become more possible. For example, some teachers form support groups within which they can share their questions, their findings, and their interpretations of meaning of their findings for future practice. Other teachers share their projects through in-service programs, at local and state conferences, or as participants at national meetings of professional organizations. Still others have challenged professional journals to consider teachers' writings as worthy of publication.

BEGIN THE CYCLE AGAIN.   Remember that reflective teachers are never satisfied that they have all the answers. By continually seeking new information, they constantly challenge their own practices and assumptions. In the process new dilemmas surface and teachers initiate a new cycle of planning, acting, observing, and reflecting.

As we have described the cycle, it might appear as if it is always very involved and takes place over an extended amount of time. While this is certainly possible in a carefully designed action research study, as we will describe later in this chapter, it is also possible for the cycle to be brief. Within the following example, for instance, we will point out how the teacher notices a problem with parent communication, spontaneously develops a plan, implements it, and then assesses it by listening to children's and parents' comments. Embedded within a more extensive cycle of reflective self-evaluation is a brief, yet complete, cycle that came about through reflection upon unintended consequences of the original plan. This exemplifies the cyclical nature of reflective self-evaluation.

As the educational community becomes more committed to providing teachers with opportunities for sharing, and as teachers become more comfortable with this new role, the likelihood of teachers' empowerment and professional autonomy increases. For the reflective teacher, these challenges become a natural and eagerly sought aspect of professional growth and development.

FOCUS BOX 12–2

Practical Application Activity

Anita has taught third grade successfully for nine years. She is known to have a well-organized classroom, students who score well on the end-of-the-year tests, and a good relationship with parents. Her lessons come mostly from the textbooks and, although not particularly creative, this rather traditional approach has suited her well during these nine years.

Recently, a new third-grade teacher has joined the faculty. She has shared with Anita some of the ideas she has learned about in her recent teacher education program. Many of these ideas, such as "writing process," "cooperative learning," and "problem solving in math" suggest a departure from the kinds of instructional strategies that Anita has come to depend upon. Anita has listened carefully to the persuasive arguments her new friend has made and, although concerned about not knowing how to make changes and about jeopardizing children's test scores, she has decided to try some new ideas and "see how it goes."

Select one new approach that Anita might focus on first. Keeping the plan-act-observe-reflect cycle in mind, suggest (1) what specific problem she might want to address, (2) what questions she might want to answer, (3) what data would be important to collect, (4) how she might collect that data, making sure to be realistic about what's possible, and (5) what possible findings might come out of such an activity. Discuss your ideas with your peers.

Reflective Self-Evaluation: An Example of Action Research

The following example describes a kindergarten teacher's year-long study of her teaching (Awbrey, 1987).[5] Although this is a more extensive and publicly shared example of reflective self-evaluation than many teachers might engage in, we believe it helps demonstrate the process and how a teacher can benefit from the experience. We have included quotes that capture the teacher's voice and have attempted to provide a comprehensive explanation of the purpose and findings of the self-evaluation; however, we encourage you to read the article in its entirety.

Maureen is a veteran kindergarten teacher, having spent 25 years teaching five- and six-year-olds. By her own account, she has tried different approaches along the way that have helped her refine her thinking and create the developmentally based program she believes is most appropriate for young children.

[5]   The excerpts are from "A Teacher's Action Research Study of Writing in the Kindergarten: Accepting the Natural Expression of Children" by M. Awbrey, 1987, *Peabody Journal of Education, 64*(2), pp. 33–64. Reprinted by permission.

> I . . . have settled in comfortably to the use of [units] for integration of the total curriculum, of learning centers to teach most basic concepts, and of many language experience activities. (Awbrey, 1987, p. 34)

What possible problem could such an experienced, confident teacher face? Remember that reflective teachers question, seek to improve, and evaluate the consequences of their decisions. And these are career-long characteristics!

A part of Maureen's *planning* for the year focused on *the problem* of how to alter her program to reflect the latest thinking on the use of a natural "writing process" approach with young children. This problem emerged as a result of keeping current with professional literature and taking graduate courses. Confronted with this new idea, she drew on her appreciation system (although in all honesty she probably didn't call it that), considered how this approach compared to her current practice and determined that, while changes would be needed if she were to implement the approach, the changes did not violate the theoretical basis of her program. She was ready to proceed.

As we noted earlier, an integral part of the planning stage is *searching for desirable solutions and evaluating their results.* However, this sounds much more linear and "recipe-like" than it actually is. A solution can at times be serendipitously chosen, based on responsiveness to an unplanned-for event. Furthermore, while a teacher might be able to evaluate some results fairly quickly, other results may take more time. In the middle of all this, new dilemmas can develop that require additional solutions. Several examples from Maureen's experience illustrate these points.

Maureen's problem required that she make several decisions about how to facilitate children's development as writers. Her solutions, drawn from several sources, focused on the types of opportunities for writing she wanted to provide, the kinds of materials she needed to add to the classroom, the ways she might make it possible for children to share their efforts, and so on. However, she could not possibly have thought of everything, as she learned on the first day of school when she asked the children to write on the back of a picture they had drawn.

> I watched apprehensively to see what would happen. The children did just as I had asked them to, turned their papers over and began to write. . . . Walker wrote ERWAKE, looked up at me, and said, "What does this spell?" I said, "What do you think it spells?" "I think it spells *wave*," he answered. He was quite satisfied, and went confidently on to write a few more letters. In the year preceding this I would have reacted to Walker's question quite differently, probably by saying, "Oh, those are most of the letters in your name put in a different order," thinking I was pointing out some important pre-reading information to him. . . . Feeling my way, not knowing what I was doing or how to begin, I believed intuitively that I should be accepting of all that the children did. (Awbrey, 1987, p. 34)

Maureen had not anticipated this situation, but based upon her knowledge of young children and her goals, she was able to offer a solution. Furthermore, she was aware that she was making a conscious choice to respond differently than she

Reflective teachers document what's happening in their class-rooms.

might have in the past; and although she thought she made the right decision, she remained open to the possibility of error and continued to look for evidence of the impact of her decision.

Maureen then *acted and observed* as she implemented her writing program, carefully making notes of the children's behavior, interactions, and comments and keeping copies of their drawings and writing. Having this wealth of information helped her evaluate what was happening, what the effects seemed to be, and what adjustments needed to be made. For instance, in the following excerpt, Maureen describes her awareness of children's sharing and "sense making" of one another's writing. However, these positive results merge with a new dilemma that needs a solution. As we mentioned previously, this illustrates a brief, yet complete, cycle of reflective self-evaluation.

> One day Lauren shared with the class her word BDCSAFBS (Brontosaurus). Everyone was envious, especially the boys. A few days later . . . Lauren looked up at me with a totally disgusted look on her face. She complained, "I can't go on to the next page. They are *all* copying my BDCSAFBS (Brontosaurus)!" Soon everyone's book contained this coveted word. . . . One day, soon after sharing her treasured word, Lauren came to school and announced to the class that she had spelled BDCSAFBS (Brontosaurus) for her mom. Her mom had said it was not right, but Lauren had responded, "Miss Maureen says it's right." Mom had then said, "Let's look it up in the dictionary." I quickly sensed . . . that it was time to send an explanatory note home to the parents. Perhaps I had been remiss by not doing it sooner, [however] my explanation that it is *right* for *her* satisfied Lauren. (Awbrey, 1987, pp. 45–46)

The careful documentation of solutions to the problems Maureen confronted continued throughout the year. By year's end, she was convinced that the consequences were desirable and would shape her decision making in the future. However, as she pointed out, new questions emerged that would require her attention with her next class. As we noted previously, reflection should be an ongoing process in a teacher's life.

Although we have cited a detailed, published example of a reflective self-evaluation, we are not suggesting that you have to be as comprehensive in your efforts. Many teachers engage in and benefit from reflective self-evaluation without formally sharing their insights with others. Next, we describe more informal applications of reflective self-evaluation.

Reflective Self-Evaluation: Informal Examples

Chris

Chris Zajac, sensitively portrayed in Tracy Kidder's (1989) *Among Schoolchildren,* is a fifth-grade teacher who rejects the status quo and constantly searches for solutions to problems. For Chris, a troubled student named Clarence presented problems the first day of school and set the stage for Chris' efforts and reflective self-evaluation throughout the year.

Although Chris did not engage in systematic data-collection, she followed the plan-act-observe-reflect cycle we have described. In the following excerpt, Kidder (1989) recounts Chris' continuing efforts to find strategies that would elicit work and good behavior from Clarence.

> By the end of the second week of school, [Chris's] pattern had become unmistakable. She remembered one day out of many like it: Clarence wouldn't work. Chris told him gently that if he didn't, he couldn't go to gym. That didn't make Clarence comply. Instead, he beat up Felipe, his best friend and usual victim, in the hallway. A scolding followed. Afterward, Clarence ripped down part of Chris's bulletin board display. Chris planned to keep Clarence after school, to try to talk to him, but he managed to get away. . . . When she felt calmer, Chris devised a new plan. . . . Clarence would win a star for each day he behaved well and did his work. He would get a special reward for three stars in a row. . . . Clarence got only one star in three weeks before Chris let that frail attempt at behavior modification drift into oblivion . . . Chris felt she couldn't let him win the little contests that he staged. . . . However, if she spent half her time and energy on Clarence, she would cheat the other children. . . .
>
> Thinking about Clarence tonight didn't lead to any new strategies. . . . Maybe she had made some progress. . . . He'd done well on this social studies test. There was always reason for hope. (pp. 98–107)

As this excerpt illustrates, Chris used her observation of Clarence's behavior, the completion of his work, and the quality of that work as a basis for deciding whether strategies were working or needed to be modified or stopped. Using this information, she decided on new plans and began the cycle again.

Kerrie

Another example application of reflective self-evaluation is provided by Kerrie, a first-year teacher studied by Bullough (1989). As a part of this study, Kerrie shared many examples of problems she confronted and solutions she attempted during her first year of teaching. She, too, demonstrated the plan-act-observe-reflect cycle. Bullough describes Kerrie's attempts to deal with students' individual differences.

> It's frustrating. . . . If I waited until everyone finished the assignment, I'd still be waiting. It's [only] the third week of school and there are stragglers. I don't know the cure, either. . . . [Four weeks later she noted:] That's always a problem, stragglers. As soon as you start something, someone is done and they've done a good job! You can't make them do it over again!"
>
> Homogeneous grouping was supposed to make teaching easier for Kerrie; it did not, although at the beginning of the year, before she was fully sensitive to the range of ability in her classes, she thought it did. . . .
>
> When she had to deal with differences, Kerrie relied on ad hoc approaches, only to find exceptions proliferating beyond a manageable level. . . . As she analyzed the situation, she realized she needed to find a middle ground, which necessitated speeding up the classes, requiring more work, and nudging her standards a bit higher. . . . "Things are different now . . . it came to me that the more work I give them the better they are. . . ."
>
> While exceptions continued to be made, they became fewer and were based on greater knowledge of and sensitivity to student potential: "There isn't a written standard, it's the feel I get from the kids. . . ." (1989, pp. 58–60)

Kerrie faced a problem that many teachers confront—how to recognize and respond to the needs of students who differ in ability and motivation. Through observing the effects of different strategies, Kerrie refined her ability to perceive whether or not a lesson was successful for the targeted students or needed to have a change of pace or direction.

Although we appreciate Chris's and Kerrie's explorations of possible solutions to the dilemmas they faced, their choices focused on technical issues and responses. Teachers confront many technical issues as part of the day-to-day reality of teaching. Reflective evaluation of the impact of those decisions clearly is an important part of what a reflective teacher does. However, one of the points we have raised in this book is the importance of considering one's decisions also in terms of educational issues and ethical commitments grounded in teaching in a democracy. The following example illustrates this dimension in a teacher's reflective self-evaluation.

Vivian

By her own account, Vivian Paley grew up with tolerant, liberal attitudes in her middle-class Jewish home. Although the only black people she knew tended to be housekeepers and service workers, she viewed herself as committed to civil rights and the integration of neighborhoods and schools. These attitudes did not mean, however, that she felt confident or comfortable in her role as a teacher of black children. In *White Teacher,* Paley (1979) chronicles her journey toward understanding children's differences, most especially race, in her kindergarten classroom.

Paley does not engage in a formal action research study; however, she carefully observes herself as she interacts with her black students. Her interactions with her black children and their parents, her observations of how children relate to one another, and her conversations with colleagues provide the basis for an informal reflective cycle. At the heart of this process is Paley's ethical commitment to understanding and celebrating the uniqueness of each child—and her growth in knowing how to transform this commitment into genuine relationships. Paley's words capture her reflection on the importance of that growth.

> Mrs. Hawkins . . . startled me when she said, "My children are black. They don't look like your children. They know they're black and we want it recognized. It's a positive difference, an interesting difference, and a comfortable natural difference. At least it could be so, if you teachers learned to value differences more. What you value, you talk about." Mrs. Hawkins never intended that these differences be used to . . . dim the uniqueness of each child. But she knew that these differences must be treasured by the black child and the white teacher.
>
> I had been unable then to speak of color and so I could not be a friend. Friendship and love grow out of recognizing and respecting differences. Strangers cover up. Color had been, for me, a sign of a stranger. I did not look into the eyes of strangers or dare to find out about their feelings. . . .
>
> It is becoming clear why my experiences with black children have meant so much to me. I have identified with them in the role of the outsider. Those of us who have been outsiders understand the need to be seen exactly as we are and to be accepted and valued. Our safety lies in schools and societies in which faces with many shapes and colors can feel an equal sense of belonging. Our children must grow up knowing and liking those who look and speak in different ways, or they will live as strangers in a hostile land. (1979, pp. 138–139)

Summary

In this chapter, we reviewed the reflective teaching cycle. We discussed reflective teaching as a basis for professional autonomy and empowerment, and as a synthesis of the processes of reflective self-evaluation. We also reviewed the application of those processes in both systematic and informal ways. We have reiterated throughout the book the view that teaching is a problem-solving endeavor, a process of deciding what you want to accomplish, what strategies are likely to help you reach those aims, what happens as a result of putting your plans into practice, and what changes need to be made to enrich your decision making and practice in the future. This cycle of planning, acting, observing, and reflecting forms the basis of the challenge and reward of teaching. Our hope, as you conclude this book, is that you feel more knowledgeable and confident in your role as a reflective teacher and that you ultimately agree with the following insight provided by Kidder (1989) about Chris Zajac:

> She belonged among schoolchildren. They made her confront sorrow and injustice. They made her feel useful. Again this year, some had needed more help than she could provide. There were many problems that she hadn't solved. But it wasn't for lack of trying. She hadn't given up. She had run out of time. (p. 331)

Further Readings

Awbrey, M. (1987). A teacher's action research study of writing in the kindergarten: Accepting the natural expression of children. *Peabody Journal of Education, 64*(2), 33–64.

Cochran-Smith, M., & Lytle, S. (1990). Research on teaching and teacher research: The issues that divide. *Educational Researcher, 19*(2), 2–11.

Corey, S. M. (1954). Action research in education. *Journal of Educational Research, 47*, 375–380.

Goswami, D., & Stillman, P. (1987). *Reclaiming the classroom: Teacher research as an agency for change.* Portsmouth, NH: Boynton/Cook.

Hovda, R. A., & Kyle, D. W. (1984). Action research: A professional development possibility. *Middle School Journal, 15*, 21–23.

Kidder, T. (1989). *Among schoolchildren.* Boston: Houghton Mifflin.

Paley, V. G. (1979). *White teacher.* Cambridge, MA: Harvard University Press.

Ross, D. D. (1984). A practical model of conducting action research in public school settings. *Contemporary Education, 55*(2), 113–117.

Ross, D. D. (1987). Action research for preservice teachers: A description of why and how. *Peabody Journal of Education, 64*(3), 131–150.

Bibliography

Adler, M. (1982). *Paideia proposal: An educational manifesto.* New York: Macmillan.

Anderson, R. C., Hiebert, E. H., Scott, J. A., & Wilkinson, I. A. (1985). *Becoming a nation of readers.* Washington, DC: National Institute of Education.

Apple, M. (1986). *Teachers and texts.* London: Routledge & Kegan Paul.

Applebee, A. N., Langer, J. A., & Mullis, I. V. S. (1986). *The writing report card.* Princeton, NJ: National Assessment of Educational Progress at Educational Testing Service.

Applebee, A. N., Langer, J. A., & Mullis, I. V. S. (1989). Crossroad in American education: A summary of the findings. The nation's report card. Princeton, NJ: National Assessment of Educational Progress. (ERIC Document Reproduction Service No. ED 309 178).

Argyris, C. (1982). *Reasoning, learning and action: Individual and organizational.* San Francisco: Jossey-Bass.

Armor, D., Conry–Oseguera, P., Cox, M., King, N., McDonnell, L., Pascal, A., Pauly, E., & Zellman, G. (1976). Analysis of the school preferred reading program in selected Los Angeles minority schools. (Report No. R–2007–LAUSD). Santa Monica, CA: The Rand Corporation. (ERIC Document Reproduction Service No. ED 130 243).

Ashcroft, L. (1987). Defusing "empowering": The what and the why. *Language Arts, 64,* 142–156.

Asher, S. R. (1973). The influence of race and sex on children's sociometric choices across the school year. Unpublished manuscript, University of Illinois.

Asher, S. R., Oden, S. L., & Gottman, J. M. (1977). Children's friendships in school settings. In L. Katz (Ed.), *Current topics in early childhood education, vol. 1* (pp. 33–61). Norwood, NJ: Ablex.

Asher, S. R., Renshaw, P. D., & Geraci, . (1980). Children's friendships and social competence. *International Journal of Psycholinguistics, 7,* 27–39.

Asher, S. R., Renshaw, P. D., & Hymel, S. (1982). Peer relations and the development of social skills. In S. G. Moore (Ed.), *The young child: Reviews of research (Vol. 3, pp. 137–158).* Washington, D. C.: National Association for the Education of Young Children.

Asher, S. R., Singleton, L. L., Tinsley, B. R., & Hymel, S. (1979). A reliable sociometric measure for preschool children. *Child Development, 15*(4), 443–444.

Ashton, P. T. (1984). Teacher efficacy: A motivational paradigm for effective teacher education. *Journal of Teacher Education, 35,* 28–32.

Ashton, P. T., & Webb, R. B. (1986). *Making a difference: Teachers' sense of efficacy and student achievement.* New York: Longman.

Awbrey, M. (1987). A teacher's action research study of writing in the kindergarten: Accepting the natural expression of children. *Peabody Journal of Education, 64*(2), 33–64.

Bagenstos, N. T. (1975). The teacher as an inquirer. *The Educational Forum, 39*, 231–237.

Bailin, S. (1988). *Achieving extraordinary ends: An essay on creativity.* Boston: Kluwer Academic Publishers.

Ball, S. J. (1987). *The micro–politics of the school: Towards a theory of school organization.* New York: Methuen.

Bandura, A. (1982). Self–efficacy mechanism in human agency. *American Psychologist, 37*(2), 122–147.

Barell, J. (1985). Removing impediments to change. In A. L. Costa (Ed.), *Developing minds* (pp. 33–40). Alexandria, VA: Association for Supervision and Curriculum Development.

Barnes, D. (1976). *From communication to curriculum.* Harmondsworth: Penguin Books.

Basal Readers and the State of American Reading Instruction: A Call for Action. (1988). Position statement, Commission on Reading, National Council of Teachers of English, Urbana, IL.

Baxter, K. B. (1974). Combating the influence of black stereotypes in children's books. *The Reading Teacher, 27*, 540–544.

Belenky, M., Clinchy, B., Goldberger, N., & Tarule, J. (1986). *Women's ways of knowing: The development of self, voice, and mind.* New York: Basic Books.

Benson, N. (1987). Citizenship and student power: Some strategies for the classroom. *The Social Studies, 78*, 136–139.

Berlak, A., & Berlak, H. (1981). *Dilemmas of schooling.* New York: Methuen.

Berliner, D. C. (1984). The half-full glass: A review of research on teaching. In P. L. Hosford (Ed.), *Using what we know about teaching* (pp. 51–77). Alexandria, Va: Association for Supervision and Curriculum Development.

Berman, P., McLaughlin, M., Bass, G., Pauly, E., & Zellman, G. (1977). *Federal programs supporting educational change. Vol. 7: Factors affecting implementation and continuation.* Santa Monica: The Rand Corporation. (ERIC Document Reproduction Service No. ED 140 432).

Blase, J. J. (1988). The everyday political perspective of teachers: Vulnerability and conservatism. *International Journal of Qualitative Studies in Education, 1*(2) 125–142.

Boggs, S. T. (1985). *Speaking, relating and learning: A study of Hawaiian children at home and at school.* Norwood, NJ: Ablex.

Bondy, E. (1984). Thinking about thinking: Encouraging children's use of metacognitive processes. *Childhood Education, 60*, 234–238.

Borko, H. (1986). Clinical teacher education and the professional teacher. In J. V. Hoffman & S. A. Edwards (Eds.), *Reality and reform in clinical teacher education* (pp. 45–64). New York: Random House.

Borko, H., & Shavelson, R. J. (1983). Speculations on teacher education: Recommendations from research on teachers' cognitions. *Journal of Education for Teaching, 9*(3), 210–224.

Bradley, P. H., & Baird, J. E. (1983). *Communication for business and the professions.* Dubuque, IA: Wm. C. Brown Co.

Brandt, R. (1987). On leadership and student achievement: A conversation with Richard Andrews. *Educational Leadership, 45*(1), 9–16.

Bredemeier, M. E. (1988). *Urban classroom portraits: Teachers who make a difference.* New York: Peter Lang.

Bridge, C. A., & Hiebert, E. H. (1985). A comparison of classroom writing practices, teachers' perceptions of their writing instruction, and textbook recommendations on writing practices. *The Elementary School Journal, 86*(2), 155–172.

Brinkerhoff, R. F. (1989). School science: Agenda for the 1990s. *Independent Schools, 49*(1), 49–57.

Brophy, J. (1981a). On praising effectively. *Elementary School Journal, 81*(5), 269–278.

Brophy, J. (1981b). Teacher praise: A functional analysis. *Review of Educational Research, 51*, 5–32.

Brophy, J. (1985). Classroom management as instruction: Socializing self–guidance in students. *Theory Into Practice, 24*(1), 233–240.

Brophy, J. (1990). Teaching social studies for understanding and higher order applications. *Elementary School Journal, 90*(4), 351–417.

Brophy, J., & Good, T. L. (1986). Teacher behavior and student achievement. In M. Wittrock (Ed.), *Third handbook of research on teaching* (pp. 328–375). New York: Macmillan.

Brown, J. S., & Burton, R. R. (1978). Diagnostic models for procedural bugs in basic mathematical skills. *Cognitive Science, 2*, 155–192.

Brown, J. S., & Van Lehn, K. (1980). Repair theory: A generic theory of bugs in procedural skills. *Cognitive Science, 4*, 370–426.

Bryan, J. (1975). Children's cooperation and helping behavior. In E. Heatherington (Ed.), *Review of child development research, Volume 5* (pp. 127–181). Chicago: University of Chicago Press.

Bullough, R., Jr. (1989). *First year teacher: A case study.* New York: Teachers College Press.

Burbules, N. C. (1988). A theory of power in education. *Educational Theory, 36*(2), 95–114.

Bussis, A. M. (1982). "Burn it at the casket": Research, reading instruction and children's learning of the first R. *Phi Delta Kappan, 64*, 237–241.

Butt, R. L., & Raymond, D. (1989). Teacher development using collaborative autobiography. Paper presented at an International Invitational Conference on "Teacher Development: Policy, Practices, and Research." Ontario Institute for Studies in Education, Toronto, Canada.

Calkins, L. M. (1986). *The art of teaching writing.* Portsmouth, NH: Heinemann.

Cangelosi, J. S. (1988). *Classroom management strategies: Gaining and maintaining students' cooperation.* New York: Longman.

Cannella, G. S. (1986). Praise and concrete rewards: Concerns for childhood education. *Childhood Education, 62*(4), 297–301.

Canter, L. (1979). Discipline: You can do it! *Instructor, 68*(2), 106–112.

Canter, L., & Canter, M. (1976). *Assertive discipline: A take charge approach for today's educator.* Santa Monica: Canter & Associates.

Carbo, M. (1987). Reading styles research: "What works" isn't always phonics. *Phi Delta Kappan, 68*(6), 431–435.

Carnegie, D. (1981). *How to win friends and influence people.* New York: Simon & Schuster.

Carpenter, T. P, Corbitt, M. K., Kepner, H. S., Lindquist, M. M., Reys, R. E. (1981). National Assessment. In E. Fennema (Ed.), *Mathematics education research: Implications for the 80s* (pp. 22–37). Reston, VA: Association for Supervision and Curriculum Development.

Carpenter, T. P., Matthews, W., Lindquist, M. M., & Silver, E. A. (1984). *Elementary School Journal, 84*(5), 485–495.

Carter, J. (1983). Characteristics of successful writing instruction: A preliminary report. *The Elementary School Journal, 84*(1), 40–44.

Cazden, C. B. (1978). Environments for language learning. *Language Arts, 55,* 681–682.

Cazden, D. B. (1986). Classroom discourse. In M. C. Wittrock (Ed.), *Handbook of research on teaching* (3rd ed.) (pp. 432–464). New York: Macmillan.

Charles, C. M. (1985). *Building classroom discipline: From models to practice* (2nd ed.). New York: Longman.

Charlesworth, R., & Hartup, W. W. (1967). Positive social reinforcement in the nursery school peer group. *Child Development, 38,* 993–1002.

Clark, C. M., & Yinger, R. J. (1977). Research on teacher thinking. *Curriculum Inquiry, 7*(4), 279–304.

Cochran–Smith, M., & Lytle, S. (1990). Research on teaching and teacher research: The issues that divide. *Educational Researcher, 19*(2), 2–11.

Collins, A., Brown, J. S., & Newman, S. W. (1989). Cognitive apprenticeship: Teaching the craft of reading, writing and mathematics. In L. B. Resnick (Ed.), *Knowing, learning and instruction: Essays in honor of Robert Glaser* (pp. 453–494). Hillsdale, NJ: Erlbaum.

Comer, J. P. (1989). Children can. In R. B. Webb & F. W. Parkay (Eds.), *Children can: An address on school improvement* (pp. 4–17). University of Florida: Research and Development Center on School Improvement.

Copeland, W. D. (1986). The RITE framework for teacher education: Preservice applications. In J. V. Hoffman & S. A. Edwards (Eds.), *Reality and reform in clinical teacher education* (pp. 25–44). New York: Random House.

Corey, S. M. (1953). *Action research to improve school practices.* New York: Teachers College Press.

Corey, S. M. (1954). Action research in education. *Journal of Educational Research, 47,* 375–380.

Cornbleth, C. (1989). Cries of crisis, calls for reform, and challenges of change. In L. Weis, P. G. Altback, G. P. Kelly, H. G. Petrie, & S. Slaughter (Eds.), *Crisis in teaching: Perspectives on current reforms* (pp. 9–32). Albany, NY: State University of New York Press.

Cornbleth, C., & Korth, W. (1984). Teacher perspectives and meanings of responsibility. *Educational Forum, 48,* 413–422.

Corsaro, W. A. (1979). "We're friends, right?": Children's use of access rituals in a nursery school. *Language in Society, 8,* 315–336.

Corsaro, W. A. (1981). Friendship in the nursery school: Social organization in a peer environment. In S. R. Asher & J. M. Gottman (Eds.), *The development of children's friendships* (pp. 207–241). New York: Cambridge University Press.

Corsaro, W. A. (1988). Peer culture in the preschool. *Theory Into Practice, 27*(1), 19–24.

Costa, A. L. (Ed.). (1985). *Developing minds: A resource book for teaching thinking.* Alexandria, VA: Association for Supervision and Curriculum Development.

Costa, A. L. (1985). Programs for teaching thinking. In A. L. Costa (Ed.), *Developing minds* (pp. 183–246). Alexandria, VA: Association for Supervision and Curriculum Development.

Covington, M. V. (1984). The self–worth theory of achievement motivation: Findings and implications. *Elementary School Journal, 85*(1), 5–20.

Cowen, E. L., Pederson, A., Babigian, H., Izzo, L. D., & Trost, M. A. (1973). Long–term follow–up of early detected vulnerable children. *Journal of Consulting and Clinical Psychology, 41,* 438–446.

Criswell, J. H. (1939). A sociometric study of race cleavage in the classroom. *Archives of Psychology,* No. 235, 1–82.

Cruickshank, D. R. (1985). Uses and benefits of reflective teaching. *Phi Delta Kappan, 66*(10), 704–706.

Cuban, L. (1986). Persistent instruction: Another look at constancy in the classroom. *Phi Delta Kappan, 68,* 7–11.

Cummins, J. (1986). Empowering minority students: A framework for intervention. *Harvard Educational Review, 56,* 18–36.

Davis, R. B. (1983). Diagnosis and evaluation in mathematics instruction: Making contact with students' mental representations. In D. C. Smith (Ed.), *Essential knowledge for beginning educators* (pp. 101–111). Washington, DC: American Association of Colleges of Teacher Education.

de Castell, S., Luke, A., & MacLennan, D. (1986). On defining literacy. In de Castell, S., Luke, A., & Egan, K. (Eds.), *Literacy, society, and schooling* (pp. 3–14). New York: Cambridge University Press.

Deci, E. L. (1971). Effects of externally medicated rewards on intrinsic motivation. *Journal of Personality and Social Psychology, 18,* 1043–1052.

Deci, E. L. (1972). Intrinsic motivation, extrinsic reinforcement and inequity. *Journal of Personality and Social Psychology, 22,* 113–120.

Denzin, N. K. (1977). *Childhood socialization.* San Francisco: Jossey–Bass Publishers.

Dewey, J. (1933). *How we think.* Chicago: Henry Regnery Co.

Dion, K. K. (1972). Physical attractiveness and evaluation of children's transgressions. *Journal of Personality and Social Psychology, 24,* 207–213.

Douglass, M. P. (1978). On reading: The great American debate. In E. W. Eisner (Ed.), *Reading, the arts and the creation of meaning* (pp. 89–109). Reston, VA: National Art Association.

Doyle, W. (1983). Academic work. *Review of Educational Research, 53*(2), 159–199.

Dreeben, R. (1968). *On what is learned in school.* Reading, MA: Addison–Wesley.

Dreikurs, R. (1968). *Psychology in the classroom* (2nd ed.). New York: Harper & Row.

Dreyfus, A., Jungwirth, E., & Eliovitch, R. (1990). Applying the "cognitive conflict" strategy for conceptual change—Some implications, difficulties and problems. *Science Education, 74*(5), 555–569.

Duffy, G. G., & Roehler, L. R. (1987). Teaching reading skills as strategies. *The Reading Teacher, 40,* 414–418.

Duke, D. L., & Jones, V. F. (1985). What can schools do to foster student responsibility? *Theory Into Practice, 24*(1), 277–285.

Durkin, D. D. (1978–79). What classroom observations reveal about reading comprehension instruction. *Reading Research Quarterly, 14,* 481–533.

Durkin, D. D. (1981). Reading comprehension instruction in five basal reader series. *Reading Research Quarterly, 16,* 515–544.

Durkin, D. D. (1984). Is there a match between what elementary teachers do and what basal reader manuals recommend? *The Reading Teacher, 37,* 734–744.

Early, M. J., Cooper, E. K., & Santeusanio, N. (1979). Mr. Fig. In *Magic Afternoon.* HBJ Bookmark Reading Program. New York: Harcourt Brace Jovanovich.

Eder, D. (1983). Ability grouping and students' academic self–concepts: A case study. *Elementary School Journal, 84,* 149–161.

Educating Americans for the 21st century. (1983). Washington, DC: The National Science Board Commission on Pre–College Education in Mathematics, Science, and Technology.

Eisner, E. W. (1979, 1985). *The educational imagination.* New York: Macmillan.

Eisner, E. W. (1983). The art and craft of teaching. *Educational Leadership, 40,* 4–18.

Eisner, E. W., & Vallance, E. (Eds.). (1974). *Conflicting conceptions of curriculum.* Berkeley, CA: McCutchan Publishing Co.

Elkind, D. (1979). Beginning reading: A stage structure analysis. *Childhood Education, 55,* 248–252.

Elksnin, L. K., & Elksnin, N. (1989). Collaborative consultation: Improving parent teacher communication. *Academic Therapy, 24*(3) 261–269.

Elsbree, W. (1939). *The American teacher.* New York: American Book Co.

Ennis, R. H. (1985). Goals for a critical thinking curriculum. In A. L. Costa (Ed.), *Developing minds* (pp. 54–57). Alexandria, VA: Association for Supervision and Curriculum Development.

Epstein, J. L. (1986). Parents' reactions to teacher practices of parent involvement. *Elementary School Journal, 86*(3), 277–294.

Epstein, J. L. (1987). Parent involvement: What research says to administrators. *Education and Urban Society, 19*(2), 119–136.

Evertson, C. M., & Emmer, E. T. (1982). Preventive classroom management. In D. L. Duke (Ed.), *Helping teachers manage classrooms* (pp. 2–31). Alexandria, VA: Association for Supervision and Curriculum Development.

Evertson, C. M., Emmer, E. T., Clements, B. S., Sanford, J. P., & Worsham, M. E. (1984). *Classroom management for elementary teachers.* Englewood Cliffs, NJ: Prentice–Hall.

Farr, R., & Tulley, M. (1985). Do adoption committees perpetuate mediocre textbooks? *Phi Delta Kappan, 66*(7), 467–471.

Feiman, S. (1979). Technique and inquiry in teacher education: A curricular case study. *Curriculum Inquiry, 9*(1), 63–79.

Feiman-Nemser, S. (1986). The cultures of teaching. In M. Wittrock (Ed.), *Third handbook of research on teaching* (pp. 505–526). New York: Macmillan.

Fisher, C. W., Berliner, D., Filby, N., Marliave, R., Cohen, L., Dishaw, M., & Moore, J. (1978). *Teaching and learning in elementary schools: A summary of the beginning teacher evaluation study.* San Francisco, CA: Far West Regional Laboratory for Educational Research and Development.

Fitzclarence, L., & Giroux, H. (1984). The paradox of power in educational theory and practice. *Language Arts, 61,* 462–477.

Flavell, J. H. (1976). Metacognitive aspects of problem solving. In L. B. Resnick (Ed.), *The nature of intelligence* (pp. 213–235). Hillsdale, NJ: Erlbaum.

Flower, L., & Hayes, J. R. (1981). A cognitive process theory of writing. *College Composition and Communication, 32,* 365–387.

Fordham, S., & Ogbu, J. (1986). Black students' school success: Coping with the burden of "acting white." *The Urban Review, 18*(3), 1–31.

Freed, A. M. (1973). *T.A. for tots.* San Marcos, CA.: Jalmar Press.

Freire, P., & Macedo, D. (1987). *Literacy: Reading the word and the world.* South Hadley, MA: Bergin and Garvey.

Frymier, J. (1987). Bureaucracy and the neutering of teachers. *Phi Delta Kappan, 69*(1), 9–14.

Gage, N. L. (1985). *Hard gains in the soft sciences: The case of pedagogy.* Bloomington, IN: Phi Delta Kappa Center on Evaluation Development and Research.

Gall, M. (1984). Synthesis of research on teachers' questioning. *Educational Leadership, 42,* 40–47.

Gallup, A. M. (1986). The 18th annual Gallup poll of the public's attitudes toward the public schools. *Phi Delta Kappan, 68,* 43–59.

Garner, R. (1987). *Metacognition and reading comprehension.* Norwood, NJ: Ablex Publishing Co.

Garrison, J. W. (1988). Democracy, scientific knowledge, and teacher empowerment. *Teachers College Record, 89*(4), 487–504.

Genishi, C., & Di Paolo, M. (1982). Learning through argument in a preschool. In L. C. Wilkinson (Ed.), *Communicating in the classroom* (pp. 49–68). New York: Academic Press.

Gersten, R., & Carnine, D. (1986). Direct instruction in reading comprehension. *Educational Leadership, 43*(7), 70–78.

Gilbert, S. E., & Gay, G. (1985). Improving the success in school of poor black children. *Phi Delta Kappan, 67,* 133–137.

Ginott, H. (1965). *Between parent and child.* New York: Avon.

Ginott, H. (1969). *Between parent and teenager.* New York: Macmillan.

Ginott, H. (1971). *Teacher and child.* New York: Macmillan.

Giroux, H. (1988). *Teachers as intellectuals.* Granby, MA: Bergin & Garvey.

Giroux, H. (1989). Educational reform and teacher empowerment. In Holtz, H., Marcus, I., Dougherty, J., Michaels, J. & Peduzzi, R. (Eds.), *Education and the American dream* (pp. 173–186). Granby, MA: Bergin & Garvey.

Giroux, H., & McLaren, P. (1986). Teacher education and the politics of engagement: The case for democratic schooling. *Harvard Educational Review, 56,* 213–233.

Glaser, E. (1941). *An experiment in the development of critical thinking.* New York: Teachers College Press.

Glasersfeld, E. von. (1987). Learning as constructive activity. In E. von Glasersfeld (Ed.), *The construction of knowledge: Contributions to conceptual semantics* (pp. 307–333). Salinas, CA: Intersystems Publications.

Glasser, W. (1965). *Schools without failure.* New York: Harper & Row.

Glasser, W. (1985). Discipline has never been the problem and isn't the problem now. *Theory Into Practice, 24*(1), 241–246.

Glatthorn, A. A., & Baron, J. (1985). The good thinker. In A. L. Costa (Ed.), *Developing minds* (pp. 49–53). Alexandria, VA: Association for Supervision and Curriculum Development.

Good, T. L. (1979). Teacher effectiveness in the elementary school. *Journal of Teacher Education, 30,* 52–64.

Good, T. L. (1987). Two decades of research on teacher expectations: Findings and future directions. *Journal of Teacher Education, 38*(4), 32–47.

Good, T. L. & Grouws, D. A. (1979). Teaching and mathematics learning. *Educational Leadership, 37*(1), 39–43.

Good, T. L., & Grouws, D. A. (1987). Increasing teachers' understanding of mathematical ideas through inservice training. *Phi Delta Kappan, 68*, 778–783.

Goodlad, J. I. (1984). *A place called school.* New York: McGraw Hill Book Co.

Goodman, J. (1984). Reflection and teacher education: A case study and theoretical analysis. *Interchange, 15*(3), 9–26.

Goodman, J. (1986). Making early field experience meaningful: A critical approach. *Journal of Education for Teaching, 12*(2), 109–125.

Goodman, J. (1987a, Oct.). The disenfranchisement of elementary teachers and strategies for resistance. Bergamo Conference on Curriculum Theory and Practice, Dayton, OH.

Goodman, J. (1987b). Factors in becoming a proactive elementary school teacher: A preliminary study of selected novices. *Journal of Education for Teaching, 13*(3), 207–229.

Goodman, J. (1988a). Democratic empowerment and elementary curriculum: A case study. Paper presented at the annual meeting of the American Educational Research Association, New Orleans.

Goodman, J. (1988b). The political tactics and teaching strategies of reflective, active preservice teachers. *Elementary School Journal, 89*(1), 23–41.

Goodman, J. (1992). *Elementary schooling for critical democracy.* Albany, NY: State University of New York Press.

Goodman, K. S. (1978). What is basic about reading? In E. W. Eisner (Ed.), *Reading, the arts and the creation of meaning* (pp. 55–90). Reston, VA: National Art Association.

Goodman, K. S. (1989). Whole–language research: Foundations and development. *The Elementary School Journal, 90*(2), 207–221.

Goodman, Y. (1978). Kid watching: An alternative to testing. *The National Elementary Principal, 57*, 41–45.

Gordon, T. (1970). *P.E.T.: Parent effectiveness training.* New York: Peter H. Wyden.

Goswami, D., & Stillman, P. (1987). *Reclaiming the classroom: Teacher research as an agency for change.* Portsmouth, NH: Boynton/Cook.

Gottman, J., Gonso, J., & Rasamussen, B. (1975). Social interaction, social competence, and friendship in children. *Child Development, 46*, 709–718.

Grant, C. A., & Sleeter, C. E. (1987). Who determines teacher work? The debate continues. *Teaching and Teacher Education, 3*(1), 61–64.

Grant, L., & Rothenberg, J. (1986). The social enhancement of ability differences: Teacher–student interactions in first– and second–grade reading groups. *The Elementary School Journal, 87*(1), 29–49.

Graves, D. H. (1977). Language arts textbooks: A writing process evaluation. *Language Arts, 54*, 817–823.

Griffin, G. (1984). Why use research in preservice teacher education: A proposal. *Journal of Teacher Education, 35*(4), 36–40.

Grimmett, P. P., MacKinnon, A. M., Erickson, G. L., & Riecken, T. J. (1990). Reflective practice in teacher education. In R. L. Clift, W. R. Houston, & M. C. Pugach (Eds.), *Encouraging reflective practice in education* (pp. 20–38). New York: Teachers College Press.

Gross, S. J. (1985). Personal power and empowerment. *Contemporary Education, 56*(3), 137–143.

Hall, G. E. (1987). The principal as leader of the change facilitating team. Paper presented at the annual meeting of the American Educational Research Association, Washington, DC.

Hallinan, M. (1984). Summary and implications. In P. Peterson, L. Wilkinson, & M. Hallinan (Eds.), *The social context of instruction* (pp. 229–240). New York: Academic Press.

Hammack, D. C., Hartoonian, M., Howe, J., Jenkins, L. B., Levstik, L. S., McDonald, W. B., Mullis, I. V. S. & Owen, E. (1990). The U.S. history report card. Princeton, NJ: National Assessment of Educational Progress. (ERIC Document Reproduction Service No. ED 315 377).

Hansen, J., & Pearson, P. D. (1983). An instructional study: Improving the inferential comprehension of good and poor fourth-grade readers. *Journal of Educational Psychology, 75*(6), 821–829.

Harari, H., & McDavid, J. W. (1973). Name stereotyping and teachers' expectations. *Journal of Educational Psychology, 65,* 222–225.

Harste, J., Woodward, V., & Burke, C. (1984). *Language stories and literacy lessons.* Portsmouth, NH: Heinemann.

Hartup, W. W., & Coates, B. (1967). Imitation of a peer as a function of reinforcement from the peer group and rewardingness of the model. *Child Development, 38,* 1003–1016.

Harty, S. (1979). *Hucksters in the classroom: A review of industry propaganda in schools.* Washington, DC: Center for Study of Responsive Law.

Hatano, G., & Inagaki, K. (1987). A theory of motivation for comprehension and its application to mathematics instruction. In T. A. Romberg & D. M. Steward (Eds.), *The monitoring of school mathematics: Background papers. Vol 2. Implications from psychology, outcomes of instruction.* (Program Rep. N. 87–2, pp. 27–66). Madison, WI: Center for Educational Research.

Hatch, J. A. (1988). Learning to be an outsider: Peer stigmatization in kindergarten. *The Urban Review, 20*(1), 59–72.

Hatton, E. (1987). Determinants of teacher work: Some causal complications. *Teaching and Teacher Education, 3*(1), 55–60.

Hayes, L. F., & Ross, D. D. (1989). Trust versus control: The impact of school leadership on teacher reflection. *International Journal of Qualitative Studies in Education, 2*(4), 335–350.

Hewson, P. W., & Hewson, M. G. (1988). An appropriate conception of teaching science: A view from studies of science learning. *Science Education, 72,* 597–614.

Hiebert, E. (1983). An examination of ability grouping for reading instruction. *Reading Research Quarterly, 18,* 231–255.

Hiebert, J. (1984). Children's mathematics learning: The struggle to link form and understanding. *The Elementary School Journal, 84*(5), 497–513.

Hill, T. C. (1982). Promoting empathy in the preschool: An important part of the curriculum. Paper presented at the annual meeting of the National Association for the Education of Young Children, Washington, DC.

Hill, T. C. (1983). The effect of self–reflection on preschool children's empathetic under-standing and prosocial behavior. Paper presented at the annual meeting of the Society for Research in Child Development, Detroit.

Hillocks, G., Jr. (1986). The writer's knowledge: Theory, research, and implications for practice. In A. R. Petrosky & D. Bartholomae (Eds.), *The teaching of writing: Eighty–fifth yearbook of the National Society for the Study of Education* (pp. 71–94). Chicago: University of Chicago Press.

Hirsch, E. D., Jr. (1987). *Cultural literacy: What every American needs to know.* Boston: Houghton Mifflin.

Honig, A. S. (1982). Research in review: Prosocial development in children. *Young Children, 37*(5), 51–62.

Hoskisson, K. (1979). Learning to read naturally. *Language Arts, 56,* 489–496.

Hovda, R. A., & Kyle, D. W. (1984). Action research: A professional development possibili-ty. *Middle School Journal, 15,* 21–23.

Hoy, C. (1986). Preventing learned helplessness. *Academic Therapy, 22*(1), 11–18.

Hoyle, E. (1986). *The politics of school management.* Toronto: Hodder and Stoughton.

Hughes, R., Tingle, B. A., & Sawin, D. B. (1981). Development of empathic understand-ing. *Child Development, 52,* 122–128.

Hunter, M., & Barker, G. (1987). "If at first . . ." Attribution theory in the classroom. *Educational Leadership, 45*(2), 50–54.

Jackson, P. W. (1968). *Life in classrooms.* New York: Holt, Rinehart, and Winston.

Johnson, D. W., & Johnson, R. T. (1987). *Learning together and alone: Cooperative, competi-tive, & individualistic learning* (2nd ed.). Englewood Cliffs, NJ: Prentice–Hall.

Johnson, D. W., Johnson, R. T., & Holubec, E. J. (1988a). *Advanced cooperative learning.* Edina, MN: Interaction Book Co.

Johnson, D. W., Johnson, R. T., & Holubec, E. (1988b). *Cooperation in the classroom.* Edina, MN: Interaction Book Company.

Johnson, D. W., Johnson, R. T., Holubec, E., & Roy, P. (1984). *Circles of learning: Cooperation in the classroom.* Alexandria, VA: Association for Supervision and Curriculum Development.

Johnson, N. B. (1985). *West Haven: Classroom culture and society in a rural elementary school.* Chapel Hill, NC: University of North Carolina Press.

Johnston, J. M. (1985). Teacher induction: Problems, roles, and guidelines. In P. J. Burke & R. G. Henderson (Eds.), *Career–long teacher education* (pp. 194–222). Springfield, IL: Thomas.

Johnston, J. M., & Ryan, K. (1983). Research on the beginning teacher: Implications for teacher education. In K. R. Howey & W. Gardner (Eds.), *The Education of Teachers: A Look Ahead* (pp. 136–162). New York: Longman.

Kantowski, M. G. (1981). Problem solving. In E. Fennema (Ed.), *Mathematics education research: Implications for the 80s* (pp. 111–130). Reston, VA: ASCD.

Kemmis, S., & McTaggart, R. (1982). *The action research planner.* Victoria, Australia: Deacon University Press.

Kidder, T. (1989). *Among schoolchildren.* Boston: Houghton Mifflin.

Kilgore, K., Ross, D. D., & Zbikowski, J. (1990). Understanding the teaching perspectives of first year teachers. *Journal of Teacher Education, 41*(1), 28–38.

Kohl, H. (1967). *36 children.* New York: The New American Library.

Korthagen, F. A. (1985). Reflective teaching and preservice teacher education in the Netherlands. *Journal of Teacher Education, 36*(5), 11–15.

Kounin, J. (1970). *Discipline and group management in classrooms.* New York: Holt, Rinehart and Winston.

Krogh, S. L. (1982). Encouraging positive justice reasoning and perspective taking skills. Paper presented at the annual meeting of the National Association of Early Childhood Educators, Washington, DC.

Kyle, D. W. (1978). Changes in basal reader content: Has anyone been listening? *The Elementary School Journal, 78*(5), 305–312.

Kyle, D. W. (1980). Curriculum decisions: Who decides what? *Elementary School Journal, 81*(2), 77–85.

Lacey, C. (1977). *The socialization of teachers.* London: Metheun.

Ladson–Billings, G. (1990). Making a little magic: Teachers talk about successful teaching strategies for black children. Paper presented at the annual meeting of the American Educational Research Association, Boston, MA.

Lampert, M. (1985). How do teachers manage to teach? Perspectives on problems in practice. *Harvard Educational Review, 55*(2), 178–194.

Lampert, M. (1986). Knowing, doing, and teaching multiplication. *Cognition and Instruction, 3*(4), 305–342.

Langer, J. A. (1984). Literacy instruction in American schools: Problems and perspectives. *American Journal of Education, 93*(1), 107–131.

Langer, J. A. (1989). Literate thinking and schooling. *Literacy Research Newsletter, 5,* 1–2.

Langer, J. A., & Applebee, A. N. (1987). *How writing shapes thinking.* Urbana, IL: National Council of Teachers of English.

Langer, J. A., Applebee, A. N., Mullis, I. V. S., & Foertsch, M. A. (1990). Learning to read in our nation's schools. Princeton, NJ: National Assessment of Educational Progress. (ERIC Document Reproduction Service No. 317990).

Lankshear, C., & Lawler, M. (1987). *Literacy, schooling and revolution.* Philadelphia: The Falmer Press.

Lasky, L. R. (1978). Personalizing teaching: Action research in action. *Young Children, 33,* 58–64.

Lasley, T. J. (1985). Fostering nonaggression in the classroom: An anthropological perspective. *Theory Into Practice, 24*(1), 248–255.

Leiter, M. P. (1977). A study in reciprocity in preschool play groups. *Child Development, 48,* 1288–1295.

Leithwood, K. A., & Montgomery, D. J. (1982). The role of the elementary school principal in program improvement. *Review of Educational Research, 52*(3), 309–339.

Lester, F. K., & Garofalo, J. (Eds.). (1982). *Mathematical problem solving: Issues in research.* Philadelphia: Franklin Institute Press.

Levin, H. M. (1986). *National Education Association SEARCH: Educational reform for disadvantaged students: An emerging crisis.* Westhaven, CT: National Education Association.

Levin, H. M. (1987). Accelerated schools for disadvantaged students. *Educational Leadership, 44*(6), 19–21.

Levy, J. (1983). Research synthesis on right and left hemispheres: We think with both sides of the brain. *Educational Leadership, 40,* 66–71.

Lieberman, A. (1988a). Expanding the leadership team. *Educational Leadership, 45*(5), 4–8.

Lieberman, A. (1988b). Teachers and principals: Turf, tension and new tasks. *Phi Delta Kappan, 69*(9), 648–653.

Lindquist, M. M. (1984). The elementary school mathematics curriculum: Issues for today. *The Elementary School Journal, 84*(5), 595–608.

Liston, D. P., & Zeichner, K. M. (1987). Reflective teacher education and moral deliberation. *Journal of Teacher Education, 38*(6), 2–9.

Little, J. W. (1982). Norms of collegiality and experimentation: Workplace conditions of school success. *American Educational Research Journal, 19*(3), 325–340.

Maeroff, G. I. (1988a). A blueprint for empowering teachers. *Phi Delta Kappan, 69*(7), 472–477.

Maeroff, G. I. (1988b). *The empowerment of teachers.* New York: Teachers College Press.

Margolis, H., & Brannigan, G. G. (1986). Building trust with parents. *Academic Therapy, 22*(1), 71–74.

Martin, J., Feldman, M. S., Hatch, M. J., & Sitkin, S. B. (1983). The uniqueness paradox in organizational stories. *Administrative Science Quarterly, 28*, 438–453.

Martin, J. R. (1976). What should we do with a hidden curriculum when we find one? *Curriculum Inquiry, 6*(2), 135–151.

Marzano, R. J., Brandt, R. S., Hughes, C. S., Jones, B. F., Presseisen, B. Z., Rankin, S. C., & Suhor, C. (1988). *Dimensions of thinking: A framework for curriculum and instruction.* Alexandria, VA: Association for Supervision and Curriculum Development.

McCaleb, J. (1979). On reconciling dissonance between preparation and practice. *Journal of Teacher Education, 30*(4), 50–53.

McCutcheon, G. (1980). How do elementary school teachers plan? The nature of planning and influences on it. *Elementary School Journal, 81*(1), 4–23.

McCutcheon, G. (1981). The impact of the insider. In J. Nixon (Ed.), *A teacher's guide to action research.* London: Grant McIntyre.

McDaniel, T. (1980). Alternatives to punishment. *Phi Delta Kappan, 61*(7), 455–458.

McDavid, J. W., & Harari, H. (1966). Stereotyping of names and popularity in grade–school children. *Child Development, 37*, 453–459.

McDiarmid, G. W. (1989). What do teachers need to know about cultural diversity: Restoring subject matter to the picture. Paper presented at the Policy Conference of the National Center for Research on Teacher Education, Washington, DC.

McFaul, S. A. (1983). An examination of direct instruction. *Educational Leadership, 40*, 67–69.

McLaren, P. (1989). *Life in schools.* White Plains, NY: Longman.

McNeil, J. D. (1984). *Reading comprehension.* Glenview, IL: Scott, Foresman & Co.

McNeil, L. M. (1988a). Contradictions of control, part 3: Contradictions of reform. *Phi Delta Kappan, 69*(7), 478–485.

McNeil, L. M. (1988b). Contradictions of control, part 2: Teachers, students and curriculum. *Phi Delta Kappan, 69*(6), 432–438.

McNeil, L. M. (1988c). Contradictions of control, part 1: Administrators and teachers. *Phi Delta Kappan, 69*(5), 333–339.

McTighe, J., & Schollenberger, J. (1985). Why teach thinking: A statement of rationale. In A. L. Costa (Ed.), *Developing minds* (pp. 3–6). Alexandria, VA: Association for Supervision and Curriculum Development.

Mead, G. H. (1930). The philosophies of Royce, James, and Dewey in their American setting. *International Journal of Ethics, 40*, 211–231.

Menacker, J., Hurwitz, E., & Weldon, W. (1988). Parent–teacher cooperation in schools serving the urban poor. *The Clearinghouse, 62,* 108–112.

Michelson, L., Sugai, D. P., Wood, R. P., & Kazdin, A. E. (1983). *Social skills assessment and training with children.* New York: Plenum.

Miller, J. (1983). *The educational spectrum: Orientations to curriculum.* New York: Longman.

Minstrell, J. A. (1989). Teaching science for understanding. In L. B. Resnick & L. E. Klopfer (Eds.), *Toward the thinking curriculum: Current cognitive research* (pp. 129–149). Alexandria, VA: Association for Supervision and Curriculum Development.

Moles, O. C. (1987). Who wants parent involvement? Interest, skills and opportunities among parents and educators. *Education and Urban Society, 19*(2), 137–145.

Moore, J. R., Mintz, S. L., & Bierman, M. (1987). Reflective inquiry: Teaching and thinking. Paper prepared for the Reflective Inquiry Conference, Houston, Texas.

Moore, S. G. (1981). Unique contributions of peers to socialization in early childhood. *Theory Into Practice, 20,* 105–108.

Morante, E. A., & Ulesky, A. (1984). Assessment of reasoning abilities. *Educational Leadership, 42*(1), 71–74.

Morgan, J. (1984). Reward–induced decrements and increments in intrinsic motivation. *Review of Educational Research, 54*(1), 5–30.

Mortimore, P., & Sammons, P. (1987). New evidence on effective elementary schools. *Educational Leadership, 45*(1), 4–8.

Mumby, D. K. (1987). The political function of narrative in organizations. *Communication Monographs, 54,* 113–127.

Murphy, J., Weil, M., & McGreal, T. L. (1987). The basic practice model of instruction. *Elementary School Journal, 87*(1), 83–95.

Murphy, J. T. (1988). The unheroic side of leadership: Notes from the swamp. *Phi Delta Kappan, 69,*(9), 654–659.

Muther, C. (1985). What every textbook evaluator should know. *Educational Leadership, 42*(7), 4–8.

National Commission on Social Studies in the Schools. (1989). *Charting a course: Social studies for the 21st century.* Washington, DC: National Council for the Social Studies.

Neil, A. S. (1960). *Summerhill.* New York: Hart Publishing Co.

Nelson-LeGall, S. (1985). Help seeking behavior in learning. In E. W. Gordon (Ed.), *Review of research in education Vol. 12* (pp. 55–90). Washington, DC: American Educational Research Association.

Nias, J. (1985). Reference groups in primary teaching: Talking, listening, and identity. In S. J. Ball & I. F. Goodson (Eds.). *Teachers lives and careers.* (pp. 105–119). Philadelphia: The Falmer Press.

Nickerson, R. S., Perkins, D., & Smith, E. E. (1985). *The teaching of thinking.* Hillsdale, NJ: Erlbaum.

Noffke, S. E., & Zeichner, K. M. (1987). Action research and teacher thinking: The first phase of the action research on action research project at the University of Wisconsin—Madison. Paper presented at the annual meeting of the American Educational Research Association, Washington, DC.

Nozick, R. (1974). *Anarchy, state and utopia.* New York: Basic Books.

Oakes, J. (1985). *Keeping track: How schools structure inequality.* New Haven: Yale University Press.

O'Brien, T. C. (1989). Some thoughts on treasure–keeping. *Phi Delta Kappan, 70,* 360–364.

Ogbu, J. (1985). Research currents: Cultural–ecological influences on minority school learning. *Language Arts, 62,* 860–869.

Oja, S. N., & Pine, G. J. (1984). *Collaborative action research: A two–year study of teachers' stages of development and school contexts.* Executive summary, Collaborative Action Research Projects. Durham, NH: University of New Hampshire.

Okun, S. H. (1977). How to be a better listener. In R. C. Huseman, C. M. Logue, & D. L. Freshly (Eds.), *Readings in interpersonal and organizational communication.* (pp. 582–586). Boston: Holbrook Press.

Ost, D. H. (1988). Teacher–parent interactions: An effective school–community environment. *The Educational Forum, 52*(2), 165–176.

Paine, L. (1988). Orientations towards diversity: What do prospective teachers bring? Paper presented at the annual meeting of the American Educational Research Association, New Orleans.

Paley, V. G. (1979). *White teacher.* Cambridge, MA: Harvard University Press.

Palincsar, A. S., & Brown, A. L. (1984). Reciprocal teaching of comprehension–fostering and comprehension–monitoring activities. *Cognition and Instruction, 1,* 117–175.

Paris, S. G., Cross, D. R., & Lipson, M. Y. (1984). Informed strategies for learning: A program to improve children's reading awareness and comprehension. *Journal of Educational Psychology, 76*(6), 1239–1252.

Paris, S. G., Oka, E., & DeBritto, M. (1983). Beyond decoding: Synthesis of research on reading comprehension. *Educational Leadership, 40,* 78–83.

Paris, S. G., & Winograd, P. (1990). Metacognition in academic learning and instruction. In B.F. Jones (Ed.), *Dimensions of thinking and cognitive instruction* (pp. 15–51). Hillsdale, NJ: Erlbaum.

Parsons, J. B. (1983). Toward understanding the roots of reflective inquiry. *The Social Studies, 74*(2), 67–70.

Pearson, P. D., & Dole, J. A. (1987). Explicit comprehension instruction: A review of research and a new conceptualization of instruction. *The Elementary School Journal, 88,* 151–165.

Pepper, F. C., & Henry, S. L. (1985). Using developmental and democratic practices to teach self–discipline. *Theory Into Practice, 24*(1), 264–270.

Perkins, D. N. (1984). Creativity by design. *Educational Leadership, 42,* 18–25.

Peters, T. J. & Waterman, R. H. (1982). *In search of excellence: Lessons From America's best run companies.* New York: Harper & Row.

Peterson, P. L. (1979). Direct instruction: Effective for what and for whom? *Educational Leadership, 37,* 46–48.

Phillips, S. U. (1983). *The invisible culture: Communication in classroom and community on the Warm Springs Indian Reservation.* White Plains, NY: Longman.

Piaget, J. (1969). *Science of education and the psychology of the child.* (D. Coltman, Trans.). New York: The Viking Press.

Piaget, J. (1972). *Psychology and epistemology: Towards a theory of knowledge.* (P. A. Wells, Trans.). London: The Penguin Press. (Original work published 1970.)

Pirkle, J. (1982). The effects of a new intervention program on the self–esteem and school behavior of third, fourth, and fifth grade elementary school students. Unpublished doctoral dissertation, University of Florida.

Popham, W. J., & Baker, E. L. (1970). *Systematic instruction.* Englewood Cliffs, NJ: Prentice–Hall.

Porro, B. (1981). Non–sexist elementary education: A research report and teacher's guide. Gainesville, FL: P.K. Yonge Laboratory School Research Monograph Series (#34).

Porro, B. (1985). Playing the school system: The low achiever's game. In E. Eisner's *The educational imagination,* 2nd edition (pp. 256–274). New York: Macmillan.

Posner, G. J., & Rudnitsky, A. N. (1982). *Course design: A guide to curriculum development for teachers.* New York: Longman.

Powell, A., Farrar, E., & Cohen, D. (1985). *The shopping mall high school.* Boston, MA: Houghton Mifflin.

Power, C., & Kohlberg, L. (1986). Moral development: Transforming the hidden curriculum. *Curriculum Review, 26*(1), 14–17.

Prawat, R. S. (1989). Teaching for understanding: Three key attributes. *Teaching & Teacher Education, 5,* 315–328.

Putallaz, M., & Gottman, J. M. (1981). An introductional model of children's entry into peer groups. *Child Development, 52,* 986–994.

Rallis, S. (1988). Room at the top: Conditions for effective school leadership. *Phi Delta Kappan, 69*(9), 643–647.

Raphael, T. E. (1982). Question-answering strategies for children. *Reading Teacher, 36,* 186–191.

The reading report card: Trends in reading over four national assessments, 1971–1984. Princeton, NJ: National Assessment of Educational Progress at Educational Testing Service.

Render, G. F., Padilla, J. N. M. & Krank, H. M. (1989). Assertive discipline: A critical review and analysis. *Teachers' College Record, 90*(4), 607–630.

Resnick, L. B. (1987a). *Education and learning to think.* Washington, DC: National Academy Press.

Resnick, L. B. (1987b). Learning in and out of school. *Educational Researcher, 16*(9), 13–20.

Resnick, L. B., & Klopfer, L. E. (1989a). Toward the thinking curriculum: An overview. In L. B. Resnick & L. E. Klopfer (Eds.), *Toward the thinking curriculum: Current cognitive research* (pp. 1–18). Alexandria, VA: Association for Supervision and Curriculum Development.

Resnick, L. B. & Klopfer, L. E. (1989b). Toward the thinking curriculum: Concluding remarks. In L. B. Resnick & L. E. Klopfer (Eds.), *Toward the thinking curriculum: Current cognitive research* (pp. 206–211). Alexandria, VA: Association for Supervision and Curriculum Development.

Reys, R. E. (1984). Mental computation and estimation: Past, present and future. *The Elementary School Journal, 84*(5), 547–557.

Richardson, V., Casanova, U., Placier, P., & Guilfoyle, K. (1989). *School children at risk.* Philadelphia: The Falmer Press.

Roff, M., Sells, S. B., & Golden, M. M. (1972). *Social adjustment and personality.* Minneapolis, MN: University of Minnesota Press.

Rogers, C. (1961). *On becoming a person.* Boston: Houghton Mifflin.

Rogers, C. R. & Farson, R. W. (1977). Active listening. In R. C. Huseman, C. M. Logue, & D. L. Freshly (Eds.), *Readings in interpersonal and organizational communication* (pp. 561–576). Boston: Holbrook Press.

Rogers, D. L., & Ross, D. D. (1986). Encouraging positive social interaction among young children. *Young Children, 41,* 12–17.

Romberg, T. A., & Carpenter, T. P. (1986). Research on teaching and learning mathematics: Two disciplines of scientific inquiry. In M. Wittrock (Ed.), *Third handbook of research on teaching* (pp. 850–873). New York: Macmillan.

Rosenholtz, S. J. (1989a). *Teachers' workplace.* New York: Longman.

Rosenholtz, S. J. (1989b). Workplace conditions that affect teacher quality and commitment: Implications for teacher induction programs. *Elementary School Journal, 89*(4), 421–439.

Rosenholtz, S. J., Bassler, O., & Hoover–Dempsey, K. (1986). Organizational conditions of teacher learning. *Teaching and Teacher Education, 2*(2), 91–104.

Rosenshine, B. (1986). Synthesis of research on explicit teaching. *Educational Leadership, 43,* 60–69.

Rosenshine, B. (1987). Explicit teaching and teacher training. *Journal of Teacher Education, 38,*(3), 34–36.

Ross, D. D. (1978). *Teaching beliefs and practices in three kindergartens.* Unpublished doctoral dissertation, University of Virginia.

Ross, D. D. (1984). A practical model of conducting action research in public school settings. *Contemporary Education, 55*(2), 113–117.

Ross, D. D. (1987a). Reflective teaching: Meaning and implications for preservice teacher educators. Paper presented at the Reflective Inquiry Conference, Houston, Texas.

Ross, D. D. (1987b). Action research for preservice teachers: A description of why and how. *Peabody Journal of Education, 64*(3), 131–150.

Ross, D. D., & Kyle, D. W. (1987). Helping preservice teachers learn to use teacher effectiveness research. *Journal of Teacher Education, 38,* 40–44.

Ross, D. D., & Rogers, D. W. (1982). Block play and social development: What do children learn as they play? Paper presented at the annual meeting of the National Association for the Education of Young Children, Washington, DC.

Routman, R. (1988). *Transitions.* Portsmouth, NH: Heinemann.

Rowe, M. B. (1974a). Wait–time and rewards as instructional variables, their influence on language, logic and fate control: Part one—wait–time. *Journal of Research on Science Teaching, 11,* 81–94.

Rowe, M. B. (1974b). Relation of wait–time and rewards to the development of language, logic, and fate control: Part two—rewards. *Journal of Research in Science Teaching, 11*(4), 291–301.

Rubin, K. H. (1972). Relationship between egocentric communication and popularity among peers. *Developmental Psychology, 7,* 364.

Ruddick, J. (1985). Teacher research and research–based teacher education. *Journal of Education for Teaching, 11*(3), 281–289.

Ryan, K. (1979). Toward understanding the problem: At the threshold of a profession. In K. R. Howey & R. H. Bents (Eds.), *Toward meeting the needs of the beginning teacher* (pp. 35–52). Minneapolis: Midwest Teacher Corps Network and the University of Minnesota.

Sanford, J. P., & Emmer, E. T. (1988). *Understanding classroom management: An observation guide.* Englewood Cliffs, NJ: Prentice–Hall.

Sarason, S. B. (1971). *The culture of the school and the problem of change.* Boston: Allyn & Bacon.

Saunders, A. (1989). Creativity and the infant classroom. In G. Barrett (Ed.), *Disaffection from school? The early years* (pp. 48–58). Bristol, PA: The Falmer Press.

Schachter, F. F., Kirshner, K., Klips, B., Fredricks, M., & Sanders, K. (1976). Everyday preschool interpersonal speech usage. *Monographs of the Society for Research in Child Development, 39*(3), 1–88.

Schieffelin, B., & Cochran–Smith, M. (1984). Learning to read culturally: Literacy before schooling. In H. Goelman, A. Oberg, & F. Smith (Eds.), *Awakening to literacy* (pp. 3–23). Exeter, NH: Heinemann.

Schoenfeld, A. H. (1991). On mathematics as sense–making: An informal attack on the unfortunate divorce of formal and informal mathematics. In J. Voss, D. N. Perkins, & J. Segal (Eds.), *Informal Reasoning and Education* (pp. 311–344). Hillsdale, NJ: Lawrence Erlbaum.

Schon, D. A. (1983). *The reflective practitioner.* New York: Basic Books.

Schuncke, G. M. & Krogh, S. L. (1983). *Helping children choose.* Glenview, IL: Scott, Foresman & Co.

Scriven, M. (1976). *Reasoning.* New York: McGraw–Hill.

Segal, J. W., Chipman, S. F., & Glaser, R. (1985). *Thinking and learning skills: Vol. 1. Relating instruction to research.* Hillsdale, NJ: Erlbaum.

Shavelson, R. J. (1983). Review of research on teachers' pedagogical judgments, plans and decisions. *Elementary School Journal, 83,* 392–414.

Shor, I. (1980). *Critical teaching and everyday life.* Chicago: University of Chicago Press.

Shultz, J. J., Florio, S., & Erickson, F. (1982). Where's the floor? Aspects of the cultural organization of social relationships in communication at home and in school. In P. Gilmore & A. A. Glatthorn (Eds.), *Children in and out of school: Ethnography in education* (pp. 88–123). Washington, DC: Center for Applied Linguistics.

Siegel, H. (1988). *Educating reason.* New York: Routledge.

Siegel, I. E. (1984). A constructivist perspective for teaching thinking. *Educational Leadership, 42,* 18–21.

Simandl, K. (1979). A one sided dialogue in defense of art education. *Art Teacher, 9*(1), 16–17.

Simon, R. (1989). Empowerment as a pedagogy of possibility. In H. Holtz, I. Marcus, J. Dougherty, J. Michaels, & R. Peduzzi (Eds.), *Education and the American dream* (pp. 134–146). Granby, MA: Bergin & Garvey.

Simpson, R. L. & Simpson, I. H. (1969). Women and bureaucracy in the semi–professions. In A. Etzioni (Ed.), *The semi–professions and their organization* (pp. 196–265). New York: The Free Press.

Sizer, T. (1984). *Horace's compromise: The dilemma of the American high school.* Boston, MA: Houghton Mifflin.

Slavin, R. E. (1987). Ability grouping and student achievement in elementary schools: A best evidence synthesis. *Review of Educational Research, 57,* 293–350.

Smith, D. C., & Neale, D. C. (1989). The construction of subject matter knowledge in primary science teaching. *Teaching and Teacher Education, 5*(1), 1–20.

Smith, F. (1977). Making sense of reading and of reading instruction. *Harvard Educational Review, 47,* 386–395.

Smith, S. (1987). The collaborative school takes shape. *Educational Leadership, 45*(3), 4–6.

Soar, R. S., & Soar, R. M. (1983). Context effects in the teaching learning process. In D. C. Smith (Ed.), *Essential knowledge for beginning educators* (pp. 65–75). Washington, DC: American Association of Colleges of Teacher Education.

Stafford, L. (1987). Parent teacher communication. *Communication Education, 36,* 182–187.

Stengel, W. (1971). *Suicide and attempted suicide.* Middlesex, Great Britain: Penguin.

Stensrud, R., & Stensrud, K. (1981). Discipline: An attitude not an outcome. *Educational Forum, 45,* 161–167.

Strange, M. C. (1978). Considerations for evaluating reading instruction. *Educational Leadership, 36,* 178–181.

Strunk, W., & White, E. B. (1959). *The elements of style.* New York: Macmillan.

Sykes, G. (1983). Contradictions, ironies and promises unfulfilled: A contemporary account of the status of teaching. *Phi Delta Kappan, 65*(2), 87–93.

Sykes, G. (1986). Teaching as reflective practice. In K. A. Sirotnik & J. Oakes (Eds.), *Critical perspectives on the organization and improvement of schooling* (pp. 229–246). Boston: Kluwer Nijhoff Publishing.

Taba, H. (1962). *Curriculum development.* New York: Harcourt Brace Jovanovich.

Tanner, D., & Tanner, L. (1980). *Curriculum development.* New York: Macmillan.

Taylor, D. (1989). Toward a unified theory of literacy learning and instructional practices. *Phi Delta Kappan, 71,* 184–193.

TenBrink, T. D. (1974). *Evaluation: A practical guide for teachers.* New York: McGraw-Hill.

Tharp, R. G. (1989). Culturally compatible education: A formula for designing effective classrooms. In H. T. Trueba, G. Spindler, & L. Spindler (Eds.), *What do anthropologists have to say about dropouts?* (pp. 51–66). Bristol, PA: The Falmer Press.

Tipps, S. (1981). Play and the brain: Relationships and reciprocity. *Journal of Research and Development in Education, 14,* 19–29.

Tobin, K., Briscoe, C., & Holman, J. R. (1990). Overcoming constraints to effective elementary science teaching. *Science Education, 74*(5), 409–420.

Tom, A. (1984). *Teaching as a moral craft.* New York: Longman.

Trueba, H. T. (1988). Culturally–based explanations of minority students' academic achievement. *Anthropology and Education Quarterly, 19,* 270–287.

U.S. Bureau of the Census (1989). Current Population Reports, Series P–23, No. 159, *Population profile of the United States: 1989,* U. S. Government Printing Office, Washington, DC.

Vallance, E. (1973/74). Hiding the hidden curriculum: An interpretation of the language of justification in nineteenth–century educational reform. *Curriculum Theory Network, 4*(1), 5–21.

Van Fleet, A. A. (1983). Teachers as cultural brokers: Historical and anthropological evidence. *Journal of Thought, 18* (3), 57–62.

Van Manen, M. (1977). Linking ways of knowing with ways of being practical. *Curriculum Inquiry, 6,* 205–228.

Vaughn, B. E., & Waters, E. (1978). Attention structures, sociometric status, and dominance: Interrelations, behavioral correlates, and relationships to social competence. *Developmental Psychology, 17*(3), 275–288.

Vaughn, B. E., & Waters, E. (1980). Social organization among preschool peers: Dominance, attention, and sociometric correlates. In D. R. Omark, F. F. Strayer, & D. G. Freeman (Eds.), *Dominance relations: An ethological view of human conflict and social interaction.* New York: Garland STPM Press.

Veal, M. L., Clift, R., & Holland, P. (1989). School contexts that encourage reflection: Teacher perceptions. *International Journal of Qualitative Studies in Education, 2*(4), 315–334.

Vobejda, B. (1987). A mathematician's research on math instruction. *Educational Researcher, 16*(9), 9–12.

Vygotsky, L. S. (1978). *Mind in society.* Edited by M. Cole, V. John-Steiner, S. Scribner & E. Souberman. Cambridge, MA: Harvard University Press.

Walsh, C. E. (Ed.). (1991). *Literacy as praxis.* Norwood, NJ: Ablex.

Wasserman, S. (1987). Teaching for thinking: Louis E. Raths revisited. *Phi Delta Kappan, 68*(6), 460–466.

Watson, B., & Konicek, R. (1990). Teaching for conceptual change: Confronting children's experience. *Phi Delta Kappan, 71*(9), 680–685.

Wayson, W. W. (1985). Opening windows to teaching: Empowering educators to teach self–discipline. *Theory Into Practice, 24*(1), 227–232.

Webb, R. B., Ashton, P. T., & Andrews, S. D. (1983). The basic skills instructional system: A manual for improving the reading and language arts skills of low achieving students. *Florida Educational Research and Development Council Research Bulletin, 17*, 1–33.

Webb, R. B., & Sherman, R. R. (1989). *Schooling and society.* New York: Macmillan.

Wehlage, G. G., Rutter, R. A., Smith, G. A., Lesko, N., & Fernandez, R. R. (1989). *Reducing the risk: Schools as communities of support.* Bristol, PA: The Falmer Press.

Weick, K. (1976). Educational organizations as loosely–coupled systems. *Administrative Science Quarterly, 21*(1), 1–19.

Weinstein, R. S. (1983). Student perceptions of schooling. *Elementary School Journal, 83*(4), 287–312.

Whitford, B. L. (1984). Some structural constraints affecting action research. *The High School Journal, 68*, 18–21.

Whitford, B. L., Schlechty, P. C., & Shelor, L. (1987). Sustaining action research through collaboration: Inquiries for invention. *Peabody Journal of Education, 64*(3), 151–169.

Wigginton, E. (1989). Foxfire grows up. *Harvard Educational Review, 59*, 24–49.

Wildman, T. M., & Niles, J. A. (1987). Reflective teachers: Tensions between abstractions and realities. *Journal of Teacher Education, 38*(1), 25–31.

Wilkinson, L. C., & Dollaghan, C. (1979). Peer communication in first grade reading groups. *Theory Into Practice, 18*, 267–274.

Williams, C. R., Neff, A. R., & Finklestein, J. H. (1981). Theory into practice: Reconsidering the preposition. *Theory Into Practice, 29*, 93–96.

Williams, R. M. (1980). Why children should draw: The surprising link between the arts and learning. In G. Wass (Ed.), *Curriculum planning* (pp. 288–290). Boston: Allyn and Bacon.

Winograd, P., & Greenlee, M. (1986). Students need a balanced reading program. *Educational Leadership, 43,* 16–21.

Women on Words and Images. (1974). Look, Jane, look. See sex stereotypes. In J. Stacey, S. Bereaud, & J. Daniels (Eds.), *And Jill came tumbling after: Sexism in American education* (pp. 159–177). New York: Dell Publishing Co.

Zahorik, J. A. (1975). Teachers' planning models. *Educational Leadership, 33,* 134–139.

Zeichner, K. (1980). Myths and realities: Field based experiences in preservice teacher education. *Journal of Teacher Education, 31*(6), 45–55.

Zeichner, K. M., & Liston, D. P. (1987). Teaching student teachers to reflect. *Harvard Educational Review, 57,* 23–48.

Zwack, J. M. (1973). The stereotypic family in children's literature. *The Reading Teacher, 26,* 389–391.

INDEX